Gaining Control
of the
Corporate Culture

Ralph H. Kilmann
Mary J. Saxton
Roy Serpa
and Associates

Gaining Control
of the
Corporate Culture

Jossey-Bass Publishers · San Francisco

GAINING CONTROL OF THE CORPORATE CULTURE
by Ralph H. Kilmann, Mary J. Saxton, Roy Serpa, and Associates

Copyright © 1985 by: Jossey-Bass Inc., Publishers
350 Sansome Street
San Francisco, California 94104

Library of Congress Cataloging-in-Publication Data
Main entry under title:

Gaining control of the corporate culture.

  (A Joint publication in the Jossey-Bass management
series and the Jossey-Bass social and behavioral science
series)
  "From October 24 to 27, the Program in Corporate
Culture, Graduate School of Business, University of
Pittsburgh sponsored a conference"—P.
  Includes bibliographies and index.
  1. Corporate culture—Congresses. 2. Organizational
change—Congresses. I. Kilmann, Ralph H. II. Saxton,
Mary J. (date). III. Serpa, Roy (date).
IV. University of Pittsburgh. Program in Corporate
Culture. V. Series: Jossey-Bass management series.
VI. Series: Jossey-Bass social and behavioral science
series.
HD58.7.G34   1985   658.4'06   85-45059
ISBN 0-87589-666-9

Manufactured in the United States of America

The paper used in this book meets the State
of California requirements for recycled paper
(50 percent recycled waste, including 10 percent
post-consumer waste), which are the strictest guidelines
for recycled paper currently in use in the United States.
JACKET DESIGN BY WILLI BAUM
FIRST EDITION
  HB Printing   10 9 8 7 6 5

Code 8535

A joint publication in
The Jossey-Bass Management Series
and
The Jossey-Bass
Social and Behavioral Science Series

To Dean H. J. Zoffer
for his continual support and inspiration

Preface

Social scientists and practitioners have focused their attention on the tangibles: "If you can easily measure it, it must be important" and "if you can observe it, it should be managed" are the unwritten rules that have prevailed. In the past few years, however, both groups have begun to recognize that some of the most important things to study and manage cannot be observed or controlled directly.

Culture is the invisible force behind the tangibles and observables in any organization, a social energy that moves people to act. Culture is to the organization what personality is to the individual—a hidden, yet unifying theme that provides meaning, direction, and mobilization. Organization charts and employee manuals are simply not enough to get members working together. Operationally, culture is defined as shared philosophies, ideologies, values, beliefs, assumptions, and norms. These are seldom written down or discussed, but they are learned by living in the organization and becoming a part of it.

Culture fills in the gaps between what is formally decreed by the organization and what actually takes place. Culture thus determines how formal statements will be interpreted and provides what the written documents leave out. The surest way to kill an organization is to have all members follow every written rule to the letter. The best way to make a company successful is to have a culture that influences all members to adopt, by tacit agreement, the most effective approach, attitude, and behavior on the job.

From October 24 to 27, 1984, the Program in Corporate Culture, Graduate School of Business, University of Pittsburgh, sponsored a conference on "Managing Corporate Cultures." The conference was the program's first major event since its founding in September 1983 and was organized to help meet the program's objectives: to promote the study of the impact of culture on "organizational" effectiveness and to disseminate the knowledge acquired so that managers could use it to increase the effectiveness of their organizations. The designation "corporate" culture was chosen because of its current popularity, not because corporate is meant to refer to a specific type of culture, such as that present at the top levels of an organization or that operating in industrial organizations. Therefore, corporate culture as used here and throughout the book refers to the culture of any organization, whether public or private, large or small. Similarly, when the conference was organized, experts in "organizational" culture were invited to discuss what is known in the field.

The experts were chosen in two ways. First, we invited eight individuals who had demonstrated a keen understanding of the topic, either through their academic research or through direct involvement with organizational efforts at managing corporate cultures, to present papers at the conference. Second, we mailed more than 12,000 announcements and calls for papers to the various professional societies that might be expected to be interested in the topic: the Academy of Management, the American Psychological Association, the Institute of Management Sciences, and the American Society for Training and Development. We expected that this would help us uncover important research currently under way but not yet published. Our expectations were more than realized: eighty-seven papers covering a very wide range of material on corporate culture were submitted to our call-for-papers competition.

These papers were subjected to a thorough review. Each paper was evaluated by at least two independent reviewers whose judgment was based on four criteria: (1) innovativeness in approach to the topic, (2) quality in developing the approach; (3) practical usefulness in guiding management action, and (4) clarity of expression for a broad audience. In cases of disagreement, the paper was reviewed by a third person, and a discussion among the editors resolved any differences of opinion. This review process allowed us to select the best ten from the total of eighty-seven papers. Editorial recommendations for revision were then sent to all authors. The invited authors' papers were subjected to the same review procedure to help them fine tune their ideas and improve their style as well.

The review process did not end with the editors, however. At the conference, all authors delivered their papers to an audience of both academics and practitioners, with thirty minutes for their presentation and thirty minutes for discussion. This encouraged the authors to clarify their thoughts for a broad audience and allowed them to benefit from active debates and immediate feedback. Moreover, since all the papers presented during the three-day conference concerned the topic of corporate culture, there was ample opportunity for each author to learn from the presentations and discussions of the other papers. As editors, we were delighted to see the thinking evolve as the conference progressed. In fact, after reviewing the revised papers, which were submitted *after* the conference took place, we could observe the impact of the conference discussions on each paper. As a result of this comprehensive editorial and interactive review process, the chapters in this book offer original ideas whose arguments are clearly conceived and well developed.

We expect that both academics and practitioners will find this collection of material invaluable. The practitioners who may be especially interested in this book include chief executive officers; senior operating executives; vice-presidents of corporate organization, planning, and development; human resource managers; personnel administrators; general managers; project managers; plant superintendents; management consultants; organizational development practitioners; management training and development practitioners; and administrators and directors of nonprofit organizations. The academics who may be especially interested in this book include faculty specializing in organizational theory, organizational behavior, organizational science, organizational development, sociology, anthropology, psychology, social work, public health, community mental health, and educational administration.

At present, both academics and practitioners are intensely interested in the topic of corporate culture. Several academic journals have sponsored special issues on organizational culture (for example, *Administrative Science Quarterly,* September 1983), and the popular press has provided cover stories as well (for instance, *Fortune,* October 17, 1983). This rare shared interest brings together two communities that frequently seem so divided: the world of ideas and the world of action. If we can bridge the communication gap with discussions on corporate culture, we may be able to do so on other important management topics as well. Clearly, the two communities need one another: the organizational sciences are irrelevant without a client to serve, and the practitioner world is apt to pay a high price for relying on the slow process of trial-and-error learning in such turbulent times.

Overview of the Contents

The twenty chapters in this volume are organized into four major parts that are especially designed to facilitate learning about this emerging field of management thought. It is best to read the chapters in order, or at least to review material from one part to the next, since the arguments build throughout the book.

In Chapter One, the Introduction, the editors discuss five key cultural themes: Does culture have an impact? How deep-seated is culture? Can an organization have more than one culture? Can culture be changed? Can culture be changed without changing other aspects of an organization? The objective of this chapter is to familiarize the reader with the fundamental issues that pervade all the chapters in this book.

Part One, "What Is Culture: Its Function and Impact," provides several chapters that attempt to define the concept of corporate culture in the broadest possible way. Numerous case histories are provided in order to give the reader an adequate background to proceed with the remaining parts of the book. Edgar H. Schein, in Chapter Two, discusses various definitions of culture and what kinds of functions culture serves at different stages of the organization's life cycle. In Chapter Three, W. Brooke Tunstall describes the major steps in the American Telephone and Telegraph Company's attempt to identify, measure, and modify its culture during its recent divestiture, perhaps the richest example of cultural transition of any American company. Alice M. Sapienza, in Chapter Four, uses two case studies to show how culture affects everything top managers see and, hence, believe is possible. Chapter Five, by Jay W. Lorsch, shows how the core beliefs of top managers can inhibit strategic change by producing "strategic myopia" so that the natural response is to keep managing in the same old way. He then presents the several steps needed to break this invisible barrier, including making beliefs visible, using outside directors, bringing in new blood, and encouraging flexibility throughout the ranks of middle management. In Chapter Six, George G. Gordon provides a most comprehensive study of the effects of corporate culture on performance by showing how the "bottom line" is influenced by top-management beliefs about "the way things are done here." Since 1970, data was collected from the top four or five levels of management covering over 500 organizations and 50,000 managers and professionals. The results indicate that there is no one "winning culture" but that characteristics of the industry, marketplace, and the organization affect what is the appropriate culture.

Part Two, "General Approaches to Understanding and Managing Culture," highlights various conceptual and methodological issues in considering how and where to look for culture in any organization. Chapter Seven, by Meryl Reis Louis, argues that there are multiple cultures in any work organization and that each culture has its own "penetration" and "orientation." She suggests "natural occurrences" and "field stimulations" as two ways of exploring these multiple cultures. Stanley M. Davis, in Chapter Eight, points out that most examinations of culture are inward looking, focusing on management and employees. He stresses the need to be outward looking, to focus on the values and beliefs a business has concerning customers, competitors, shareholders, suppliers, government, and the society at large. Similarly, Harry J. Martin, in Chapter Nine, considers how cultures can be maintained through employee selection *and* through fostering the culture's compatibility with the organization's immediate environment. Chapter Ten, by Tim R. V. Davis, examines the formation of corporate culture at lower levels in the hierarchy, emphasizing how cultures form in opposition to management: us versus management; us versus the work; us versus other departments, and us versus the customer. In Chapter Eleven, Ian I. Mitroff and Ralph H. Kilmann argue that one of the keys to understanding any culture involves the examination of taboos, the strongest set of inappropriate behaviors defined in any society. They explore several types of "unthinkables" that corporations find taboo even to discuss.

Part Three, "The Dynamics of Cultural Change," considers the process by which cultures form and evolve in any organization. Understanding the evolutionary aspects of culture helps us to find the right points at which management might undertake to change culture, to purposely alter the natural course of cultural events. In Chapter Twelve, W. Gibb Dyer, Jr., offers a model to represent the complex processes and conditions underlying cultural change derived from the histories of five organizations. The model shows several interconnected stages that center around the leadership of the company: Does a perceived crisis call into question the leadership's abilities and practices? How is the leadership crisis resolved? Vijay Sathe, in Chapter Thirteen, also considers the role of the leader and crises in cultural change, but he examines the question of who the deviants are and how they are treated. Chapter Fourteen, by Alan L. Wilkins and Kerry J. Patterson, emphasizes that cultures cannot be changed by using methods that focus on rational planning, nor by imposing the values of a few upon the many, nor by eliminating the muddling and growing time required to change human institutions. Since culture consists of the three core elements of equity, collective competence, and facilitation and encouragement of collective competence, management must let people grow toward the culture they desire. In Chapter Fifteen, Terrence E. Deal reflects on the deep sense of individual and collective loss that lurks beneath the surface of any change in culture. The fundamental human fears seem to be death and life without meaning; since cultural change can touch upon both of these fears, Deal suggests that various rites are necessary to help people assuage these fears, heal wounds, and "mend the torn fabric of meaning."

Part Four, "Specific Methods for Changing Culture," focuses on the approaches, methods, and tools that managers can use to deliberately change and manage culture. Robert F. Allen, in Chapter Sixteen, describes a four-phase systematic program for changing cultures: (1) analysis of organizational culture and norms, (2) leadership training and introductory workshops, (3) systematic modification of the culture, and (4) feedback, evaluation, and further modification. He highlights the barriers that must be overcome for this program to work, such as placing blame, establishing win-lose norms, seeking simplistic solutions to complex problems, instituting crash programs, fostering learned helplessness, and making promises that cannot be kept. In Chapter Seventeen, Ralph H. Kilmann also focuses on behavioral norms as a way to assess and change the corporate culture in any organization. He outlines a five-step, participative process to do this: (1) examining actual norms, (2) articulating new directions, (3) establishing new norms, (4) identifying culture-gaps (the difference between actual and desired norms), and (5) closing culture-gaps. Chapter Eighteen, by Harrison M. Trice and Janice M. Beyer, defines rites as sets of organized and planned activities that have practical and expressive consequences for organizational members. They show how cultural change can be assisted by the use of rites such as rites of passage, degradation, enhancement, renewal, conflict reduction, and integration. In Chapter Nineteen, Nirmal K. Sethia and Mary Ann Von Glinow argue that the organizational reward system is a concrete and powerful tool, readily amenable to managerial control, for managing corporate culture. Four types of rewards (financial, job content, career, and status) are matched to four types of cultures (Apathetic, Caring, Exacting, and Integrative) in order to encourage and reinforce the best performance and morale of organizational members.

Chapter Twenty, the Conclusion, considers whether the topic of corporate culture is merely a passing fad or whether it represents a more fundamental shift in attempts to understand the complex, multifaceted organizations of today. We lean toward the latter, provided that managing culture is not approached as a quick-fix solution to a complex and changing problem. If culture is managed along with all the other elements of management theory, such as strategy, structure, reward systems, skills, and human resource management, then culture may become an important factor in an integrated program for improving corporate performance.

Acknowledgments

Many people played a key role in making possible both the conference and this book. Dean H. J. Zoffer and Executive Associate Dean Andrew R. Blair provided the impetus to form the Program in Corporate Culture and to embark on its first major project. We also appreciate the help of the Division of Executive Development, particularly the assistance of Jeanette Engel, in managing the hotel arrangements. Professors Raghu Nath, John Prescott, and Craig Russell were most effective in chairing several sessions at the conference. Arthur Baron and William Peace contributed significantly to identifying critical issues for the practitioner panel.

Kathy Robbins, administrative secretary for the Program in Corporate Culture, efficiently and effectively managed all the preparations for the conference and the manuscript, including conference registration and all correspondence. Karen Hoy was extremely helpful in preparing the printed conference announcement and the registration brochure. Several doctoral students provided invaluable assistance in reviewing manuscripts and managing particular aspects of the conference: Larry Boone, Teresa Joyce, Jeff Pinto, and Betty Ann Velthouse.

Lastly, we would like to express our appreciation to all the contributors to this book for their ideas and insights. In addition we acknowledge the active involvement of the approximately two hundred participants at the conference who asked important and probing questions at every session.

Pittsburgh, Pennsylvania   Ralph H. Kilmann
July 1985   Mary J. Saxton
                                            Roy Serpa

Contents

The Authors

Ralph H. Kilmann is professor of business administration and director of the Program in Corporate Culture at the Graduate School of Business, University of Pittsburgh. He received both his B.S. and M.S. degrees in industrial administration from Carnegie-Mellon University and his Ph.D. in management from the University of California at Los Angeles. Kilmann is a member of the American Psychological Association, the Academy of Management, and the Institute of Management Sciences. Since 1975, he has served as president of Organizational Design Consultants, Inc., a Pittsburgh-based firm specializing in the five tracks to organizational success.

Kilmann has published more than one hundred articles and books on such topics as organizational design, strategy, structure, and culture; conflict management; and organizational change and development. He is the developer of the MAPS Design Technology and codeveloper of several diagnostic instruments, including the Thomas-Kilmann Conflict Mode Instrument and the Kilmann-Saxton Culture-Gap Survey. His most recent publication, *Beyond the Quick Fix: Managing Five Tracks to Organizational Success* (1984), describes his complete, integrated program for creating and maintaining an organization's high performance and morale. Kilmann has applied this program for planned change to federal agencies, universities, hospitals, professional organizations, and numerous corporations in the top fifty of the *Fortune* 500.

Mary J. Saxton is a part-time lecturer and a Ph.D. candidate in organizational studies at the Graduate School of Business, University of Pittsburgh. She received her B.A. degree in psychology and Spanish from the State University of New York at Cortland and her M.B.A. degree from the University of Pittsburgh. She is currently completing her dissertation on measuring organizational culture. Since 1982, Saxton has been associated with Organizational Design Consultants, Inc.

Saxton is a member of the American Psychological Association, the Academy of Management, and the Association for Consumer Research. Her research activities focus on organizational culture, organizational design and development, and individual reaction and adaptation to organizational change. She is the codeveloper of the Kilmann-Saxton Culture-Gap Survey.

Roy Serpa is director of commercial development for Borg-Warner Chemicals, Inc. He began his career as a chemical salesman, and for the past twenty years he has held several marketing, business development, and general management positions. During the past ten years Serpa has been extensively involved with new business ventures, technology transfer on an international basis, and acquisitions. He has presented several lectures and has published articles on marketing, innovation, entrepreneurship, business ethics, and the free enterprise system.

Serpa received his B.S. degree in textile chemistry from Southeastern Massachusetts University and his M.B.A. degree from the University of Pittsburgh. He is a member of the American Management Association, the Commercial Development Association, and the Academy of Management. Serpa is an advisory trustee for the Free Market Education Foundation. In addition, he is a visiting lecturer at Texas A&M University and the University of Houston.

Robert F. Allen is president of the Human Resources Institute and graduate professor of policy sciences and psychology at Kean College in New Jersey. He received his B.A. degree in behavioral sciences from the State University of New York at Plattsburgh and his M.A. degree in clinical psychology and his Ph.D. degree in clinical and social psychology from New York University. Allen completed his postdoctoral work at Columbia University and New York University. His most recent book, *The Organizational Unconscious* (1982), describes the normative systems process of cultural change and reviews a number of its most recent applications.

Janice M. Beyer is professor of organization and human resources in the School of Management at the State University of New York at Buffalo. She received her B.A. degree from the University of Wisconsin in music and her M.S. and Ph.D. degrees from Cornell University in organizational behavior. She is currently chairperson of the Organization and Management Theory Division of the Academy of Management and editor designate of the *Academy of Management Journal.* She contributed the chapter, "Ideologies, Values, and Decision Making," to the *Handbook of Organizational Design* by Paul Nystrom and William H. Starbuck.

Stanley M. Davis is a research professor of management at the School of Management at Boston University. He is a member of the board of directors of Management Analysis Center and serves on the advisory board of Index Systems; both of these consulting firms are headquartered in Cambridge, Massachusetts. Davis frequently serves as a consultant on matters of management and organization for domestic and multinational corporations. His most recent book is *Managing Corporate Culture* (1984).

Tim R. V. Davis is an associate professor of management in the James J. Nance College of Business Administration, Cleveland State University, where he teaches strategy, policy, and general management. Davis received his B.A. degree in business and behavioral sciences from Bowling Green State University and his M.A. degree in management and organizational communication and his Ph.D. in management, organizational behavior, organizational theory, and personnel from the University of Nebraska. Davis has also taught at Colorado State University. Before embarking on his teaching career, he worked for ten years in brand management, advertising, and sales. He has served as a consultant to various service organizations and public agencies. His current research interests include the management of service businesses, the study of managerial behavior, natural learning processes, and management development.

Terrence E. Deal is a professor of education at Peabody College, Vanderbilt University. He received his B.A. degree in history and physical education from Laverne College, his M.A. degree in educational administration from California State University at Los Angeles, and his Ph.D. degree in educational administration and sociology from Stanford University. Deal has coauthored five books, including *Corporate Cultures: The Rites and Rituals of Corporate Life* (with Allan Kennedy, 1983) and *Modern Approaches to Understanding and Managing Organizations* (with Lee Bolman, 1984).

W. Gibb Dyer, Jr., is an assistant professor of organizational behavior at Brigham Young University. He received both his B.S. degree in psychology and his M.B.A. degree from Brigham Young University; his Ph.D. degree in organization studies was awarded by the Massachusetts Institute of Technology. His primary research interests are organizational culture, coping with change, and managing family-owned businesses. Articles on managing change in family businesses that Dyer has recently coauthored with Richard Beckhard have been published in *Organizational Dynamics* and *Sloan Management Review*.

George G. Gordon is partner and director of planning and development at Hay Associates. He received his B.A. degree from Rutgers University in psychology and his B.S. and Ph.D. degrees from Purdue University in industrial psychology. In

1970 he joined Hay Associates, and in 1975 he established Research for Management, a subsidiary focusing on survey research. In his work at Hay, Gordon both consults directly with clients and develops new consulting processes that can be applied by Hay consultants worldwide. His most important work is *Managing Management Climate* (with W. M. Cummins, 1979).

Jay W. Lorsch is the Louis E. Kirstein Professor of Human Relations and the chairman of the Advanced Management Program at the Graduate School of Business Administration at Harvard University. He received his A.B. degree from Antioch College, his S.M. degree from Columbia University, and his D.B.A. degree from Harvard University. Lorsch is the author or coauthor of twelve books, the best known of which are *Organization and Environment* (with P. Lawrence, 1967), *Organizations and Their Members* (with J. Morse, 1975), and *Managing Diversity and Interdependence* (with S. A. Allen III, 1976). His newest book is *Decision Making at the Top: The Shaping of Strategic Direction* (with G. Donaldson, 1983).

Meryl Reis Louis is an associate professor at the School of Management at Boston University and a research associate at the Center for Applied Social Science. She received her B.S. degree in management, her M.S. degree in management theory, and her Ph.D. in organizational sciences, all from the Graduate School of Management at the University of California at Los Angeles. She is a member of the editorial review boards of *Administrative Science Quarterly,* the *Academy of Management Review,* and the *Organizational Behavior Teaching Review.* Louis's research focuses on career transitions, sense-making practices in work settings, the culture of the workplace, and the sociology of social science.

Harry J. Martin is an assistant professor of management at Cleveland State University. He received his B.A. and M.A. degrees in psychology from Oregon State University and his Ph.D. degree from Southern Illinois University at Carbondale in organizational psychology. Martin's research interests include the relationship between power and leadership effectiveness and the impact of status on decision making. His most important work to date reports on the development of a scale designed to measure the need for social approval; this article, "A Revised Measure of Approval Motivation and Its Relationship to Social Desirability," will be published in a forthcoming issue of the *Journal of Personality Assessment.*

Ian I. Mitroff is the Harold Quinton Distinguished Professor of Business Policy in the Department of Management and Organization at the School of Business Administration, University of Southern California. He received his B.S. degree in engineering physics, his M.S. degree in structural mechanics, and his Ph.D. degree in engineering science and the philosophy of social science, all from the University of California, Berkeley. Mitroff has published over 140 papers and 7 books in the areas of business policy, corporate culture, managerial psychology and psychiatry, strategic planning, and the philosophy and sociology of science. His most recent book is *Corporate Tragedies: Product Tampering, Sabotage, and Other Catastrophes* (with R. Kilmann, 1984).

Kerry J. Patterson is the vice-president of Interact Performance Systems and a lecturer in organizational behavior at Brigham Young University. He received his B.S. and M.A. degrees in organizational behavior at Brigham Young University. He is currently working on his Ph.D. degree at Stanford University. Patterson's research focuses on interpersonal script acquisition. He is also involved in producing videotape instructional programs on problem solving in groups, the management of meetings, and performance review. These types of videotapes have been used to train tens of thousands of managers across the United States.

Alice M. Sapienza is an assistant professor of management in the Department of Health Policy and Management at the Harvard University School of Public Health. She received her B.S. degree from Stonehill College in chemistry, her M.A. degree from Boston College in English, and her M.B.A. and D.B.A. degrees from the Graduate School of Business Administration at Harvard University. Her research interests include the study of collective cognitive structures of top managers and their effects on decision making and executives' views on and attempts to manage their corporate cultures.

Vijay Sathe is an associate professor at the Graduate School of Business Administration at Harvard University. He received his B.S. degree from the University of Poona, India, and his M.S. degree from the University of Wisconsin at Madison, both in mechanical engineering. His Ph.D. degree in organizational behavior and his M.B.A. degree are both from Ohio State University. His recent book, *Managerial Action and Corporate Culture* (1985), is based on a graduate course he developed and has taught at Harvard for the last three years.

Edgar H. Schein is the Sloan Fellows Professor of Management at the Sloan School of Management at the Massachusetts Institute of Technology. He received his B.A. degree in general education from the University of Chicago, his M.A. degree in social psychology from Stanford University, and his Ph.D. degree in social psychology from Harvard University. Since 1957 he has worked as a consultant for major corporations on such issues as corporate culture, human resource planning, management development, organization development, and process consultation. His most recent book is *Organizational Culture and Leadership: A Dynamic View* (1985).

Nirmal K. Sethia is a visiting scholar in the Department of Management and Organization at the School of Business Administration, University of Southern California. He received his B. Tech. degree in electrical engineering from the Indian Institute of Technology in Bombay, his M.S. degree in electrical engineering from the University of Wisconsin at Madison, and his Ph.D. degree in organizational behavior from the Indian Institute of Technology in Bombay. Sethia's most recent writings focus on the implications of organizational culture for innovation.

Harrison M. Trice is a professor in the School of Industrial and Labor Relations at Cornell University. He received his B.A. degree in sociology and speech from Louisiana State University and both his M.A. degree in social psychology and his Ph.D. degree in sociology from the University of Wisconsin. Trice's publications in his main area of interest include the "Role of Ceremonials in Organizational Behavior," (with James Belasco and Joseph Alutto in *Industrial and Labor Relations Review,* 1969) and *Implementing Change* (with Janice M. Beyer, 1978). In addition to the study of rites and ceremonials, Trice's research interests include the implementation of organizational innovation and the evaluation of organizational interventions.

W. Brooke Tunstall is corporate vice-president for organization and management systems of the American Telephone and Telegraph Company. He received his B.E. degree in industrial engineering from Johns Hopkins University. His major research interests include organizational design and implementation, management systems, and corporate culture. His most significant publication is a recent book on the American Telephone and Telegraph Company divestiture, *Disconnecting Parties: Managing the Bell System Break-Up* (1985).

Mary Ann Von Glinow is an associate professor in the Department of Management and Organization at the School of Business Administration, University of Southern California. She received her B.A. in political science from Bradley University and her M.B.A. and M.A. in public administration and her Ph.D. in management science from Ohio State University. Von Glinow has published numerous articles on her research in journals such as *Organizational Behavior and Human Performance, Management Science,* and the *Academy of Management Journal.* Her research focuses on both the management of high technology and professional employees and systems of performance appraisal, reward, and feedback.

Alan L. Wilkins is an associate professor of organizational behavior at Brigham Young University. He received his B.A. degree in Spanish and his M.B.A. degree from Brigham Young University and his Ph.D. degree in organizational behavior from Stanford University. Among his publications are an article co-authored with William Ouchi in *Administrative Science Quarterly* (1983) entitled "Efficient Cultures: Exploring the Relationship Between Culture and Organizational Performance" and a forthcoming book on culture that develops the theme he and Kerry J. Patterson present here.

Gaining Control
of the
Corporate Culture

One

Introduction:
Five Key Issues in
Understanding and
Changing Culture

Ralph H. Kilmann
Mary J. Saxton
Roy Serpa

Which are the well-run companies? Are they the star performers so often referred to in articles about good management and organization—GE, GM, IBM, Texas Instruments? Not to mention the Mitsubishis, Sonys, ICIs, Phillipses, and Siemenses of the world? Whatever your list, a discussion of what makes these firms tops will involve notions of their strategic sense, their clear organization, their management systems, and their excellent top people. Even then, a description generally ends up with statements about some vague thing called corporate "style" or "culture." Apparently, the well-run corporations of the world have distinctive cultures that are somehow responsible for their ability to create, implement, and maintain their world leadership positions [Schwartz and Davis, 1981, p. 30].

1

The idea of managing corporate cultures is still quite new to most practitioners. At best, most managers have a vague sense of what the term *corporate culture* means: something having to do with the people and the unique quality or character of organizations. But ask how culture can be identified and, if found dysfunctional, changed, and most managers are at a loss. Some may talk about holding awards ceremonies to praise excellent performers or family picnics to bring employees together. For the most part, however, their knowledge of how to manage culture is even fuzzier than their definitions. This lack of knowledge about corporate culture is in sharp contrast to managers' intricate knowledge of goals, strategies, organization charts, policy statements, and budgets—the more tangible aspects of their organizations.

The purpose of this book is to bring together the "state of the art" of corporate culture from those who have been defining and managing it for several years—academics, managers, and consultants. As stated in the preface, the chapters in this book are written by those who are at the leading edge of this topic, selected either by special invitation or by the results of a special research competition on "Managing Corporate Cultures." The objective behind this selection process was to bring together a very excellent, timely, and cohesive body of original work.

To develop the selected chapters to their fullest potential, several available avenues were utilized. First, extensive editorial comments were provided to all authors to help them refine their chapters for publication. Second, each author delivered a thirty-minute presentation to a conference audience of academics and practitioners, followed by another thirty minutes of discussion and debate. This one-hour focus on each presentation is extensive compared to the time allocations typical at most professional meetings. Thus, each chapter benefited from several different sources of feedback.

The editorial process did not stop there, however. The conference also provided all participants with a unique learning experience: everyone witnessed the evolution of certain key cultural themes as the three-day conference unfolded. In fact, these key themes took on new meaning as the participants became more articulate and sophisticated in understanding the concept of corporate culture. Literally, one had to be at the conference to experience this special kind of active learning—to see how everyone struggled to make better sense of the nebulous topic before them. As the editors of this book, we can see how the conference discussions, in addition to our initial editorial recommendations for revision, have directly influenced the content and form of the final chapters.

The purpose of this introductory chapter is to highlight the five key themes that will be discussed in the remainder of this book: (1) Does culture have an impact on an organization? (2) How deep-seated is culture? (3) Can an organization have more than one culture? (4) Can culture be changed? (5) Can culture be changed without changing other aspects of an organization? These themes are addressed in one or more of the chapters in this book and, for the most part, transcend any collection of chapters. This introductory chapter allows us to highlight all five themes in ways that could not be done in any of the other chapters, nor could this chapter have been written without the benefit of the conference experience—without the gift of productive conversation and active learning.

Does Culture Have Impact?

There is not much point in attempting to study or change a thing called *culture* if it does not affect what goes on in organizations. An important assumption guiding all our discussions on this topic, therefore, is that culture *does* affect organizational behavior and performance. We find it useful to distinguish three interrelated aspects of impact: direction, pervasiveness, and strength.

The *direction* of impact is the course that culture is causing the organization to follow. Does culture influence behavior so that organizational goals are accomplished, or does culture push members to behave in ways that are counter to the formal mission and goals of the organization—is culture moving the organization in the right direction? If, for example, an organization's culture says, "don't rock the boat," yet it is innovation that is required for success in the organization's fast-paced, competitive environment, then the impact of that culture is in the wrong direction.

The *pervasiveness* of impact is the degree to which the culture is widespread, or shared, among the members of the group. Is the culture seen the same way by all members—is it highly pervasive—or is the culture seen very differently by different members within the organization? If each member of a work group is being influenced to behave in a different way, for example, the work group will not be able to act as a unit and will be immobilized. Whether each group in an organization (divisions, departments, and work groups) should have the same culture is another issue, and this will be discussed further later. For now, we will recognize that the members of any group must share a common view if the group is to act effectively.

The *strength* of impact is the level of pressure that a culture exerts on members in the organization, regardless of the direction. Do members feel compelled to follow the dictates of the culture, or do they feel that the culture only mildly suggests that they behave in certain ways? The social energy captured in culture can range from very weak to very strong. If a culture only mildly suggests what to do, the direction of the culture is largely inconsequential. However, a strong culture that puts considerable pressure on each person to behave in certain ways must be managed correctly; the consequences of a strong culture that channels behavior in the wrong direction—against the formal goals and objectives—can be devastating, and, conversely, a culture that captures the group's energy and imagination and moves activity in the right direction will help the organization accomplish its goals.

These three aspects of impact affect the performance of the organization. A culture has *positive* impact on an organization when it points behavior in the right direction, is widely shared among the members of work groups, and puts strong pressure on group members to follow the established cultural guidelines. Alternatively, a culture has *negative* impact on an organization when it points behavior in the wrong direction, is widely shared among group members, and exerts strong pressure on group members. If a culture is mobilized against the mission of the organization, it is better for the organization to have a weak culture (wrong direction, but not strong or pervasive among group members) than to have a mobilized counterculture (wrong direction, but very strong and pervasive). Considerable research is needed to learn how these different aspects of impact, separately and in combination, affect the performance and morale of different types of organizations in different settings. The empirical study by Gordon (Chapter Six) provides the most comprehensive study to date on the impact of corporate culture on performance in different industries, and Sapienza (Chapter Four) and Lorsch (Chapter Five) demonstrate how culture affects the strategic decisions made by top management and, hence, corporate performance.

How Deep-Seated Is Culture?

Culture can be defined as the shared philosophies, ideologies, values, assumptions, beliefs, expectations, attitudes, and norms that knit a community together. All of these interrelated psychological qualities reveal a group's agreement, implicit or explicit, on how to approach decisions and problems: "the way things are done around here." A key issue in discussions of corporate culture, however, is just how deep-seated these shared qualities are. The degree to which a culture is consciously and overtly rather than unconsciously and covertly manifest has much to do with how easily the culture can be studied and, ultimately, managed.

Culture is manifest in behavioral norms, hidden assumptions, and human nature, each occurring at a different level of depth. (Schein (Chapter Two) and Dyer (Chapter Twelve) also suggest the usefulness of viewing culture at different levels.)

Behavioral norms are just below the surface of experience; they are the unwritten rules of the game. Norms describe the behaviors and attitudes that the members of a group or organization pressure one another to follow. Norms, by definition, are not written but are transmitted from one generation of employees to another by stories, rites, rituals, and, particularly, sanctions that are applied when anyone violates a norm. Examples of norms are: don't disagree with your boss, don't rock the boat, do the minimum to get by, don't socialize with the boss, only wear dark business suits to work, don't share information with other groups, treat women as second-class citizens, cheat on your expense account, don't trust anyone who seems sincere, look busy even when you are not. When asked, most individuals can list the norms that operate in their work groups and can even suggest what new set of norms would be more effective for achieving higher performance and morale. Such discussions can also lead to the management of norms, as when members develop agreed-upon ways to change the old, dysfunctional (actual) norms into new, adaptive (desired) norms. Allen (Chapter Sixteen) and Kilmann (Chapter Seventeen) concentrate on this just-below-the-surface aspect of corporate culture.

At a somewhat deeper level lie the hidden assumptions—the fundamental beliefs behind all decisions and actions—that underlie culture. These assumptions pertain to the nature of the environment and to what various stakeholders—competitors, the government, financial institutions, prospective employees—want and need, how stakeholders make decisions, and which actions stakeholders are likely to take both now and in the future. For example, some assumptions that might be shared among the members of a group or organization are: no new competitor will enter the industry, the economy will steadily improve, the government will continue to restrict foreign imports, the consumer will buy whatever the firm produces, employees will continue to accept the same working conditions, new technology is more important than finding out what customers really desire, and what made the organization successful in the past will make the organization successful in the future.

These kinds of assumptions certainly have affected the types of decisions organizations have made in the past—strategic as well as day-to-day decisions—and will surely affect decisions in the future. Vested interests are always attached to critical organization decisions, such as which strategic directions to follow, which new products to market, and which new investments to make. Not surprisingly, it is difficult for most individuals to accept that the assumptions underlying their important decisions are no longer valid; if their assumptions are not valid, their previous decisions and the decisions they are proposing for the present may be invalid as well. In the extreme case, people may prefer to cling to their old assumptions rather than examine them and find out that most of their efforts have been in vain. Assumptions, therefore, are more difficult to examine and change than behavioral norms. To examine norms requires examination of day-to-day behavior as people interact with other members of the organization, but to examine assumptions requires examination of all previous decisions and actions —a much more threatening undertaking. Sathe (see Chapter Thirteen) provides the most explicit discussion of culture as conscious and unconscious assumptions.

At its deepest level, culture is the collective manifestation of human nature—the collection of human dynamics, wants, motives, and desires that make a group of people unique. Some properties of human nature, for example, can be generally shared among group members, although each group differs in the strength and nature of these qualities: mental capacity (only a few variables can be understood and analyzed at one time), memory (time erases the clarity and recall of events), and objectivity (psychological needs bias the interpretation of both current and past events). To understand how any group functions, therefore, we must understand which issues it is likely to emphasize or ignore, what information it is likely to select to retain, and how it is likely to distort information.

Other properties of human nature that can be shared among group members might include the following: people are often insecure, and their negative feelings of self-worth result in numerous defensive reactions and dysfunctional coping styles; some people have a strong desire for power and control and thus find it difficult to take any action that increases their dependency on their organizations; people resist change when their security and positions are threatened; and people do not universally have the ability to learn—sometimes all they can do is fight to survive. If we wish to understand how a group functions, we must also appreciate how human nature affects the way in which the group approaches new problems and opportunities. Various habitual reactions by the group cannot be fully explained by behavioral norms and hidden assumptions about the organization's environment. Rather, we must look to the unconscious dynamics of human nature in group settings.

Certain psychological characteristics, if widely shared among group members, permit the existence of behavior that is dysfunctional from the points of view of both the organization and its members. It seems that human fear, insecurity, oversensitivity, dependency, and paranoia eventually motivate members to protect themselves by being cautious, by minimizing their risks, and by going along with cultures that build protective barriers around work units and around entire organizations. Unfortunately, it is difficult to get group members to discuss these psychological dynamics and how they affect their interactions with the group. Generally, there are strong defense mechanisms that prevent individuals from seeing or discussing these unconscious motives and habits. Indeed, psychological defenses help individuals hold on to the belief that they themselves are rational, good, and pure and do not give in to primitive desires or nonrational approaches to problems. It is always the *other* groups and *other* organizations in which dysfunctional qualities are found. Because it is so difficult even to bring people to discuss deep-seated characteristics that affect work-group behavior, it is especially difficult to effect change in this area. Deal (see Chapter Fifteen) is most explicit in coming to grips with this deepest level of culture; he shows how the loss of meaning and the fear of dying are evoked during any change in an individual's life, including organizational change. Mitroff and Kilmann (see Chapter Eleven) suggest that an organization's taboos—those areas forbidden to discussion or action—provide the foundation of culture by ensuring social order and meaning.

We believe that it is most fruitful to view culture as manifesting itself at *all* of these levels through behavioral norms, hidden assumptions, and human nature. The critical question is: must we study and change culture at all levels to manage culture effectively? Clearly, more research and experience are necessary to answer this question. In the meantime, however, we can offer the following guidelines.

It seems that the most penetrating definitions of culture emphasize the deepest level of human nature or at least refer to shared but unstated assumptions, ideologies, philosophies, and values. Such definitions of culture also imply that it is very difficult to create culture change in any complex organization. Wilkins and Patterson (see Chapter Fourteen) make the strongest case for the inertia of corporate culture. This deeper perspective also tends to be advocated by academics who may be more concerned with understanding the concept of culture than with managing culture. These advocates of the deeper perspective seem to assume that change methods will naturally follow once we agree on definitions. However, many executives and people throughout organizations have difficulty openly discussing their assumptions, ideologies, philosophies, and values. In fact, organization members describe these discussions of culture as "academic."

At the other extreme are those definitions of culture that emphasize the more shallow levels—that emphasize the "rules of the game" and behavioral norms—although organization members usually can actively discuss culture at this level with minimal feelings of threat and discomfort. Defining culture primarily as behavioral norms allows managers and consultants to identify, assess, and change corporate cultures—at least at that level. These more pragmatic approaches, not surprisingly, are generally advocated by both academics and consultants who have been involved in programs to change work-group and organizational cultures. Allen (see Chapter Sixteen) and Kilmann (see Chapter Seventeen) illustrate methods for changing cultures with actual experiences of culture change. They assume that a comprehensive definition of culture will emerge *after* we know more about culture in situ. Thus, although the deeper approaches initially seem to be more penetrating, in practice they seem to be impractical; and although the more superficial approaches at first appear to disregard the more fundamental bases of culture, in practice they appear to offer some specific handles for managing culture.

We believe that the question of what is the proper depth at which to define, study, and manage culture does not require an either/or answer; culture is not based in human nature *or* hidden assumptions *or* behavioral norms. Future research can examine whether all three levels can be integrated so that practitioners can have a broader understanding of what causes or underlies behavioral norms as well as access to methods for managing the various manifestations of corporate culture.

Can an Organization Have More than One Culture?

However culture is defined and whichever level of depth is examined, it is important to consider whether an organization has one set of shared norms, assumptions, or qualities of human nature, or whether, instead, the organization has multiple cultures. Assuming one culture per organization would mean that it makes little difference which members or work groups are observed or questioned as to the organization's culture. Everyone could provide the same response. Alternatively, if there are multiple cultures, then culture must be studied and changed in different ways. When we look at a culture's pervasiveness, we are concerned with whether the members of a particular group all share the same culture; we say an organization has multiple cultures when different *groups* in the organization have different cultures, but each of these multiple cultures may be pervasive within its own domain. Louis (see Chapter Seven) provides the most thorough discussion on multiple cultures by examining both vertical and horizontal slices of culture in organizations. T. Davis (see Chapter Ten) is especially concerned with distinguishing between cultures at the top and cultures at the bottom of organizations.

We have found that managers and consultants who endorse a Theory X approach to managing people (or creating change in general) are more likely to assume the existence of only one culture—the culture that exists in top-management circles (McGregor, 1960). Just as top management determines the mission, strategy, and structure of the organization, it determines the cultural norms, values, beliefs, and assumptions of the organization. An excellent example of this traditional approach is illustrated by a *Fortune* cover story, "Corporate Culture Vultures" (Uttal, 1983), which reviewed only culture change programs in which consultants worked with top executives to design and sell single, new cultures to the members of organizations.

Consultants and managers who endorse a Theory Y approach to managing people and creating change generally assume that multiple cultures are likely to exist in most organizations. They tend to recognize differences between work groups as well as between individuals. Their view is that although an organization may have certain core values that are endorsed by all the members, the histories, incidents, people, and problems of each division, department, or work group shape culture differently in each situation. Culture is not a property of individuals (as, for example, personality is); it develops, however, when even a few people come together in a small group setting. The group is where culture first forms and then evolves, and it is also a key leverage point for changing an organization's cultures.

Whether an organization should have more than one culture can be decided not just by the organization's approach to managing people (Theory X versus Theory Y), but by the organization's goals and environment. Although considerable research on this topic still needs to be done, some guidelines can be drawn. First, an organization with a single product line facing a very homogeneous market might best be served by a culture that is uniform throughout the organization and that emphasizes behavior consistent with what is needed for success. Second, an organization with multiple products or services each facing a different market may require different cultures for its various business units, divisions, and departments. Here, it would be important for each division to have a culture that encourages the behavior, values, beliefs, and assumptions consistent with what is required for success in each case. S. Davis (see Chapter Eight) and Martin (see Chapter Nine) examine how corporate cultures fit with the expectations of various stakeholders and how cultures encourage adaptability to changing environments.

How different organizational structures fit different

types of environments, referred to as *differentiation,* has been examined by Lawrence and Lorsch (1967). For organizations to develop overall plans, policies, and procedures to coordinate differentiated divisional cultures, some superordinate culture, such as the need to coordinate efforts, share information, and comply with corporate policies and directions, must be shared among all divisions. A shared culture at the corporate level facilitates integration.

Having single organizational cultures shaped at the top-management levels made more sense in the past when the business environment was more stable and homogeneous than it is now. The complex and changing environments of the present and, most likely, the future, call for organizations to become more complex, diversified, and differentiated to survive, and multiple organizational cultures can help organizations be more effective. Certainly, the empirical study by Gordon (see Chapter Six) suggests that there is not a single "winning" culture, but the best culture is the one that is best adapted for success in an organization's particular business environment.

Can Culture Be Changed?

Whether a given culture can be changed depends on how deep-seated the culture is and whether multiple cultures exist. The deeper the level at which culture change is required and the more cultures there are in the organization, the more difficult and time consuming the culture-change process. Certainly, it is easier to conduct a change effort in the same way in every department and division in the organization than to design and implement a unique approach in each case.

When culture change involves changing surface-level behavioral norms, it can occur with relative ease because members can articulate what behaviors are required for success today in contrast to those required yesterday. In addition, closing the gap between actual and desired norms is easier if the desired norms are essentially the same throughout the organization—if the environment is homogeneous. Even when multiple cultures exist, requiring different changes in each work group, change is still easier to effect when the focus of culture change is on behavioral norms rather than hidden assumptions or human nature.

The *process* of identifying and changing culture is also affected by the level and number of cultures in the organization. Specifically, managing the deepest layers of cultures differently in each work unit requires a participative approach—a derivative of Theory Y. Top management, with or without the aid of consultants, cannot dictate changes in assumptions about human nature and the business environment or in the content of these assumptions in each unit of the organization. However, the top-down approach to culture change—a derivative of Theory X—might be feasible when a single corporate culture exists (those at the top thus *could* be accurate in their view of the desired culture) and if the focus is on changing norms and not assumptions. For example, Trice and Beyer (see Chapter Eighteen) outline how various types of rites and ceremonies can be designed and implemented by top management to either reinforce or alter particular behaviors. Similarly, as reported by Sethia and Von Glinow (see Chapter Nineteen), a top-down approach to changing the reward system and thus encouraging different behaviors is also feasible.

How long a change in culture will last and how firmly the change is ingrained in the behavior and decision-making processes in the organization also are related to the process of culture change. On the one hand, top-down approaches to changing behavioral norms result in changes that are difficult to sustain, even though such changes may be easy to bring about; top-down approaches generally result in overt compliance to what is mandated, not covert acceptance. On the other hand, participative approaches to changing underlying assumptions, although difficult and time consuming to implement, are likely to result in changes that last and are felt in everything that organization members do; participation yields overt commitment to and covert acceptance of what the group decides.

Which approach to culture change, then, should be used? Again, an either/or choice is not required. A feasible approach is to conduct some early culture change at the norm level, using a top-down approach, if necessary, to encourage the organization members to begin behaving in new ways. After the new culture achieves some successes, time can be devoted to changing the deeper, more fundamental aspects of culture so the change will be sustained. Now a participative approach can be used to fine-tune the culture change to the unique circumstances of each work unit as well as to challenge assumptions regarding the organization's environment and the essence of human nature. Thus, over time, all three levels of culture can be addressed, and the culture change desired by the organization and its members can be sustained. Tunstall (see Chapter Three) describes how American Telephone and Telegraph, formerly the largest company in the world, is undergoing dramatic culture change at all levels so the company can succeed in its new, highly competitive environment.

Can Culture Alone Be Changed?

Can culture change be accomplished by concentrating only on culture, or must other aspects of the organization be altered along with culture—both to enable culture to change at all and to sustain culture change into the future? Is culture an independent quality of the organization, or is culture intimately connected and linked to all other aspects of the organization?

Viewing the organization as analogous to a simple machine suggests that culture is independent. Just as a defective part can be replaced without altering the functioning parts of a machine, culture can be studied and treated independent of the rest of the organization. Alternatively, viewing the organization as an open system—as an interconnected, *living* organism whose parts are connected and dependent on each other—suggests that culture cannot be managed as a thing apart from the rest of the organization. All parts of the organization are altered by any culture change; in fact, these other parts may become dysfunctional and problematic unless they are taken into consideration by the managers and consultants responsible for culture change.

To better understand the view of organizations as interconnected organisms, let us consider an effort to establish new behavioral norms that is not supported by corresponding changes in the reward system. Once the culture change is in force (whether effected in a top-down or a participative manner), organization members would soon realize that the reward system is still rewarding their old behaviors, not the new behaviors encouraged by the new norms. If the reward system is not changed appropriately, or if the reward system cannot be changed (because it is mandated by corporate headquarters), members would soon be confused, frustrated, and perhaps angered by the conflicting signals being sent to them by the new culture and the performance appraisal system. These feelings would undermine both the cultural change and the reward system.

Although the metaphor of the organization as a simple machine was perhaps useful to explain the inner workings of organizations when the world itself was simpler and more stable, in today's complex environment, rapid change and instantaneous information worldwide not only shrinks the size of the world but interconnects all its parts as well. As a result, the metaphor of the organization as an open, living, interconnected system better describes the organization of today. Any efforts to effect culture change, therefore, could create more problems than are being solved if culture change is not looked at and managed from a systems perspective. When studying and changing culture, (1) the consequences of a culture change on all aspects of the organization (strategy, structure, reward systems, skills, work procedures, and so on) and (2) how all of these aspects may need to be altered to support culture change must be considered. Thus, all aspects of the organization, because they are interconnected, can be viewed by managers and consultants as leverage points for fostering positive culture change in the organization. Reward systems, work procedures, strategies, objectives, training programs, and work teams can be adjusted to ensure that the new culture takes hold and lasts (Kilmann, 1984).

The chapters in this book concentrate on managing corporate culture, often to the exclusion of all of the other manageable parts of the organization. It is important, however, that we keep in mind all of our other knowledge about managing and changing our complex organizations, even as we focus on the neglected topic of managing corporate cultures. .

Conclusion

The remainder of this book concentrates on what culture is, how to study culture, how cultures change, and how to change cultures. A final chapter offers some concluding comments, where we will again return to the issue of how culture is related to all other aspects of the organization. Here we will see that for culture to be the guiding force for revitalizing organizations, culture change must be systemic, well-planned, and integrated with all aspects of the organization. Otherwise, culture change will fail, and the topic of culture will disappear as have all the other quick-fix approaches to organizational renewal (Kilmann, 1984). Our belief is that culture is too important to the effective functioning of organizations to be dismissed as yesterday's fad. Culture is the glue that not only holds our organizations together, but our theories about them as well.

References

Kilmann, R. H. *Beyond the Quick Fix: Managing Five Tracks to Organizational Success.* San Francisco: Jossey-Bass, 1984.

Lawrence, P. R., and Lorsch, J. W. *Organization and Environment.* Boston: Division of Research, Graduate School of Business Administration, Harvard University, 1967.

McGregor, D. *The Human Side of Enterprise.* New York: McGraw-Hill, 1960.

Schwartz, H. M., and Davis, S. M. "Matching Corporate Culture and Business Strategy." *Organizational Dynamics,* Summer 1981, pp. 30-48.

Uttal, B. "The Corporate Culture Vultures." *Fortune,* Oct. 17, 1983, pp. 66-72.

Two

How Culture Forms, Develops, and Changes

Edgar H. Schein

A few years ago the concept of corporate or organizational culture was hardly mentioned by anyone but a few social scientists. Today it is one of the hottest topics around because many consultants and managers would like to believe that organizations can become more effective if they build or develop the "right" kind of culture. Furthermore, it is alleged by some that organizations can change dysfunctional cultures into ones that are better adapted to the environmental realities that the organizations face. Finally, it is argued that "strong" cultures are somehow more likely to be associated with effectiveness than are "weak" cultures, and that strong cultures can be deliberately created (Ouchi, 1981; Deal and Kennedy, 1982; Peters and Waterman, 1982).

The research on which this chapter is based was supported by the Office of Naval Research, Organizational Effectiveness Group, under contract NR 170-911. A more detailed account of some of the ideas presented here can be found in my book *Organizational Culture and Leadership: A Dynamic View* (San Francisco: Jossey-Bass, 1985). This chapter elaborates on the particular issues of culture change.

17

So the hunt is on for "right" and "strong" cultures, but the dilemma is that we do not know exactly what we are hunting for or what kinds of guns, traps, or other devices we should use to make the catch. And it is not at all clear that we would know what to do with the catch if we pulled it in. Many different definitions of organizational culture can be found, and many different models are advocated for creating, managing, or changing culture—or even for circumventing culture, just in case culture turns out to be an unfriendly animal.

Even if we learn how to decipher organizational culture, it is not at all clear that full knowledge of our own culture will help us change it. Sometimes self-awareness is a source of anxiety and discouragement, and sometimes self-awareness destroys the mystique of what we have. On the other hand, lack of insight into our own culture leaves us vulnerable to forces of evolution and change which we may not understand and which we may have difficulty controlling.

The dilemma can be seen clearly when we analyze the effects of the introduction of new technologies such as the information, control, and decision support systems that the computer has made possible. Such systems have the effect of forcing managers and employees to confront aspects of their culture that they had never thought about before. For example, the introduction of electronic mail makes managers confront the question of how they prefer to relate to each other and what assumptions they hold about decision making. In one organization, for instance, managers came to realize that they depended on face-to-face contact and frequent meetings. They chose to hold on to this way of working and, instead, subverted the electronic mail system.

In another organization, the introduction of personal computers on all executive desks made it possible for senior managers to be fully informed about all aspects of their organization, a power that they used to question lower-level managers about any deviations they noticed. This produced so much resentment, hiding of information, and even falsifying of information that the system had to be modified to introduce time delays into the information flow. Senior management saw data one day later than did lower-level management so that the latter could investigate any variances and find out the reasons for them before senior management demanded answers.

Insight into cultural matters also clearly affects the creation and implementation of strategy. Not only does culture limit the strategic options that are conceivable to an organization, but strategies cannot be implemented if they run against powerful cultural assumptions. This can be seen most clearly in an organization in transition from an engineering-based to a marketing-based operation. Not only is it difficult for the ex-engineer to conceive of marketing in the way that the professional marketer perceives this function, but the implementation of a marketing strategy may be undermined by the kind of people who are in the sales force, the incentive systems operating, the issues that executives pay attention to, and so on.

Yet the economic situation of an organization may dictate a strategy that requires some culture change, so we need to understand the conditions under which change is possible, and we need insight into how to manage the process of culture change. In thinking about such possibilities of change, we must not forget that culture as a concept was invented by anthropologists to describe those elements of a social system that were, in many senses, the *least* changeable aspects of that system.

These issues will be approached here by reviewing a model of corporate culture that emphasizes how culture is learned. If we are to influence and change the dynamics of culture, we must first have a clear model of the origins of culture.

A Dynamic Model of Organizational Culture

The simplest way to think about the culture of any group or social unit is to think of it as the total of the collective or shared learning of that unit as it develops its capacity to survive in its external environment and to manage its own internal affairs. Culture is the solution to external and internal problems that has worked consistently for a group and that is therefore taught to new members as the correct way to perceive, think about, and feel in relation to those problems. Such solutions eventually come to be assumptions about the nature of reality, truth, time, space, human nature, human activity, and human relationships—then they come to be taken for granted and, finally, drop out of awareness. The power of culture is derived from the fact that it operates as a set of assumptions that are unconscious and taken for granted.

The kinds of problems that any group faces can best be conceptualized as issues of external survival and internal integration. Any new company, whether it has just been formed or is the product of a merger, must develop, if it is to survive in its external environment: (1) a sense of its own mission or primary task, some reason for existing; (2) some concrete goals that are, typically, derived from the primary mission; (3) some means for accomplishing those goals through the development of appropriate organizational structures and decision-making processes; (4) some means of monitoring progress through the development of information and control systems; and, (5) some means of repairing structures and processes if they are not accomplishing the goals.

In order to function at all, however, the group must have (1) a common language and shared conceptual categories; (2) some way of defining its boundaries and selecting its members, a process typically embodied in the recruitment, selection, socialization, training, and development systems of the organization; (3) some way of allocating authority, power, status, property, and other resources; (4) some norms for handling interpersonal relationships and intimacy, creating what is often called the *style* or *climate* of the organization; (5) criteria for dispensing rewards and punishments; and (6) some way of coping with unmanageable, unpredictable, and stressful events, a problem usually resolved by the development of ideologies, religions, superstitions, magical thinking, and the like.

Note that organizational culture is the embodiment of solutions to a wide range of problems. We must never make the mistake of assuming that when we have described one salient aspect of a given organization, such as how people are managed, we have then described the whole culture. To describe a whole culture we must confront each of the external and internal issues that have been identified.

Organizations are also to some degree integrated by even more basic assumptions about broad human issues—about fundamental matters of organizational and environmental relations, the nature of human nature, the nature of human activity and relationships, and, most important, the nature of reality and truth—that embody fundamental concepts of time, space, and the nature of things.

We call these matters *assumptions* rather than *values* because we tend to be unconscious of them, to take them for granted and to view them as automatically true and non-negotiable. Whereas values can be debated and discussed, basic assumptions cannot. We are up against a basic assumption when our observations or questions are treated as stupid, crazy, or too absurd for response—such as when someone questions whether the world is round, whether it is necessary to make a profit, and so on.

Once a group has had enough of a history to develop a set of basic assumptions about itself, the culture can be viewed as existing at three levels, as shown in Figure 1. At the most superficial level are artifacts and creations, the visible behavioral manifestations of underlying concepts. They are easy to see but hard to decipher. If every office at Company A has an open door, if people wander into each others' offices and argue a lot, what does that mean? The artifactual visible and audible environment can provide clues, but rarely does it provide answers. If we attempt to describe it in broad categories we usually end up describing the style or climate of the organization.

The next level, values, has more credibility. If we ask people *why* they do what they do, we will elicit values and begin to understand the reasons behind some of their behaviors. We may learn that doors are open because the president of the company ordered them open in the belief that everyone should always be accessible. We may learn that people talk to each other because communication is highly valued, and that people argue a lot because they are required to agree on decisions before they act. We may also learn that middle managers are quite

Figure 1. The Levels of Culture.

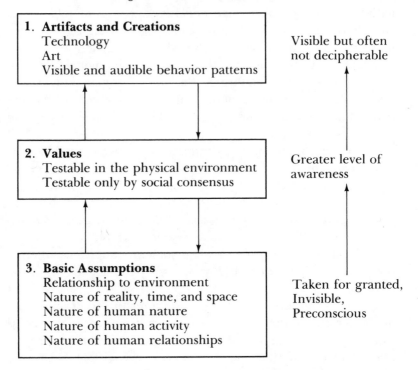

frustrated because decision making takes too long, but when they try to become more efficient and disciplined, "something" in the environment, something they cannot identify, resists.

When we have a sizable body of information about values, we can begin to see why the organization works the way it does, and often improvements immediately suggest themselves at this level. But we have not yet really confronted the essence of the culture at all. The values we have encountered are themselves only manifestations of the culture, not what we could think of as the driving force or essence of the culture. At this level we may be seeing the "ideology," "philosophy," "charter," or basic "credo" of the organization.

What really drives or creates the values and overt responses are the learned underlying assumptions of level three. As a group or organization solves its collective problems, it always operates with some world view, some cognitive map, some hypotheses about reality, and, if it has success in solving those problems, that world view comes to be seen as correct and valid. It changes from a hypothesis or a value into an assumption, and, if it continues to work, it gradually drops out of awareness altogether.

Because of the human need for consistency and order, the basic assumptions of a group gradually form a pattern, assuming that the group has a long enough life for this process to happen. Culture thus can be described as the *pattern* of *underlying assumptions,* a pattern that is implicit, taken for granted, and unconscious unless called to the surface by some process of inquiry.

If we continue to probe into Company A, for example, we will discover that the underlying reason that people have open doors and frequent meetings is the shared assumption that truth can only be determined by some process of testing ideas on each other. This assumption about truth is combined with the assumption that anyone can have good ideas but no one is smart enough to assess his or her own ideas, not even the boss, and, hence, mutual testing is the only way to determine truth, even if that takes time and energy.

By contrast, if Company B has many locked offices and few meetings, the organization's basic assumptions may be that each manager's job is considered to be that manager's personal turf, not to be interfered with unless there is clear evidence of failure, and then only the boss has a right to intrude with suggestions and corrective measures. Whereas in the first organization there is information overload and frustration over slow decision making because too many people can get into the act, in the second organization there is frustration over the inability to get innovative information from one part of the organization to another. The suggestion that there should be a system of lateral communication simply never gets off the ground because it is assumed that the manager will be threatened and insulted if information is offered when none has been asked for.

Assumptions can grow up about the nature of a successful product, what the marketplace and customers are like, which functions in the company really are the most important, what is the best form of organization, how people should be motivated and managed based on Theory X or Theory Y assumptions, whether or not individuals or groups are the ultimate unit of the organization, and so on for each of the issues of external survival and internal integration. It is the basic paradigm that these assumptions create that is the most basic and most important layer of an organization's culture.

How Culture Is Learned

Culture is learned essentially through two interactive mechanisms: anxiety and pain reduction—the social trauma model—and positive reward and reinforcement—the success model.

Suppose that an individual founds a new group. This group will encounter from the beginning the basic anxiety that comes from uncertainty as to whether or not the group will survive and be productive and whether the members will be able to work with each other. Cognitive and social uncertainty is traumatic, leading group members to seek ways of perceiving, thinking, and feeling that they can share and that make life more predictable. The founder may have his or her own preferred ways of solving these problems and these may become embedded in the group, but only if the group shares in the solutions and sees how they work can we think of cultural learning (Schein, 1983, 1985).

In addition to these initial traumas, every new group will face crises of survival in its early history. As members share the perception of the crisis and develop ways of handling it, they learn to overcome the immediate discomfort and also ways to avoid such discomfort in the future. When a situation arises that is similar to a prior crisis, it will arouse anxiety and cause the group to do what it did before in order to reduce the anxiety. It will avoid as much as possible reliving the actual discomfort and pain if it can be avoided by ritualistic ways of thinking, feeling, and behaving.

If a young company facing extinction because of a product failure, for example, learns that it has underengineered its product and then survives by careful redesign of the product, it may well learn that to avoid such trauma in the future, it should engineer products more carefully in the first place, even though that is costly. Whatever works to save the organization is learned as the way to avoid future trauma. Members of the organization begin to think of careful engineering as "the way we do things around here," and they teach new, incoming engineers that "we should always design products very carefully" because of the now unconscious assumption that this is the way to win in the marketplace.

The problem with this learning mechanism is that once people learn how to avoid a painful situation, they continue to pursue this course without testing to see whether the danger still exists. The company that now carefully engineers everything cannot find out whether customers now would accept a less well-engineered and less costly product. Trauma-based learning is hard to undo because it hinders testing for changes in the environment. Cultural assumptions learned by this means can thus be thought of as defense mechanisms that the group has learned to cope with anxiety and potential trauma (Jaques, 1955; Menzies, 1960).

Learning theorists also note that trauma-based learning is so stable because not only does the ritualized response avoid the pain, but the actual reduction of the anxiety is itself very rewarding. Thus, some ways of thinking about organizational problems produce the immediate comfort of anxiety reduction, even though those ways of thinking may be dysfunctional in terms of adaptation to a rapidly changing environment. And if those ways of thinking have become ingrained as basic assumptions about the nature of the world, it is no small task to change them.

The second major learning mechanism is positive reinforcement. People repeat what works and give up what does not. If a young company begins with its founder's belief that the way to succeed is to provide good service to customers or to treat employees as the organization's major resource or always to sell the lowest-priced product in the marketplace, and if action based on that belief succeeds in the marketplace, then the group will learn to repeat whatever worked and gradually to accept this as a shared view of how the world really is, thereby creating a piece of its culture.

This learning mechanism is different from trauma-based learning in that it produces responses that continually test the environment. If the environment changes so that strategies that previously were consistently successful no longer work, the group will quickly discover this, and their strategies will be reexamined and changed. This learning mechanism can, however, produce behavior that is very resistant to change if the environment is inconsistent, producing success at one time and failure at another time. Unpredictable, intermittent reinforcement leads to very stable learning just as trauma does.

Once we have adopted a model for learning culture, the question of whether every organization has a culture can be answered in terms of whether or not it has had an opportunity for such social learning to occur. For example, if staff turnover has been low, especially for key positions, and if people have a history of intense experiences with each other, a collective, shared way of thinking can develop very quickly, as it often did in wartime in military units. Thus, it can be postulated that the strength, clarity, and degree of integration of a corporate culture or subculture is directly proportional to the stability of the membership of the group, the length of time the group has been together, and the intensity of the collective learning that has taken place.

If we adopt such a view of how corporate culture is learned, we can see that a strong culture cannot simply be created by executive action. Such a culture evolves through shared history, not managerial decisions to have a strong culture. We can also define subcultures from this perspective. Any group within an organization has the potential of developing its own culture if it has stable membership and a history of joint problem solving. Thus, we would expect to find within a given organization a variety of cultures based on functions, geography, rank, project teams, and so forth that, from the point of view of the total organization, can be thought of as subcultures, just as the total corporate culture, if there is one, can be thought of as a subculture vis-a-vis the larger society in which the company operates.

Self-Awareness and Culture Change

Given this model of organizational culture, what are the pros and cons of gaining insight into the underpinnings of a culture and how does this relate to culture change? The answer depends on the circumstances in which the organization finds itself, as Table 1 illustrates—assuming that an organization's culture is different at different stages of development (Davis, 1982), and that the kind of change that is possible depends upon the flexibility of the organization and the degree to which it is ready to change, either because of some externally induced crisis or some internal forces pushing toward change (Schein, 1980; Dyer, 1984). Table 1 shows three major developmental periods that can be identified in organizations and for each period presents hypotheses as to what the major culture issues are, how much self-awareness is crucial, and what change mechanisms are likely to be operating.

Birth and Early Growth

The early stage of an organization includes a whole host of substages and processes and can last anywhere from a few years to a few decades. At this stage the organizational culture serves the critical function of holding the organization together while it grows and matures. It is the glue that permits rapid growth and the influx of many newcomers. During this stage we might expect to see strong socialization processes that almost become control mechanisms, and we might observe strong defensiveness about the organizational culture because members recognize how critical the culture is as a force for integration.

At this stage the culture can be seen as a distinctive competence, and as a source of identity and strength. Assumptions about distinctive competence can involve the organization's products, processes, and structure. It can even involve the rela-

Table 1. Growth Stages, Functions of Culture, and Mechanisms of Change.

Growth Stage	Function of Culture	Mechanism of Change
I. *Birth and Early Growth*		
• Founder domination, possible family domination	• Culture is a distinctive competence and source of identity • Culture is the "glue" that holds organization together • Organization strives toward more integration and clarity • Heavy emphasis on socialization as evidence of commitment	1. Natural evolution 2. Self-guided evolution through therapy 3. Managed evolution through hybrids 4. Managed "revolution" through outsiders
Succession phase:	• Culture becomes battleground between conservatives and liberals • Potential successors are judged on whether they will preserve or change cultural elements	
II. *Organizational Midlife*		
• New-product development • Vertical integration • Geographic expansion • Acquisitions, mergers	• Cultural integration declines as new subcultures are spawned • Crisis of identity, loss of key goals, values, and assumptions • Opportunity to manage direction of cultural change	5. Planned change and organizational development 6. Technological seduction 7. Change through scandal, explosion of myths 8. Incrementalism

III. *Organizational Maturity*
- Maturity of markets
- Internal stability or stagnation
- Lack of motivation to change

• Culture becomes a constraint on innovation
• Culture preserves the glories of the past, hence is valued as a source of self-esteem, defense

9. Coercive persuasion
10. Turnaround
11. Reorganization, destruction, and rebirth

Transformation option:

• Culture change necessary and inevitable, but not all elements of culture can or must change
• Essential elements of culture must be identified, preserved
• Culture change can be managed or simply be allowed to evolve

Destruction option:
- Bankruptcy and reorganization
- Takeover and reorganization
- Merger and assimilation

• Culture changes at basic levels
• Culture changes through massive replacement of key people

tionships among the members of the organization, as was the case in one young and rapidly growing company in the lawn service business that chose its employees—not its customers or stockholders—as its primary stakeholders. All the company's truck drivers, secretaries, and maintenance people were fully instructed in the economics of the business on the theory that this would make them feel totally committed and professional and that they thus would see to it that customers were found and were treated well. When this company was faced with the need to diversify, it was the employees who proposed a new series of services based on their ability to sell those services to customers whom they had developed on their own. The continued success of this company hinges on its ability to maintain its employees' identification with its core mission, even among a work force that is rapidly growing.

Self-awareness is critical in that it is important for members to recognize what their source of strength really is, but the process of achieving that insight is not easy because people only want to look at the positive and desirable qualities of the culture at this stage. A company may have gotten where it is by ruthless competition in the marketplace and ruthless weeding out of incompetents within the organization, but it does not necessarily want to accept that image as its distinctive competence and source of strength.

During the period when the founder or the founder's family is still dominant in the organization, we can expect little change in the culture but considerable effort to clarify, integrate, maintain, and evolve the culture, primarily because it is identified with the founder. Culture *change* becomes an issue only under two conditions: the company runs into economic difficulties, forcing key managers to re-evaluate their culture, or succession from the founder to professional managers forces assessment of what kind of managers to pick.

How then does culture change during this stage? Four mechanisms can be identified.

Mechanism 1: Natural Evolution. If the organization is not under too much external stress and if the founder or founding family are around for a long time, the culture simply evolves according to what works best over the years. Such evolution involves two basic processes: general evolution and specific evolution.

General evolution toward the next stage of development is the result of diversification and increasing organizational complexity, differentiation, and integration. In addition, the elements of the culture that operate as defenses are likely to be retained and strengthened over the years.

Specific evolution is the adaptation of specific parts of the organization to their particular environments. Thus, a high technology company may develop highly refined research and development skills, while a consumer products company may develop highly refined marketing skills. Such differences reflect important underlying assumptions about the nature of the world as well as the actual growth experiences of the organizations.

Mechanism 2: Self-Guided Evolution Through Organizational Therapy. If culture is, in part, a defense mechanism to avoid uncertainty and anxiety, then it should be possible to help an organization assess the strengths and weaknesses of its culture and modify the culture if that is necessary for effective functioning and survival. Therapy that operates by creating self-awareness permits cognitive redefinition to occur and thereby can produce dramatic changes. This process requires outsiders to help unfreeze the organization, provide psychological safety, analyze the present defensive nature of the culture, reflect back to key people in the organization how the culture seems to be operating, and further the process of cognitive redefinition (Schein and Bennis, 1965; Schein, 1969).

When this process works, usually because the client is highly motivated to change, dramatic shifts in assumptions can take place. One company, for example, could not make a crucial transition because of its history of defining marketing in very limited terms as "merchandising" and, hence, seeing little value in the function. The assumption that marketing was of little importance led to the hiring of ineffective marketers and the loss of the good ones that the company had. Only when key executives gained real personal insight into how they defined marketing and then redefined the function in their own minds were they able to adopt the assumption that marketing could help the company succeed.

Most practitioners of planned change and organizational development subscribe to the therapeutic and self-awareness model. The assumption has to be made that the system is unfrozen—that is, that there is motivation to change and a readiness for self-awareness, however much discomfort this might entail. Organizations sometimes have to get into real trouble, however, before they recognize their need for help, and then they often do not seek the right kind of help. Sadly, organizations are no different in this regard than individuals.

Mechanism 3: Managed Evolution Through Hybrids. One process that operates in many companies is captured by the feeling "we don't like what the boss is doing to change the place, but at least he is one of us." If the organization's leaders recognize the need for some change but do not quite know how to create it, they begin systematically to select for key jobs those members of the old culture who best represent the new assumptions that the leaders want to implement.

One rapidly growing company, for example, was faced with the problem of moving from the assumption that everybody should think for themselves and exercise local option, to the assumption that some decisions must be made at the top and then implemented by subordinates in an efficient and disciplined way. To achieve this new way of operating, the chief executive officer increasingly selected for senior management positions younger managers who had grown up with and who believed in more disciplined ways of doing things, in this case, managers with a manufacturing background.

Formal management succession when the founder or founding family finally relinquishes control provides an opportunity to change the direction of the culture if the successor is the right kind of hybrid, representing what is needed for the organization to survive, yet being seen as acceptable "because he is one of us" and therefore also a conserver of the important elements of the old culture. An interesting special case is the outsider who is "groomed" as the successor to the founder by being asked to serve for a number of years on the board of directors and thereby become partially acculturated.

Mechanism 4: Managed "Revolution" Through Outsiders. It is not uncommon in the succession process of a young and growing company to turn to outsiders to fill key positions on the grounds that the organization needs to be more "professionally" managed—that is, needs to bring in modern management tools that the founder is often perceived to lack. Turning to outsiders is also the most likely course if the company is in economic difficulty because of inefficiencies perceived to be associated with the old culture.

Dyer (1984) has studied this change mechanism in several organizations and has found what appear to be the key conditions necessary for this process to work. Assuming that the outsider is really seen as different, not merely a hybrid, it would appear that the following scenario is typical. First, the organization develops a sense of crisis because of declining performance or some kind of failure in the marketplace and concludes that it needs a new managerial approach. At the same time, some of the powerful supports of the old culture are weakened—the company may go public, for example, thus reducing the power of a few owners. An outsider is brought in with different assumptions, many of which immediately conflict with the old culture, causing skepticism, resistance, and possibly even sabotage of the new leader's program. If organizational performance improves and if the new leader is given credit for the improvement, he or she will survive, and new assumptions will begin to operate. "We don't like his approach, but we can't argue with the fact that he made us profitable once again, so maybe we have to try the new ways." If improvement does not occur or the new leader is not given credit for what improvement does occur, he or she will be forced out. Sometimes this cycle has to be repeated several times with different outsiders before new assumptions begin to take hold.

Organizational Midlife

The cultural issues of organizational midlife are very different from those of the earlier stage of growth. The organization is established and must now maintain itself through a continuous process of growth and renewal. Whether or not to pursue growth through geographic expansion, development of new products, opening up of new markets, vertical integration to improve its cost and resource position, mergers and acquisitions, divisionalization, or spin-offs becomes a major strategic issue.

Whereas culture was nourished during the growth period, it is likely that the most important elements of the culture are now embedded in the structure and major processes of the organization, and consciousness of the culture and deliberate attempts to build, integrate, or conserve the culture hence are less important. The culture that the organization acquired during its early years now is taken for granted. The only elements that are likely to be consciously fostered and articulated are the credos, dominant values, company slogans, written charters, and other public pronouncements of what the company wants to be and claims to stand for, its *espoused* values and theories (Argyris and Schön, 1978).

At this stage it is difficult to decipher the culture and make people aware of it because it is so embedded in routines. It may even be counterproductive to make people aware of it unless there is some crisis or problem to be solved. Managers view culture discussions as boring and irrelevant, especially if the company is large and well established.

At this stage there may be strong forces toward cultural diffusion, toward loss of integration because powerful subcultures have developed in the system and because it is difficult to maintain a highly integrated, uniform culture in a large, increasingly differentiated organization. Furthermore, it is not clear how important it is for all of the elements of the culture to be uniform and integrated. Some conglomerates, for example, have spent much time wrestling with the question of whether to attempt to preserve or, in some cases, to try to build a common culture among their various businesses. Is such an effort worth its costs? Is there a danger of imposing a culture on a subunit that does not fit its situation at all? On the other hand, if subunits are all allowed to develop their own cultures, what is the competitive advantage of being a single organization?

Geographic expansions, mergers, and acquisitions all require careful assessment to determine whether the cultures being integrated or merged are, in fact, compatible. The major conclusion to be drawn about this stage, then, is that culture is a complex issue with numerous facets and ramifications. It could almost be argued that at this stage there are so many possible conditions that might require management of cultural issues that the leaders of mature, healthy companies should be required to understand as much as possible about cultural dynamics. If they then must manage their business through growth, diversification, an acquisition, or a merger, they would have the necessary insights and skills to diagnose and manage the cultural aspects of the situation.

Such insights and skills become especially important when external or internal conditions change and create a crisis. At such times, leaders need to know more than the espoused values of their organizations. They need insight into the foundations of the existing culture so they can surmount any limitations on strategic options it may impose, and they need the skills to bring about culture change.

Mechanism 5: Planned Change and Organizational Development. Much of the work of organizational development practitioners involves the knitting together of diverse and warring subcultures, helping the dominant coalition or the client manager figure out how to integrate constructively the multiple agendas of different groups (Beckhard and Harris, 1977). Thus, conflicts between headquarters and field staffs, between divisions, between functional groups, or, in a matrix system, between functional groups and project groups, and so on all require an understanding of the company's culture and intervention that creates mutual insight and develops a commitment to superordinate company goals. Such commitment always seems to involve both self-awareness and insight into the assumptions of other groups with which there is conflict.

Such therapeutic intervention generally is thought of as part of the work of organizational development, but planned-change programs generally must go beyond producing insight to help leaders manage the actual change process—from unfreezing the organization through the change stage itself to refreezing the organization once more (Schein, 1980).

Mechanism 6: Technological Seduction. The introduction

of new technologies causes culture change in two ways. The introduction of new behavior patterns disrupts the social and interpersonal relationships that have been built up around the old technology and thus forces an examination and reevaluation of the assumptions on which those patterns were built. Therefore, anytime we change a part of the technical system of an organization, we are forcing the assumptions to surface that might otherwise remain implicit.

In addition, technological change usually involves new assumptions about the nature of the organization's mission, goals, means, measurements, and remedial actions. Such assumptions are built into the technology itself but may not be recognized until the technology is in place. Both of these change mechanisms can be seen when we examine the introduction of computerized information and decision-support systems. By linking people through an electronic mail system and by making information widely available to people at all levels in the organization, the assumptions of how people relate to each other and how information is used as a power base are forced into the open. Managers who prefer face-to-face relationships must either subvert the new technology or give up that way of working. People who want to protect the power base that having special access to information gives them must either subvert the technology or find new types of information that are not so easily entered into the computerized system.

A computerized system also brings with it assumptions about the nature of information that may or may not be congruent with prior assumptions: that information can be quantified and coded into computer categories, that having more information is better than having less, that accuracy of communication is enhanced by reducing face-to-face negotiation, that having information available in many places at the same time is desirable, and so on. Beneath these assumptions may be more fundamental ones about the nature of the business that will not be examined until the system is in place.

The insightful manager of change may deliberately introduce new technology to unfreeze the system, but the insightful member of the organization may resist the technology for the same reason: because it will upset relationships and cause cultural change, which the employee views as potentially undesirable. Seduction then becomes an apt metaphor for the effect of the technology on organization members.

Mechanism 7: Change Through Scandal, Explosion of Myths. As a company matures it develops a positive ideology and a set of myths about how it operates, what Argyris and Schön (1978) have labelled "espoused theories," while at the same time it continues to operate by other assumptions, which they label *theories-in-use* and which more accurately reflect what actually goes on. For example, an organization may claim that it takes individual needs into consideration in making geographical moves yet make it virtually impossible for people to refuse reassignment because of the assumption that individuals who refuse de facto take themselves off the promotional track. An organization may claim that it uses rational decision-making techniques and market research when introducing new products yet may allow the biases and pet projects of certain key managers to prevail.

It is where such incongruities exist between espoused theories and theories-in-use that this change mechanism operates most clearly. Nothing changes until the consequences of the theory-in-use create a visible, public scandal that cannot be hidden, avoided, or denied. A senior executive who has been posted to a position he did not want commits suicide, and his note makes it clear that he felt the company pushed him into it. A product fails in the market place or turns out to be unsafe, and members of the organization leak the fact that their own research had revealed the problem before the product was brought to market. Such events suddenly expose an element of the culture in such a way that it is immediately reassessed as incongruent. Strong policies are then immediately put in place to change the assumption that was in operation.

This mechanism tends to be more evolutionary than managed, so it may be more properly noted as an event that causes change than as a tool for organizations to use. It is possible, however, to imagine scenarios in which managers actually engineer scandals in order to induce some of the changes they want.

Mechanism 8: Incrementalism. Incrementalism is achieved when all of a manager's decisions are consistently biased toward a new set of assumptions, even though individually each decision is a small change. The concept was introduced by Quinn (1978) to describe what he saw as the actual process by which strategy is implemented in organizations. Key leaders do not create massive changes even when they have a clear idea of where they eventually want to end up. Instead they look for opportunities to make small changes, constantly test how these worked, and concentrate on the opportunistic utilization of fortuitous events to move the system in the desired direction.

Such a process changes the culture slowly over a long period of time, especially if one set of such incremental decisions is the replacement of people in key positions by people with different assumptions. Executive selection and staffing processes are, in this sense, one of the most powerful agents of culture change.

In summary, organizational midlife is the period when managers have the most choice as to whether and how to manage cultural issues and is therefore the time when they need to be most aware of how to diagnose where the organization is and where it is going. As organizations face increasingly turbulent environments, *flexible* cultures, cultures that encourage diversity rather than uniformity, may well be more advantageous than *strong* cultures.

Organizational Maturity

The last stage of development is perhaps the most important from the point of view of culture change, because some organizations find that pieces of their culture—or even their entire culture—become dysfunctional in a dynamic, competitive environment. If a company has had a track record of success with certain assumptions about itself and the environment, it is unlikely to want to challenge or reexamine those assumptions. Even if it brings them to consciousness, it tends to want to hold on to them because they justify the past and are the source of organization members' self-esteem. Such assumptions now operate as filters that make it difficult for key managers to understand alternative strategies for survival and renewal, no matter how clear the data and argument. Even if alternative strategies are understood, they often cannot be implemented because the new concepts are not comprehended or accepted down the line in the organization.

A company that has built its success on basic research, for example, may see itself confronted by a world in which it is not clear that there is much left to be invented, where patents have run out, and where younger, more flexible competitors are threatening. The company needs more innovative marketing strategies, but the culture is built around research, and the creative marketers have a hard time getting the attention they need from senior management. The research department itself needs to become more responsive to the marketplace, but it still believes that it knows best. Even those senior managers who can see the dilemma are caught in the culture in that they cannot really challenge and overrule the powerful research people. On the interpersonal side, the culture dictates that a job is a person's own fiefdom. To ask for help or to accept it are both signs of weakness. To offer help or information is potentially insulting in that it implies that the recipient does not know his or her job. Everyone is for change, but no one knows how to bring it about, and the anticipated anxiety of real self-examination effectively keeps change from happening.

In this kind of situation, the choices are between rapid transformation of parts of the culture so the organization can become competitive once again, creating what can be thought of as a *turnaround,* or destruction of the group and its culture through some process of *total reorganization* via a merger, acquisition, or bankruptcy proceedings. In either case some strong, new change managers will be needed first to unfreeze the organization and then to implement a program of change. The first steps will often involve coercive forces.

Mechanism 9: Coercive Persuasion. The concept of coercive persuasion, originally developed through studies of prisoners of war in Korea (Schein, 1961), argues that if the people to be changed can be physically or psychologically restrained from leaving, they can be made more susceptible to whatever changes are to be made. Thus, if an uncomfortable culture change is to be undertaken, people will be more likely to accept it if they have no choice—no alternative jobs to go to, the loss of stock options or pension benefits, the threat of being blackballed with other potential employers, and so on.

If exit can be prevented, the change manager can escalate the amount of change and can count on more willingness to tolerate the discomfort of change. At the same time, if the rewards of success follow quickly on the heels of this change, a real momentum toward new cultural assumptions can be generated. The change manager here needs great insight and skill to manipulate the restraining forces and incentives, a skill that is the essential characteristic of successful turnaround managers.

Mechanism 10: Turnaround. Turnaround is really the use of many of the other mechanisms of change to alter a situation where the present culture has become to some degree dysfunctional. The first condition for change through some kind of turnaround is that the organization's culture must be unfrozen. Either because of external realities that threaten organizational survival or because of new insights and plans on the part of the board of directors or the dominant management coalition, the organization must recognize that some of its old ways of thinking, feeling, and acting are obsolete.

If the organization is unfrozen in this sense, change is possible if there is a turnaround manager or team with a clear sense of where the organization needs to go, a model of how to change the culture to get there, and the power to implement the model. If any of these is lacking, the process will fail. We know from organizational-change theory that the key both to unfreezing an organization and to managing change is to create enough psychological safety to permit members to bear the anxieties that come with reexamining and changing parts of their culture. The turnaround management team must have the insight and skill necessary to manage a range of change mechanisms without arousing defensive resistance. If the replacement of people in key positions is required, for example, this must be managed in such a way that it is seen as necessary and carried out so that some of the most basic cultural assumptions are pre-served.

Turnarounds usually involve all organization members, so the old culture and its dysfunctional qualities become clearly visible to everyone. The process of developing new assumptions then is a process of cognitive redefinition through teaching and coaching; changing the structure and processes where necessary; consistently paying attention to and rewarding evidence of learning the new ways; creating new slogans, stories, myths, and rituals; and in other ways coercing people at least into new be-havior (Schein, 1983). All of the change mechanisms may come into play, but it is the turnaround manager's ability to coerce that is the key to turnarounds.

Mechanism 11: Reorganization, Destruction, and Rebirth. Little is known or understood about this process, so little will be said about it here. Suffice it to say that if the group that is the carrier of a given culture is eliminated or destroyed, that culture is also destroyed, and whatever new group begins to function builds its own, new culture. This process is traumatic and therefore not typically used as a deliberate strategy, but it may be necessary if economic survival is at stake.

Conclusion

There are five mistakes that need to be avoided in think-ing about organizational culture.

1. *Do not oversimplify culture.* Culture is more fundamental than behavior patterns and values; it is the basic assump-tions that define the learned reality of a given group.
2. *Do not forget how culture is learned.* If trauma-based learn-ing underlies the culture, remember that people will resist change.
3. *Do not limit your thinking about areas of culture content.* Culture goes beyond human relations into fundamental concepts of reality, truth, social structure and organization design, how decisions are made, and so on.
4. *Do not assume that culture change is simple.* It involves at

least the eleven mechanisms outlined here—and probably many more.

5. *Do not assume that more culture or stronger culture is better.* What is better depends on the stage of evolution of the company and its current state of adaptiveness. Instead of seeking that elusive, possibly nonexistent, and possibly dangerous thing—a strong culture—try to understand and use the strengths of the existing culture.

If we give culture its due, if we take an inquiring attitude toward the deciphering of culture, if we respect what culture is and what functions it serves, we will find that it is a potentially friendly animal that can be tamed and made to work for us.

References

Argyris, C., and Schön, D. A. *Organizational Learning: A Theory of Action Perspective.* Reading, Mass.: Addison-Wesley, 1978.

Beckhard, R., and Harris, R. T. *Organizational Transitions.* Reading, Mass.: Addison-Wesley, 1977.

Davis, S. M. "Transforming Organizations: The Key to Strategy Is Context." *Organizational Dynamics,* Winter 1982, pp. 64-80.

Deal, T. E., and Kennedy, A. A. *Corporate Cultures: The Rites and Rituals of Corporate Life.* Reading, Mass.: Addison-Wesley, 1982.

Dyer, W. G. "The Cycle of Cultural Evolution in Organizations." Unpublished paper, Sloan School of Management, Massachusetts Institute of Technology, 1984.

Jaques, E. "Social Systems as a Defense Against Persecutory and Depressive Anxiety." In M. Klein, P. Heimann, and R. Money-Kyrle (eds.), *New Directions in Psychoanalysis.* London: Tavistock, 1955.

Menzies, I. E. P. "A Case Study in the Functioning of Social Systems as a Defense Against Anxiety." *Human Relations,* 1960, *13,* 95-121.

Ouchi, W. G. *Theory Z.* Reading, Mass.: Addison-Wesley, 1981.

Peters, T. J., and Waterman, R. H., Jr. *In Search of Excellence:*

Lessons from America's Best-Run Companies. New York: Harper & Row, 1982.

Quinn, J. B. "Strategic Change: Logical Incrementalism." *Sloan Management Review,* 1978, *20,* 7–21.

Schein, E. H. *Coercive Persuasion.* New York: Norton, 1961.

Schein, E. H. *Process Consultation.* Reading, Mass.: Addison-Wesley, 1969.

Schein, E. H. *Organizational Psychology,* 3rd ed. Englewood Cliffs, N.J.: Prentice-Hall, 1980.

Schein, E. H. "The Role of the Founder in Creating Organizational Cultures." *Organizational Dynamics,* Summer 1983, pp. 13–29.

Schein, E. H. *Organizational Culture and Leadership: A Dynamic View.* San Francisco: Jossey-Bass, 1985.

Schein, E. H., and Bennis, W. G. *Personal and Organizational Change Through Group Methods.* New York: Wiley, 1965.

Three

Breakup of the Bell System: A Case Study in Cultural Transformation

W. Brooke Tunstall

When business historians of the future survey the past, they may commemorate the 1980s as the decade of the cultural revolution in corporate America. Unquestionably, today's lively interest in the concept of organizational culture and in what writer Bro Uttal (1983, p. 66) calls "the soft, bewildering human underpinnings of business" flared suddenly both in intensity and in fashion with the advent of the decade, and it has shown little inclination to fade away.

Not surprisingly, perhaps, business managers themselves have not been the front-line forces in the corporate cultural revolution, notwithstanding the pressures to adapt their enterprises brought on by deregulation, rapid economic shifts, foreign competition, new technologies, and emerging changes in the marketplace. Rather, a circle of insightful business-school educators and consultants have led the way, not only in recognizing the critical importance of organizational culture in the fortunes of the business enterprise but also in exploring the possibilities of evaluating and changing culture to make it consonant with and supportive of the corporation's strategy.

44

To date, the road to such possibilities is still neither broad nor well marked. In fact, there is not as yet even a clear consensus on how to define culture, although a number of different approaches have been suggested. However, most authorities do appear to agree with the observation in *Disconnecting Parties*: "Like nations, corporations evolve distinct cultures from a rather complex interaction of factors, including past and present experiences, structural characteristics and corporate leaders" (Tunstall, 1985, p. 144). Loosely defined, a company's culture is the "amalgam of shared values, behavior patterns, mores, symbols, attitudes, and normative ways of conducting business that, more than its products or services, differentiate it from all other companies. Cultural uniqueness is a primary and cherished feature of organizations, a critical asset that is nurtured in the internal value system" (Tunstall, 1985, p. 144).

As *The New York Times* (Salmans, 1983, p. D1) reported: "Now corporate culture is the magic phrase that management consultants are breathing into the ears of American executives"—and it appears that many executives are beginning to listen. Indeed, more each year are recognizing that culture, however defined, might play as significant a role as structure or strategy in the long-term performance of the company.

To many executives, two lessons seem especially clear: First, in a relatively stable business environment, the elements of a well-entrenched and adhesive corporate culture are supportive of the company's mission and success and thus should be nurtured and encouraged. Second, and conversely, in the face of significant change, these very same elements may threaten adaptation—and, thus, corporate fortunes—if they are not modified to fit new business realities.

Unquestionably, no corporate enterprise has been more regularly cited than American Telephone and Telegraph Company—AT&T—as a paradigm of both phenomena, and not without cause. For the better part of a century, the Bell System possessed a corporate culture that, as much as any other factor, created the energy to drive the entire enterprise. It was a culture uncommon not only in its singleness of purpose and its creation of a sense of family but also in its demonstrable contributions to corporate success. Then, in the mid 1970s, the inexorable march toward deregulation of the telecommunications industry began to unfold and with it came a recognition that internal changes were needed at AT&T. Among them, of course, were attendant "cultural" changes in value systems, behavior patterns, and corporate symbols.

In the midst of these gradual changes came the Justice Department Consent Decree, which required the breakup of the Bell System by horizontal divestiture of its local exchange companies. That divestiture decree served as a potent catalyst to the normally slow chemistry of cultural change.

Not surprisingly, observers of corporate culture from academe, business, and the media soon were citing AT&T as a living business case study—a virtual laboratory of cultural change in "real time"—not only because of the challenge faced by AT&T's management in adjusting a clear-cut, well-established cultural heritage to an entirely new business environment but also because of the critically compressed time frame in which the change had to occur.

Of course, AT&T's transformation does not precisely exemplify future cultural changes in other industries. In fact, the breakup of the Bell System will probably stand forever as a singular business event, set apart from other rearrangements of corporate structure not only by the numbers of people affected and the sheer size of divested resources but also the nature of its integrated, continental network and the historic service relationship between Bell and the nation. (When expressed in financial terms alone, the scope and complexity of this unique, $125-billion business "happening" tend to be obscured. It is considerably more graphic to note that all of the Bell System's resources—including 24,000 buildings; 177,000 motor vehicles; 1,000,000 employees; 142,000,000 telephones; and 1,700,000,000,000 miles of cable, microwave radio, and satellite circuits—had to be apportioned equitably into nine separate, fully operational, and viable corporate operations, down to the last cable pair in the local switching office.)

Nonetheless, the breakup of the Bell System provided an extraordinary opportunity for testing cultural concepts, perhaps first among them the contention of *Corporate Cultures* authors Terrence Deal and Alan Kennedy (1982, p. 13) that the "business environment is the single greatest influence in shaping a corporate culture."

Beyond question, the change in AT&T's business environment covered such a range of extremes between regulation and competition that surviving the deregulation transition posed enormous managerial challenges in and of itself. Moreover, at the precise moment that the corporation faced the enormity of its own dissolution, the telecommunications industry became an arena of overheated, high-tech competition, with powerful foreign and domestic firms swarming through suddenly opening windows of opportunity into a previously protected marketplace.

To survive the transition, to continue its century-old tradition of success, AT&T required the erection of decidedly nontraditional management and operating structures on the foundations of traditional strengths. At the midpoint in the Bell System's disaggregation, AT&T chairman Charles L. Brown told his senior managers:

> Just as we have to sharpen our marketing focus, just as we have to shorten the journey of our products from the laboratory to the marketplace, just as we have to produce goods and services more cost-effectively, we also have to quicken our pace and sharpen our day-to-day management. We have to come to decisions faster. We have to lean more toward action than study. We have to learn to take more risks, and, where we fail, to cut our losses. We have to open the channels of communication, so that ideas for improvement, cost savings, new opportunities come to the fore in timely fashion and don't die on the organizational ladder. A more swift, more responsive, more accountable style of management will be required.
>
> In short, we need to establish and maintain an internal environment that commands excellence, that encourages a spirit of entrepreneurship, and that rewards individual accomplishment.

Several months earlier, the chairman had exhorted AT&T's managers "to reshape, reorient, adapt the corporation's culture to changing times and different needs." Now he had set forth a blueprint for that change and presented it with a new sense of urgency.

No characteristic of organizational culture is cited more frequently and with better cause, however, than its remarkable resistance to change. (In fact, a 1980 *Business Week* cover article incorporated this difficulty into its very definition of corporate culture, calling it "the hard-to-change values that spell success or failure" ["Corporate Culture . . . ," p. 148]).

Nonetheless, changes had to be effected to bring the value systems and expectations of AT&T into congruence with the corporation's changing environment and to prepare its employees for the grueling competitive battles looming ahead.

In considering how this might be accomplished, this writer postulated in *The Sloan Management Review* (Tunstall, 1983, p. 18) that management of cultural adaptation within AT&T—indeed, within any major corporation—would essentially require a three-step process:

> First, management must understand the meaning and impact of corporate culture and must ascertain, often through empirical methods, the elements of its own culture;

> Second, the "cultural wheat must be separated from the chaff." Decisions must be made about which elements support future goals and strategies, and thus must be retained, and which elements are no longer appropriate, and must be changed;

> Third, appropriate actions must be taken to effect the required changes in a way that leaves the desirable elements unaffected.

It is interesting and instructive to examine the change at AT&T retrospectively along these three dimensions.

Cultural Elements

As noted, AT&T had a strong and mature culture—a culture whose elements had long been cited as a critical foundation for service and success. Thus, the first of the three steps required little creative effort. Bell's historic culture blended a constellation of mutually reinforcing attributes, the most prominent of which were dedication to customer service, lifelong careers, up-from-the-ranks management succession, operational skills, consensus management, level consciousness, and a strong focus on regulatory matters.

All of these attributes evolved to support one superordinate goal: universal service. In fact, everything related to the culture was affected by this goal: the kinds of people Bell companies hired, the shared value systems of Bell companies, and the infrastructure of processes to run the business.

These elements, all geared to providing high-quality service at affordable prices to everyone in the United States, comprised the cultural glue that united Bell people in mission and in pride, regardless of rank or station.

Cultural Wheat from Chaff

Rarely had corporate mission and corporate culture been so ideally matched. However, with divestiture, certain bedrock values—so indispensable in the regulated past—had to be discarded, or at least reshaped and redirected, while others had to be nurtured carefully through the great transition.

The significance of this winnowing of values was broadly recognized. In fact, management authority Richard T. Pascale (1984, p. 27) advised: "The primary task for AT&T leadership is to redefine its values—to identify 'magnetic north.' " He added, "You need not abandon old values in wholesale fashion; but values cannot retain their validity in the new environment unless they are reinterpreted in the context of the customer and the marketplace." Of course, any tampering with the value system had to be executed with great care. If employees began to question whether the corporation had their best interests at heart—or, indeed, whether the corporation's commitment to customer service was diminishing—the company would be challenged by a severe setback that could not be easily repaired.

Thus, as AT&T's family of one million was broken apart, management had to demonstrate consistently that it continued to care about each employee as an individual and, at the same time, to continue to foster the service doctrine as a strong corporate value. This historic vision of fairness and service, of loyalty and unity, and of the value of operational and technical skills and safety standards were among the most prominent aspects of the culture that needed to be protected. As Tony H. Bonaparte, dean of the Pace University School of Business, noted: "All of these are of incalculable importance in lubricating sound human relationships which are so crucial to managing task assignment and teamwork in a complex and sophisticated modern organization" (1984, p. 24).

. AT&T instead allowed other cultural characteristics to be changed. For example, as the corporation moved toward a fully competitive environment, the mind-set and methodologies of its managers shifted toward a market orientation. The "steady state" organizational structure, for half a century so ideally suited to a regulated world, now adapted and readapted to meet the changing needs of a competitive future. (As noted in *Disconnecting Parties* [Tunstall, 1985, p. 98], "Chiefly, AT&T needed a new framework for its organization—in its simplest form, a drastic decentralization and downsizing of the corporate staff and the formation of two large sectors: one to conduct the regulated part of the business, and the other the unregulated part.") The corporate value system had to recognize and reward a more entrepreneurial type of manager. The routes to managerial authority, for so long concentrated in line telephone operating jobs, had to be broadened to include more characteristic routes upward, to include marketing and sales, finance, and production and engineering.

Effecting Change

A consulting-firm president (Langley, 1984, p. 32) noted, "AT&T stands ready to mortgage its future if it doesn't reshape its culture to meet the new competitive battles ahead," and few within AT&T's principle management cadre disagreed. Yet no AT&T manager was charged specifically with management of the culture, no committee was named to plan alterations of its underlying values. The reasons appear to be threefold. First, the culture was so broad, so pervasive and deeply rooted, that no single manager or committee could be responsible for changing it. Rather, change had to begin at the top; then everyone had to be enlisted in the effort.

Second, the enormity of effort required to pull off the breakup, which involved the full-time efforts of no less than 30,000 people system-wide, made such demands on managerial time and energy that a formalized cultural effort was all but precluded.

Third, and perhaps most critical, the very nature of organizational culture is that it changes by evolution rather than by edict. As one *AT&T Magazine* editor (Kinkead, 1984, p. 9) observed, a new corporate culture is like a new wine, with several developmental stages. "Rough manipulation will not improve it, nor will it benefit from benign neglect. Only through good judgment and delicate handling can it achieve its full promise."

Nonetheless, change was high on the list of priorities of the corporation's principle managers, and, both in word and deed, they moved to effect that change.

"If we are able to adapt our marvelous culture to a different environment—and if we remember that the business in the '80s cannot be run by memory—we can set the course for the next century," Chairman Brown said ("The Premium Now . . . ," 1982, p. 15). His closely watched speeches themselves became vehicles for stimulating such adaptation. Even before divestiture was announced, for example, he laid the ancient "Ma Bell" sobriquet to rest, calling it inadequate to describe a high-technology business. After the early 1982 signing of the Consent Decree, he used the occasions of other speeches to establish a new mission for the business, a new bias toward action, an entire new system of corporate positions and expectations.

The overt actions of the corporation, of course, spoke at least as persuasively to employees as the chairman's words.

Changes in the system of management, including its many management processes, its organizational structure, and its management style, began to reorient cultural norms. New recruiting aims were implemented to suit the shifting human requirements of the business. New kinds of management training, calculated to anticipate and respond to strategic issues in a rapidly changing business environment, were introduced for the first time into the corporate managerial experience. A new corporate headquarters at 550 Madison Avenue rose to replace the wonderful old classic structure at 195 Broadway, whose architecture and ambiance were both themselves symbols of another era.

In the final months before the January 1, 1984, divestiture date, the corporation announced a surprising array of competitive steps that only months before would have been undreamed of. In August 1983, AT&T introduced a new corporate identity, mission statement, and organizational structure. In November, it offered early retirement packages to 13,000 people in order to streamline its force. In December, AT&T Technologies organized into six new lines of business, creating profit-center management groups along market and product lines.

In the same months, the corporation announced a number of unprecedented joint ventures. In August, for example, AT&T entered into a joint venture agreement with Phillips of the Netherlands to market switching and transmission equipment in Europe. The following month, AT&T Communications and Netcom Enterprises won a multimillion dollar contract to provide broadcast coverage of the Olympic Games throughout Europe. In November, AT&T established links to Wang and Hewlett-Packard to produce compatible computer equipment, and a month later, AT&T bought a 75 percent stake in Olivetti so the two firms could distribute and manufacture each other's products.

With regard to products and services, AT&T was no less busy in the months just prior to January 1, 1984. In October alone, the corporation adapted its Number 5 electronic switch for international customers, then announced its Merlin Communications System, its first new product specially designed for

the small business market. The following month, AT&T un-
veiled its new "Caller Card" phone, which uses a card instead of
voice or a dialing-card number.

In a mid-1982 article in the *Harvard Business Review*,
Thomas S. Robertson, Scott Ward, and William M. Caldwell
(1982, p. 24) noted: "For companies fresh off the regulatory
treadmill, success will come from abandonment of the regulation mentality and adoption of a competitive frame of mind."
At AT&T, a new identity; entirely new lines of business; a
streamlined managerial force; the introduction of new products
and services; and an array of joint ventures, both domestically
and abroad, in fields as disparate as transmission equipment,
broadcasting, computers, and word processing spoke volumes
about AT&T's recognition that business as usual could be the
high road to irrelevance. Perhaps more than anything else the
management might have done, said, or written, these actions
had a significant impact on the company's culture; they began
to build into the value system a "competitive frame of mind."

Looking Back to See Ahead

In late 1983, when it became clear that divestiture would,
in fact, be achieved on schedule, AT&T's management breathed
a collective sigh of relief and took stock of the impact of events
on the corporation's people.

The initiative began at the very top when Chairman
Brown asked retiring AT&T president William Ellinghaus to
look into the matter of cultural change—in fact, to investigate
and find answers to one central question: "Have we adequately
addressed the impact of divestiture on our culture and our people?" The stated objective of the resulting study was to provide
senior management with the means not only to understand the
dislocations and strains caused by divestiture but also to determine what new initiatives might be required to adapt current
cultural values to the new environment.

Of course, no generally accepted conceptual model exists
for identifying the elements of corporate culture, especially
when those elements are still in a state of radical evolution. A

number of interesting, often highly creative approaches have been suggested, including Stan Silverzweig and Robert Allen's normative systems evaluation, Howard Schwartz and Stanley Davis' Corporate Culture Matrix, and Professor Ralph Kilmann and Mary Saxton's promising Kilmann-Saxton Culture-Gap Survey. In addition, many less formal approaches have been suggested. For example, Andrew Pettigrew (1979) advises the researcher to look for "social dramas" within the corporation. James J. O'Toole (1979, pp. 22, 23) suggests "hiring a social anthropologist for six months to immerse himself in the enterprise, and emerge with an ethnology of the corporation." Thomas J. Peters (1978) suggested analyzing how time is spent by key executives, organizational interlinks and review procedures, and what reports and meetings are about.

All are attractive ideas. However, the experiences and the dislocations within AT&T had been as unprecedented as they were vast and transforming, and, in addition, the time frame allotted for the study was critically short. Thus, when the study was assigned to this writer for staff direction, it seemed inescapably necessary to custom design an approach.

Ultimately, a broad, three-element approach to the study was taken. First, William Ellinghaus wrote a personal request to twenty key executives in the company asking for their detailed assessments of the impact of divestiture on AT&T's culture and for their recommendations. Second, exhaustive interviews were conducted with leading management consultants familiar with Bell's history, the trauma of its disaggregation, and its current condition. Third, a comprehensive survey sought answers and impressions from the "soul" of the organization: a scientifically selected sample of employees drawn from all levels and divisions of the organization.

The survey questionnaire, distributed to 6,000 employees, was comprised of twelve basic questions seeking responses to 116 different items. One, for example, examined confidence levels in such factors as the company's and the employee's future, the effectiveness with which the company was being managed, and the company's dedication to quality service. A second question examined the personal effects of divestiture on the employee. A third asked employees to rank in importance such values as spirit of service, teamwork, community involvement, and aggressiveness in the marketplace. Other questions explored employees' feelings and attitudes about top management, about the degree to which—for better or worse—divestiture impacted their jobs and their work, about their levels of satisfaction with certain elements of their jobs (such as employment security, pace of change, pay, and benefits), about the quantity and quality of information they receive, about the amount of stress they feel, and about the prospects of the "new" AT&T in a competitive world.

The response to all three elements of the study was extraordinary. All of the executives queried wrote carefully considered and highly detailed memoranda, more than a few of which reflected the pain they had witnessed and felt during divestiture.

The interviews with the consultants—among them such well-known authorities as Michael Maccoby, Stanley Peterfruend, Harry Levinson, and Frank Stanek—provided important and highly objective perspectives, often from original points of view. Significantly, the consultants agreed almost unanimously that the corporation's traditional system of values had been placed under great strain by divestiture, that substantial uncertainty still existed among employees at all levels with regard to the "new AT&T" and its opportunities, and that changes in the culture needed to take place, to include a less hierarchical orientation, less level consciousness, less consensus management, and less avoidance of risk. Moreover, they made quite specific recommendations as to how the corporation's values and management style could be altered to effect these changes, ranging from democratizing the management and increasing executive visibility to steps that would lead to recreating the corporate sense of identification and pride that had been lost in the divestiture process.

However, the richest source proved to be the response to the employee questionnaire, from which measurable patterns and reactions were discerned for the corporation as a whole and for each subsidiary unit. (Significantly, a larger percentage of employees responded to the survey—without any followup prompting—than had answered any other survey in the corporation's abundant history of employee opinion sampling.)

A Thirteenth Question

Of course, divestiture had been an intensely human and often emotional experience for AT&T people; thus, the design of the questionnaire had to permit responses that might not readily lend themselves to quantification. Consequently, a thirteenth question, inviting a free-form written response, was included. It asked: "What were your feelings as the new year and the new AT&T era dawned on January 1, 1984? Feel free to share your thoughts, about the passing of the old Bell System, the birth of the new AT&T and its impact on you as you begin work this year."

The response exceeded anything AT&T's professional attitude surveyors had ever seen. Question 13 had been included as a kind of catch-all item designed to pick up anything the other questions failed to evoke. But more than 3,400 respondents—57 percent of those surveyed, a remarkable response—took time to write about their feelings and experiences, often in considerable detail. It was as if they had been waiting for an opportunity to tell someone in authority of their sadness, anger, and outrage at divestiture, of their stubborn pride in their heritage, and of their mingled hopes and concerns about the future.

By reviewing a few randomly selected responses to question 13, it is possible to reconstruct at least a sense of what AT&T employees felt, including their feelings of ambivalence, about the corporate trauma called divestiture:

> Angry, sad, a little scared about my future. Divestiture was a triumph of lawyers, bureaucrats, and financial manipulators over producers and servers.

> I felt like I had gone through a divorce that neither my wife nor my children wanted. It was

forced upon us by some very powerful outside forces and I could not control the outcome. It was like waking up in familiar surroundings (your home) but your family and all that you held dear was missing.

I felt sad and somewhat resentful because the government has been absolutely wrong on the question of competition. Foreign telephone companies think the U.S. is crazy for breaking up AT&T. . . . Yet I think young managers will see challenge and opportunities.

A sense of loss . . . we were screwed by the federal government.

My feelings were ambivalent. . . . I was numb but I neither rejoiced nor shed a tear. The old AT&T and the operating companies were great places to work. The new AT&T will also be a good place to work. With so many people with such a long-standing ethic of quality of service, it can't help but be that.

Working through divestiture was exciting, challenging and hard, productive work. The aftermath has been a letdown. Once the estate is settled, things may sort out.

The wealth of information gathered from the three assessment approaches was, to the degree possible, quantified. All answers to the twelve objective questions on the employee questionnaire were computerized so that overall responses could be examined along many diffierent lines. (It was thereby ultimately possible to ascertain the relative degrees of importance, expressed numerically, that employees attached to a wide variety of values, set against the relative ranking of those values as current strengths within the divested corporation, such that perceived gaps between importance and strength could be clearly seen. In addition, changes in attitudes toward such critical factors as job security, company loyalty, employee treatment, and service commitment could be quantified on specific percentage bases, for management and nonmanagement people, and by units within AT&T.)

All data were subjected to in-depth review and analysis and considered along with the thousands of comments inspired by question 13, comments that brought to life and reconfirmed the conclusions that issued forth from the quantified statistical data. The results were as revealing in their consistency as in their considerable substance.

The Findings: Bad News, Good News

Key executives, knowledgeable outsiders, and the rank and file virtually all agreed that divestiture had a vast and unsettling impact on employees and on their shared value system —their collective culture. There was anger, frustration, a sense of personal loss. Yet there also was a strong resolve, a commitment to get on with the management of the new company in a new age and to make it a success. This is not to say that differences were not perceived between employment levels, between organizational units, or between subcultures. But with regard to AT&T's overarching cultural attributes, there was a reassuring consistency of response along virtually every important dimension surveyed.

The findings of the study were summarized as follows:

1.   The shock that accompanied the breakup and the subsequent burdensome workload required to implement an order felt to be wrong for the company, the customer, and the nation at large took a heavy toll on AT&T people. A high percentage said they had found it physically and emotionally taxing and that it had taken too much time from their families.

2.   There was almost overwhelming concern among employees everywhere regarding AT&T's ability to continue to provide high-quality service, given the demise of "end-to-end responsibility" caused by the divestiture and the possible

drag toward service mediocrity resulting from prospective price wars.

3. The collective confidence of the employee body had been badly shaken by the divestiture experience. Consequently, employees tended to feel less secure about their jobs (a realistic concern, to be sure) and about their career opportunities in what they perceived as a "new ball game."

4. Employees wondered about AT&T's ability to compete, given the newness of the competitive environment and the remnant regulatory constraints still imposed on the corporation.

5. Encouragingly, employees recognized and accepted the need for a new priority of values. With regard to characteristics most vital to the future success of the company, for example, market aggressiveness, technological innovation, profitability, and fast response to customer needs outranked company loyalty, lifelong careers, up-from-the-ranks management succession, consensus management, and community involvement—all high fliers in the regulatory environment of yesteryear.

Summing up, immediately after the divestiture experience there was a kind of identity crisis for AT&T people. A soft, collective voice almost could be heard saying: "I knew the old Bell System, its mission, its operation, its people, its culture. And I knew my niche in it. In that knowledge, I had identity and confidence about my company and myself. Now I work for a new company, one fourth its former size, with only a partial history and no track record. With the loss of our mission—universal service—and the fragmentation of the very business of providing telephone service, I find myself asking, 'Who are we?' 'Who am I?' "

This very real sense of loss was counterbalanced in many ways by a pervasive excitement and anticipation about the challenges of a new era. Furthermore, an ever-abiding pride in still being a member of AT&T was crowned with the belief that AT&T would be a "winner" if given time and a level playing field by Washington.

Most important, AT&T people had taken to their hearts the precise new pro-competitive values senior management believed should be emphasized. No commentary on a felicitous cultural shift could be more dramatic than the acceptance of these new values over others long embedded in and thoroughly characteristic of the corporate value system.

As this author and his colleagues pored over the study results, it became clear that we had reached inside the corporation and felt its living heart. We had noted in the past (Tunstall, 1983, p. 17) that "culture within the corporation is difficult to pin down, nearly impossible to quantify or measure, and remarkably resistant to change." Now, however, we realized that organizational culture *can* be measured, that it *can* be quantified, if the best techniques and concepts of the social scientists are combined with a meaningful understanding of the corporation's constituencies—and most especially, its employees —within whom the culture substantively resides.

Mr. Brown Takes Charge

In all of the diverse literature on corporate culture, one common tenet is that cultural change must be led from the top. The transformation of AT&T offered dramatic confirmation. Almost eighteen months earlier, Mr. Brown had told an audience at the Harvard Business School that "though corporate strategies can be recast overnight, a corporate culture cannot be laid aside like an old suit that is no longer considered stylish." He added that "our job now is to adapt our culture to changing times and different needs. The challenge will be to change our culture without changing the character of our business."

Now, with the Ellinghaus Report in hand, Mr. Brown moved to take personal charge of management's response to that challenge. He began by transmitting copies of the report to the top fifteen officers of AT&T—his "cabinet." The cover note apprised the cabinet members of a special meeting and signalled its importance. "I am interrupting my vacation for this meeting," the note pointed out. "We clearly have work to do."

Held in early March, 1984, the meeting comprised a frank

discussion of the impact of divestiture on the corporation's people, the action steps that had been taken to date in connection with adapting the culture, and what further initiatives might be needed. The discussion was extremely fruitful, not only in providing the substance for cultural change but also in enlisting the support of the top executive team in the change process.

Characteristically, there was no rhetorical fanfare about the Ellinghaus Report nor were there broad pronouncements about cultural change. However, the report and the meeting proved extremely useful to senior management in preparing them to take actions aimed at reestablishing a sense of mission, identity, confidence, and self-renewal after the divestiture trauma. The study had accomplished its purpose.

Appropriately, the first steps were informational in nature. They included:

1. Broad distribution of a talk by Chairman Brown entitled "A New Vision for AT&T." In this talk, Mr. Brown articulated AT&T's new mission (to bring the Information Age to everyone), outlined new strategies and aims, and discussed how the style of management had to change for the company to succeed in the new environment.
2. A company-wide transmission of a videotape featuring a panel of top corporate officers, including Mr. Brown, answering questions about the new AT&T from a group of employees.
3. A series of in-house publications featuring articles on the new AT&T (a sample of titles makes clear their thrust: "AT&T: One Company, One Mission, One Measure"; "Corporate Headquarters, Owner and Manager"; "No One Will Show You The Way").
4. A procession of talks by officers to AT&T employees articulating the new vision, goals, and desired behaviors and values (for example, the new bias toward action, risk taking, individual initiative, and so forth).
5. Announcement of a series of week-long corporate forums for the top 800 executives to help them develop a total understanding of the new company and its environment.

(Top executives also would appear weekly for dialogues on the corporation's identity, mission, management style, expectations, and challenges in a deregulated world.)

6. Development of a two-volume document, entitled "AT&T's Management System," to provide a comprehensive picture of the corporation's new organization, the relationships between various units, the underlying principles and values, and, finally, major decision processes—all critical contributors to the corporate culture. (Planned for release in mid 1984, the document was intended to increase employees' understanding of how the new AT&T functions and, therefore of who AT&T now is.)

7. Sponsorship of an advertising program directed essentially at AT&T's external constituencies but which proved to be equally useful in aiding the change process inside the corporation. The outstanding advertisements in this program portrayed AT&T as a quality information/communications competitor and thus reinforced the internal initiatives, giving employees a heightened sense of identity and pride.

8. Formal recognition by several units of outstanding achievements in matters that encouraged new behavior (for example, Eagle Awards for marketing ideas or super sales, Golden Boy awards for exemplary customer service, and cost-equivalent awards for accepted ideas for cutting costs).

Continuum for Change

It has often been observed that cultural change cannot be delegated to the employee information department; that, indeed, substantive change grows more directly and more predictably out of what the corporation does than what it says. This is undeniably true.

Nonetheless, the information activities outlined here helped to substantiate and solidify the alteration of employee views and values already in progress. Simultaneously, a steady drumbeat of additional, often extraordinary actions by the corporation—all exemplifying a new predisposition to engage in competitive behavior—broadened and continued the process. In March 1984 alone:

- AT&T Technologies entered the computer marketplace with the 3B family of products, the broadest introduction of mini- and microcomputers in the industry's history.
- AT&T Communications began offering its long-distance discount programs.
- AT&T Information Systems introduced System 75 for small offices.
- AT&T Information Systems joined Rockwell International, Honeywell, and Data General in searching for ways for computers to swap data with telephone switching equipment.
- AT&T Consumer Products consolidated its repair operations to gain efficiencies and meet customer needs.

Other changes soon followed, including an across-the-board 20 percent cost reduction program; the unveiling by AT&T Technologies of its first personal computer; and, for the first time in AT&T's history, a freeze on salaries of all managerial personnel, a move affecting 114,000 employees.

Significantly, not one of these actions would have taken place in the Bell System as recently as three years previously. Indeed, Ma Bell did not live here anymore!

A Pluralistic Process

By mid 1984, divestiture had begun to fade; it was not forgotten, any more than the traditional Bell System heritage has been forgotten, but it was, of necessity, left behind. As one writer (Pascale, 1984, p. 27) observed, "Organizations, like people, often deal best with loss by moving on." So it was with Bell System people.

What lay ahead was the exciting challenge of creating the next stage of AT&T's long history, a challenge requiring that AT&T adapt itself as successfully to the competitive environment as it had evolved itself to prosper under regulation.

To respond successfully to this challenge would, as Chairman Brown had said, require that the corporation change its culture without changing the character of the business. To do so not only would serve customers and shareowners, but also pay

tribute to millions of Bell employees of years past who had dedicated themselves to the achievement of universal service.

As shown in the Ellinghaus study, that process is well
launched. However, it would be inaccurate to portray the scene
as an total, overnight cultural transformation. To assume that
the entire employee body of 350,000 people had arrived at an
entirely new cultural orientation would be far off the mark. As
Professor James J. O'Toole (1981, p. 139) noted, culture
change "is a pluralistic process, not a monolithic one." It will
take time for the new values to permeate the new AT&T. But
the start is an encouraging and productive one, bearing witness
to the assertion that the company is, as its ads proclaim, "reaching out in new directions." It is, as well, an extraordinary event
—perhaps the high-water mark—in the corporate cultural revolution of the 1980s.

References

Bonaparte, T. H. "Forum for Change." *AT&T Magazine,* 1984,
    1 (1), 24.
"Corporate Culture: The Hard-To-Change Values that Spell Suc-
    cess or Failure." *Business Week,* Oct. 27, 1980, pp. 148–160.
Deal, T. E., and Kennedy, A. A. *Corporate Cultures: The Rites
    and Rituals of Corporate Life.* Reading, Mass.: Addison-
    Wesley, 1982.
Kinkead, R. "Pulling Together Is the Way to Go." *AT&T Maga-
    zine,* 1984, *1* (1), 8-9.
Langley, M. "AT&T Has Call for a New Corporate Culture."
    The Wall Street Journal, Feb. 28, 1984, p. 32.
O'Toole, J. J. "Corporate and Managerial Cultures." In C. L.
    Cooper (ed.), *Behavioral Problems in Organizations.* Engle-
    wood Cliffs, N.J.: Prentice-Hall, 1979.
O'Toole, J. J. *Making America Work.* New York: Continuum,
    1981.
Pascale, R. T. "Forum for Change." *AT&T Magazine,* 1984,
    1 (1), 26-27.
Peters, T. J. "Symbols, Patterns and Settings: An Optimistic
    Case for Getting Things Done." *Organizational Dynamics,*
    1978, *7* (2), 2-23.

Pettigrew, A. "On Studying Organizational Cultures." *Adminis-trative Science Quarterly,* Dec. 1979, *24* (12), 570-581.

"The Premium Now Is on Leadership." *Bell Telephone Maga-zine,* 1982, *1,* 12-15.

Robertson, T. S., Ward, S., and Caldwell, W. M. "Deregulation: Surviving the Transition." *Harvard Business Review,* July-Aug. 1982, pp. 20-24.

Salmans, S. "New Vogue: Company Culture." *The New York Times,* Jan. 7, 1983, pp. D1, D27.

Tunstall, W. B. "Cultural Transition at AT&T." *Sloan Manage-ment Review,* 1983, *25* (1), 15-26.

Tunstall, W. B. *Disconnecting Parties: Managing the Bell Sys-tem Break-up—An Inside View.* New York: McGraw-Hill, 1985.

Uttal, B. "The Corporate Culture Vultures." *Fortune,* Oct. 17, 1983, pp. 66-72.

Four

Believing Is Seeing: How Culture Influences the Decisions Top Managers Make

Alice M. Sapienza

Organizational Culture Defined

Organizational culture has indeed become, as noted some-what flippantly in the *Wall Street Journal,* "a trendy topic in management circles lately" ("AT&T Has Call . . . ," 1984, p. 32). Because the term is often used loosely, it is important that *organizational culture* be defined by those investigating and managing this phenomenon. One definition I have found useful is that of an English businessman, Sir Geoffrey Vickers, who described organizational culture as a *shared appreciative system;* that is, "a set of readinesses to distinguish some aspects of the situation rather than others and to classify and value these [in a certain way]" (1965, p. 67). I think it is clear from this descrip-tion that, for Vickers and for many managers and academics, one of the most important facets of organizational culture is the

I wish to express my gratitude to the top managers at both sites discussed in this chapter. Without their cooperation, this study would not have been possible.

system of *shared beliefs* ("set of readinesses") that predisposes people to see the world ("to distinguish some aspects of the situation") in a certain way.

Organizational beliefs would be merely interesting if they did not appear to affect organizational performance, as illustrated by the following examples from the business press. In early 1982, *Business Week* examined at length the "profound transformation" of the computer industry ("Moving Away From Mainframes," 1982, p. 78). Briefly, analysts noted that, as technology improved, market demand shifted from mainframes (once the staple product) to mini- and microcomputers. But not every computer manufacturer recognized that the world was changing. Remarked the president of Sperry Univac about managers' predisposition to see only the mainframe aspects of the world: "We need to change this mainframe culture" (p. 80). Certain shared beliefs had to some extent predisposed managers to remain "so preoccupied with large centralized computers" that they failed to make the right decisions for the changing environment (p. 80). As a result, profits had dropped, and stock market prices were depressed.

Dr. James J. Renier, vice chairman of Honeywell, Inc., and president of Honeywell Information Systems, declared in a November 21, 1983, letter to the *Honeywell World,* an employee newspaper, soon after taking those positions, that the organization must "change to a culture of democracy if we want a decent crack at success." He explained that managers' shared beliefs in authoritarian management had to some extent predisposed them to keep information "very close to the vest," resulting in situations in which people did not have "*all* the data [they needed] to make decent decisions." Again, financial performance was below the desired level.

Finally, AT&T's culture has also come under scrutiny. The *Wall Street Journal* described this corporation's problem as a "clash of corporate cultures" ("AT&T Marketing Men . . . ," 1984, p. 1). Managers from the manufacturing side of the original Bell System were thought to share certain beliefs that to some extent predisposed them to "internal service standards and corporate traits that were appropriate to a regulated environment" ("AT&T Has Call . . . ," 1984, p. 32). Managers from the marketing side of the new AT&T (many of them from other companies) were thought to share certain beliefs that to some extent predisposed them to "competitive zeal . . . , risk taking . . . ," and attention to customer demands in a "deregulated future" ("AT&T Has Call . . . ," 1984, p. 32). The result was "battle after battle between these two segments" ("AT&T Marketing Men . . . ," 1984, p. 16). And resolution of the conflict between these two sets of shared beliefs was "cited as the single element more critical to AT&T's success than either strategy or structure" ("AT&T Has Call . . . ," 1984, p. 32).

This chapter focuses on organizational culture as shared beliefs and the influence such beliefs appear to have on top management decision making. Two case studies illustrate the following "morals":

1. Organizational culture as shared beliefs can determine in large measure what managers see and thus how they respond to their world.
2. The language that managers use, especially their metaphorical language, arises out of their shared beliefs and can be a powerful shaper of organizational strategy.

The following discussion of the two case studies is organized into four subsections. The first subsection reviews the background of the research (sites, methodology, results), and the second subsection briefly summarizes the data on the environmental event that was available for managers to see. The third subsection describes one core belief of each top management group, and the fourth subsection illustrates how these core beliefs appeared to influence the ways in which managers perceived and responded to the environmental data.

To preserve the confidentiality of the organizations, the case studies have been disguised.

Research Background

In October 1982, legislation that attempted to change the economics of a major service industry in one state went into effect. Because managers had to design and implement a financial strategy that would meet the requirements of this law by September 30, 1983, this author had a unique opportunity to study how shared beliefs influenced their perceptions of the law and their responses to it. The objective of the research was twofold: (1) to produce a rich description of the beliefs, perceptions, and responses of two groups of top managers; and (2) to examine the resulting data for *differences* that would illuminate the effects of beliefs on perceptions and responses.

Sites. Two organizations as closely matched as possible were chosen for this study: they were located within a few blocks of each other in a busy urban area; they filled similar regulatory, political, technological, and demographic niches; and their managers were subjected to the same fiscal pressures of the new state law. The organizations were close in age and financial performance as well. They came into being within a few years of each other at the turn of this century and, by 1982, were separated by less than $6 million in net revenues (out of about $200 million total). It is pertinent to the conclusions to note that neither organization was unionized, and both paid competitive wages in that area.

The two top management groups were also similar. Each group consisted of about seven people of roughly the same age, most of whom had been working together a minimum of six years. The chief executive officer of each institution was in his fifties and had held that position for at least ten years. Both groups were widely respected in the industry as "good managers," and the institutions were known for quality service outside the state as well.

Methodology. Shared beliefs do not readily lend themselves to examination. As Malinowski said: "[There] is a series of phenomena of great importance which cannot possibly be recorded by questioning or computing documents. Let us call them the *imponderabilia of actual life*" (1953, p. 20).

Managers cannot be asked what they believe but must be observed believing. Thus, this author spent almost seven consecutive months "living with" the two top management groups and observing nearly all of their regularly scheduled meetings. The final research data included nearly a thousand pages of verbatim conversations, past and current published material on each organization, and observations over the course of one year of such "imponderabilia" as managers' behaviors and artifacts of organizational culture (titles, logos, spatial arrangements, and so forth).

Results. The most important conclusions to be drawn from the analyses of these data were the two "morals" noted earlier. First, managers at each institution shared a core ideology, or beliefs about the fundamental qualities of the institution, qualities encapsulating the organization's very reason for being. These core beliefs predisposed managers to see the world in a certain way. In a real sense, sometimes believing was seeing. Second, following from managers' core beliefs, metaphoric language helped to create a reality to which managers responded strategically. A complete description of these results can be found in Sapienza (1984).

As the next subsection illustrates, the environmental event—the state legislation that became effective on October 1, 1982—attempted to change the economics of the industry by changing incentives.

The Environmental Event

Beginning in 1968, a state agency had been charged with overseeing the prices and costs in the industry. However, by 1980 average industry costs in the state were 40 percent higher than those in the rest of the nation, and the state's business round table became actively involved in cost containment efforts. Although members of the round table at first "preached cost containment, [they] did not want regulation" (former chairman of the state oversight agency).[1] But after many months of discussion, the round table finally agreed that legislation was the only way "to change incentives. [The proposed bill] will provide the right incentives and rewards to all parties" (roundtable chairman).

Some of the more important incentives of the bill ham-

---

1. Quotations in this chapter, unless otherwise noted, are from verbatim transcripts of meetings and interviews with managers by the author.

mered out by a coalition of state legislators and business round table members were these:

1. Annual operating costs of each organization would be set in advance by the state agency. This provision of the bill changed the traditional method of reimbursement from a retrospective to a prospective basis. It also provided a strong incentive for industry managers to trim expenses because, if end-of-year expenses were less than the prospectively determined amount, that difference could be kept, and future rates would not be affected. (Formerly, future rates were lowered if organizations showed a certain profit level at the end of each fiscal year.)
2. If management could offer a product whose marginal revenue exceeded its marginal cost, that profit could also be kept without affecting future rates.
3. Because the law would be in effect for three years (from October 1, 1982, through September 30, 1985), managers in the industry had some financial stability in that base costs would be known for three years. As a third incentive, then, managers could devise a strategy to reduce operating costs and offer products in the first year that would allow them to invest and compound the profits for three years without affecting rates during that period.

The legislation was defined as a "charge control law," and reactions were emphatic on both sides. The regulators' view was that the new law, in rewarding economically prudent administration, would help eliminate the waste that, to them, had been inherent in industry budgeting. A former chairman of the state oversight agency predicted that the changes would "be comparable to administrative changes in the education field, where administrators who cannot adapt to the new economics do not survive, and [organizations] which cannot adapt . . . face bankruptcy and consolidation."

Industry executives, on the other hand, believed that the new law meant either layoffs or not filling the jobs of workers who leave. They also feared that it would hamper introduction

of new technology, because every time a new product is introduced, the rates would be raised.

The above briefly summarizes key data on the environmental event available to industry managers through public
media, industry association publications, and internal memoranda. Managers of the two research sites were exposed to at
least this information during specially called executive meetings.

The next subsection describes one of the core beliefs of
managers at each institution. As will be illustrated later, core
beliefs appeared to influence how managers perceived this legislation and thus how they responded to it.

The Core Ideology of Top Managers

Institution A. One core belief of managers at Institution
A was that employees should be well cared for. For example,
one director said: "We've tried to make this place—not just an
organization. We call ourselves a family, and we try to really live
that image from the bottom up." Explained another: "The
spirit of the place is different. . . . [We] care. Look at the employee talent show—it was mobbed." The month of December
was entitled "employee appreciation month," and the most
talked-about event was a free meal in the company cafeteria,
served by top managers in aprons and chef's hats. When one
manager proposed that this tradition be scaled down to a free
meal anytime during the week, the executive vice president remarked: "But then the *meaning* is gone! You might as well do
nothing." Noted the president: "If [employees] feel dumped
on and that we're not caring for them, they won't care for us."

An ambitious in-house training program was offered to all
levels of employees. In describing the philosophy behind training, the director of human relations told the top-management
group: "Training establishes an atmosphere where the employees
feel the organization *cares* for their growth. Such programs en-
gender their realization of caring and feeling on the part of the
organization."

Institution B. At Institution B, one core belief of top

managers was that clients should be put "above all other concerns, . . . almost irrespective of cost." Said the chief financial
officer: "The client is first and foremost. Quality issues are
more prominent, more ingrained in the management structure."
One director who had been with the organization over forty
years offered this perspective: "We've become inculcated with
what [Institution B] *did* and that was to put the client on a
very high priority level." Managers felt that "throughout almost
a hundred years [one] characteristic has remained unchanged:
The client has *first priority.*"

Reflecting this core belief, Institution B was one of only
four organizations in the state out of a total of 120 designing a
particular sophisticated service (Institution A was not involved
in this effort). During the first three years of its introduction,
this service was expected to cost the institution about $46,000
per client. However, management had unanimously voted to go
into that business because it was consistent with the institution's "tradition of always putting the needs of the individual
client above all other concerns."

Managers of Institution B viewed efforts to reduce the
rate of industry cost inflation as specifically threatening to their
core belief. In the words of one manager: "The . . . industry is
beset with increasing encroachment by regulation." This encroachment, Institution B's managers felt, "continues to threat-
en our ability to provide the highest quality [product for our
client]."

The next subsection describes how managers perceived
the legislation—environmental event—and how they responded
to it. As will become apparent, there can be a remarkable difference between what managers *can* perceive and what they *do*
perceive, and this difference may stem from managers' shared
beliefs.

Perception and Response of Top Managers

The Perceptual Ground. A Russian contemporary of Pav-
lov, L. S. Vygotsky, maintained that "[all] human perception
consists of categorized rather than isolated perceptions . . .

[based on] the internalization of culturally produced sign systems [i.e., language]" (Vygotsky, 1978, p. 33). Simply speaking, perception *is* categorization (Rosch and Lloyd, 1978; Berger and Luckmann, 1966).

How does categorization occur? One researcher found that it follows the principle of cognitive economy—that is, managers strive for maximum information in a category with minimum cognitive effort—and that "names evolve first for basic-level objects" (Rosch, 1978, p. 35). She goes on to explain that basic-level characteristics of, for example, the state legislation can be sorted into natural discontinuities, and categories will be formed at these junctures. As Quine had pointed out earlier: "[People] sort things into kinds. . . . What are [perceived] are significantly structured wholes" (1973, p. 1).

Top managers of the two organizations collectively sorted their perceptions of the legislation according to five basic categories (or clusters of "kinds"):

1. *What* the legislation is (definition).
2. *Who* is responsible for the legislation (agent attribution).
3. *Why* the legislation came about (causality).
4. *What* the legislation is intended to accomplish (*intent*).
5. *How* the legislation will affect us (*impact*).

These five categories both "reduce information load" and "maximize the similarity of objects within the cluster and the dissimilarity of objects from different clusters" (Tversky and Gati, 1978, p. 91).

Using the text of the legislation along with generally accepted commentaries on the law by state regulators, the industry association, and the community of industry managers, data on the environmental event can be sorted into the same five categories. These categories constitute the perceptual ground—the objective data—with which the actual perceptions of top managers can be compared.

1. *What:* Charge-control law.
2. *Who:* State regulators and business round table.
3. *Why:* Industry costs in state were too high.

4. *Intent:* Reduce rate of industry cost inflation; cut waste in the system.
5. *Impact:* Layoff or attrition; could be bankruptcy; innovation will be constrained.

As the following paragraphs reveal, managers' perceptions did not always map the available data.

Perceptions of Institution A's Top Managers. When top managers at Institution A collectively sorted their perceptions of the law into these five categories, their language was straightforward and their categorization very close to the perceptual ground in four of the five categories. However, when these managers categorized one *impact* of the law—layoff or attrition—they categorized it as "suffering," "hurt," and "pain" for employees. In nearly every discussion of the legislation, this imagery was paramount.

Said the executive vice president: "The last thing I want to do is to cause any suffering for employees. And to lose your job is suffering." The chief financial officer stated over and over: "Whatever we do will hurt." All agreed: "There's no way to come up with cuts without real pain." Even more vividly one manager recounted: "Grown men have come in *in tears* to see if they'll still have a job!" And another responded: "We need to remain *so* cognizant of the anxieties and pain that are out there."

For these managers, layoff or attrition clearly threatened their core belief in taking care of their employees. This belief acted like a lens through which managers "saw" one characteristic of the legislation (for discussion of this phenomena, see Newell and Simon, 1972; Claxton, 1980). Because of the strong emotion with which they held this core belief, managers perceived a heightened image of reality and depicted that reality using metaphors of suffering and pain.

To put managers' perception of "suffering" in context, the worst-case budget reduction at Institution A (assuming no revenue offsets) was equivalent to a layoff of eighty full-time employees. This was less than 3 percent of total staff and probably less than normal annual turnover.

Perceptions of Institution B's Top Managers. When top

managers at Institution B sorted their perceptions of the law into the five categories, their language was straightforward and their categorization very close to the perceptual ground in two of the five categories. However, when these managers categorized the *definition,* the *agents,* and the *intent* of the law, their perceptions were quite different and their language was characterized by vivid imagery.

For example, managers did not define the law as "charge control." Instead, at their first meeting after the law went into effect the president stood up at a flipchart, drew a box, and stated: "What they've really done is put us in a box." The implication? He continued: "If you add something, you have to take something away."

Responsible agents were identified as the state regulators and the business round table but were conceptualized as the attacking and anonymous "they." Said one manager: "They [the business round table] just realized they tasted blood, and they'll be out for more." Similarly: "They don't forget. They'll kill you in the long run!" To managers, "their" intent was obvious: "They want to wipe us out!"

For these managers the definition, agents, and intent of the law clearly threatened their core belief in putting the client "above all other concerns, . . . almost irrespective of cost." This belief acted like a lens through which managers "saw" these characteristics of the legislation. Because of the strong emotion with which they held this core belief, managers perceived a heightened image of reality and depicted that reality using the metaphors of box, attack, and capture.

To put managers' perception of the law as a box in context, it was noted earlier that a major incentive of the bill was to introduce products whose marginal revenues exceeded marginal costs. Early on, the chief financial officer attempted to correct the president's connotation ("if you add something, you have to take something away"). He said: "If you put in a service that produces a profit, there's really no limit to these increases." In other words, the law did not impose such rigid boundaries on their strategic options.

Without arguing that there is only one best strategy for

an institution, let us consider what an economically rational, value-maximizing response to this legislation might include (see, for example, Porter, 1980). Using the incentives included in the legislation, managers could (1) reduce expenses below the prospectively set total by going after the biggest expense line item (in this as in other service industries that item was labor, and the industry association recommended that annual wage increases be tied to the expected inflation index), (2) introduce products whose marginal revenues exceeded marginal costs, and (3) generate as much surplus from tactics one and two as possible and invest this money over three years.

What the following paragraphs reveal is that managers responded not just to "objective" reality but, more important, to that reality created by their shared beliefs and depicted in metaphoric language.

Responses of Institution A's Top Managers. At Institution A, managers responded in an economically rational manner *up to a point.* They introduced a service expected to yield $300,000 in marginal revenues the first year. Other decisions appeared to be based not on economic rationality but on their perception that one impact of the law was "suffering." The director of human relations stated: "I'm going to recommend that we *not* cut the salary program"—that is, reduce perquisites or tie the increase to the inflation index. More emphatically, she went on: "I'm going to recommend, after a lot of agonizing, that we meet the budget by layoff. There's a narrower effect—of defined duration—in contrast to the very broad impact of salary adjustments. . . . And [our salary policy must] support our emphasis on *caring.*"

Managers at Institution A in fact decided to give as large a salary increase as possible: 8 percent. Said the executive vice president about this decision: "We wanted . . . to give employees a pat on the back." Because of the revenue-generating service and because of budget reductions in areas other than salaries and wages, no employees were laid off during the first year of the new law. (Total staff was reduced by nineteen people [less than 1 percent] through attrition.) In addition, managers did not attempt to generate as large a surplus as possible by making

all expense cuts the first year, nor did they attempt to compound the surplus over three years. Rather, they decided to "go
at" the budget reduction process each year as "more intelligent
than wreaking havoc all over." Commented the chief financial
officer: "I subscribe to: 'lay back and don't do it [cut people]
until it's your last resort.' "

Responses of Institution B's Top Managers. Like their
counterparts at Institution A, Institution B managers followed
an economically rational strategy *up to a point.* They went
after the biggest line item, labor, by tying annual pay increases
to the inflation index, at that time 5 percent. (In fact, the executive vice president urged managers to try to give less than the
index.) They also reduced total staff by 4 percent through attrition and levied a 3 percent across-the-board budget cut on all
departments. Managers chose that budget target to achieve in
the first year the reductions needed for three years. In line with
the incentives, managers intended to compound the savings for
the duration of the legislation.

However, in line with their core belief in putting the client "above all other concerns," managers also invested heavily
in the new service discussed earlier that would cost the institution $46,000 per client. And, in line with their perception of
the legislation as a box, they attempted *to make room* for that
service by taking something out. For example, one manager said
about this service: "[We] know *that* takes up 80 percent of the
box!" Thus, said the executive vice president: "We're going to
have to make sure that the costs are extremely well spelled
out, and the [board has] to understand that this would have to
be funded by *giving up* something else" (emphasis added). The
president commented: "We're asking everybody to look for 3
percent savings. And we think if we can get it—and we intend to
get it—we can keep it and use it for other things" (such as the
new service).

Comparison of Responses

When the decisions of the two top management groups
are compared, they appear almost diametrically opposed. At Institution A, managers decided (1) to give as large a salary increase

as possible, (2) to introduce a sizable revenue-generating service, and (3) not to generate as much surplus as possible nor to compound over three years what surplus did occur. At Institution B, managers decided (1) to give as small a salary increase as possible (the inflation index or less), (2) to introduce a sizable revenue-losing service, and (3) to levy an across-the-board budget reduction to generate as much surplus as possible the first year.

Although structural factors often constrain managers' decisions so that two organizations would not be expected to respond alike, such factors did not appear to play a very important role in this investigation. For example, no structural factor required managers at Institution A to give as large a salary increase as they did. As stated earlier, both institutions paid competitive wages; neither institution was unionized, and unionization was not considered an immediate possibility. Likewise, no structural factor required managers at Institution B *not* to introduce revenue-generating products (but on only two occasions did the author hear that even mentioned as an option). Instead of structural constraints, the influence of shared beliefs appeared to be the cause of the major differences in responses (see also Donaldson and Lorsch, 1983). Let us review the managers' decisions again from this perspective.

Of all the data on the law, only the impact of layoff or attrition roused strong emotions among managers of Institution A. Why? Managers shared a core belief that one fundamental quality of their institution was caring for employees. Layoff or attrition (or reducing employee perquisites) was therefore perceived to be "suffering," "hurt," and "pain." This metaphoric categorization of the law became for managers what is called an *intersubjective reality* (for discussion of this phenomena, see Mead, 1934; Berger and Luckmann, 1966; Argyris and Schön, 1978). That is, part of what managers perceived about the legislation was not supported by the objective data. Their subjective perception was nonetheless real to them and constituted part of the reality to which they responded.

By the same token, the definition, agents, and intent of the law roused strong emotions among managers of Institution B. Why? Managers shared a core belief that one fundamental quality of their institution was putting the client first. A law that would control their charges and restrict their ability to put the client above monetary concerns was therefore perceived to be a "box" in which they had been captured. Although not supported by the objective data, managers shared this intersubjective reality and responded to it.

(As noted, one manager at Institution B, the chief financial officer, who had been with the institution for only four months at the time, did question the implications of this categorization. However, he was not successful in changing managers' intersubjective reality. Nearly five months after this interchange, at a major planning meeting, the executive vice president drew a series of boxes on a flipchart. He explained to the group that each box "represents department capacity" and went on to say: "[If we can] identify how much of the unused capacity [the new service] takes up, we can see if we can do it within existing resources." Otherwise, commented the president: "If . . . we find we can't fit [this service] into the unused portion, then we can go back to [department managers] and say: 'We'll have to cut back . . . in order to do [this]." The chief financial officer did not correct them.)

Consequences of Culture

Top managers of both institutions A and B traded one incentive of the law because of their shared beliefs. At Institution A, managers did not attempt to reduce expenses as much as they could have in the first year and invest the difference over the term of the legislation. Instead, because of their core belief, they decided to give an 8 percent average salary increase and tackle budget reductions each year. As noted, the recommended wage inflator was 5 percent. If we assume a total salary expense of $100 million, there was an *opportunity cost* of $3.9 million attached to the managers' shared belief in caring for employees [(8 percent − 5 percent) × $100 million compounded at 9 percent over three years].

At Institution B, managers did not emphasize revenue-generating products. Instead, because of their core belief (and the resulting perception of the law as a box), they tried to "fit in" a revenue-losing product by taking something out. If we assume that forty clients were served by the new product in its first year (actually, managers expected to phase in this volume over three years), there was an *opportunity cost* of $2.4 million attached to the managers' shared belief ($46,000 × 40 clients, compounded at 9 percent over three years). In addition, we would have to factor in the lost opportunity of potention revenue-generating products to arrive at the total consequences of this shared belief.

Finally, consider the lost opportunity of Sperry-Univac's late entry into the minicomputer market. If we could estimate the financial consequences of decisions made by managers as a result of their predisposition to see only the mainframe aspects of the world, they would be enormous.

Conclusion

In the case studies, organizational culture as shared beliefs appeared to influence the decisions top managers made. Because managers at Institution A *believed* in caring for employees, they *saw* one impact of the law to be "suffering" for employees and acted to alleviate that suffering. Because managers at Institution B *believed* in putting the client first, "almost irrespective of cost," they *saw* the result of the law to be the creation of a rigid and unyielding "box" and acted in accord with that image. If we go back to Vickers' definition of organizational culture as a "set of readinesses," it is clear that in each organization top managers were *predisposed* to distinguish some aspects of the legislation in a certain way. Believing was sometimes seeing.

Note also that vivid imagery characterized the language with which managers articulated their perceptions and, in fact, appeared to influence their strategic decision making. As Lakeoff and Johnson note: "We draw inferences, set goals, make commitments, and execute plans, all on the basis of how we in part structure our experience, consciously and unconsciously, by means of metaphor" (1980, p. 158; see also Nisbett and Ross, 1980). Because of managers' shared beliefs, certain metaphors appeared to resonate with each group and to create an intersubjective reality (see Schön, 1963; Ortony, 1979; Smith and Simmons, 1983). At Institution A, managers based their response to the law on their perception (and metaphor) of the law as suffering for employees. At Institution B, they based their responses on their perception (and metaphor) of the law as a box. In both cases, metaphors helped to create the reality to which managers responded strategically.

Organizational culture as shared beliefs thus appeared to influence the decision making of the two top-management groups in the following way:

1. Shared beliefs influenced how managers perceived certain aspects of the legislation.
2. Shared beliefs influenced the language that managers used to articulate their perceptions.
3. Decision making entailed a response to the intersubjective reality created in part by managers' shared beliefs and depicted in metaphoric imagery. Strategy was designed in some measure to adapt the institution to a metaphorical reality.

References

Argyris, C., and Schön, D. A. *Organizational Learning: A Theory of Action Perspective.* Reading, Mass.: Addison-Wesley, 1978.

"AT&T Has Call for a New Company Culture." *Wall Street Journal,* Feb. 28, 1984, p. 32.

"AT&T Marketing Men Find Their Star Fails to Ascend as Expected." *Wall Street Journal,* Feb. 13, 1984, pp. 1, 16.

Berger, P. L., and Luckmann, T. *The Social Construction of Reality.* New York: Anchor Books, 1966.

Claxton, G. (ed.). *Cognitive Psychology: New Directions.* London: Routledge & Kegan Paul, 1980.

Donaldson, G., and Lorsch, J. W. *Decision Making at the Top: The Shaping of Strategic Direction.* New York: Basic Books, 1983.

Lakeoff, G., and Johnson, M. *Metaphors We Live By.* Chicago: University of Chicago Press, 1980.

Malinowski, B. *Argonauts of the Western Pacific.* New York: Dutton, 1953.

Mead, G. H. *Mind, Self, and Society.* Chicago: University of Chicago Press, 1934.

"Moving Away From Mainframes." *Business Week,* Feb. 15, 1982, pp. 78–87.

Newell, A., and Simon, H. A. *Human Problem Solving.* Englewood Cliffs, N.J.: Prentice-Hall, 1972.

Nisbett, R., and Ross, L. *Human Inference: Strategies and Shortcomings of Social Judgment.* Englewood Cliffs, N.J.: Prentice-Hall, 1980.

Ortony, A. (ed.). *Metaphor and Thought.* Cambridge, England: Cambridge University Press, 1979.

Porter, M. E. *Competitive Strategy.* New York: Free Press, 1980.

Quine, W. V. *The Roots of Reference.* La Salle, Ill.: Open Court, 1973.

Rosch, E., and Lloyd, B. B. (eds.). *Cognition and Categorization.* Hillsdale, N.J.: Lawrence Erlbaum, 1978.

Sapienza, A. M. "Believing Is Seeing." Unpublished doctoral dissertation, Graduate School of Business Administration, Harvard University, 1984.

Schön, D. A. *Displacement of Concepts.* London: Tavistock, 1963.

Smith, K. K., and Simmons, V. M. "A Rumpelstiltskin Organization." *Administrative Science Quarterly,* 1983, *28,* 372–392.

Tversky, A., and Gati, I. "Studies of Similarity." In E. Rosch and B. B. Lloyd (eds.), *Cognition and Categorization.* Hillsdale, N.J.: Lawrence Erlbaum, 1978.

Vickers, G. *The Art of Judgment.* London: Chapman & Hall, 1965.

Vygotsky, L. S. *Mind in Society.* Trans. and ed. by Michael Cole. Cambridge: Harvard University Press, 1978.

Five

Strategic Myopia: Culture as an Invisible Barrier to Change

Jay W. Lorsch

In a book concerned with corporate culture, it is important to recognize that culture affects not only what managers believe within the organization but also the decisions they make about the organization's relationships with its environment—in other words, its strategy. In fact, the central argument of this chapter is that culture has a major impact on corporate strategy. To clarify this position, we must first define two key concepts— *culture* and *strategy*—terms widely used by scholars and managers but often without a clear explanation of their precise meaning.

Culture will be used here to mean the beliefs top managers in a company share about how they should manage themselves and other employees and how they should conduct their business. These beliefs are often invisible to the top managers, but they nevertheless have a major impact on their thoughts and actions.

Strategy will be used here to mean the stream of decisions taken over time by top managers that, when understood as a whole, reveal the goals they are seeking and the means they are using to reach them. Such a definition of strategy differs from the common business use of the term in that it does not refer to an explicit plan. In fact, by this definition strategy may be implicit as well as explicit.

Focusing on the connection between culture and strategy is critical because at no time in recent history have top American managers been confronted with such a wide array of challenges to the traditional strategies of their companies:

- Regulatory changes have significantly altered the nature of competition in industries as diverse as airlines, trucking, banking, insurance, and telecommunications.
- Advancing electronic technology has spurred competition in the computer industry itself and also has made the computer a key competitive weapon for financial services, retailing, and telecommunications companies.
- The cost of technological and product development has caused even the giants of the aircraft industry to undertake joint ventures with foreign partners, formerly their competitors.
- Automotive companies facing changing consumer tastes and intense foreign competition are restructuring product lines, improving quality and productivity, and adopting foreign business partners.
- Similarly, managers in a wide range of mature industries, from steel to consumer durables, are reexamining and changing traditional manufacturing and distribution policies to remain competitive in the world market.

There is considerable evidence that such pressures will accelerate in the years ahead, given the rapid rate of technological change, the increasing interdependence of global markets, and continuing regulatory change in the United States. This means that many top managers increasingly will find that they are confronted with major questions of how to position their companies in new businesses and how to change fundamentally their firms' strategies in their existing businesses.

In the face of such pressures for strategic change, a major goal for managers must be avoiding missteps and shortening the time required to develop successful new strategic approaches. Unfortunately, strategic repositioning historically has been a long and complex process, even in highly successful companies, and one that is heavily influenced by the company's culture (Donaldson and Lorsch, 1983). The following examples illustrate the point.

- A consumer food company recognized in the late 1950s that changing consumer tastes were making its major products obsolete. It took more than fifteen years and two generations of top management to successfully reposition the company into growing businesses that built on the company's strengths in consumer marketing.
- A manufacturer of industrial supplies became aware in the late 1960s that the market for its major product was shrinking because of the development of new processing technologies. Top management needed almost a decade to develop and implement a strategy that today makes the company again successful as a source of supplies to its customers.
- In the early 1970s the top management of a growing electronics firm rejected as too risky a proposal from the engineering department and middle managers to manufacture and market a mainframe computer with innovative new features. It was almost ten years before top management found a suitable way to position itself successfully in the computer industry.

The top managers in these examples are among the most successful in their industries—they made major strategic changes that allowed their companies to remain financially healthy and growing in changing times—and still they required many years to change the direction of their companies.[1]

1. The author and two colleagues interviewed extensively the financial, planning, and operating executives who constituted the top management team of twelve major industrial firms. The firms were chosen on

The Difficulties of Achieving Strategic Change

Some might argue that all the time required to achieve strategic change is a direct result of management's poor analytical skills or its failure to use the latest tools for strategic planning. But the facts point to a different conclusion.

Most obvious, strategic changes necessarily involve many actions that require months or years to accomplish. Old businesses may have to be divested or closed. New products may have to be developed by scientists and engineers. Market tests may be required. Manufacturing facilities may have to be built or modified. If the company chooses to expand its business through acquisition, time is required to locate appropriate companies, negotiate agreements, and successfully integrate the acquired companies with the parent.

More subtle but equally important, strategic change requires a basic rethinking of the beliefs by which the company defines and carries on its businesses. In successful companies, it was found, there exists among top managers a system of beliefs —a culture—that underlies these strategic choices. This system has usually developed over many years. As a top manager in one firm stated: "It is a closed loop. You make the argument that in the beginning of the company, the founders wanted to make certain products, which in turn led to our way of managing which reinforced our products. It all hangs together. It isn't the result of any intellectual process but it evolves. The pattern of principles which emerge out of a lot of individual decisions is totally consistent and it is a fabric which hangs together and leads to success."

As this executive also points out, the beliefs in each successful company truly are part of a system. Each individual

---

the basis of several criteria, the most obvious being long-term corporate success. The interviewers also spoke with some of the division managers who were subject to the discipline of the planning and goal-setting process, as well as with past and present chief executives. The rationale for the selection of these companies and a detailed analysis of the findings of these interviews are discussed in Donaldson and Lorsch, 1983.

premise fits into a pattern or cultural whole that has guided managers' decisions during many years of corporate success.

Managers learn to be guided by these beliefs because they have worked successfully in the past. As one chief executive officer (CEO) said: "If you have a way that's working, you want to stay with it. . . . This is not the only way to run a company, but it has sure worked for us."[2]

Executives in successful companies become emotionally committed to these beliefs because they often have spent their entire careers in their companies and have learned their beliefs from valued mentors and have had them reinforced by success at various stages of their career. This history of long association with their companies is true not only of the CEOs in the twelve companies studied but of most Fortune 500 companies (Burck, 1976). The president of another company provided a specific example: "My predecessor became president about 1947. In our staff meetings he'd say, 'We're caught between two giants—the retailers and our suppliers.' We're the little unit in between. We need to grow so we can exercise power on both sides. I don't remember a staff meeting in the early 1950s when an officer didn't make some mention of this point. It led directly to our concern with growth."

These beliefs cover a range of topics: what the firm's financial goals should be, in what businesses the firm can succeed, how marketing should be done in these businesses, what types of risks are acceptable and which are not. But at the core of each system of beliefs is top management's particular vision of its company's distinctive competence. This vision is management's own assessment of the capabilities and limits of the company's employees, its market position, its financial resources, and its technological base. In sum, it is management's core beliefs about what the company is capable of accomplishing.

A system of beliefs in a typical company is illustrated in Figure 1. It includes beliefs about capital-market expectations, about the internal organization, and about product-market com-

2. The quotations in this chapter, unless otherwise noted, are derived from the author's personal research, and the sources are confidential.

Figure 1. Commodity Products Company: Top Management Culture.

Beliefs About Capital-Market Expectations

- Return on equity should be X%, which places us among the upper ⅓ of all manufacturing companies.
- Market share should steadily improve.
- Dividends should *never* be cut and should be X% of earnings.
- X credit rating should be maintained, and debt should be kept at less than X% of capital.

Strategic Vision

We can be the strongest and top-ranked company in our industry but will not diversify outside it.

Beliefs About Product-Market Competition

- Our geographic location provides us with a cost advantage.
- We must offer better service than competitors to our customers.
- Major customers like big suppliers committed to the industry.
- We must improve profit position through lower costs, not higher prices.
- Market share is important, but not through low prices.
- We must compete on innovation in processes and basic products, not in price.
- We must expand and modernize plants for the long haul.

Beliefs About Internal Organization

- We must have the strongest management structure in the industry.
- We must foster harmony and preserve the family feeling within the company through all levels of employees, including those in the union.
- We must keep employees who believe in the industry happy because the industry is what we are good at.
- We must preserve the drama and emotion of the industry.
- We want to keep management accessible and participating.
- Top management must always include at least one person who understands manufacturing processes and operations.
- Good coordination between sales and manufacturing gives us the ability to serve customers better than the competition.

petition. Briefly, beliefs about capital-market expectations reflect management's convictions about what is necessary to keep investors and lenders satisfied, given management's strategic vision of staying in a mature industry. Beliefs about product-market competition reflect management's notion of why and how the company can succeed in a highly competitive, mature industry. Beliefs about internal management reflect the approaches that management thinks will lead to competitive success and that therefore will meet capital-market expectations.

These beliefs can inhibit strategic change in two ways. First, they can produce a strategic myopia. Because managers hold a set of beliefs, they see events through this prism. Frequently they miss the significance of changing external conditions because they are blinded by strongly held beliefs. For example, the management of the industrial supply manufacturer mentioned earlier was rudely awakened to the decline of its major product by a dramatic market study. The current CEO of the company recalled: "Back in the 1950s, a member of the finance department made a study of the industry which showed that it was in a mature phase. This was the first time that the company had done such a study and management was shocked by its implications that the industry and the company would stop growing. From that point on everyone became concerned about the problem and what they were going to do about it." In retrospect, management recognized that it could have seen the decline several years earlier.

Even when managers can overcome such myopia, they respond to changing events in terms of their culture. Because their beliefs have been effective guides in the past, their natural response is to stick with them. For example, the food processing company mentioned earlier studiously avoided opportunities to grow internationally. Why? An early international failure convinced its top managers that such expansion was outside of the company's distinctive competence. Their vision was: "We can succeed with products that are marketed to consumers in the United States. We understand them." While top managers are usually able to recognize the practical difficulties involved in accomplishing a major strategic change, they are much less likely to recognize that their deeply held beliefs represent an invisible barrier that must be penetrated if strategic change is to take place.

The Process of Strategic Change

An examination of strategic change as revealed in the study of twelve successful companies illustrates how the invisible carrier of culture can be overcome. In those companies where major strategic change was necessary because of changing market conditions, managers for a time did suffer from strategic myopia. The severity of this ailment depended on how long and how well the old culture continued to achieve top management's financial goals. Persistent problems in achieving desired financial goals was in each case the trigger that made managers aware that something was wrong with their beliefs. The pattern of beliefs that had worked well no longer did so.

Incremental Change. The initial response to this discovery was a period of questioning various individual premises. Could the problem be fixed by minor modification of the belief system? In some instances, these incremental changes succeeded in correcting the problem. For example, in one company, adverse financial results in 1974 and 1975 especially alarmed top management because they were then investing heavily in a major new product. They either had to take on more long-term debt or abandon the new product. Either option meant departing from an important belief. Two executives recalled the dilemma: "We were using our debt capacity too fast. The momentum of our capital expenditures program was carrying us out too fast, especially in one business where the outlook had been changing negatively. We had to decide what was useful to the future of the company. . . . Well, in '74–'75 survival was the name of the game. The first thing we had to do was perpetuate the company and not let it get away from us, but [the new product] represented the future and we couldn't let that go. It was a technological breakthrough. It was a big chip to bet on."

In the end, top management altered its beliefs about what

was an acceptable level of long-term debt so the company could continue the development of the new product. In the past, such new products had fueled the company's growth. To depart from the principle that major new products assured the future health of the company would have shattered management's central cultural vision of the company's distinctive competence. It was far easier to bend a less-central principle than one at the core of top management's culture.

Such incremental changes in top management's beliefs occur periodically in most successful companies. One belief or another is altered, but the basic fabric of the culture remains the same. However, in the rapidly changing world of the 1980s, more fundamental changes are likely to be required. This was the case in several of the companies studied. While their top managers tried initially to adjust to market changes through incremental actions, they found that such small steps did not achieve the desired results. This led to much more serious departures from past strategic beliefs and practices, which ultimately changed the fundamental nature of their belief system.

Fundamental Change. Top managers went through several distinct but interrelated stages in their thoughts and actions, as they led their companies in fundamentally new directions.

The first stage grew directly out of earlier attempts at incremental changes. Top managers gradually developed a shared awareness that fundamental changes in their culture would be necessary to ensure corporate survival. Because top managers were so emotionally committed to their beliefs, an awareness of the need for fundamental change did not come easily. During this early phase, top managers could engage in months of what psychiatrists would label *denial.* They chose to ignore the possibility that key beliefs could and should be modified. But gradually in each firm an awareness did develop among top managers that external events had changed permanently and that incremental steps would not solve their problems. Drastic changes in the whole pattern of beliefs were needed.

This recognition was followed by a period of confusion. While all the top managers could agree that the old beliefs were not working, there were often as many ideas about what to do next as there were top managers. No one idea attracted wide support. Strategic planners and their concepts offered little help, because the confusion went to the heart of top managers' own judgments about such matters as what the firm's distinctive competence had been and could be in the future.

So long as the firm's financial viability is not seriously in question, the period of confusion can continue for many months or even years. One executive described such a period in his company's past: "We acquired business after business. There was no real support so it failed. We flubbed around. People said we should be in a [particular business] because it had growth, but we never picked out what segment and the president and chairman weren't comfortable with the program."

With an awareness of the need for major change in strategic direction but confusion about what to do, top management was ready for new leadership, and each company's board of directors apparently shared that view. In each case, the board turned to new leadership to find a path out of the period of confusion. In all but one instance the new CEO was promoted from within, however, he always represented a new generation of management with fresh ideas. Because these CEOs were generally insiders, they also understood and appreciated the old pattern of strategic beliefs. This was important because their major task was to find a clear, new direction out of the existing confusion, building as much as possible on their companies' strengths.

Developing a Strategic Vision. The first steps out of the confusion took place inside the heads of the new CEOs and may have even predated their ascension to corporate leadership. They each developed a personal set of ideas about what their companies could become. Their next tasks were to elaborate on and clarify this strategic vision and to rally other top managers and the larger management organization to it. For a while their activities in this regard were largely mental and verbal: thinking, talking, and listening to their subordinates.

A company executive described this phase: "What we did in the mid-sixties was to assess the management group. We stepped back. There were several sessions with top management out of the office. It was a self-assessment. It was top management assessing itself and saying we didn't see the good prospects for technology in [a basic consumer products business] we had hoped for. If we had anything to bring to new industries, it was our ability to think about customers, how to do market research, market planning, etc." Out of such discussions evolved a vision shared among the top managers about what the company's distinctive capabilities could be in the future. In the instance of this executive's company, it was to become a manufacturer and marketer of a wide range of nondurable, brand-name products to United States consumers and to do this in such a way that the company would be an "all-weather company," one that would do well in all phases of the business cycle.

In each company the CEO and his associates developed a unique vision. What these strategic visions had in common, however, was that they took fundamentally new ideas and meshed them with some old beliefs about how to compete effectively, how to manage employees, and how to manage corporate finances. Such a fusion of old and new resulted in realistic new strategies because it reflected the best assessment executives could make about their own and their company's capabilities. Psychologically, it made sense because it enabled executives to retain as many beliefs from their old culture as possible, even as they headed off in new directions. Because the new CEO and his colleagues were almost all career-long employees of their companies, it was comfortable to adhere to at least some old beliefs, and this minimized their resistance to strategic change.

In fact, one of the two major accomplishments during this phase was overcoming the persistent doubts among the executives about departing too far from established beliefs. The other accomplishment was refining and clarifying the direction that was to carry the firm forward. Once clarification was achieved, initially by thought and discussion, ideas then had to be converted into concrete decisions. Such decisions signalled the final stage of the process: experimentation.

Experimentation. Like scientists in a laboratory, executives in the successful companies studied experimented with their new ideas. Gradually and in increments they committed money and people to the new direction. (This view of strategic change as an incremental process is also confirmed by James Brian Quinn, [1980].) An executive in a consumer products company described this phase: "During the 1960s we had four out of every five capital investment dollars going into acquisitions. There were many new venture teams going and we got into quite a number of businesses. We were searching for new business."

In this particular company, experimentation took the form of both acquisitions and internal development. For example, part of the company's new vision was opening retail shops so it could sell directly to the consumer. A number of different types of stores were opened. Results were evaluated and new ideas tried, but none of the ideas really caught fire. Frustrated but not discouraged by several years of experimentation, the company's executives discovered a small chain of stores that they could acquire and which already embodied many of the ideas that, as a result of its internal development efforts, management had concluded were important. These four stores were acquired and today have been expanded into a nationwide network of 300 outlets. The success of this acquisition led to other acquisitions to repeat the pattern with other products.

The top managers in the industrial supply company went through a similar process. They began a search for products that could build upon their strong sales force and distribution network. A number of small acquisitions were made. Some were kept and others divested. Gradually, again over several years, top managers learned what products fit their vision and which did not. For example, it became clear to them that consumable supplies were desirable products and that highly technical products were less desirable.

In some of the companies top managers also learned through experimentation that their new vision would not work. A forest products company provides an example. Even though their company was a good performer in its industry, top managers, frustrated by slow growth and low profitability in the base business, concluded that diversification into unrelated businesses would benefit the company. Several acquisitions were made, and the company operated these new businesses for several years. Results were only mediocre, however, and top management concluded that its vision of the company as a diversified conglomerate was not viable. Instead, they began experimenting with new products more closely related to their core business.

These examples illustrate one reason that fundamental strategic change can consume years: it simply takes a long time for top managers to convert abstract ideas into concrete realities that succeed. As they do so, they learn new beliefs that combine with the old ones they retain, and so they reshape the pattern of the company's culture and strategy. Like their predecessors, they become committed to a system of beliefs that work. Experimentation gradually subsides, and top management finds itself with a stable pattern of beliefs that have created new corporate success, but which are fundamentally different from those with which they started the process of strategic change.

Breaking Through the Invisible Barrier

What can managers do to speed up the process of strategic change in an era that demands more rapid adaptation to constantly changing realities? Of course, managers are in part limited by the amount of time required for certain elements of strategic change—acquisition, diversification, new-product development, test marketing, and so forth—particularly if one agrees that the experimentation so characteristic of strategic change in successful companies helps minimize major missteps in choosing a new direction. But, as we have seen, there is another major drag on the speed with which strategic changes occur: this is the invisible barrier of the top managers' culture. Is it possible for managers to retain the benefits of strong beliefs, yet still be able to change them rapidly? To this author, the answer is yes.

One key factor is top managers' acceptance of the importance of flexibility and innovation as a major premise in their company's culture. Whatever else they hold sacred, they must recognize that in the world of the 1980s and beyond, the need for strategic change will be a constant. However else top managers define their unique strategic vision, they must recognize this fact. But such a commitment will be meaningless unless it can be converted into activities and actions that cause managers to use this conviction to examine and challenge their other strategic premises. Several ways of assuring that this happens are suggested by the experience of the successful companies studied.

Making Beliefs Visible. In a few of these companies, top managers had put their major beliefs in writing. In one, for example, central beliefs were available for employees, customers, and visitors to read in a printed brochure distributed widely throughout the company's offices, visitors' waiting rooms, and so forth. Similarly, at Johnson and Johnson (a very successful company but not included in the study), the company's credo hangs on the walls of most executives' offices (Aguilar, 1983). Such formalized statements, while they may not capture all aspects of a company's culture, do remind managers that their decisions are guided by certain principles.

The important lesson to be drawn from these attempts to develop formal statements of beliefs is that the invisible beliefs can be made more visible in this way. Of course, displaying these beliefs publicly may or may not be a sound idea, depending upon whether managers feel they contain proprietary ideas. But that is not the critical point. What is important is that top managers can and should make their implicit beliefs explicit, at least to each other. If managers are aware of the beliefs they share, they are less likely to be blinded by them and are apt to understand more rapidly when changing events make aspects of their culture obsolete.

In companies that, like most of those we studied, do not have such explicit statements, top managers should undertake a culture audit so that they are aware of their beliefs before they confront an event that forces them to reassess those beliefs. A culture audit requires top management to develop a consensus about its shared beliefs. The process starts with each member of the group answering questions such as those in Table 1. Indi-

Table 1. Culture Audit.

Beliefs about Goals

1. About what financial objectives do we have strong beliefs based on traditions and history (e.g., return on assets, rate of growth, debt/ equity ratio, bond rating, dividend policies)?
2. How, if at all, are these beliefs about financial goals related to each other (e.g., growth should be financed internally, which means no long-term debt and limited dividends)?
3. What other goals do we believe to be important (e.g., to be in the top quartile of Fortune 500 companies; to be the best in our industry; to be a responsible corporate citizen; to be an "all-weather" company)?

Beliefs about Distinctive Competence

4. What do we believe to be the appropriate scope of our competitive activity (e.g., we can manage any business; we can succeed in domestic consumer products; we can succeed with products based on our technological expertise; we can only succeed in the paper industry; we can manage our business worldwide)?
5. To what earlier experience can we trace these beliefs?
6. Do these beliefs reflect a realistic assessment of the competence of our management and company?

Beliefs about Product-Market Guidelines

7. What broad guidelines do we believe our managers should follow in competing in product markets (e.g., have one or two share in each market; provide the best-quality product; compete on service, not on price)?
8. To what, if any, earlier historical events can these principles be traced?
9. Are these guidelines valid today in our various businesses?

Key Beliefs about Management Employees[a]

10. What do we believe employees want or deserve in exchange for their effort (e.g., safe working conditions, stable employment, high wages, share of profits, equity ownership)?
11. What beliefs do we hold about the importance of employees to company success (e.g., our scientists are key to innovation; we want managers and employees to work as one big team; committed employees lead to satisfied customers)?

---

[a]Although these are not, strictly speaking, strategic beliefs, they are important to understand because they are so closely related to strategic premises.

vidual answers to these questions can then be compared and discussed among top managers. Through this process, beliefs that are shared can be identified and codified.

In answering the questions on the culture audit, it is critical that the emphasis be on what managers believe as evidenced by their actual practices, not on an idealized view of the company. This is especially important in the wake of management's current obsession with excellence and corporate culture, a by-product of which has been a spate of statements of corporate philosophy. While these may be admirable statements of top management's intentions, they may have little to do with the strategic beliefs that actually guide top managers' actions, beliefs that the culture audit attempts to identify.

An effective culture audit cannot be delegated. It must involve the company's major decision makers, including the CEO. Managers must be willing to commit the thought and time, probably several days, first to answer the questions on the audit individually, and then to compare and discuss their responses with their colleagues until a consensus is reached.

As they go through this process, managers should be able gradually to identify the consistent pattern of their culture and the ways in which beliefs are related. If the audit is successful, top managers will have made the once invisible barrier of culture visible so that they can deal with it more rapidly in the face of change, retaining beliefs that still are valid and discarding those that are not.

Assuring Flexibility

Making culture explicit is one way to facilitate more rapid strategic change. But what is also required are other ways to stimulate top managers to maintain a commitment to flexibility, whatever else they believe. Successful companies use a variety of means to accomplish this.

Top Managers Without Portfolio. One device is the presence of a very senior and experienced top manager whose role is to raise questions, challenge beliefs, and suggest new ideas. Such managers, who often have the title of vice-chairman, generally have few other responsibilities. At first glance it might seem that they have been shunted out of line management, but a more careful examination reveals that these "managers without portfolio" are valued members of the top management group.

Always very intelligent and experienced, often skeptical and questioning, they interact constantly with other top managers, challenging beliefs and suggesting new ideas. While they understand and are committed to the existing culture, their presence in the management group helps keep it fluid and dynamic.

The qualifications for such a post may seem unique, and there is no way to assure that such a person is available to every top management group. Yet the presence of such managers in several of the successful companies studied suggests that the CEOs understood the value of intelligent dissent and creativity in their top management team.

The Role of Outside Directors. Outside directors can also play an important part in assuring strategic flexibility. While they usually are affiliated with companies for long periods of time and may therefore fall prey to many of top management's beliefs, they are also enough removed to provide objectivity and raise important questions about the appropriateness of these beliefs in changing times. While many top managers hold the view that strategic decisions are the sole purview of management, outside directors can, even with limited time and information, play an important role in keeping top managers alert to their culture and to changing external events. This may be done informally or, as in some companies, may be formally assigned to a board strategy committee.

Bringing in New Blood. Another way to ensure cultural flexibility is to bring in an outside manager at a very senior level. Such an individual brings a new perspective and objectivity, but to be successful this senior manager must effectively solve two problems. First, any newcomer brings a set of beliefs from his or her prior experience; what worked with a previous employer may now be part of a dearly held set of principles. To be effective in a new setting, the newcomer needs to develop an awareness of these beliefs. Second, the new executive needs to develop an awareness of the culture of the new company. If its beliefs have been explicitly stated, the transition is easier; but if not, the newcomer will have to be an alert detective. Poor understanding of existing beliefs can cause the new manager unwittingly to step on too many sensitive toes and to be rejected before he or she has any impact on the organization.

Flexibility Down the Line. Another way to ensure flexibility at the top is to encourage flexible thinking at subordinate levels of management. This can ensure that succeeding generations of top management will be less blindly rigid in their adherence to cultural traditions. It can also offer a new perspective to the present top managers as ideas bubble up from subordinate levels.

Two different routes can be used to encourage flexibility among middle managers. One is to stimulate new ideas within the organization. An in-company education program for middle managers, with outside experts as instructors, is one frequently employed means. Another is encouraging systematic rotation of managers among functions and businesses. In this way, their perspectives can be broadened. Such inside activities always have the inherent limitation that new ideas are learned from company colleagues in the context of the company's culture.

The second way to encourage flexibility among middle managers avoids this pitfall. Subordinate managers with high potential are provided an opportunity to broaden their perspectives outside the company. University executive education programs are one vehicle for achieving this. Whatever else they achieve, they do broaden the perspective of participants through contact with peers from other companies. Business and government exchange programs, like the White House Exchange Fellowships, can accomplish the same objective. Another tactic used successfully is encouraging managers to travel to companies in other countries to learn new methods and gain a broader perspective. Such programs have been used recently by several companies to challenge the beliefs and broaden the perspectives of manufacturing executives. The result has been improved manufacturing practices that depart from traditional methods.

No matter how top managers decide to broaden their subordinates' perspectives, they must be ready to encourage initiatives and innovations after their subordinates have completed their experiences. Flexibility will only flourish if top managers, through their own words and actions, reward initiators of innovation and allow experimentation.

Change and Stability

Our focus has been on how top managers can overcome the invisible barrier of culture to speed up the process of strategic change. As necessary as this will be in the future, we must not lose sight of the positive value of a strong culture. In the successful companies studied, these belief systems were critical components of corporate success, providing guidance to managers as they made complex decisions. As long as external conditions do not change dramatically, culture is an invaluable aid to speedy and coherent strategic choices. Even when conditions change dramatically, many old beliefs describe the essence of the company's character and competence, and they cannot be abandoned without a high cost.

Thus, the real challenge for top managers is to encourage flexibility while still respecting and valuing the existing culture. Awareness of this culture is a necessary prerequisite to achieving this balance. Therefore, it may be a critical key to corporate survival in the dynamic decades ahead.

References

Aguilar, J. F. "Johnson & Johnson (A)." Harvard Business School Case 9-384-053, 1983.

Burck, C. G. "A Group Profile of the Fortune 500 Chief Executive." *Fortune,* May 1976, pp. 173–177, 308, 311–312.

Donaldson, G., and Lorsch, J. W. *Decision Making at the Top: The Shaping of Strategic Direction.* New York: Basic Books, 1983.

Quinn, J. B. *Strategies for Change: Logical Incrementalism.* Homewood, Ill.: Richard D. Irwin, 1980.

Six

The Relationship of Corporate Culture to Industry Sector and Corporate Performance

George G. Gordon

Although corporate culture is receiving considerable attention in recent business literature, most of the information has been anecdotal, with little reference to consistent research across companies. As a step toward filling this gap, the following material draws upon relevant data collected by Hay Associates in hundreds of companies from 1970 to the present. The research indicates that culture is real, is measurable, and bears a significant relationship to company performance. It also suggests some ideas about the conditions under which corporate culture can be changed.

Measuring Culture

Since 1970, Hay Associates has been conducting studies of all types of organizations under the rubric of "management climate." Our operational definition of the term *climate* has been quite different from that of many others. For instance, Schwartz and Davis use the more common definition of climate as "a measure of whether people's expectations about what it *should* be like to work in an organization are being met" (1981, p. 33). In other words, climate is usually equated with attitude surveys that measure *satisfaction* with various aspects of the job environment. In our surveys, we have systematically collected the *perceptions* of individuals in the top four or five levels of management about how their companies operate. They are not asked whether or not they are "satisfied" with aspects of their job environments or whether their expectations about the organization are being met. Rather, their perceptions of how their companies function reflect the value systems or cultures of these companies as seen through management's eyes.

We chose to study culture through this upper-level group because we believe that the corporate values held by management are reflected in behavior throughout an organization. For instance, if a chief executive officer (CEO) is strongly committed to the concept that profitability is driven primarily by cost control and is further committed to stability and growth of quarterly earnings, it is unlikely that a single unit, department, or division will develop a culture that values programs that are innovative, long-term, and expansionary, but risky.

Further, if a company wishes to modify its culture, we believe that the thrust must come from the top. Although there is little disagreement that cultures are resistant to change or that ultimately the commitment of large numbers of people is necessary, our own observations indicate that a company's culture can change, but only through the perseverance of its leaders. It is they who set the direction, reinforce the values, and raise the consciousness of the organization to what it must be rather than what it has been.

Our surveys provide a wealth of data about some very important elements of culture and include responses from over 50,000 managers and professionals in over 500 organizations. Most often, we collected data through a census of the top four or five levels of management from the CEO down, rather than examining samples of people at all levels. By focusing on the top of the pyramid, we obtained a clear picture of some of the major values driving the company being examined. This chapter reviews some of the findings of our studies. In particular, it examines the relationships between culture and industry sectors and between culture and corporate performance. Finally, it addresses a central question: Can a company's culture be changed if top management wishes to do so?

Industry Characteristics

The book *In Search of Excellence* (Peters and Waterman, 1982) posits a number of characteristics of successful companies, many of which are strongly cultural in nature. Such central values as an orientation toward the customer and encouragement of innovation seem to characterize these companies. There is, however, a relatively narrow focus in the range of companies considered. For the most part, they are either high tech companies, consumer products companies, or both. These companies operate in highly dynamic marketplaces, where consumer tastes, societal values, economic fluctuations, and technological developments require frequent changes in products or market positioning and a rapid response to competitive developments.

But there are many other organizations that do not operate in so dynamic an environment. For instance, utilities, mining companies, hospitals, and governmental organizations are not as affected by short-term changes in consumer preferences. An oil company, which may have to invest hundreds of millions of dollars to acquire, explore, and develop a new source of supply, will have to commit to that action without getting to the marketplace, or even beginning to realize a return, for perhaps eight to ten years. In this environment, some of the principles advanced by Peters and Waterman (1982), such as introducing an innovation into a marketable product through a series of small steps, seem much less appropriate. In the extreme case, an electric utility, a monopoly, which is expected to bring a single product to market in a totally reliable fashion, would seem to require a very different set of values if it is to meet its mission effectively.

With these distinctions in mind, we explored the question of how much influence a company's business has upon its culture. Specifically, we contrasted a group of utilities with a group of companies operating in a dynamic marketplace ("dynamic-marketplace companies") on a series of cultural issues.

The issues as well as the questionnaire employed are described more fully in the book *Managing Management Climate* (Gordon and Cummins, 1979). For purposes of the present analysis, the eight dimensions described there were expanded to eleven on the basis of inter-item correlations. This "purified" each dimension as much as possible for research, rather than consulting, purposes. The dimensions are:

- Clarity of direction: the extent to which the company emphasizes creating clear objectives and plans to meet them.
- Organizational reach: the extent to which the company sets venturesome goals and approaches its business innovatively.
- Integration: the extent to which units are encouraged to operate in a coordinated manner. This is an indicator of horizontal interdependence.
- Top management contact: the extent to which employees get clear communication and support from upper management. This is an indicator of vertical interdependence.
- Encouragement of individual initiative: the extent to which freedom to act, innovation, and risk taking are emphasized.
- Conflict resolution: the extent to which employees are encouraged to air conflicts and criticisms openly.
- Performance clarity: the extent to which the company makes performance expectations clear to employees.
- Performance emphasis: the extent to which the company is demanding of employees, expecting high levels of performance from them and holding them personally accountable for results.
- Action orientation: the extent to which the timeliness with which decisions are made, a sense of urgency to get things done, and a responsiveness to changes in the marketplace are emphasized.
- Compensation: the extent to which employees perceive the company as paying competitively and fairly as well as relating that pay to performance.

- Human resource development: the extent to which companies provide opportunities for employees to grow and develop within the company.

Utilities vs. Dynamic-Marketplace Companies

The utilities identified in our data base include fourteen electric, gas, and local telephone companies. In order to have a reasonably homogeneous sample, the dynamic-marketplace companies were limited to manufacturers, all in highly competitive marketplaces and all with products that employ some element of high technology. Using this definition we were able to identify eighteen such companies in our data base.

Figure 1 contrasts the cultural values of the two groups of companies. Survey scores are converted to percentiles that position each company's average response against a data base of all types of companies. An industry percentile is then composed of the unweighted average of the percentile scores of all the companies in that industry.

Clearly, the utility profile indicates that some values are emphasized much more than others. Within functionally organized utilities there appears to be a high need for stability, which is reflected in relatively high scores on integration, top management contact, compensation, and human resource development. The greater the degree of interdependence, either horizontally or vertically, the more voices will be heard in any decision, and the less the organization will move off in any significantly different direction. Similarly, a focus upon retaining and developing future management from within reinforces continuity in how things are done. In effect, utilities have created cultures that value stability and for that reason alone find it difficult to change. The changing economics of and demand for energy have therefore had a devastating effect on many utilities whose managements have been unable to make even minor changes in their beliefs about how to manage their companies.

The most dramatic contrasts between the two groups are the much lower value placed on organizational reach within

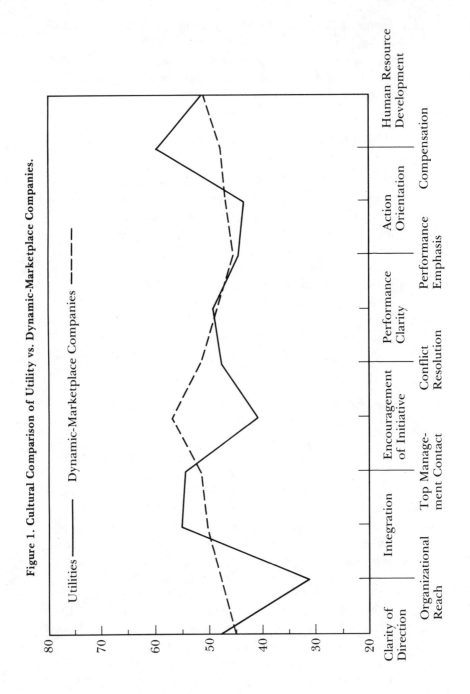

Figure 1. Cultural Comparison of Utility vs. Dynamic-Marketplace Companies.

Utilities ——— Dynamic-Marketplace Companies -------

Percentile

80 70 60 50 40 30 20

Clarity of Direction

Organizational Reach

Integration

Top Management Contact

Encouragement of Initiative

Performance Clarity

Performance Emphasis

Action Orientation

Compensation

Human Resource Development

Conflict Resolution

utilities ($p < .02$)[1] and the greater value placed on the use of individual initiative by the dynamic-marketplace companies ($p < .002$). Obviously, the dynamic-marketplace companies must be able to change much more rapidly than utilities and have created cultures much more attuned to adaptation in all parts of their organizations.

Utilities. What do the most successful utilities look like? To answer this question we first entered our data base for the utilities we had surveyed and obtained data on their profitability for the year the survey was conducted and for two subsequent years. We compared this with the industry's average profitability for those same years and isolated six companies that were clearly high performers and contrasted them with four that were clearly operating below the industry average (putting aside those that had average or mixed performance). Given the small number of companies involved, the ability to detect significant differences is severely limited. For this reason, the discussion includes findings that are marked, but which do not achieve conventional levels of statistical significance.

Figure 2 shows fairly similar profiles for the high and low performers, although the overall profile for the more successful companies is consistently higher. What most differentiates them statistically are the two dimensions relating to interdependence, integration ($p < .12$) and top-management contact ($p < .03$); openness in dealing with conflicts and criticisms ($p < .01$); emphasis on clarity of performance expectations ($p < .07$); and concern for the development of people ($p < .03$). Clearly, the cultures of these successful companies are oriented toward a high degree of interdependence and long employee tenure, both of which cushion the organizations against radical change.

Interestingly, encouragement of individual initiative and organizational reach are relatively low for both groups of companies. In this industry, where stability of operation is very important, great emphasis on individual initiative could well be counterproductive; it is much more important that all employees understand their jobs and how they are expected to perform

1. Two-tailed t test for independent samples.

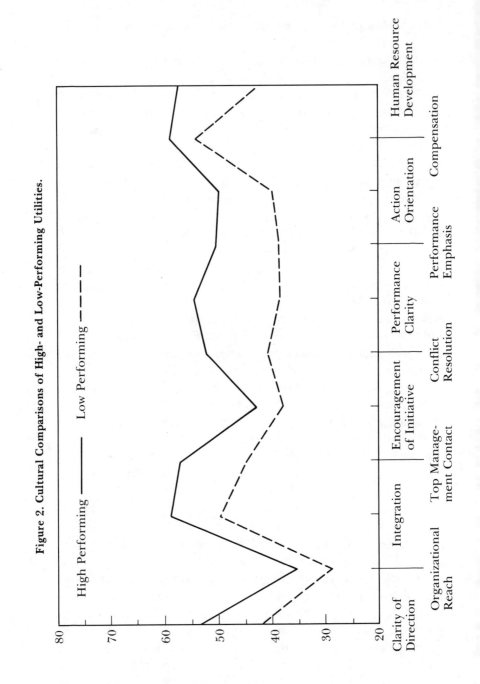

Figure 2. Cultural Comparisons of High- and Low-Performing Utilities.

them (that they have performance clarity). In a like manner, even the successful companies place a very low value on organizational reach, dramatically underscoring the importance of stability to these companies.

Dynamic-Marketplace Companies. Figure 3 compares companies that operate in a more dynamic marketplace. The eighteen companies studied were compared in terms of profitability and growth in revenues, since growth is a much more important factor for these companies than it is for a utility. Success in this group was therefore defined as exceeding industry peers in both dimensions for the year of the survey and for two subsequent years. The five companies that met this dual criterion were then compared with the thirteen that did not (mixed performers).

As indicated in Figure 3, the profile for the high-performing group is very different from that of high-performing utilities. The dominant values for high-performing utilities are integration, top management contact, compensation, and human resource development, but these are all subordinate values for successful dynamic-marketplace companies. Indeed, the most dominant value of the high-performing dynamic-marketplace companies seems to be a drive to make the company bigger and different than it was previously. This tendency to reach out at the company level is reinforced at the individual level through a strong concentration on individual initiative, an open environment, and a bias toward action.

Financial Institutions

We also explored cultural characteristics in an industry undergoing considerable change—the financial industry. For many years, banks and insurance companies have been very insular, conservative, and certainly unthreatened by the world around them. Suddenly, a series of developments—including government deregulation, competition from new entrants, economic volatility, and technological advances—are changing the entire picture of product and market opportunities. The data, combining results from thirty-one banks and insurance com-

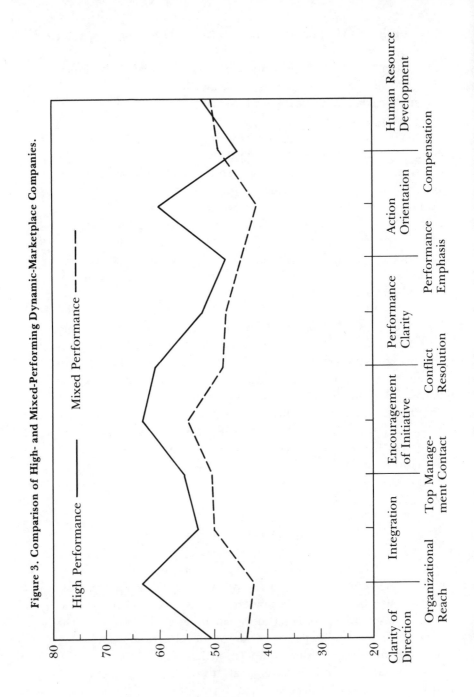

Figure 3. Comparison of High- and Mixed-Performing Dynamic-Marketplace Companies.

panies studied between 1975 and 1982, thus relates to an industry in transition. Eight companies were identified as clearly successful and twelve as clearly unsuccessful in terms of performance as compared to their peers. The others, not represented in Figure 4, were closer to the averages for their industries.

High performers concentrate much more on stretching the company qualitatively and quantitatively ($p < .02$) and taking action ($p < .02$) rather than delaying through indecision, lack of coordination, and so on. The high performers are also much more apt to encourage employees to take the initiative ($p < .02$) in figuring out what they can do to move the company ahead. Thus, the profile of successful financial institutions is not greatly different in these respects from that of the dynamic-marketplace companies. Low performers, on the other hand, seem to have the dominant characteristics of utilities: low stretch and initiative.

Although the leaders of the better-performing financial institutions appear to communicate well and support the actions of those below them (for management contact, $p < .15$; for conflict resolution, $p < .15$), they place little emphasis on clarity of performance standards or performance demand at the individual level.

This pattern might be looked at as that of a group of companies in the middle of a learning curve. It appears that the biggest challenge facing any CEO in this transition is to change the mentality (spelled *culture?*) of the company from one that favors a stable, conservative, slow-moving organization to one that favors a rapid, responsive, adaptive organization. Apparently, the first steps taken in successful organizations have been to make management believe the company can be much more than it was yesterday and to remove the barriers to action. As Edwards indicates in *The Cultural Crisis in Banking,* "practices and procedures [were] designed to satisfy internal needs for safety, order and the next visit of the state or federal examiner" (1983, p. 12). In the stable pre-1970s environment, this culture may have been functional, but it is clearly less so today. Removing the impediments to action, therefore, appears to be a major goal of successful companies in the financial arena.

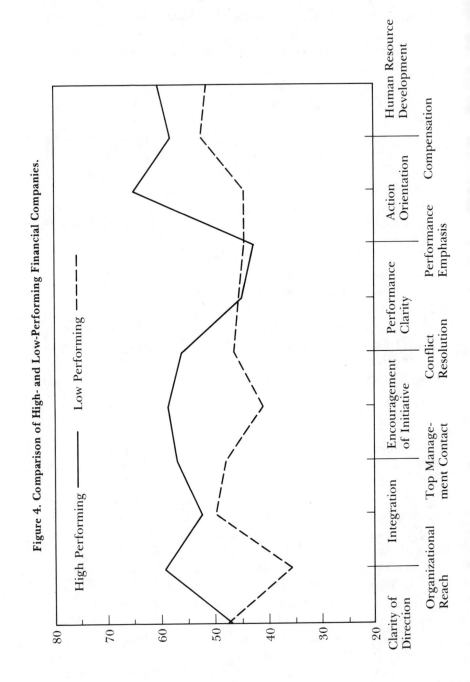

Figure 4. Comparison of High- and Low-Performing Financial Companies.

Industry Summary

Clearly, different industries have developed different cultural patterns to suit their business demands. In those industries requiring stability over time, the dominant values support long employee tenure, redundancy in decision making, limitations on the ability of any individual to move the company off on a tangent, and so on. Those companies at the other end of the spectrum, companies that must respond rapidly to changes in tastes, technology, and competitor's actions, create quite a different culture. The emphasis here is on the constant drive to keep the company out in front of the competition and the reliance on individuals to perform.

What implications do these findings have for actions such as motivation and organization? Certainly, financial rewards would differ if they were geared to reinforce different cultures. Short-term incentives and high-risk compensation packages would certainly be appropriate in dynamic-marketplace companies. In utilities or other long-term oriented companies (for example, resource companies), compensation that rewarded efforts that promoted stability and long-term growth would be more appropriate, both from a business and a cultural standpoint.

The way in which a company is organized and the way people operate within that structure is a very strong determinant and expression of the company's culture. In the pre-divestiture days of the Bell System, no matter which operating company this author visited, we would meet in a large conference room, and not only the seats at the table but also the seats placed around the walls would be occupied. Before any program was settled upon, a myriad of units would have to be consulted, and the program would have to be designed to fit the needs, mission, or capabilities of each. This did not result in rapid decision making, but it did result in reliability. When the program was implemented, it was implemented consistently down to the last affected employee—just as when we pick up a phone, we get a dial tone, not just some of the time but virtually all of the time.

This extreme example of functional integration is obviously not appropriate to a company such as 3M that operates in many marketplaces with hundreds of products. Rather, allowing individual units to operate as small, entrepreneurial businesses allows that company to maximize its responsiveness to the opportunities in its many different markets. Yet, even in the free-swinging, dynamic marketplaces, a company as committed to entrepreneurism as Johnson & Johnson ("Changing a Corporate Culture," 1984) finds it necessary to change its culture to foster greater cooperation across business units as some of its businesses mature and as it attempts to develop other businesses for the future. Thus, the "right" culture may have a time frame and may have to be reevaluated when an organization is faced with a need for major business changes.

Can Cultures Be Changed?

A recent *Fortune* article (Uttal, 1983) casts doubt on whether cultures can change. But none of the sources quoted apparently made any systematic search among companies to determine where such change had been tried or how successful the results had been. Most of the hundreds of companies we have studied over fifteen years have certainly not been *attempting* to change their cultures in any significant way. Yet, in the course of this experience, we have come across some who have attempted such change—some successfully and some unsuccessfully. A case study can illustrate an instance where significant change took place.

Home Life Insurance Company (its real name, which is being used with the permission of the management) was founded in 1860 and is headquartered in New York City. Today, it has about $2 billion in assets, revenues of about $400 million, and about 3000 employees. Our investigation of culture at Home Life began in the spring of 1982 when the company wished to look into the feasibility of an incentive program for its senior executives. A culture study was conducted to test the "fit" of incentives with the current culture, followed up by a similar study the next year.

Although our interviews and data collection focused on

the present, each manager interviewed began by contrasting the current and previous approaches to management. From these interviews, we constructed a picture of a company that previously had very directive leadership from the top. All major decisions had been made by, or in close consultation with, the chairman. Further, the company did not have a formal planning process involving any significant number of people. Rather, problems or opportunities were handled as they arose. Budgeting was rudimentary and identified neither profit centers nor true cost centers. Executives' salaries were low, but, considering the constraints on managers' freedom to act, were probably in line with what was expected from the positions.

The company's strategic focus had been on (1) whole-life products, (2) a conservative approach to the group lines, and (3) a very small pension business. The company placed overwhelming emphasis on its agency force, gearing its strategy around the well being of that force, primarily through generous compensation arrangements. Given the competitive environment, this strategy had allowed the company to prosper. It had built a very strong cash surplus and had a modest-sized, but effective, career agency distribution system. By the mid 1970s, however, with a wave of new products hitting the marketplace from competitors, agent loyalty began to wane; the company failed to provide its agents with a range of products to meet the competition. Meanwhile, soaring medical costs created enormous problems for the group health business.

It can be inferred that the board of directors foresaw a need for fundamental change since it reached out to Prudential Life Insurance Company and recruited Ken Nichols to become president of Home Life. All those interviewed pinpoint the beginning of change to Nichols' assumption of the CEO role in September 1981, upon the retirement of the previous chairman.

A series of very aggressive actions were taken to change both the substance of the company and its culture. Briefly, some of these actions were:

- Replacing or reassigning almost all of the executive officers with individuals who valued delegation and innovation.
- Forcing delegation.

- Communicating the state of the company as widely as possible and as frequently as possible, including, for the first time, to field agents.
- Initiating monthly area meetings to broaden the prespective of the company's officers.
- Instituting a planning and budgeting process with both top-down and bottom-up elements.
- Changing the product emphasis to a broader individual-life portfolio, a greater emphasis on pensions, and a repositioning of group products.
- Emphasizing service to agents and customers and reinforcing this emphasis with standards, reporting systems, and recognition of outstanding accomplishments.
- Reducing response times for product introductions, interest rate changes, and so forth.
- Creating a consolidated pension department.

The effectiveness of these actions can be judged on two planes: first, is the culture changing; and, second, is change being reflected in the company's performance? Since both studies were conducted to gauge the company's readiness for incentive compensation, the surveys did not cover a full range of cultural issues. A number of key elements *were* included, however, and the results for both studies are presented in Figure 5.

Clearly, there are some very substantial differences between the two sets of results. The differences exceed ten percentile points for clarity of direction, organizational reach, encouragement of individual initiative, and performance clarity. Because the data for the two surveys includes many of the same people, the samples are not independent, and individuals cannot be paired to determine the correlation between the two samples. Thus, statistical tests have not been applied to these data, but the dimensions listed earlier appear to reflect meaningful changes. This is especially true in light of the fact that in similar surveys taken a year apart in thirteen different companies, the average change on ten items was $-.57$ percentile points with a standard deviation of 5.5 points.

Even in mid 1982, when many of the actions to be taken

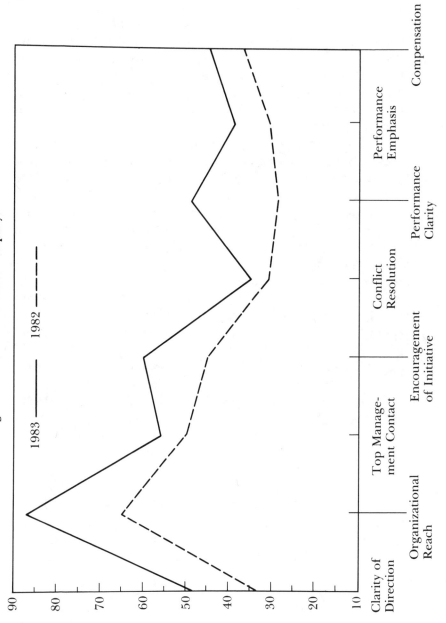

Figure 5. Home Life Insurance Company.

were still on the drawing board, management perceived that the company was reaching out very ambitiously in its corporate goals. But at that early time, there had been little clear statement of direction and expectations and limited encouragement to employees to use their initiative in helping the company out of its problems. Within a year, management reported much greater emphasis on each of these elements.

Today, the company has adopted the outlines of a significantly changed culture. It is a culture in which individual contributions are valued and encouraged. To better stimulate the "right" contributions, information exchange is viewed as central to the company's management processes. Part of that information is detailed communication of the company's very ambitious aspirations and its progress toward achieving them. Externally, the client and agent occupy a central role in the company's value system. But today, the key approach to both is *service and flexibility,* with everyone in the company constantly reminded of those values. It seems clear that those who continue to hold some of the previous values and modes of behavior are fighting against a strong emerging culture.

Gauging the impact of these changes on corporate performance is difficult because of the short time period. The pension department was not created as a separate entity until late 1982, and most of the individual new-product introductions did not take place until early 1983. Yet even in this short interval the impact of a new leadership and its ambitious expectations for the company can be sensed in its performance. Premium income, which was flat between 1978 and 1981, rose 15 percent in 1982 and another 12 percent in 1983. More specifically, in 1983 the organizational and product changes resulted in a 42 percent increase in income from premiums from new sales of individual-life insurance and a 120 percent increase in pension income.

Certainly, one case study does not settle the question of cultural change, yet it sheds light on an issue that is critical if the study of corporate culture is to be seriously pursued. If managers cannot guide their companies through planned cultural change, the subject has limited practical utility and may be of only academic interest. Through happenstance, we have seen a handful of companies where very significant cultural change has occurred. Because these are real-world instances of opportunity, it is impossible to test cause and effect hypotheses, but intuitively we are led to the conclusion that such change *is* caused by management focusing on *creating* the change. In fact, we have seen at least as many instances where management has *not* focused on change and *no change* has been observed in subsequent surveys.

But whether or not management wishes to address corporate culture specifically, it seems patently evident that every company still *has* a culture, which is perceived by its members and which provides direction for the many specific things that people will or will not do. This point is underlined in Figure 6, which shows the responses of management in five separate regions of a geographically decentralized company. Before the study was done, the recently appointed CEO reported that "we don't have a culture here." Clearly, the consistency of perceptions from region to region belies this statement.

Discussion and Conclusions

The research relating industry characteristics, cultural patterns, and performance strongly suggests that there is no one "winning culture." Rather, factors such as the characteristics of the industry and the marketplace and the diversity, size, and market position of the organization define the broad outlines of an appropriate culture. Utilities, dependent upon stability of performance, do not attempt to create very entrepreneurial, free-wheeling environments, with their concomitant cultural values of innovation and action orientation, but instead concentrate on teamwork and reliability. Just the opposite is true for dynamic-marketplace companies, where the former values are heavily emphasized.

Within these broad, industry outlines, the most successful companies tend to place a higher value on somewhat different factors than do those that are less successful. For instance, we find the most successful utilities placing more emphasis on de-

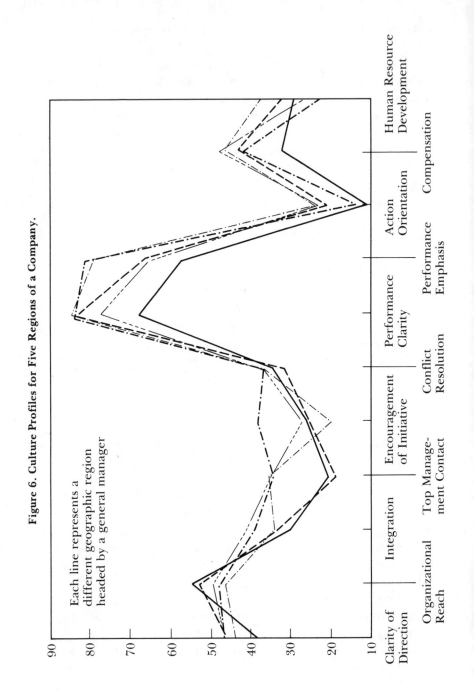

Figure 6. Culture Profiles for Five Regions of a Company.

Each line represents a
different geographic region
headed by a general manager

Percentile

fining individual performance expectations. This contrasts sharply with dynamic-market companies, in which the most and least successful are differentiated mostly by the extent to which managers perceive the company as setting its sights very high.

Finally, observation suggests that a company's culture can be changed in a planned way. Although this chapter reports on only one such company, we have in the course of our consulting observed a number of companies where such was the case. The companies where we have seen major changes take place seem to share certain common characteristics. First, the CEO has a vision of what the company can be. This vision is clearly understood and shared by those reporting directly to the CEO. In some cases, this need to have executive management share the vision has resulted in the replacement of many individuals; in other cases only a few executives were changed.

Second, the vision is translated into the key elements that are necessary for the accomplishment of that vision. These elements are usually integrally tied to the strategic plan. For instance, if the vision calls for the company to be recognized as the leader in quality or service, aspects of quality and service are delineated and appropriate measurement systems developed to track them. These measures are revealed and communicated widely—through contests, formal and informal recognition, monetary rewards, and similar devices. Thus, a new value system is not only developed but heavily reinforced.

Finally, where significant culture change has taken place, the CEO and executive management were obsessive about communicating as widely as possible to employees at all levels. These communications included three basic elements:

1. The state of the business and its competitors, the outlook for the future, and other information that someone with a keen interest in the fortunes of the company would want to know.
2. The vision of *what* the company is to become and *how* it will achieve this.
3. The progress of the company in the areas that are identified as key to the realization of the vision.

This view of leadership's central role in changing culture may seem to conflict with the organizational development tenet that for change to occur the focus must be on getting people to "buy in" at all levels of the organization. This conflict is only partially substantive and probably stems from the fact that most organizational development efforts focus on tactical issues (for example, how to get manufacturing managers and research and development engineers to understand each others' potential contributions). The view of culture presented here is strategic insofar as it focuses on the ability of the total enterprise to function effectively in various business and marketplace environments.

On the one hand, we agree, and indeed we have observed that in some companies the leadership is badly out of touch with the organizational values that influence the bulk of managers as well as the larger group of nonmanagement employees. But these are not the companies in which we see planned cultural change being accomplished. Good leadership is "in touch" with the dominant values of the company and recognizes the need to have people understand and "buy in." These leaders create the processes and momentum to make that happen.

On the other hand, leadership, by definition, is still in charge, and it has the option of removing key individuals who cannot or will not adapt to changes in the way the company is to be managed. The instances in which we have observed the most dramatic one- to two-year changes take place have all involved bringing in *some* new executives and certainly changing the jobs of others. The same principle holds true at any level. The astute leader, however, will foster the implementation of programs designed to *gain* committment at all levels rather than attempt a wholesale replacement of people.

We do not advocate a world in which organizations change their cultures frequently. Such changes are difficult and always involve some degree of pain. They should probably be undertaken only where the external environment demands the change. AT&T operated very effectively for 100 years with a single, well-defined culture. Only when its basic mission was changed by the various arms of the government did the leaders begin to question the viability of that culture.

Again, the key to cultural change appears to lie with a company's leadership. Thomas J. Lipton, whom we can all associate with the company of the same name, asserted that every organization is, in reality, the lengthened shadow of its leader. It seems clear, furthermore, that this statement does not apply solely to founders or to flamboyant, charismatic individuals; it applies also to the leaders who find it necessary to remold their companies at any particular point in their history—leaders who have the determination and perseverance to effect change.

References

"Changing a Corporate Culture." *Business Week,* May 14, 1984, pp. 130-138.

Edwards, R. D. (ed.). "The Cultural Crisis in Banking." *United States Banker,* Oct. 1983, *94,* 10-18, 90.

Gordon, G. G., and Cummins, W. M. *Managing Management Climate.* Lexington, Mass.: Lexington Books, 1979.

Peters, T. J., and Waterman, R. H., Jr. *In Search of Excellence: Lessons from America's Best-Run Companies.* New York: Harper & Row, 1982.

Schwartz, H. M., and Davis, S. M. "Matching Corporate Culture and Business Strategy." *Organizational Dynamics,* 1981, *10* (1), 30-48.

Uttal, B. "The Corporate Culture Vultures." *Fortune,* Oct. 17, 1983, pp. 66-72.

Seven

Sourcing Workplace Cultures: Why, When, and How

Meryl Reis Louis

This chapter has two goals. The first is to drive home the point that it matters that there are, potentially, multiple cultures in any given work organization. We will explore when and how the occurrence of multiple cultures matters and identify issues with which individuals (such as managers, employees, consultants, and researchers) might concern themselves to better negotiate such instances. The second goal is to point out that strategies for detecting cultures in work settings must be appropriate to the nature of the phenomenon. We will see that cultures as "shared tacit knowledge" are not easily revealed through normal methods of asking questions and making observations in everyday, "business-as-usual" situations. We will explore some examples of places to look and ways to probe that promise to be more useful for deciphering workplace cultures.

Definitions

What is meant by *sourcing and bounding a workplace culture*? Why are these ideas needed? When are they useful?

Sourcing is the identification of the roots or primary site of shared understandings. *Bounding* is the identification of the extent, reach, or penetration of shared understandings. The two issues entwine. Let us look at some examples.

Suppose we are concerned with caution as a shared understanding at AVCO Bank of Anytown. Perhaps we, as the management team, have come to recognize that we are losing business to our competitors because of the caution of various bank representatives, including our loan officers. In this example, we might ask whether the source of caution as a shared understanding is (1) AVCO Bank as an organization, (2) the banking industry, (3) Anytown as a community, (4) lending officers as an occupational group, or (5) lending officers as a subgroup within AVCO Bank in particular.

The source of AVCO's caution, or any other shared understandings, makes a difference when we are trying to manage or alter those shared understandings. We need to find the roots of the shared understanding if we hope to bring about lasting change. The boundaries of AVCO's caution also make a difference when we are newcomers trying to get along in our new organizational setting. We may need to know the extent to which caution is acceptable in the organization, to know where caution applies and where it does not, when negotiating situations we encounter as new members of AVCO.

But what of a more theoretical rationale for the tasks of sourcing and bounding? Surely there must be some philosophical basis for such tasks beyond the pragmatics of "passing" as a member of an organization or managing within it. Let us first consider the components of a definition of culture—not the components of *culture* but the components of a *definition.* Consider a typical dictionary definition of culture: "the totality of socially transmitted behavior patterns, arts, beliefs, institutions, and all other products of human work and thought characteristic of a community or population; a style of social and artistic expression peculiar to a society or class" (*American Heritage Dictionary,* 1976, p. 321).

Culture refers, first, to some content (that is, shared understandings, artifacts, behaviors); second, to a group; and third, to the relationship between the group and the content, a relationship of distinctiveness and specificity. Culture refers to the shared understandings peculiar to and specific to a group.

Until now, practitioners and researchers of organizational behavior have overlooked two of these three components of the definition of culture—the group and relationship—in the rush to grasp the content component of culture.

In doing so, they are following in the footsteps of the anthropologists, who, by and large, did not concern themselves with sourcing and bounding, with identifying the group to which some shared understandings were peculiar. But the situation anthropologists traditionally have faced differs in important ways from the situation we face in examining cultures in modern organizations. Early anthropologists studied cultures in settings that were remote and isolated. It was relatively safe to assume that shared understandings identified were rooted in the setting and fairly pervasive across members of the community. Thus, geographical and historical isolation alleviated much of the need to identify the groups to which certain shared understandings were distinctive.

In the situations that practitioners and researchers of organizational behavior face, geographic and historical isolation of groups does not exist, so we need to establish the source and bounds of culture, to determine the group whose culture is at issue.

What are the characteristics of organizations as settings that may foster the development of shared understandings? What is the nature of sites within work settings that afford the opportunity for distinctive cultural content to develop? Some properties of organizations and the sites within them that may be "culture-bearing milieux" are:

- Work settings bring together on a recurring basis a fairly stable set of members.
- Work settings provide opportunities for affiliation, through which people may develop friendships and social and support systems.
- In work settings, people are linked together through shared tasks.

- Organizations and units within them represent constellations of interests, aims, and missions.

Awareness of such properties may highlight situations beyond traditional work settings through which shared understandings may emerge. Given the prevalence of settings characterized by such properties, there is little wonder that so many different layers of culture are present within any single organization. The idea of a cultural "blank slate" within modern work organizations makes little sense.

Given that organizational settings represent potential sites for shared understandings and that it seems worthwhile to untangle the sources and bounds of shared understandings (that is: Whose culture does this shared understanding belong to? What culture is distinctive here? How far does this understanding extend?), what are the processes of sourcing and bounding a culture?

Processes of Sourcing and Bounding

In this section, potential sites or pockets of shared understandings that may be found in work settings will be identified, and the diagnostic issues to pursue in sourcing and bounding such shared understandings will be outlined.

Some understandings might be distinctive to people at one *level* of the organization. Some assumptions may be shared only among top executives, for example. Shared understandings may also develop among members of a *vertical slice* of the organization. For instance, any particular product division of a conglomerate may have an esprit quite different from that of other divisions of the organization. A *horizontal slice,* such as all of a certain classification of personnel—systems engineers, for instance, or accountants—no matter what division they belong to, may also develop shared understandings. A *department* also may have common understandings different from those of other departments within the organization.

For that matter, any *group* that gathers over time and meets other of the criteria discussed here may develop common understandings distinct from those of other groups of the same general type. A group of workers, for instance, meeting on Thursdays over lunch for a bridge game over a span of several years may differ from similar groups in what they consider to be the appropriate topics of conversation, playing etiquette, means of inviting new players, degree of loyalty to one another on matters of office politics, and social contact away from work.

Aside from these sites of potential culture and pockets of shared understandings within work settings, there are several sources of culture that are external to the organization. To distinguish among them, the terms *intraorganizational* and *transorganizational sites of culture* are used to refer to internal and external sites or sources of culture, respectively.

Transorganizational sources of shared understandings that may be found within work organizations include the *national* culture of the society in which the organization is located. *Ethnic* cultures of groups of workers as well as the *local geographic community* may contribute shared understandings. In addition, *professions* and *occupational* groups may develop particular behaviors and attitudes. For instance, lawyers throughout General Motors may share understandings quite distinct from those shared by other workers at General Motors. Those understandings may have little to do with General Motors itself or with the automotive industry but are derived mainly from this group's socialization and affiliation as lawyers. The *industry* to which an organization belongs may also contribute shared understandings. At AVCO Bank, discussed earlier, the banking industry may exert a stronger influence on the attitudes and behavior of AVCO members than anything specifically related to AVCO as a particular banking organization. Thus, there are threads of shared understandings entwining individuals on many different levels, through many different affiliations of daily life at work and elsewhere. Thus, it is difficult to determine where any particular understanding comes from or is rooted and how widely within a work setting the understanding is shared or extends.

How can the roots and extent of cultures be traced? What diagnostic issues can help source and bound shared understandings? These questions can be addressed by assessing the sociological, psychological, and historical aspects of the *penetration* of any shared understandings. The sociological aspect of penetration involves its *pervasiveness*: How far and wide does the culture reach? Across how many departments and through how much of the organization does it extend? Do people in sales and people in production subscribe to the same understanding of "what matters"—for example, does the Avis Rent-A-Car slogan "We Try Harder" get the same support in the sales department as it does in the maintenance department? These are the kinds of concerns that must be addressed in assessing the sociological penetration of culture.

The psychological aspect of cultural penetration relates to its *homogeneity* or the consistency of understandings within it. Once we have determined that sales and maintenance people at Avis do both support the company's slogan, we need to find out whether the interpretations of the slogan differ in any significant ways across departments. Is the meaning of the slogan used to support the same behaviors across departments, or is it used to justify vastly different actions and orientations? Are meaning and use consistent across physical space?

The historical aspect of cultural penetration refers to its *stability* or *consistency* across time: "For how long has this culture been in effect?" This helps us determine how firmly entrenched the group's understandings are and is thus particularly important when any culture change is contemplated.

Imagine having a Geiger counter that beeps according to its proximity to the roots of a culture, so that as we walk around in a work setting, the sound from the Geiger counter becomes quite loud as we approach the origins of some particular shared understanding in which we have an interest, and it diminishes as we move away from this point. Now imagine that this Geiger counter has a knob with three positions representing three different channels on which the device can operate. Imagine that it can pick up signals reflecting the sociological, psychological, and historical dimensions so that the pervasiveness, homogeneity, and stability of an understanding is registered in sound. This metaphor offers a sense of what we are trying to accomplish when we source a culture.

What else do we need to know to source and bound a culture? Given the possibility of multiple cultures—or subcultures—within a given work setting, it is useful to determine the *direction* and *target* of any set of shared understandings. Just as individuals and groups may orient themselves in relation to others by "moving toward," "moving against," or moving in a neutral fashion, so, too, do subcultures. Some subcultures may enhance overall organizational understandings and aims, some may undermine other groups or the organization as a whole, and some may be oriented in no particular way toward other groups or the organization per se. Managers who want to alter their organizations may thus focus their efforts on changing those subcultures that are oriented against overall organizational aims. Knowing which groups enhance or are neutral toward other cultures within the organization should help managers avoid disruption or the squandering of resources on benign cultures.

How to Look for Workplace Cultures

The way we look for and at workplace cultures depends on our underlying purpose. Two purposes are the primary forces behind most interest in organizational culture. Different strategies are appropriate for pursuing each purpose.

One reason for pursuing workplace culture is to understand a particular workplace. A manager or a consultant may want to improve performance within an organization, or a new employee may want to "get up to speed." In these cases, knowing the culture per se is somewhat incidental; knowing the *setting* is the true aim, and knowing the local culture is instrumental or helpful in coming to know the setting. When we want to master a setting, we are concerned with "what it is really like here." Part of the process of defining what a setting is like is comparative: what it is like is at base a concern with how it is *different* or unique from other settings. The process of inquiry is a process of extraction.

A second purpose for studying workplace culture is to understand culture, to understand "normal" aspects of cultural phenomena in and across work settings. What any one setting is like is irrelevant in this inquiry; what is common across settings is the concern. Again, a comparative process is employed, but the emphasis is on identifying what is *common* rather than what is unique. The process of inquiry is a process of sifting.

Given these two broad purposes, what strategies are appropriate for searching out workplace cultures? Because organizational cultures are sets of shared and largely *tacit* understandings, the regular methods of asking questions and observing behavior are not sufficient for detecting workplace cultures. Tacit knowledge is not readily amenable to either direct questioning or observation. We are not looking for behaviors but, rather, for fundamental assumptions carried at an unconscious level. Thus, the nature of cultural understandings requires special means and ingenuity on the part of the cultural detective.

Organizational culture is more likely to be accessible in some situations than in others. Disruptions, for example, often reveal possible cultures in a particular setting, where knowing the setting is the aim. When a major reorganization is impending or in progress—for example, when there is a merger or acquisition or when a new chief operating officer enters the organization—members of the organization are likely to feel somewhat uncertain, perhaps even fearful about "how things will turn out." Upper and middle management may be more able to articulate "what really matters around here and why" under threat of new leadership than they were before the change. The entry of several new members into a work group may also be a situation that makes old-timers more aware of their shared understandings. Such disruptions might well be made use of to locate and isolate workplace cultures. If we want instead to understand organizational cultures generically rather than to understand a particular setting, we could look at disruptive situations across several settings using comparative case analysis.

Disruptions can be looked on as *natural occurrences* within an organization. Another set of natural occurrences through which culture can be studied can be clustered under the label *contrasts*. Individuals in situations of contrast have access to the themes and contents of workplace cultures at a more conscious level than is usual. Newcomers to an organization are in a situation of high contrast. Newcomers are likely to be more aware of the understandings associated with both the settings they are entering and the settings they have left than are insiders in either place, so tapping the experience and insights of newcomers is revealing. Newcomers, as individuals experiencing contrast, can be helpful in gaining knowledge of the workplace cultures of a particular organizational setting or in developing understandings applicable across work settings. When the aim is specific to one setting, talking with several newcomers to that setting often reveals themes common to the setting. Generic understandings, characteristics of culture across settings, can be revealed by questioning newcomers to diverse organizational settings.

Another individual in a high-contrast situation is the boundary spanner. Boundary spanners, by definition, have their feet in the doors of several different settings. Consultants and field researchers are boundary spanners whose insights may further understanding of workplace cultures.

Another way to gain access to the tacit knowledge associated with organizational cultures is to probe the culture rather than to wait for natural occurrences. Such probes could be called *field simulations,* artificially created instances in which tacit knowledge may be made explicit. A *group production,* for example, may help us understand a specific setting. In a group production, a group works together on a task in which they must employ common understandings, and this process is recorded. For instance, a group may create a montage, a humorous questionnaire, or a biography that reflects the unit in question and captures "what is unique here." The group could be videotaped at work on the task to reveal what controversies arose and how they were resolved, what was invoked as justification for keeping in or leaving out any bit of information, which categories were used to build the group product, which categories were readily agreed upon, and so on. After completion of the product, the videotape could be replayed to prompt discussion about the group's shared understandings. This debriefing could also be videotaped so that second-order rationales and the fleshing out of controversial items could be recorded for further insight into the culture later. Comparisons of the group product sessions across groups also could be pursued, but the strategy is most useful as a starting point in ferreting out key understandings associated with a particular setting.

To help us understand the cultures of work settings in the more general sense, another type of field simulation, *guided reflections,* could be employed. In this simulation, a group of individuals from different settings are asked to recall their experiences of various settings and then, as a group, to identify common themes across settings. This process reveals the ways in which processes of organizational cultures are developed and managed as well as how they are transmitted to new members and various other cultural phenomena.

Culture thus is discovered in two ways. To understand culture generically, individuals from different settings are probed; to gain access to the tacit knowledge that constitutes a particular workplace's cultures, individuals within that workplace are observed through both natural occurrences and field simulations.

Summary

It was once widely assumed that each organization had a single, pervasive culture. Few now make that assumption; instead, most people now recognize that subcultures are prevalent within work settings. Few people, however, know how to detect these cultures or when and why to be concerned with them.

This chapter has shown that:

- The source and bounds, the roots and extent, of cultures matter when we are planning change or when we are faced with a new setting and situation.
- The source and bounds of cultures can be revealed through questions about penetration (recall the image of the Geiger counter detecting the pervasiveness, consistency, and stability of shared understandings) and orientation (the targeted direction) so that dysfunctional rather than benign cultures can be changed.

- Accessing tacit knowledge requires special strategies, such as appreciation of natural occurrences and field stimulations, that can shed light on particular settings or on workplace culture in general.

Eight

Culture Is Not
Just an Internal Affair

Stanley M. Davis

Most of the commentary about corporate culture is inward looking. It focuses on internal aspects of management and organization and is addressed mainly to employees within the corporate hierarchy. It seldom has an external focus, and it thus generally avoids serious linkage to global and industry economics and to business strategy.

When investigating an organization's culture, it is useful to distinguish between *internal* and *external* values and beliefs. External values and beliefs are those that relate to how to run a *business*, and internal values and beliefs are those that relate to how to run an *organization.* An external focus reveals the values and beliefs a business has about its customers, competitors, shareholders, suppliers, the government, society at large, and all other relevant stakeholders—not just its employees.

The purpose of this chapter is to demonstrate the need not only for an internal focus but also for an external focus in the study and management of corporate culture. This will be accomplished by exploring the impact of five external constituencies—customers, competitors, government, the public, and shareholders—on corporate culture.

Before exploring this impact, a definition of the terms mentioned in this chapter would be helpful. Corporate culture is the pattern of shared beliefs and values that shapes the meaning of an institution for its members and provides them with the rules for behavior in their organization. Every organization has its own word or phrase to describe what it means by culture; some of these are: being, core, culture, ethos, identity, ideology, manner, patterns, philosophy, roots, spirit, vision, and way. To most managers, these terms mean much the same thing. Managers also tend not to distinguish between values (what is important) and beliefs (what is true), and in this chapter these terms are used interchangeably. However, a basic distinction is made between a company's fundamental beliefs and its daily culture. The first reflects what the company is and what it stands for as a business enterprise; the second reflects the beliefs of everyday life. The fundamental beliefs provide the context for the practical beliefs expressed in the daily culture. Fundamental beliefs give direction to daily beliefs, and both are part of what we now call corporate culture. (For a more elaborate discussion of these distinctions, see Davis, 1984.)

Customers and Corporate Culture

The customer is probably a company's most important external constituency and, therefore, should be the most important stakeholder in determining a corporation's culture. This is true not because of the marketing belief that a company must first and foremost consider the customers' needs, but because the economics of industry dictate what the customer is going to want in the future and hence what the culture will have to become. If there is going to be an economic shift and a company knows what the direction of this shift is going to be, then that company can know in advance what an appropriate culture will be. And, since it takes considerable time to develop that appropriate culture, the smart company will begin to manage the change in its culture at the same time that it begins to manage the change in its strategy: as soon as it perceives a significant change in the marketplace.

An example from the high-technology world of office automation and information services will help make the point. Let us look at a hypothetical, though typical, high-tech firm. An inventor-entrepreneur starts a company that grows successfully for several years. In the culture that develops within this company, product technology is king. Service is built into the product core, not into "superficialities" or into aftermarket hand-holding. The belief is: service the product, not the customer. The customer focus thus is reactive; customers' problems are solved only after they have occurred. Phrases such as "commitment to the customer" and "customer satisfaction" are not intrinsic to the company culture. The systems and structures that develop support a sales orientation rather than a service focus. The sales department exists to support the engineering department, and neither is particularly concerned with supporting the customer.

This kind of culture is common to companies that deal in new technologies and whose totally new products have created their own markets from nothing. These companies make magical "black boxes," generic products for undifferentiated markets. Computing a number, sending a message, or copying a letter is the same task, whether it is done in a hospital, a government agency, or a business corporation; a number is a number is a number, a letter is a letter is a letter. Besides ensuring success, early entry into the market that they have largely created also firmly establishes the values and beliefs that guide the organization.

During the early period of our hypothetical company, the requirements of the business and the values of the culture are well aligned. Business growth and success, however, mask future problems. As the business requirements change, the culture has to change accordingly. Typically, the economy shifts more quickly than do cultures. When the economy changed for our high-tech company, it was left with generic products in a market that is now demanding differentiated products; it was left with stand-alone units in a market that is now demanding inte-

grated systems and networks. The undifferentiated market of
the early period now is comprised of a multiplicity of customer-
specific segments and niches. Our firm thus has a technology-
driven culture from the past that is inadequate to meet the customer's market-driven demands of the present and future.

To meet the requirements of the future business environment, the company must build a culture that is more customer
oriented. Such an approach must include customer satisfaction
about:

- The product's reliability
- The product's quality
- The product's price-performance ratio
- The company's sensitivity to customer needs
- Applications of the product
- Service

The internal aspects of the corporate culture will have to be
built around these external needs of the customer.

The picture of the typical high-tech company is even
more complicated. In the early days of high-tech companies,
services were probably a very small proportion of the total business, perhaps less than 10 percent of sales and a 10 percent
drain on profits. In the last decade or two, services have become
the fastest growing segment of these businesses, outstripping
the contribution from products in both sales and profitability.
The planning department in these companies now probably says
that in another decade, nonproduct sales will represent at least
one-third of total sales and as much as half of the profits. That
is the external, economic reality of the future. All too often,
however, the internal, cultural reality of the present blinds companies to the message that their cultures will have to change
radically, that they will have to add a market focus to their
product focus and then manage both simultaneously. They will
also have to add a service orientation to their technological orientation and keep both healthy at the same time.

Even while shifting their focus to meet new demands,
however, these companies will also want to preserve the mature,

generic end of their businesses. This means that they will need to maintain the more traditional cultures in one part of their firms, and move rapidly away from it in other parts.

Competition and Corporate Culture

Competitive analysis is as appropriate in examining a company's culture as it is in examining a company's strategy.

When people are asked to define a business, they usually mention products and services, markets, and resources. The critical element they often leave out is the competition. Similarly, despite all the attention being given to corporate culture, analyses of competitors' cultures is seldom discussed.

Some industries, of course, are less competitive than others. Regulated industries, for example, usually pay more attention to the regulators and to the public, whom the regulators represent, than to the competition. The more competitive the business, however, the more important it is for companies to differentiate their products or services from their competition's. If company A's strategy is based on price or being a low-cost producer, then it will have to build a culture to reflect that strategy. Efficiency will be emphasized, pennies will be pinched, seconds will be shaved off manufacturing time, and labor-saving technologies will be employed wherever possible.

By differentiating their cultures from those of their competitors, companies also help differentiate their products. Let us consider, for example, three competing department stores, one of which promotes quality; another, fashion; and a third, price. Each organization should translate its values into other elements in the company. In hiring policies, for example, each company should look for its key trait in the way candidates dress. Further, the first company will prize low turnover and long tenure in its workforce, while the second may accept turnover and prefer youthful employees; the third company will pay less than its competitors. Based on the particular values of these organizations, different cultures will develop, each supporting a different strategic position.

Some companies have a culture that eschews competitive

analysis altogether. One chief operating officer told this author: "I know that the business schools teach the importance of competitive analysis, but if I waited for our competitors to react to changes in the market, and then reacted to their reactions, we'd never be the market leader that we are. I don't ignore the competition, but I can't afford to pay too much attention to them either."[1]

Entrepreneurs frequently build cultures in their firms that ignore competitors. This may be because professional managers are taught to develop strategies to guide their actions, whereas entrepreneurs' strategies arise out of their actions; the relationship between strategy and action is reversed. When strategies flow from actions, strategies merely codify what has already taken place and are therefore enemies of innovation. This is a radical notion, and it breeds a radically different culture. Large corporations that want to develop internal entrepreneurs will never do so if they require strategic plans before they allow these "intrapreneurs" to act.

The emphasis that was accorded to strategy and structure in the 1960s is now, in the 1980s, accorded to strategy and culture; the focus on strategy has shifted from formulation to implementation. The core values and guiding beliefs of an organization are the cultural precepts upon which strategies are formulated. It is the fundamental culture, however, that will determine how well strategies are implemented. Competitors' broad corporate strategies are generally well understood by one another, but what is often not understood, and what often makes the difference in competitive performance, is how these competitors' cultures affect the implementation of their strategies. It is thus important that any competitive analysis examine competitors' cultures as well their strategies.

Government and Corporate Culture

Monopolies, of course, do not have to worry about competitors or their strategies or cultures; however, they do have to

1. Quotations in this chapter, unless otherwise noted, are derived from the author's personal research, and the sources are confidential.

pay attention to the government. Regulated industries are often in the same position. The more regulated an industry, the more the cultures of companies in that industry will be shaped by attentiveness to government affairs rather than by attention to either customers or competitors.

In the petroleum industry, for example, depletion allowances, windfall-profit taxes, environmental controls, and the threat that government may break up large, integrated oil companies have all had a major impact on managers' beliefs and behaviors.

Before the creation of the Organization of Petroleum Exporting Countries (OPEC), for example, these kinds of controls created a mentality that emphasized discounted cash flow rather than profits. The prevalent belief was that an earlier event is better than a later event, that the present value of a sold barrel of oil was worth more than the future value of that oil should it stay in the ground. With this set of beliefs, almost all major capital resources were allocated to developing production facilities, and all companies scrambled to pump as much oil out of the ground as they could. Gas stations were opened on every corner, sometimes on all four corners, to operate as a "disposal system."

Discounted cash-flow analysis is frequently used by managers with an engineering background. It has the virtue of a mathematical model. The danger is that if the wrong assumptions and numerical values are entered into the model, the results will be misleading. In times of economic change in an industry, there is an increased possibility that incorrect assumptions and numbers will be used and, therefore, a greater danger that managers will be misled.

After the creation of OPEC, oil prices shot up so high that companies that were self-sufficient in crude oil made huge profits. One cultural trait that developed in the industry at this time was throwing money at problems. In part, this trait grew out of the capital intensity of the business. Each time a company drills a hole, it costs in the neighborhood of $50 million, and there is only perhaps a 10 percent chance that oil will be found. Spending big thus is built into the petroleum business.

American oil companies now had two major worries. One was that petroleum is a nonrenewable resource—so they invested in alternative energy sources. The other was that the government might break them up—so they threw even more money into nonenergy diversification; they went into metals, minerals, chemicals, department stores, packaged goods, and so on. The logic behind diversification of the oil companies may have been sound, but the track record of the oil companies' new enterprises has been poor. The oil-patch culture has not been successful outside of its original home.

Petroleum companies tend to work together more than do companies in other industries. Almost all oil and gas activities are done in cooperation with competitors at a cost of hundreds of millions of dollars or more, so companies work hard to get along with one another. As one oil executive put it, "You lose more by being uncooperative than you gain by being antagonistic. The industry requires intercompany cooperation; therefore there is no nastiness in the marketplace."

In summary, OPEC, industry economics, and government regulation all affected the oil companies more than did their customers and competitors; and they affected the oil companies' cultures as well as their strategies.

The Public and Corporate Culture

Many industries have been deregulated in recent years and this, too, affects the cultures of the companies involved. Some corporations, such as Mobil and Citicorp, have taken very aggressive and public positions about the deregulation of their industries. This attention to public opinion is an explicit part of their strategy; it also enters into the cultures of some firms. Bank of America is one such company where community involvement is a major element of the company's culture.

A. P. Giannini built the Bank of America as "a bank for the little guy." As Jim Miscoll, head of the bank's California division, explained in a company newsletter, the bank was founded "to create, manage, and recycle economic value for as many people as possible, in as many places as possible, so that more people can live better economically. In short—better living through banking." Bank of America succeeded so well that it now has 1,500 branches in California, one within a mile of 90 percent of the state's population.

When deregulation and the electronic age came to banking, many of the company's cherished values began to be questioned. Banks, for example, began to segment their customer bases, especially along lines of income and life-style. This raised a serious question for Bank of America: if they were truly still "a bank for the little guy," how could they treat the person with a small account differently than the person with a large account? Wouldn't this segmentation drive a wedge between their actions and their vision and heritage? What actually occurred is that segmentation allowed the bank to serve its customer better, according to the particular needs of each; the traditional focus on Joe Public did not disappear, but it did have to change with the times.

Another change at Bank of America involved its full-service concept. Historically, each branch delivered the full range of bank services. This was a tremendous burden, which the bank wanted to move away from. But how could it do so without abandoning its valued culture of full service? Again, the bank reinterpreted its traditional beliefs to fit current realities. The company found that the average person was willing to go a mile and a half for an automatic teller machine, up to ten miles to secure a car loan, and as much as twenty miles to get the best home mortgage. It therefore concentrated each service in one branch within an appropriate geographic range. This enabled Bank of America both to cut costs and to give better service because it could concentrate specialists in each service at different branches.

These examples are intended to show how the public—potential customers as well as existing customers—may be valued in a corporate culture, even in the face of major changes in a company's external environment.

Shareholders and Corporate Culture

Although it might seem that shareholders have a powerful influence on the internal culture of a corporation, this is not actually the case. In the 1930s, Adolphe Berle and Gardiner Means (1937) demonstrated that ownership and management had been forever split asunder in the majority of American corporations, with control going inexorably to the managers. This is still the case today, and shareholders have little or no impact on the formation of corporate culture.

The only two instances in which management pays serious attention to shareholders are when ownership is closely held by an individual or a family, or when management is afraid of a takeover. The family firm, no matter how large the corporation, is a peculiar case, and it will not be addressed here. The corporate takeover, however, deserves a brief mention.

From an internal perspective, a takeover has a powerful effect on the culture of the company affected; it either strengthens the culture or weakens it, but it rarely leaves it untouched. When an unfriendly takeover threatens, management "pulls in the wagons"; it no more wants to liquidate the corporate culture than it wants to liquidate the corporate business, even if this is in the best interest of the shareholders.

The shareholders' lack of effect on corporate culture indirectly adds weight to the reality that cultures are invariably set by management at the top and transmitted down through the ranks. When an unfriendly takeover threatens, management responds, not the rank and file.

A takeover is a threat to the management's values and beliefs as much as to its power and pocketbooks. If management succeeds in heading off a takeover, this may strengthen the company's once-endangered culture. More often than not, however, it seems that a takeover threat fundamentally weakens a company's culture because it exposes what is unhealthy in the culture, thus destroying the old without building anything new. A targeted firm, like an acquired firm, rarely maintains its old culture intact.

Conclusions

The purpose of this chapter has been to show what can be gained in the study and management of corporate culture by focusing on the impact of conditions and stakeholders external to the firm. This impact is greatest on companies' beliefs about how to run a *business,* more than on their beliefs about how to run an *organization.*

When the economic environment changes, firms alter their strategies to meet the new circumstances. Similarly, the values and culture of these firms must also be realigned; when business requirements change, culture has to change accordingly. Implementation of change takes longer than formulation, however, so it is wise for businesses to begin to change their cultures at the same time that they begin to change their strategies.

Management of business institutions has been criticized in recent years for insularity and short-term self-interest. These are serious accusations because continued economic weakness can undermine a democratic society. The recent preoccupation with corporate culture has been similarly insular and near-sighted, focusing too much on internal conditions. We should all pay more attention to the role of customers, competitors, and stakeholders besides employees when we chart corporate culture.

References

Berle, A. A., and Means, G. C. *The Modern Corporation and Private Property.* New York: Macmillan, 1937.

Davis, S. M. *Managing Corporate Culture.* Cambridge, Mass.: Ballinger, 1984.

Nine

Managing Specialized Corporate Cultures

Harry J. Martin

Corporate culture can be defined as a set of commonly held attitudes, values, and beliefs that guide the behavior of an organization's members. In many organizations, corporate cultures are developed from the philosophies of top management and maintained through the acceptance of these philosophies by the organization's members. If a majority of the firm's employees do not subscribe to the values embodied in the organization's culture, it will not have a long-term or pronounced effect on member activity. This is true whether management wants to strengthen existing values and beliefs or to change the culture to reflect new ones. When addressing either culture development or change, executives should consider (1) the impact of recruitment and selection systems on culture and (2) the degree of compatibility between the organization's culture and existing environmental conditions.

This is particularly important for those organizations that have or are seeking "specialized" cultures; that is, organizations that promote one dominant philosophy to which all members are expected to subscribe. The greater the number of administrative levels that adhere to the culture, the greater the number of horizontal units that are affected by it, and the longer the culture has been in existence, the more pervasive the culture will be. Such organizations, where a limited number of deeply held values dominate, can also be viewed as having "thick" cultures. "Thin," or unspecialized, cultures, on the other hand, accommodate multiple value systems where there are few shared assumptions and where division or departmental cultures are the dominant influences on member behavior (Sathe, 1983).

The purpose of this chapter is to explore the impact of selection and environmental compatibility on the maintenance of corporate cultures. This will be accomplished by studying the cultures of two organizations headquartered in Cleveland, Ohio: Lincoln Electric Company and Progressive Corporation. Both organizations have well-defined, specialized cultures that originated in the philosophies of past and present executives. They also have recruitment and selection systems designed to maintain their cultures. In addition, both organizations face environmental changes that have caused top management to maneuver to maintain the existing cultures. This chapter will first provide a brief description of these organizations and their respective cultures and then address the role of selection and environmental compatibility in the maintenance of culture.

Lincoln Electric Company: Background and Culture

Lincoln Electric Company is the world's largest manufacturer of arc-welding equipment—primarily electric welding machines and electrodes. The company employs approximately 2400 workers in its two main plants near Cleveland. Lincoln is reported to have a 25.4 percent share of the welding equipment market (more than twice that of its nearest competitor), and that figure is expected to remain stable through 1987 (Ashyk, 1984). It also markets its products through more than seventy company-owned distribution centers in thirty-six states and claims to have one of the largest distribution networks in the country. Lincoln has been so successful that it dictates the price structure of the welding industry.

The company was founded in 1895 by John C. Lincoln. James F. Lincoln, John's younger brother, joined the firm in 1907 and is largely responsible for the company's innovative labor practices and unique culture. He was a firm believer in the principles of hard work and individual initiative. These principles are reflected in the company motto: "The actual is limited; the possible immense." Lincoln also believed that those who work hard and perform well should share in the benefits of their labor. Each employee is expected to be loyal to the firm, and the company is obligated to share the benefits gained from improved sales and productivity. It was long Lincoln's position that the welfare of the firm and its customers is related directly to the welfare of the employees (Lincoln, 1951, 1961).

In 1914, for example, James Lincoln established a committee of elected employee representatives to advise him on company operations. In 1915 the company gave each employee a paid life insurance policy. An employee's association was established in 1919 to provide health benefits and social activities. A piecework wage system providing paid vacations and cost-of-living adjustments was in place by 1923 and, in 1925, an employee stock purchase plan was initiated. By 1944, Lincoln employees benefited from a number of progressive personnel programs, including a pension plan, a policy of internal promotion, and guaranteed employment. Perhaps the best-known aspect of the "Lincoln System" is the Lincoln bonus plan.

In 1934 the company was faced with reduced sales and increasing demand from employees for more hours of work. In an effort to boost productivity, an annual bonus plan was adopted whereby employees could boost their compensation significantly, depending on their base salary and merit rating and overall company profits. That year the bonus averaged 30 percent of wages and, since then, a bonus has been paid every year, sometimes amounting to 50 percent of wages. In 1981 Lincoln's incentive bonus plan paid an average of $22,008 per employee over and above regular wages and benefits ("Lincoln Electric Fills Socks . . . ," 1981).

The values of hard work, loyalty, security, sharing, and thrift that are at the core of Lincoln's culture survive today. For example, in addition to the advisory committees and compensation and benefit systems already mentioned, the organization emphasizes equality. All employees use the same plant entrance and eat in the same cafeteria. There are no assigned parking spaces and no separate office buildings. The corporate offices have few, if any, status distinctions. Desks and office furnishings are uniform and seem to date from the 1940s. There are few private offices and few of the amenities one would normally expect to find in a corporate headquarters. Not even the president's office is carpeted. A visitor gets the impression that everything is functional and well maintained but that not a penny is spent on unnecessary or frivolous furnishings.

These values are also evident in the manufacturing areas. Employees always seem to be busy and engaged in purposeful activity. There is very little social interaction or wasted time. Plenty of in-process inventory is available at each work station so that employees get the feeling that there is plenty to do. Most workers take no coffee breaks, and little supervision is required.

The corporate culture is also reflected in the structure of Lincoln Electric. Communication channels to management are open, and no doors are closed to workers. Lincoln never has had an organizational chart and encourages people to take problems to whomever they feel is best equipped to help them. Supervisors have wide spans of control because there is little need for routine supervision.

In summary, the culture at Lincoln is based on the strong convictions of the company's founders and is well developed vertically, horizontally, and historically. It is similar in many ways to what Sethia and Von Glinow (see Chapter Nineteen) call an "integrative" culture. The culture is pervasive and affects the company's structure, compensation systems, physical facilities, relations with customers and stockholders, and personnel policies as well as the daily behavior of managers and employees.

Progressive Corporation: Background and Culture

Progressive Corporation is an insurance company that writes specialty property-casualty and credit-related insurance. It markets its products nationwide and in Canada and, in 1982, was ranked sixty-ninth by A. M. Best Company in net premiums written (A. M. Best Co., 1983). Progressive began in 1937 and was incorporated as an insurance holding company in 1965. Progressive currently owns fourteen operating subsidiaries and has two mutual insurance company affiliates. The company has consistently exceeded growth rates for the industry; its compounded annual growth rate is currently 25.8 percent, while the industry average is 11.2 percent. A. M. Best ranked Progressive second among property-casualty firms in premium growth for the period 1977–1982 (A. M. Best Co., 1983). The company strives to be a leader in the insurance industry and is responsible for numerous innovations in the nonstandard property-casualty field.

Like Lincoln Electric, Progressive also has a culture that emphasizes hard work and personal initiative. Its culture also reflects the philosophies and values of top management, especially the company's chairman and chief executive officer, Peter B. Lewis. Mr. Lewis has guided the firm since 1966 and is largely responsible for the firm's ambitious goals and bold personnel policies.

Progressive has challenging goals that are clearly stated and communicated to all employees. For example, Progressive seeks to achieve an after-tax return on shareholders' equity of at least 15 percentage points above the rate of inflation. The company also has ambitious growth plans and seeks to achieve an annual increase in insurance premiums written that is at least 15 percentage points above inflation. In the area of underwriting profitability, Progressive expects insurance operations to produce a profit margin of 4 percent or more.

To achieve these objectives, the company places a major emphasis on individual effort and performance. "Progressive's fundamental premise is that we will succeed by having excellent people motivated to do excellent work. We believe we can outperform our competitors by having superior people in every job and by creating an environment in which each person can make his or her maximum contribution" (The Progressive Corporation, 1982, p. 9). The company emphasizes long work hours and expects employees to work overtime. Lewis has been quoted as saying, "We know there is an absolute correlation between hard work and success. Progressive wants to be the best insurance company in the United States. That objective can be achieved only if we work harder and smarter than anybody else. Thus, we revere hard work. . . . We evaluate people downward if they don't work overtime. That's a fact. We don't make any bones about it" ("It's a Super Bowl Winner . . . ," 1981, p. 7-C).

Progressive's work-hard culture pays handsome rewards much as Lincoln Electric's does. Compensation at Progressive is in the top 25 percent for all industry and near the top for the insurance field. In addition, the company rewards performance and encourages initiative by granting people a great deal of discretion and responsibility. "Every individual has a set of written objectives upon which he or she is evaluated regularly. This evaluation system enables us to know how each is performing, match monetary reward with specific results, and give greater responsibilities more quickly to those who demonstrate they can handle them" (The Progressive Corporation, 1982, p. 9). This is evident in the fact that the average age of the company's top seventy-two managers is thirty-four.

In summary, the culture of Progressive Corporation is similar in many respects to that of Lincoln Electric. Both emphasize hard work and above-average compensation based directly on performance. Both place a high value on employees and their contribution to the firm's success. Both place great emphasis on individual initiative. Employees are given clear and challenging goals along with the responsibility necessary to achieve these goals. Finally, both companies want to be leaders in their industries and are headed by people committed to this goal. However, the relative emphasis on individual as opposed to group success makes the culture at Progressive more like Sethia and Von Glinow's "exacting" culture (see Chapter Nineteen).

Since both Lincoln Electric and Progressive know exactly what they want their cultures to be like, finding employees who fit or are willing to adapt to their specialized cultures is instrumental to the maintenance of these cultures.

Selection Systems

Managers have long been concerned with developing systems that attract and retain qualified people (see, for example, Lorsch and Morse, 1974). In addition, researchers in the areas of vocational choice and career management (for example, Lofquist and Dawis, 1969) and selection (for example, Schneider, 1976; Wanous, 1977, 1980) have been concerned with the match between individual skills and interests and job requirements and organizational reward systems. For example, the theory behind the concept of realistic job previews (see, for instance, Wanous, 1975a, 1975b) suggests that potential employees should have access to information regarding the true nature of job offerings so they can remove themselves from the selection process if they perceive a poor fit between their needs and rewards associated with the job. It has also been suggested that interviewers and others involved in the selection process should evaluate the fit between a candidate's needs and interests and the duties of the job (Schneider, 1976).

If an organization has or is seeking a specialized culture, then culture should be an additional consideration in the assessment of fit between individual needs and job demands. Many organizations have, like Lincoln Electric and Progressive Corporation, successfully included this consideration in their selection systems. For example, Delta Airlines has a culture that favors people who prefer a "family atmosphere," are team players, and are not looking for a fast rise to the top. The company carefully screens job applicants to make sure they embrace Delta's cultural values. At Honda of America Manufacturing Company's plant in Marysville, Ohio, a teamwork approach that minimizes distinctions between management and labor is favored. To ensure that employees support "the Honda way," great care is taken in evaluating job applicants. An employee is hired only after screening by two three-person panels, and all six people must approve the applicant (Jensen, 1983). At Sony Corporation's Rancho Bernardo, California, facility, a family atmosphere is also encouraged. Here, employees who lack extensive experience in manufacturing settings are selected. Preference is given to hiring recent high school graduates and housewives who are "blank" with regard to familiarity with factory systems (Jensen, 1984). It can be inferred that individuals such as these might be more accepting of Sony's culture than workers with experience with other manufacturing cultures.

Lincoln Electric also is concerned with the degree of correspondence between individual needs and the organization's culture. A committee of vice presidents and supervisors interviews each applicant who passes an initial screening by the personnel department. Final selection is made by the supervisor who has the job opening after an additional interview.

Lincoln's reputation is well known among workers in the Cleveland area, and the waiting list for entry-level positions is long. Examination of turnover figures indicates that turnover is high during the first year of employment in spite of the company's selection efforts. Apparently, some individuals are unable to adapt to Lincoln's culture even though they are knowledgeable about it before being hired. However, turnover is low among employees who remain with Lincoln longer than one year, and this is especially true for those who joined Lincoln before they were twenty-five years old or who did not have extensive experience with other manufacturing systems prior to being hired. This suggests that acceptance of specialized cultures, such as those of Lincoln and Sony, is more likely if employees have not developed strong expectations regarding the climate in manufacturing settings before being hired.

Progressive Corporation also has a well-developed recruitment and selection system. In 1976 Progressive began a policy of recruiting MBAs from the top business schools in the country for entry-level management positions. Top managers are actively involved in the recruiting process, and applicants are carefully screened. "We recruit people whose personal achievements and levels of motivation are likely to make them important individual contributors. Identifying and hiring such people is difficult but critical to our continuing success. Therefore, top management is personally involved in recruiting" (The Progressive Corporation, 1982, p. 9). Even though the culture and work-hard attitudes of the company are explained to candidates in a type of "realistic culture preview," Lewis estimates that between one third and one half of these young recruits leave the firm. One Stanford University graduate who left after six months said to Lewis, "I'm resigning because it was like you told me it would be." Lewis has stated, "People don't believe it [the demanding culture] until they get here" ("It's a Super Bowl Winner . . . ," 1981, p. 7-C). To lower recruiting and turnover costs, Progressive has recently begun to recruit top MBAs who also have two to five years of business experience.

The experiences of Lincoln Electric, Progressive Corporation, and other companies suggest that recruitment and selection systems, although not perfect tools, are an integral part of promoting acceptance of corporate culture. It also appears that satisfaction and turnover can be improved if applicants have realistic expectations regarding cultural demands and rewards. Thus, selection systems should receive special attention from executives in organizations seeking to maintain specialized cultures.

This discussion should not lead the reader to the conclusion that all specialized cultures are "good" and that only those candidates that "fit the mold" should be selected. Stagnation and "groupthink" (Janis and Mann, 1977) are potential threats associated with such selection systems. However, if a specialized culture has been determined to be "right" for the organization, then candidate-culture fit becomes an important issue.

Environmental Compatibility

The question of when a specialized culture is appropriate for an organization is closely related to the issue of environmental compatibility. The strengths of a specialized culture lie primarily in the culture's contribution to uniformity, predictability, and control. Flexibility and accommodation of varied modes of behavior are generally not the hallmarks of specialized cultures. Therefore, environmental change is particularly troublesome for them. For example, economic decline in the airline industry during 1981–1982 presented special problems for Delta Airlines because of the company's policy of not laying off employees. The drain on resources associated with 1000 under-utilized employees on the payroll was enormous ("Airline Woes . . . ," 1982). Should Delta change its culture? Is its specialized culture an advantage or a disadvantage in such a situation?

While managers and scholars have long been interested in the impact of the environment on corporate strategies (see, for example, Bourgeois, 1980; Gluck, Kaufman, and Walleck, 1980) and organizational structure (see, for example, Duncan, 1979; Ford and Slocum, 1977; Osborn, Hunt, and Jauch, 1980), the impact of the environment on the maintenance of corporate culture has been largely overlooked. Decline in a company's resource base, increased competition, economic cycles, changes in technology, and new product innovations can each have pronounced implications for a company's culture as well as for its structure and strategies. American Telephone and Telegraph, Hewlett-Packard, Xerox, and Chase Manhattan are but a few examples of companies that met serious environmental challenges that forced alteration of their strategies and cultures. This raises two key questions: "For what types of environments are specialized cultures best suited?" and "When should a culture change to meet the demands of a changing environment?" While there are no simple answers to these questions, the cases of Lincoln Electric and Progressive Corporation provide opportunities to explore these issues.

Lincoln Electric found itself in a position similar to Delta Airlines during the recent recession. A two-year slump in the welding industry resulted in a 25 percent reduction in sales with only a slight recovery in 1983 (Ashyk, 1984). With declining sales, the size of the bonus pool shrank. In 1981 the bonus pool was $59.1 million; it dropped to $41.2 million in 1982 and slid even further, to $26.6 million, in 1983. Lincoln guarantees a minimum of thirty hours per week in wages for employees who have been employed over one year. Thus, not only had the bonus fund declined, but the company was faced with an under-utilized work force.

The management at Lincoln did not feel that a change in culture was warranted because the change in its environment did not appear to be either (1) fundamental or (2) permanent. However, action was needed to maintain the culture during this time of strain.

In an attempt to boost sales and employ people more productively, two vice-presidents instituted a sales training program. Under this plan, manufacturing employees could volunteer for a concentrated training course and be reassigned to a sales office. None of the newly trained salespeople were compensated for moving expenses; however, over 100 employees volunteered with the spirit of helping the company during difficult times.

Even though great care is given by management to the issue of equity at Lincoln Electric, under economic strain this issue has become even more critical. In February 1984, a group of 600 manufacturing employees gathered to complain about working conditions at the company. At the top of the list was the complaint that they had been working for eighteen months at thirty hours per week while some salaried employees had been working full-time with no reduction in pay. To help diffuse the situation, William Irrgang, Lincoln's chief executive officer, and other top executives agreed to make adjustments in salaries and to respond to the other issues raised.

While such maneuvers on the part of management will help maintain the culture, nothing short of economic recovery will solve the problem of a shrinking bonus pool. However, because there have been no fundamental or permanent changes in products, competition, legal restraints, or technologies, it should only be a matter of time before such a recovery occurs. Meanwhile, management is using the specialized nature of the company's culture (specifically, its pervasiveness and emphasis on loyalty, thrift, and sacrifice for the common good) to encourage patience and perseverance on the part of the organization's members. Thus, in Lincoln's case the culture appears to be a source of strength rather than weakness.

Progressive Corporation's culture has also been placed under strain during this period. The recession and increased competition have required additional efforts to keep growth high. Since Progressive's culture emphasizes responsibility, challenge, and upward mobility, there is an inherent potential for conflict between young, aggressive recruits and older, experienced staff. If opportunities for growth are cut off by the environment, the culture may fail to serve the interests of the organization's members and become ineffective.

Realizing this, Lewis and his colleagues have taken extraordinary efforts to keep the company growing. For example, the number of operating companies was increased from nine in 1981 to fourteen in 1983 to increase flexibility and create new positions. The company was restructured to emphasize divisions based on product lines rather than geographic regions. Moves were made out of restrictive markets, such as Michigan, and into others with greater potential, such as Florida. In addition to selling to independent agents, the company began a program of direct sales, and more sales offices were opened outside of Ohio. Progressive's management team has also placed greater emphasis on strategic planning, with particular attention to industry trends, new distribution channels and market opportunities, and changing regulations.

While these moves to adapt structure and strategies to a changing environment may be viewed as timely and appropriate, the question of culture change should also be addressed. Unlike Lincoln Electric, the movement of major insurance companies into Progressive's traditional businesses could be viewed as a fundamental and permanent change in its environment. It may be that, like the old structure and strategies, the existing culture is ill equipped to handle the new situation—for example, is the emphasis on rugged individualism still appropriate given the new demands on the organization, or would an emphasis on cooperation and teamwork be more functional?

It appears that if top management has a specialized corporate culture, such as Lincoln Electric's or Progressive Corporation's, then as much attention should be given to the effects of environmental conditions on culture as is given to their effects on strategy or structure. Key areas where the culture is dependent on the environment should be identified and contingency plans made to reduce the strain on culture if changes in these environmental components should occur. However, if the change is both fundamental and permanent, then management must evaluate whether a change in culture is needed to restore compatibility with the environment. Given the expense and turmoil associated with culture change (see, for example, Uttal, 1983), the reluctance of management to change culture is understandable. But maneuvers to maintain compatibility with the environment when basic culture change is required will only serve to distract executives while postponing the inevitable. If the environment does not favor the dominant value system in a specialized culture and if management is unable to keep the culture functional and restore compatibility, then the company is in danger of losing the acceptance of the culture by its members.

Summary

Specialized corporate cultures have numerous advantages, including strong member commitment to the values inherent in the culture. However, such pervasive cultures are less tolerant of divergent values, which creates potential problems with morale and turnover. Careful recruitment and selection of members predisposed to accept an existing or new culture should minimize these problems. However, another disadvantage is the inability of specialized cultures to adapt rapidly to changing environmental conditions. The advantages of uniformity and commitment must be balanced against the disadvantages of potential stagnation and reduced flexibility. It appears that specialized cultures may be better suited to environments where fundamental changes have a low probability of occurrence because as much effort is required to maintain specialized cultures as is required to create them. The managements of Lincoln Electric Company and Progressive Corporation appreciate this fact.

References

A. M. Best Co. "1982 Premium Growth of the 100 Leading Property/Casualty Companies." *Best's Insurance Management Reports,* May 2, 1983, Release No. 14.

"Airline Woes Catch Up with Delta." *Business Week,* Nov. 8, 1982, pp. 131–133.

Ashyk, L. "Lincoln's Welding Market Share to Stay Secure 'til 1987, Says Study." *Crain's Cleveland Business,* Jan. 30, 1984, pp. 2, 21.

Bourgeois, L. J. "Strategy and Environment: A Conceptual Integration." *Academy of Management Review,* 1980, *5,* 25–39.

Duncan, R. "What Is the Right Organization Structure?" *Organizational Dynamics,* 1979, *7,* 59–80.

Ford, J. D., and Slocum, J. W. "Size, Technology, Environment, and Structure of Organizations." *Academy of Management Review,* 1977, *2,* 561–575.

Gluck, F. W., Kaufman, S. P., and Walleck, A. S. "Strategic Management for Competitive Advantage." *Harvard Business Review,* July–Aug. 1980, *58,* 154–161.

"It's a Super Bowl Winner in Its Field." *Cleveland Plain Dealer,* June 23, 1981, pp. 1-C, 7-C.

Janis, I. L., and Mann, L. *Decision Making.* New York: Free Press, 1977.

Jensen, C. "Japanese-Style Work Code Works in America, Too." *Cleveland Plain Dealer,* Mar. 13, 1983, pp. 1-E, 3-E, 9-E.

Jensen, C. " 'Family' Keeps Sony in Tune in California." *Cleveland Plain Dealer,* Apr. 15, 1984, pp. 1-D, 6-D.

"Lincoln Electric Fills Socks with $59 Million." *Cleveland Plain Dealer,* Dec. 5, 1981, p. 2-B.

Lincoln, J. F. *Incentive Management.* Cleveland, Ohio: The Lincoln Electric Co., 1951.

Lincoln, J. F. *A New Approach to Industrial Economics.* New York: Devin-Adair, 1961.

Lofquist, L. H., and Dawis, R. V. *Adjustment to Work.* New York: Appleton-Century-Crofts, 1969.

Lorsch, J. W., and Morse, J. *Organizations and Their Members: A Contingency Approach.* New York: Harper & Row, 1974.

Osborn, R. N., Hunt, J. G., and Jauch, L. *Organization Theory.* New York: Wiley, 1980.

The Progressive Corporation. *Annual Report.* Cleveland, Ohio: The Progressive Corporation, 1982.

Sathe, V. "Implications of Corporate Culture: A Manager's Guide to Action." *Organizational Dynamics,* Autumn 1983, *12,* 4–23.

Schneider, B. *Staffing Organizations.* Glenview, Ill.: Scott, Foresman, 1976.

Uttal, B. "The Corporate Culture Vultures." *Fortune,* Oct. 17, 1983, pp. 66-72.

Wanous, J. P. "A Job Preview Makes Recruiting More Effective." *Harvard Business Review,* Sept.-Oct. 1975a, *53,* 16, 166, 168.

Wanous, J. P. "Tell It Like It Is at Realistic Job Previews." *Personnel,* 1975b, *52* (4), 50-60.

Wanous, J. P. "Organizational Entry: Newcomers Moving from Outside to Inside." *Psychological Bulletin,* 1977, *84,* 601-618.

Wanous, J. P. *Organizational Entry.* Reading, Mass.: Addison-Wesley, 1980.

Ten

Managing Culture
at the Bottom

Tim R. V. Davis

Like most organizational research, the study of organizational culture is mainly from a managerial standpoint (Wilkins and Ouchi, 1983; Sathe, 1983; Koprowski, 1983). This emphasis is understandable. The prospect of changing the corporate culture has exciting implications for improving organizational performance. Already, consultants are attempting to engineer improvements in organizational culture as a means of increasing the effectiveness and profitability of firms (Deal and Kennedy, 1982). While management may have an obvious interest in new ideas that can improve performance, such ideas often receive a different reception at the lower levels of the organization. One reason for this is that frequently an entirely different culture exists at the lower levels.

Organizational culture has generally been treated as a unitary, homogeneous entity; only a few articles have examined organization subcultures or countercultures. Gregory (1983) examined the different views of Silicon Valley held by technical professionals with different functional specialties and Riley

(1983) compared the differences in the use of political symbols by two subgroups of two professional organizations. Martin and Siehl (1983) compared the dominant culture of General Motors with the subcultures created by John DeLorean during his term as a division head at the company. Seldom has the research and writing on organization culture given any attention to the different perspectives of management and lower-level employees. Intensive case studies (Gouldner, 1954; Dalton, 1959; Blau, 1963) have indirectly exposed the nature of organizational culture at the lower levels, but most of these studies have been written from a managerial perspective.

The study of organization culture is incomplete without taking into account the prevailing culture that influences organization members in lower-level jobs. The people at the bottom that actually make the product or deliver the service are, arguably, equally as important as managers at the top. People in nonmanagerial positions often view both their jobs and the experience of working quite differently from those in managerial positions. An analysis of the culture of the lower-level employees can be undertaken from a normative, pro-management perspective or from a radical, pro-worker perspective; here, the attempt will be made to present both points of view. First, the views of lower-level employees and the bases on which lower-level subcultures form will be examined. Second, some of the ways in which management attempts to influence lower-level cultures will be evaluated. Third, consideration will be given to some of the social differences between managers and lower-level employees that tend to keep these two groups apart.

Views of Work at the Lower Levels

When a researcher commences a study of leadership or motivation, few people question where these concepts came from or whose perspective organizational behavior is being viewed. These terms tend to be accepted as definitive, objective ways of describing behavior. Recent criticisms of the conceptualization process are making organizational scholars more aware that these terms are not unbiased descriptions but interpretations of behavior from a managerial perspective (Mitroff and Turoff, 1974; Evered and Louis, 1981).

While the researcher's tendency to view organizational behavior from a particular fixed perspective may sometimes be an impediment to fuller understanding, the practicing manager is compelled to view his or her world in managerial terms. The manager's ability to operate effectively in thought and deed stems, in part, from an unquestioning belief in the legitimacy of this role. The managerial point of view accepts that authority, status, and rewards mainly derive from one's position in the hierarchy and that a manager has a right to make decisions affecting those in lower-level positions. All managers must, in varying degrees, subscribe to this if they are to succeed and advance in their jobs.

Workers in nonmanagerial jobs frequently do not accept their underprivileged status willingly. An uneasy tension often exists between the managers and the managed. Those in nonmanagerial jobs find it difficult to accept the justice of a system in which managers have superior pay, prestige, and privilege as well as the power to tell them what to do. This produces a sense of resentment, which is heightened by the often monotonous, routine, and dull nature of many lower-level jobs. Nonetheless, such a view is considered radical because it runs counter to the dominant culture—the managerial perspective—which is the prevailing way of thinking in organizations.

The radical view of work finds expression in the past writings of Karl Marx and in the recent works of Braverman (1974), Heydebrand (1977), Nord (1974), and Clegg and Dunkerly (1977). Much of these writings focus on the division in organizations between the managerial and the working class and the alienating effects of specialized jobs at the lower levels. Organization members in lower-level jobs are often united in a common distrust of management and an identification with actions and antics that can alleviate the boredom of excessively narrow jobs. In addition, organization members sometimes unite against other departments whose interests conflict with theirs or against customers, who are considered disruptive and unreasonable. A common formative element of culture at the lower organizational levels is the sharing of a common antagonism against the dominant managerial culture or against other subgroups internal to or external to the organization. This produces a sense of solidarity and provides a core set of values or beliefs that justify all sorts of behaviors and attitudes. The influence of antagonistic relations with management, the work itself, other departments, and customers will each be examined to see its effect on the formation of a cohesive lower-level subculture.

Us Vs. Management. An obvious example of group cohesiveness based on a strong orienting value is the antagonistic relationship that may exist between labor and management. Often, all actions taken by management are viewed by labor as threatening. In those situations where management exercises autocratic control, organization members may feel a greater sense of division and separation. The work of Argyris (1964) and Blauner (1964) provides examples of situations in which organizational culture at the lower levels formed as a defense against management. In some instances, the nature of labor-management relations produces overt compliance but covert defiance where organization members conform in public but gripe in private to their peers. Here, workers may not reject directives and orders issued by management outright, but they may show their recalcitrance and disavowal of upper-level authority in more covert ways.

For instance, the term *skiving* is widely used among employees in British firms to mean intentionally evading or avoiding work (Davis, 1979). Lower-level employees frequently describe each other as "skiving" and often regard this as something of an accomplishment. Behaviorally, skiving means being inaccessible in different parts of the building when tasks are assigned, prolonging trips out of the office, and drawing out errands that have to be run or messages that have to be delivered. It involves being in the work area and pretending to be busy, drawing out tasks, and extending coffee and lunch breaks. In other words, the notion of skiving gives recognition to what is often overlooked: that people frequently "work at not working."

Another response of lower-level employees to excessive

managerial control is the practice of covering things up and not admitting to errors and mistakes. "You have to cover things up occasionally. When something goes wrong and there's a screw up, I don't tell him [the supervisor] unless I know he's going to find out from someone else. If I'm accused of making a mistake, I rarely admit that it is my fault unless it's obvious. This time I wasn't sure if he knew it was me. When it's obvious that it's my fault, I try to show an appropriate level of concern but also make it clear that I'm currently too busy to have time to worry about it. Much of what goes wrong around here never becomes an issue if you keep quiet about it. In other words, it will frequently blow over if you act like nothing is wrong" (Davis, 1979, p. 9).

This kind of deceptive behavior is frequently encouraged when management is authoritative and punitive and shows little concern and understanding for lower-level employees' points of view. In union plants, the "we-they" orientation is especially strong. Here, the distrust and hostility toward management is often openly expressed instead of being suppressed in front of superiors.

Typists, secretaries, clerks, and those in other nonmanagerial positions share similar experiences in offices (Ann, 1970; Benet, 1972). Employees in these positions also voice complaints about inferior status and oppressive treatment. In most cases, office workers are not unionized, so there is often little formal resistance to management. Instead, office workers huddle together like their counterparts in factories and express concerns and criticisms among themselves but conform in the presence of management. Again, their lack of commitment is felt in indirect ways.

Professionals in lower-level jobs are usually subject to less ignominious treatment. Frequently, they are in staff departments and viewed as expert resource people in their particular specialties. The management of lower-level professionals tends to be less heavy handed (McCall, 1981).

Us Vs. the Work. In some cases, the main target of employee concern is not treatment by management but the nature of the work itself. Here, aspects of the job draw employees together. Walker and Guest's study (1952) of automobile workers in an assembly plant and Roy's study (1959) of machine operatives in a factory both provide examples of how attitudes and behaviors tend to evolve as adjustments to the nature of the work. The workers in Walker and Guest's study spent a great deal of time in informal conversations and humorous exchanges to avoid "going nuts" on the assembly line. Roy's classic study of machine operators located in an isolated part of a factory shows how a work group can develop its own unique culture to enable organization members to get through the same job, day after day. Here, the work group had its own distinctive language and its own set of ritualistic acts that were observed at the same approximate times each day. Foremost among these was the proferring of varieties of fruit at set intervals that could only be refused at risk of offending other group members. These ritualistic games and the constant banter among group members had evolved to reduce the monotony and boredom of the job, but frequently it took on more importance than the work itself. A particularly bad "put down" by a fellow group member could ruin an employee's day. Group members invested considerable time and energy thinking up new pranks and avoiding being shown up in front of their peers.

While certain types of assembly jobs and factory work are gradually being replaced by robots and computerized machines, some of the new jobs created by technological change in both factories and offices may be equally monotonous and tedious. Automated information processing is making the presence of video display terminals (VDTs) as ubiquitous as the typewriter in offices and factories. Many lower-level employees spend interminable hours reading information on a screen or monitoring signals from machines and equipment ("Terminal Tedium . . . ," 1983). The tedium of machine-paced information processing is becoming a unionizing issue for many office workers.

Us Vs. Other Departments. Another basis on which organization members band together is their opposition to other departments or particular individuals that they consider to be troublemakers. Certain departments tend to have running conflicts with one another. For instance, production department staffs frequently have constant battles with people in sales. Production wants to keep machinery and equipment evenly loaded and running smoothly, while sales wants large orders filled at a moment's notice. Similar conflicts exist between purchasing and production over delays in needed materials or between account- ing and sales over the accurate completion of paperwork for customer orders. Frequently, organization members at the lower levels have to handle these routine conflicts on a daily basis. Sympathizing with one another and sharing war stories gives people in the same department a feeling that they are not alone in dealing with "those idiots" in the other department.

Typists, clerks, and word-processing staff in service de- partments who work for different line departments share similar experiences. Frequently, conflicts occur over whose work de- serves priority and which deadlines to meet first. Some man- agers are particularly demanding and difficult to work for. Frequent discussion of these and other difficulties help these lower-level employees vent steam and develop a bond of mutual understanding.

Us Vs. the Customer. Many lower-level employees spend the better part of their days working with customers either in person or on the phone. Sales people, bank tellers, switchboard operators, receptionists, customer-relations personnel, cashiers, checkout clerks in supermarkets, bus drivers, and waiters and waitresses all constantly interact with customers or clients. Peo- ple in these positions must deal with a great variety of people, in various moods, making all manner of requests (Gold, 1983). Cus- tomers, whose patience has been worn thin from standing in lines or being kept waiting, are frequently rude and disrespect- ful. Employees in these positions find themselves caught be- tween customers, who are unappreciative, and managers, who always seems ready to criticize and rarely ready to recognize the extra efforts made to satisfy difficult people. When a store is out of stock of an item, the customer complains to the sales clerk, even though the clerk has nothing to do with the prob- lem. For the customer, the sales clerk is the store. These front- line people must bear the brunt of customer criticisms and complaints (Sasser, Olsen, and Wyckoff, 1978) while manage- ment remains insulated in offices off limits to customers.

Here, the organizational culture at the lower levels is

characterized by battle-hardened cynicism and a shared resentment of customers who are perceived as difficult and overly demanding. Lower-level employees, numbed by hour after hour of doing the same thing, become unexpressive, indifferent, and machine-like. The behavior of the lower-level government bureaucrat in the unemployment office, bureau of motor vehicles, post office, or welfare office is the public sector equivalent of this (Lipsky, 1980). The main difference here is that upper management exerts little pressure, so service is often delivered at the employees' speed and convenience.

Managing Lower-Level Cultures

The formative elements of culture at the lower levels are the shared beliefs and values with which organization members strongly identify. These become the accepted ways of interpreting experience and the standard topics of conversation. It is these focal values and shared beliefs that give members a sense of kinship and belonging that they do not get from their outcast status in the dominant managerial culture. While lower-level employees may resent their work, other departments, and the customer, their major problem always lies with management. When severe differences arise and performance suffers, management must try to intervene and try to set things right.

The formation of separate cultures at the bottom of the organization can be destructive for various reasons. Managers and lower-level workers can fight instead of collaborate. Contempt for the work can result in destructive tactics, tardiness, absenteeism, and turnover, as well as reduced quality and lowered rates of productivity. Conflicts between departments can produce bottlenecks, annoying delays, and internal inefficiencies. Customer service can deteriorate, causing reduced sales, increased customer complaints, and loss of goodwill.

Closing the Gap with Lower-Level Cultures. One of management's main goals is to close the gap between the two cultures and reduce the separation and isolation felt by those in lower-level jobs. What are some of the methods available for changing organizational culture? Without making any attempt to be exhaustive, ten managerial practices that directly or indirectly can be expected to influence the lower-level culture will now be examined.

1. *Attempting to Change the Major Organizational Values.* As part of their competitive strategy, some business organizations attempt to promote corporate-wide values. For instance, Dana Corporation emphasizes productivity and cost reduction, and United Airline emphasizes customer service (Peters and Waterman, 1982). These values are designed to permeate all levels of the organization and therefore constitute an approach to influencing lower-level culture.

As competitive conditions change, organizations are forced to change their values. For instance, Johnson & Johnson's push into the high technology medical supply field required a movement away from a highly decentralized system of product divisions to a more centralized system in which greater collaboration was encouraged between some of the newer, growing divisions, particularly in marketing and research and development ("Changing a Corporate Culture . . . ," 1984). Similarly, over the years PepsiCo, in its constant battle with Coca Cola, has attempted to change from a lethargic, placid firm to an aggressive, competitive company. One of its methods for doing this has been to encourage more aggressive, assertive behavior within all levels with interdivisional competitions and interdepartmental team sports ("Corporate Culture . . . ," 1980).

While changes in key values initiated by top management can give an organization a clearer sense of purpose, such changes may be greeted less than enthusiastically at the lower levels. The view that a job can be changed by getting people to think differently about it has its limits. Some jobs will always be tedious and irksome, regardless of how they are labeled. Why should low-level employees change their orientation to their jobs just because top management wants them to?

The alteration of major beliefs and values almost invariably changes the culture of an organization; however, organization members need to know how they will benefit before they will be willing to change. Frequently, such changes may be more cosmetic than substantive. Values at the lower levels may be more readily changed indirectly by other practices than by direct attempts to tell people what to think about their jobs.

2. *Supervisory Training.* First-level supervisors generally have the most direct contact with lower-level employees and therefore have potentially the most influence. Good supervisory practices—clarifying performance, setting attainable goals, providing feedback, reinforcing good performance—can greatly affect organizational culture at the lower levels (Mondy, DeHay, and Sharplin, 1983). Training does not guarantee good relations; however, training does, at least, show supervisors what is needed and expected. It also demonstrates that management values the lower-level employee. Fostering a consistent, professional approach to management should be viewed favorably at the lower levels.

3. *Better Labor and Personnel Practices.* The character of labor relations and personnel practices also influences the extent to which the lower-level worker feels integrated into the rest of the organization. The existence of a formal grievance process; fair disciplinary procedures; equitable distribution of overtime, wages, and benefits in line with industry standards; open job posting; and opportunities for job training can all influence the lower-level employee. Such practices are the best way a non-union plant can demonstrate why a union is not needed.

4. *Improved Customer Service.* The rapid growth of the service sector of the economy, especially franchising, places increasing numbers of lower-level employees in direct contact with customers. Generally, with manufacturing businesses, the only employees with direct contact with the customer are the sales and delivery people. In consumer-service businesses, lower-level employees generally deliver the company's service and thus greatly influence the customer's perception of the quality of the service (Lovelock, 1984).

Operations research has been used to analyze and improve many aspects of service delivery and customer contact (Schmenner, 1984; Sasser, Olsen, and Wyckoff, 1978). The total service to be provided to the customer is broken down into specialized jobs and standard operating procedures that limit the discretion of the employee. In this way, the service provided to the customer as well as the interpersonal contact delivered with it are virtually identical each time. This tends to reduce irregularities in the services delivered and, to some extent, to reduce complaints about inconsistent or inequitable treatment. The lower-level employee's job is less fraught with tension and becomes easier to perform.

5. *Restructuring and Enriching Jobs.* A traditional method for reducing the problem of excessively boring, specialized jobs has been to restructure these jobs so that they are less monotonous to perform. Job enrichment has been used successfully by companies like Saab and Bell Telephone. In the latter case, job satisfaction increased, and absenteeism and turnover declined (Ford, 1969). The main problem with this approach is that the job content often simply is not there to create a really satisfying task. An additional problem at Bell Telephone was that a significant number of employees did not want their jobs enriched. Also, in some cases positive results are short lived as a monotonous routine again establishes itself. Clearly, job restructuring could have a positive influence on organizational culture at the lower levels, but it may be at the expense of the improved productivity that specialization was designed to achieve.

6. *Participative Management Programs.* Participative management programs attempt to involve lower-level employees in decisions affecting how their jobs are done. It is a widely used method for increasing collaboration and commitment at the lower levels. It has the twofold benefit of producing ideas that can raise productivity and giving lower-level employees a genuine feeling that they can contribute to the organization. Many of the participative management programs presently being used are variants of Japanese quality circles (Munchus, 1983). Although the research results are mixed, participative management schemes could have a marked influence on organizational culture at the lower levels because organization members can actively influence the way things are done. The problem with this approach is that participation is usually acceptable only to the point where decisions do not conflict with management's views. Unless workers are allowed to contribute in meaningful ways, they may view the whole exercise as a sham.

7. *Job-Rotation Programs.* The practice of rotating work-

ers through different jobs can have the benefit of teaching additional skills to employees as well as reducing the monotony of working at a single job. A problem with this approach is that some employees prefer not to switch jobs, though this problem can be mitigated if the program is voluntary. Some firms use pay as an inducement to get workers to learn new jobs. They view workers as more valuable if they are able to fill in while others are absent. While job rotation programs frequently create administrative headaches, a well-run program may well have a positive influence on organizational culture at the lower level.

8. *Job Sharing.* Job sharing has some of the same benefits and drawbacks of job rotation. It is usually used to avoid layoffs and spread the work around during lean times. Companies such as Delta Airlines, J. C. Penney, and Lincoln Electric, which are reluctant to lay off people at any time, use this approach. During tough times, employees value job security highly. The practice of job sharing can be a powerful demonstration to lower-level employees of management's concern that everybody be kept employed.

9. *Improved Benefits.* Traditionally, pay was considered the only benefit needed by lower-level employees in return for their services. Today, many companies offer a greatly expanded compensation package, including subsidized education, day-care services for children, stock ownership, profit sharing, major medical insurance, dental and eye insurance, and athletic facilities on the premises (see Levering, Moskowitz, and Katz, 1984). While these benefits may not directly influence how work is done, they certainly can signify management's commitment to lower-level employees.

10. *Better Physical Conditions and Amenities.* Lower-level employees often work in polluted factories and cramped offices while management works in spacious, carpeted, air-conditioned quarters. According to Edelman (1978), lower-level workers tend to be socially discredited by their physical setting. The physical environment tends to create status or class differences between managers and workers that help affirm the hierarchical order. Many companies are now concerned about the quality of work life; the physical environment has improved in

factories and offices, and management is becoming more aware of how the physical environment influences behavior (Becker, 1981). Physical amenities may be considered hygiene factors (Herzberg, 1966) as well as to influence how lower-level employees feel about their jobs and about management.

Once again, the discussion of these ten managerial practices is far from comprehensive. Given the subjective nature of the concept of organizational culture, we can only talk in approximate terms about methods for changing it. Many other managerial techniques and methods could conceivably influence lower-level culture; however, the problem of closing the gap is not necessarily going to be solved by how well-selected managerial techniques and practices are applied. All these methods may do some good, but they are unlikely to be successful if more fundamental conflicts exist. Nothing is worse than the kind of nagging adversarial relations that exist in many organizations between managers and subordinates. By far the biggest problem is the antagonism felt toward managers.

Differences that Keep Managers and Lower-Level Employees Apart

The Role of Concepts and Symbolic Interpretations of Behavior. Conflicts within organizations frequently arise over competing definitions and interpretations of behavior. Notorious among these is the tendency for managers to view their subordinates' behaviors negatively because they are unable to construe any symbolic relationship between the outward appearances of their subordinates' behaviors and the tasks their subordinates are charged with. This occurs largely because what a person is actually doing is rarely obvious from observation alone. People tend to perceive each other as doing different things. Even something as apparently simple as someone talking on the phone can be given multiple interpretations. For the superior, it may be: "He's socializing on the phone again—I don't believe it!" For the subordinate, it may be: "This call's worth the time; it may eventually lead to a sale."

At work, management tends to provide the dominant accounts of organizational events. In disputes arising between managers and lower-level employees, the views of management are frequently the only interpretations accepted. In those instances where managers and subordinates disagree on the interpretation of events, the symbolic accounts of behavior held by management perform an important controlling function, which is used to elicit compliance from organization members. If employees reject these views or show apparent disrespect for them in their conduct, they are unlikely to remain members of the organization.

This does not mean, however, that countervailing interpretations of events cease to exist. Organization members may give tacit acceptance ("lip service") to these accounts but continue to view events in terms of their own concepts of reality. Organization members may justify "skiving" because they consider their work dull and boring; management makes no allowance for this view. Likewise, workers may justify "covering up" because all errors are punished; concealment is viewed as the best means of self-protection. In both cases, symbolic interpretations of events are at stake. Both parties—manager and subordinate—consider their views to be equally legitimate.

What seems questionable here is whether management's purposes are really better served by rejecting these alternative views of reality, or whether managers and lower-level employees might be able to work more effectively together if these differing viewpoints were accepted. While the tendency to enforce one interpretation of events may produce immediate compliance, the long-term costs are dysfunctional communication and deceptive practices that may outweigh any short-term advantages.

Many of the concepts that we use to describe organizational behavior actively promote adversarial relations. For instance, terms like *subordinate,* or expressions like "working for you," not "working with you," denote unequal status among organization members and thus create division. Managers assume they are superior to "subordinates" and expect to be treated as superior. If they do not get this respect, they will often become antagonistic toward their subordinates. The use of concepts like *partner, team member,* or *colleague* do not de-note unequal status and may promote better relations between managers and those in lower-level jobs.

These conflicts and difficulties present a formidable prob-lem because they are incorporated into the very language we use each day and the ingrained assumptions we hold about work and organizational behavior. The functions that concepts serve in regulating organizational behavior have been ignored in most research. The role that different conceptual views perform de-serves much closer attention, however, and needs to be made the subject of more intensive research (Mitroff and Turoff, 1974).

Cultural Conflicts Deriving from Social Values and Social Differences. In society as a whole, there is a tendency to glorify managers and to denigrate or deprecate those in lower-level jobs (Presthus, 1962). Managers are treated as a superior class, just as officers are in the military. Success is defined in terms of a per-son's level in the hierarchy (Packard, 1962).

Many people in lower-level jobs do not define their suc-cess in terms of their position at work, nor do they define their success primarily in terms of their job or career. Frequently, they do not want to put in long hours, be shifted around the country, have no weekends, and put their money and their time into earning degrees and diplomas (Terkel, 1974). They want a clear separation between their work and home life and to spend time on hobbies, with their spouses, and with their children. In many corporate jobs, these things are not possible if career suc-cess is to be achieved; employees must choose between job success and their personal, off-the-job goals (Margolis, 1979). The assumption is that choosing anything but job success is the wrong choice. Nevertheless, every organization needs a cadre of people that are content to remain at or near the bottom, that do their jobs year after year, that are loyal and dependable, and that do not want a higher spot in the hierarchy and bear no resent-ment toward people in more senior jobs. These people deserve respect for their long years of dependable service. Instead, how-ever, people who remain at the bottom often are treated as lack-ing ambition and drive and are considered failures. Managers may view them as disloyal, lazy, and insufficiently motivated if they refuse to work overtime for the company, instead of viewing them as having different priorities and values.

Many senior managers are not concerned about closing the gap between themselves and nonmanagers; they would prefer to widen it as evidence of their own elevated status. "Those in lower-level jobs started with an equal chance," they say. "They deserve to be where they are; let 'em live with it." Senior managers reinforce this point of view by preaching the necessity of leaving lower-level jobs and cutting relationships with former colleagues (Whyte, 1957). The relationship between managers and workers is often not improved by young management trainees who work briefly at lower levels ("Fitting New Employees . . . ," 1984). Frequently, they are viewed as "upstart college kids." New college graduates are usually totally unprepared for the reality of entry-level jobs and they go into a type of culture shock. Management trainees that are rotated through lower-level jobs often cannot wait to get out of them and take their "rightful places" as managers. Often, they despise the work and look down on the people that do it.

Frequently, there are educational differences between managers and lower-level employees as well as differences in life-styles, language, dress, grooming, and demeanor that set the two groups apart (Stewart and Faux, 1979). These cause communication and relationship problems that neither party is particularly eager to overcome. The lack of communication and the shallowness of relationships often mean that both parties relate to one another on the basis of stereotypes that serve to make their relationship even worse.

In the long run, one way to ameliorate the problem of social differences between different levels of employees is to try to realign the different value systems through training and education. Unfortunately, business education gives little attention to the role of stereotypes in the company culture and how damaging they can be. In any case, the experience of the lower-level employee is usually totally neglected, and education focuses on management, not nonmanagement, viewpoints. More attention needs to be given to the ideology of work (Anthony, 1977;

O'Toole, 1981) and to the work experience from the perspective of the lower-level employee.

Conclusion

In concluding, several qualifications need to be made.
First, no claim is being made that all organizations have distinct and separate lower-level cultures. Some organizations are
highly integrated, with no discernible differences in values and
perspectives among different levels of employees. Second, a
sharp distinction often cannot be made between management
and nonmanagement personnel. Some lower-level managers may
feel more empathy with nonmanagerial personnel than with
senior managers. Third, no claim is being made that all lower-
level cultures are alike, even though this chapter has focused on
plausible similarities. Finally, it is not being suggested that subcultures that are unalike are necessarily bad for the organization;
in some cases, differences provide the tension necessary to keep
an organization alert to alternative opportunities.

The purpose of this chapter has been to explore organizational culture at the lower levels, to look at orienting views and
strongly held values that tend to draw organization members
together, and to examine some of the main problems of managing
lower-level employees. Lower-level cultures that diverge from
the mainstream managerial culture can have a damaging influence on an organization and may require management to take
steps to close the gap. Recent examples of industries where this
has been necessary are the steel, automobile, and airline industries, where serious differences between managers and lower-
level employees have made it very difficult for some companies
to adjust to changing economic conditions.

Some of the ways in which management can influence
lower-level cultures have been discussed along with the drawbacks and deeply rooted differences that tend to keep managers
and lower-level employees apart. Particular emphasis has been
placed on the role of concepts in influencing organizational behavior and guiding organizational research. Most research tends
to investigate organizational behavior from a managerial per-

spective. Research is needed that looks at behavior from the lower-level employees' perspective, and the findings of this research need to be incorporated into courses on management and organizational behavior so that future managers have a better understanding of the lower-level employees' point of view. The crucial competitive difference between firms is frequently the productivity of lower-level employees. Management needs to keep a close eye on organizational culture at lower levels for its effect on overall corporate performance.

References

Ann, J. "The Secretarial Proletariat." In R. Morgran (ed.), *Sisterhood Is Powerful.* New York: Random House, 1970.

Anthony, P. D. *The Ideology of Work.* London: Tavistock, 1977.

Argyris, C. *Integrating the Individual and the Organization.* New York: Wiley, 1964.

Becker, F. D. *Workspace: Creating Environments in Organizations.* New York: Praeger, 1981.

Benet, M. K. *The Secretarial Ghetto.* New York: McGraw-Hill, 1972.

Blau, P. M. *The Dynamics of Bureaucracy.* Chicago: University of Chicago Press, 1963.

Blauner, R. *Alienation and Freedom.* Chicago: University of Chicago Press, 1964.

Braverman, H. *Labor and Monopoly Capital: The Degradation of Work in the Twentieth Century.* New York: Monthly Review Press, 1974.

"Changing a Corporate Culture: Can Johnson & Johnson Go from Band-Aids to High Tech?" *Business Week,* May 14, 1984, pp. 130–138.

Clegg, S., and Dunkerley, D. (eds.). *Critical Issues in Organizations.* Boston: Routledge & Kegan Paul, 1977.

"Corporate Culture: The Hard-To-Change Values That Spell Success or Failure." *Business Week,* Oct. 27, 1980, pp. 148–160.

Dalton, M. *Men Who Manage.* New York: Wiley, 1959.

Davis, T. R. V. *Evolving Theory from the Organization Mem-*

ber's Definition of the Situation. Paper presented at the 20th annual meeting of the Western Academy of Management, Portland, Ore., Apr. 1979.

Deal, T. E., and Kennedy, A. A. *Corporate Cultures: The Rites and Rituals of Corporate Life.* Reading, Mass.: Addison-Wesley, 1982.

Edelman, M. *Space and Social Order.* Madison: Institute for Research on Poverty, University of Wisconsin, 1978.

Evered, R., and Louis, M. R. "Alternative Perspectives in the Organizational Sciences: Inquiry from the Inside and Inquiry from the Outside." *Academy of Management Review,* 1981, *6* (3), 385-395.

"Fitting New Employees into the Company Culture." *Fortune,* May 28, 1984, pp. 28-30, 34, 38, 40, 43.

Ford, R. N. *Motivation Through the Work Itself.* New York: American Management Association, 1969.

Gold, C. S. *Solid Gold Customer Relations: A Professional Resource Guide.* Englewood Cliffs, N.J.: Prentice-Hall, 1983.

Gouldner, A. W. *Patterns of Industrial Bureaucracy: A Case Study of Modern Factory Administration.* New York: Free Press, 1954.

Gregory, K. L. "Native View Paradigms: Multiple Cultures and Culture Conflicts in Organizations." *Administrative Science Quarterly,* 1983, *28* (3), 359-376.

Herzberg, F. *Work and the Nature of Man.* Cleveland, Ohio: World Publishing Co., 1966.

Heydebrand, W. "Organizational Contradictions in Public Bureaucracies: Toward a Marxian Theory of Organizations." *Sociological Quarterly,* 1977, *18* (1), 83-107.

Koprowski, E. J. "Cultural Myths: Clues to Effective Management." *Organizational Dynamics,* 1983, *12* (2), 39-57.

Levering, R., Moskowitz, M., and Katz, M. *The 100 Best Companies to Work for in America.* Reading, Mass.: Addison-Wesley, 1984.

Lipsky, M. *Street-Level Bureaucracy: Dilemmas of the Individual in Public Service.* New York: Russell Sage, 1980.

Lovelock, C. H. *Services Marketing: Text, Cases, and Readings.* Englewood Cliffs, N.J.: Prentice-Hall, 1984.

McCall, M. W. *Leadership and the Professional.* Technical report no. 17. Greensboro, N.C.: Center for Creative Leadership, 1981.

Margolis, D. R. *The Managers: Corporate Life in America.* New York: Morrow, 1979.

Martin, J., and Siehl, C. "Organizational Culture and Counter-culture: An Uneasy Symbiosis." *Organizational Dynamics,* 1983, *12* (2), 52-64.

Mitroff, I. I., and Turoff, M. "On Measuring the Conceptional Errors in Large-Scale Social Experiments: The Future as Decision." *Technological Forecasting and Social Change,* 1974, *6* (4), 389-402.

Mondy, R. W., DeHay, J. M., and Sharplin, A. D. *Supervision.* New York: Random House, 1983.

Munchus, G. "Employer-Employee Based Quality Circles in Japan: Human Resource Policy Implications for American Firms." *Academy of Management Review,* 1983, *8* (2), 255-261.

Nord, W. "The Failure of Current Applied Behavioral Science—A Marxian Perspective." *Journal of Applied Behavioral Science,* 1974, *10* (4), 557-578.

O'Toole, J. J. *Making American Work—Productivity and Responsibility.* New York: Continuum, 1981.

Packard, V. *The Pyramid Climbers.* London: Longmans, 1962.

Peters, T. J., and Waterman, R. H. *In Search of Excellence: Lessons from America's Best-Run Companies.* New York: Harper & Row, 1982.

Presthus, R. *The Organizational Society.* New York: Vintage, 1962.

Riley, P. "A Structuralist Account of Political Culture." *Administrative Science Quarterly,* 1983, *28* (3), 414-437.

Roy, D. F. " 'Banana Time': Job Satisfaction and Informal Interaction." *Human Organization,* 1959, *18* (4), 158-168.

Sasser, W. E., Olsen, R. P., and Wyckoff, D. D. *Management of Service Operations.* Newton, Mass.: Allyn & Bacon, 1978.

Sathe, V. "Implications of Corporate Culture: A Manager's Guide to Action." *Organizational Dynamics,* 1983, *12* (2), 5-23.

Schmenner, R. W. *Production/Operations Management Concepts and Situations.* Chicago: SRA, 1984.

Stewart, M. Y., and Faux, M. *Executive Etiquette.* New York: St. Martin's, 1979.

Terkel, S. *Working.* New York: Pantheon, 1974.

"Terminal Tedium: As Computers Change the Nature of Work, Some Jobs Lose Savor." *Wall Street Journal,* May 26, 1983, p. 16.

Walker, C. R., and Guest, R. H. *The Man on the Assembly Line.* Cambridge, Mass.: Harvard University Press, 1952.

Whyte, W. H. *The Organization Man.* New York: Doubleday, 1957.

Wilkins, A. L., and Ouchi, W. G. "Efficient Cultures: Exploring the Relationship Between Culture and Organizational Performance." *Administrative Science Quarterly,* 1983, *28* (3), 468–481.

Eleven

Corporate Taboos as the Key to Unlocking Culture

Ian I. Mitroff
Ralph H. Kilmann

One of the variables that is key to understanding the concept of culture in general and to understanding any culture in particular is the notion of taboo (Leach, 1973, 1976). Every culture has a concept of taboo. Taboo variously covers such things as (1) those items that a people are forbidden to eat (for example, dogs and cats), (2) those items that a people are forbidden to touch (for example, corpses), (3) those topics that a people are generally forbiddden to discuss or which are regarded as unpleasant to talk about (for example, child abuse), (4) those topics that a people are generally forbidden to study and to research (for example, interspecies biological experiments), (5) those places that a people are generally forbidden to enter (for example, special religious shrines), and (6) those persons with whom it is generally prohibited to have a sexual relationship (for example, one's children).

Taboo is so powerful because it lies at the very heart of a

culture's basic sense of meaning and order. One of the principal functions of taboo is to set up clear boundaries of behavior. On one side of a boundary, certain acts are permitted, and on the other side, certain other acts are not permitted. As a result, topics and items associated with taboo create the deepest anxieties in a culture's members. There is a fear that even by discussing, just by acknowledging, that there are certain things that are taboo, we will have committed an action that is prohibited by the taboo itself.

A simple example is food. There are no logical reasons per se why some cultures deem it acceptable to eat dogs and cats and others do not. The reasons are not logical but cultural— or rather, what a person deems logical or compelling is itself influenced by that person's culture. Thus, in Western societies, dogs and cats are seen as extensions of the human world since they occupy a psychological and cultural space that is very close to people, that is, they are kept as pets. The unspoken cultural rule in Western societies is that whatever is psychologically close to people as human beings is not a proper thing for eating. Thus, cows can be eaten because, except for those who live on farms and have a cow for a pet, people do not form daily, close attachments to cows.

One of the most powerful ways to gain insight into the cultures of organizations is to study their taboos. In our case, we have been doing this as a byproduct of a larger study of corporate tragedies, that is, those events that, if they happen to an organization, are extremely traumatic to it or may even spell its demise. Of all the events in recent memory, one in particular stands out that best captures the nature of what we mean by *corporate tragedy*: the poisoning of bottles of Tylenol. Ever since the Tylenol tragedy occurred, we have been engaged in a study of the wider range of tragedies that can befall business organizations in general. The Tylenol case is just one example of the larger class of tragedies that we call "the unthinkable."

Our study of corporate tragedies shows that although it is virtually impossible to prevent all tragedies from occurring, *one can think of nearly every aspect of such unthinkable acts prior to their occurrence.* Further, we believe that thinking about the unthinkable is absolutely vital if a business is to be in a position to cope effectively with such tragedies if they do occur. "Coping" is thus the key word; complete prevention is not.

However, our study shows that even talking to general managers about the topic of corporate tragedies is extremely threatening and anxiety provoking. The topic brings out reactions that reveal a desire to avoid acknowledging the basic existence of the phenomenon and an unwillingness to develop strategies to cope with it. It appears that corporate tragedies are to an organization what child abuse is to a family; that is, it is culturally taboo even to talk about them. Families and organizations alike would prefer these phenomena to go away rather than face up to them squarely and deal with them. In both cases, what we are fighting are denial and resistance, even when the perfect tools for coping with or managing such phenomena are at hand.

In this chapter, three basic questions will be addressed: (1) can a list of the basic kinds of unthinkables that can beset any business be created?; (2) why is the unthinkable so much more prevalent in today's world?; and (3) what, if anything, can businesses do to cope more effectively with the unthinkable— that is, what can businesses do to face and cope with taboo topics? It should be clear that all three questions involve the concept of culture, whether it is at the general level of society or specific to a particular organization. All three questions pertain to how human beings have organized their world and have constructed institutions to manage it. Certain cultures, it seems, are more effective in acknowledging the existence of tragedies and in managing them than others.

Categorizing Evil and Tragedy

We have identified four basic types of unthinkables that have been happening in businesses recently (Mitroff and Kilmann, 1984). We make no claim that these four cover all of the kinds of unthinkable acts that could ever occur. Indeed, it is itself unthinkable that any one could ever know all there is to know about the unthinkable.

We do claim, however, that these four are sufficient to start any organization thinking about the worst things that could happen to it. Any organization that fails to think seriously about every one of these is literally playing with disaster.

The four types of tragedies and examples of each are:

1. Tampering, the evil from without: the case of Tylenol.
2. Harmful defects, the evil from within: the case of Rely tampons.
3. Unwanted compatibility, the evil of the parasite: the case of Atari.
4. Projection, the evil in the mind's eye: the case of Procter and Gamble's logo.

Tylenol

On September 29, 1982, two brothers, Adam and Steven Janus, and Mary Kellerman, of two different suburbs outside of Chicago, died from taking Extra-Strength Tylenol capsules. Cyanide, a deadly poison, had been injected into the capsules. All in all, eight victims were to be linked directly to cyanide-laced Tylenol capsules.

The cost in human lives alone was enough of a tragedy, but the monetary cost to Johnson & Johnson (J&J), the parent company of McNeil, the maker of Tylenol, was also absolutely staggering. J&J recalled some 31 million bottles of Tylenol with a retail value of over $100 million. As a consequence, its third-quarter earnings dropped from 78 cents a share in 1981 to 51 cents in 1982. Securities analysts projected that over-the-counter sales of Tylenol products, normally $100 million, would drop by 70 percent in the fourth quarter of 1982. In1983, Tylenol had been projected to earn half a billion dollars in sales. After the tragedy, analysts predicted that J&J would be fortunate if the product earned half of that (Moore, 1982, p. 49; Mitroff and Kilmann, 1984, p. 3).

If the initial tragedy that occurred to J&J was unthinkable, then its subsequent recovery was absolutely astounding. It confounded nearly all the experts who predicted nothing less than complete demise of the brand name. By 1983, Tylenol had recovered to capture a 32 percent share of the $1.3 billion analgesic market—the largest share of the market, and only a few percentage points less than the 37 percent it had before the tragedy. This is especially remarkable given the fact that its share plummeted to 7 percent at the height of the tragedy (Navarro, 1983, p. 2; Mitroff and Kilmann, 1984, p. 107).

Still, the major dimensions of this tragedy—the loss of lives and the loss of tremendous amounts of money—stand out in sharp relief. If these are not enough to get any business that is susceptible to this kind of tragedy to think seriously about it, then perhaps nothing will. And perhaps an organization that does not want to think about it is not worth saving at all. Any organization that is so callous and so oblivious to its environment will probably fall prey to some serious tragedy sooner or later.

P&G's Rely

Every manufacturer of every product lives with the constant, dreaded fear that someday he will awaken and find that his product was responsible for widespread destruction, harm, suffering, and even death. What's worse, the fear is that this will occur because of no intended fault of his own, no actions on the part of evil external actors such as occurred in the case of Tylenol, but because lurking somewhere within his product is an unknown, unforeseen ticking time bomb. Buried somewhere within his product is an unknown and unintended set of evil properties. Given enough time for these properties to incubate, or a set of operating conditions vastly different from those under which the product was designed, the product becomes a lethal killer.

In September 1980, after a wave of unfavorable publicity, Procter & Gamble (P&G) was forced to withdraw its Rely tampons from the market because of their association with toxic-shock syndrome, a lethal illness. According to a 1981 *Fortune* article, "government researchers reported that over 70 percent of toxic-shock patients in one study had worn [the] single brand [Rely]" (Sherrid, 1981). While P&G's top scientists strongly disputed the government's findings, the company nevertheless took a $75 million loss on its Rely business. Although Rely accounted for less than 1 percent of P&G's total annual sales of over $10 billion, removing the product from the market still cut $0.91 off P&G's net earnings per share in 1980 ("Toxic Shock, Horror Mystery," 1980, p. 100).

What is especially frustrating about the Rely case is that, other than an "association" with tampons in general and with P&G's Rely in particular, no one knows for sure why tampons "cause" toxic shock syndrome; in fact, there is no definitive proof that they do.

In many ways, the Rely case is similar to the Tylenol case. Both involve unknown killers. A central, mainstay product from which the business derives a significant amount of its income and for which the public has considerable brand recognition and loyalty is designed with the intention of doing good. The properties of the product are then drastically altered by the injection of foreign substances into it. The product is then converted into an agent for doing evil to its unsuspecting consumers. As a result, both the consumers and the producers of the product suffer considerable loss. Virtually every organization is vulnerable to this kind of loss, tragedy, and threat.

The difference between the two cases is that in the case of Tylenol the killer was an evil *human* agent external to the business, whereas in the Rely case the killer was a *biological mechanism* that was triggered by the interaction between the physical properties of the product and the biological properties of its users.

Atari

Suppose that your business was founded on the image of a provider of good, clean entertainment for the entire family. Suppose also that someone made an unauthorized "adult" or X-rated component that was compatible with your product. This unauthorized component could only be used in conjunction with your product or something equivalent to it. This happened to Atari, the maker of video games and equipment.

American Multiple Industries of Northridge, California,

released an "adult" game cartridge called Custer's Revenge. In the "game," a naked General Custer dodges flying arrows and various obstacles to have intercourse with (or to rape, as some outraged groups have contended) an Indian woman whose hands are tied behind her back to a stake. Even in a world where so many human tragedies and outrageous acts occur that we all become jaded or numbed, one still has to marvel at the kind of mind that has the "imagination" to create such monstrosities, let alone the gall to call them "games" to justify their existence.

P&G's Logo

According to two recent best-selling books on management (Deal and Kennedy, 1982; Peters and Waterman, 1982), Procter & Gamble is an example of one of America's "excellent" companies. It is also one of the best examples of an organization with a strong culture. Supposedly, one of the distinguishing marks of a strong culture and a successful organization is an unwavering commitment to the customer. The customer not only comes first in such organizations but is the raison d'être of the organization. P&G learned early in its history the value of a distinctive logo in communicating its strong commitment to "listening to its customers."

Imagine the shock, then, when P&G learned that a religious sect had declared that P&G was in cahoots with the devil because the "man in the moon" symbol—a picture of a man wearing a "sorcerer's" cone-shaped hat with a half-moon symbol surrounded by several stars—was clearly a sign of the devil.

Such incidents are far from isolated. Sears-Roebuck, the nation's largest retailer, also was accused of being in league with the devil. According to a report on the ABC-TV program "20-20," the first three digits on all of Sears' innumerable plastic credit cards were "666," and, according to certain religious groups, the number "666" is how the devil shall be recognized.

In many, many ways this category of the unthinkable is the most remarkable of all. It involves one of the most incredible features of the human mind: its seemingly endless ability and need to project onto other people, and even onto inanimate objects, some of the deepest symbolic urges that emanate from the innermost recesses of the human psyche. It is difficult enough for companies to protect their products from invasion by foreign, unknown, or unintended substances, or even from unintended uses, but how can companies protect themselves from the invasion of *thoughts*?

Why the Unthinkable Is Happening More

It is, unfortunately, infinitely easier to describe the unthinkable than it is to say why today's world is more susceptible to it or to specify how it can be managed. Still, there are three factors in particular that seem, in one way or another, to be responsible either for the greater likelihood of the occurrence of the unthinkable or for the inability of most businesses to cope with it in a more effective manner. These three factors are: (1) The radically changed nature of today's business environment—that is, today's world is vastly different from anything that was encountered in previous eras; (2) the fact that contemporary or traditional education in business has not kept pace with the radically changing nature of the world—in particular, that traditional education is woefully inadequate in preparing both students and practitioners to think about the unthinkable; and (3) the fact that the overwhelming majority of today's organizational cultures are not developed to cope with the unthinkable.

Factor One: The World Has Changed. It is vitally important to appreciate that the environment in which today's businesses operate is radically different from that of previous eras. Today's businesses are not only affected by more forces than ever before, but the forces themselves are more volatile, quickly changing, and unpredictable than ever before. The forces operating in earlier times were not only fewer in number but easier to understand and more stable and longer lasting. In earlier times it could be said with reasonable assurance that the major forces operating on an organization were principally the stockholders and management itself. As a result, it was easier both to formulate a strategy for running a business and to stick to it. In contrast, the forces today are almost too numerous to list, let alone to keep track of: government regulatory agencies, labor unions, suppliers, competitors, international cartels, educational institutions, the news media, financial institutions, environmentalist groups, consumer interest groups, and so on. Any one of these forces can exert a tremendous influence on a business.

These broader forces are called *stakeholders* because any one of them may have a direct stake in the running of a business. What a business does or can do either affects or is affected by what every stakeholder is like. Consider as a single example the stakeholder, *competitors*. What International Business Machines (IBM) does in the personal computer field certainly affects what Apple Computer Company, Texas Instruments, and other similar companies do, and, in turn, what these companies do affects what IBM does. No business is an island unto itself in today's world.

With the unparalleled growth in the number of stakeholders potentially affecting any business comes uncertainty and a lack of predictability. It is harder to develop a business plan based on complete, certain knowledge. It is harder to know exactly from where a force in the environment might come or what the exact nature of the force might be.

All of this, of course, is a direct reflection of an increasingly complex society. In the words of one insightful social critic, Philip Slater (1974), American society is transforming itself from a *community* into a *network*. The differences between the two are profound and essential to grasp.

A community tends to be a small, tightly knit group of people who all recognize, even if they do not know, one another on sight. One of its most essential properties is that it embraces people of all kinds who must interact with one another.

The members of a community depend on one another and are akin to the members of a large, extended family. Rich or poor, smart or dull, all must be accepted, and all are necessary to keep a balanced perspective on life.

Networks, on the other hand, tend to be homogeneous cultures. Increasingly, America is organized into a series of overlapping networks. Within each network, people communicate—increasingly, by computer or some other impersonal means—with others similar to themselves. Since the members of a network tend to think more alike than do the members of a community, they tend to share the same strengths as well as blind spots. As a result, they are blinded to forces within the environment that are not naturally a part of their network. As a consequence, they are vastly more susceptible to disruptions emanating from forces outside of the network, that is, from the broader societal culture.

There is one more factor that needs to be mentioned. A society that is organized into networks tends to be more permissive than one that is organized into communities. Indeed, it is difficult, perhaps impossible, to say which comes first: permissiveness or networks. Whichever is the case, each fosters and supports the other.

Networks foster permissiveness because they allow a greater range of behavior—and therefore more deviant behavior—to operate in a society. Every society or community has psychopaths and sociopathics; however, a network is more vulnerable than a community to their effects because it is less directly in contact with such people than is a community, where the deviant or oddball members are more likely to be known, observed, cared for, and even tolerated. As a result, social deviants are more likely to be true members of the community. The paradox is that the more we have attempted to exclude and isolate criminals and psychopaths from our networks, the more susceptible to them we have become.

There is no single class of stakeholders to which businesses today are more vulnerable and yet least prepared to recognize, understand, or manage than that of psychopaths (see Mitroff and Kilmann, 1984, pp. 49-61). Business today faces not just a world that has become infinitely complex because the number of stakeholders is greater than ever before, but a group of stakeholders that is more bizarre and evil than anything it has ever confronted.

Factor Two: The State of Management Education. With very few exceptions, management education today largely trains students to solve problems that are predicated on a simple, orderly, stable view of the world, and such problems, unlike those in the real world, generally have only one correct solution.

As a result of the constant exposure to such exercises, the view is reinforced—dangerously so, in our belief—that all problems have but a single correct answer. This is generally not true in the real world. Furthermore, the solutions to such artificial problems tend to be measured by their impact on a single criterion: the "bottom line." As a result of prolonged exposure to this kind of thinking, most students and practitioners of management today are unprepared to face the kinds of challenges that the unthinkable presents. They are prepared neither intellectually nor emotionally to face the immense challenges that the unthinkable poses.

Let us consider the emotional challenges first. Most managers with whom we have discussed the unthinkable find the entire topic too depressing to consider seriously. It is clear that they would prefer to dismiss the whole phenomenon—to wish it away—than to grapple with it seriously. However, whether managers like the phenomenon of the unthinkable or not is irrelevant. The unthinkable is increasingly a part of our world and, as such, must be dealt with. The fact that current managers do not wish to face the unthinkable should be taken as a serious sign of a gross defect in the way we currently educate managers. We have failed miserably to develop real strength in them, the emotional toughness to face the real problems with which they are presented.

The intellectual challenges are no less formidable. They also reveal another aspect of the emotional challenges.

Unlike artificial exercises, problems in the real world can *always* be looked at in more than one way. Indeed, the more serious the problem, the more it demands to be viewed from as many different standpoints as possible so that essential aspects of it are not missed. The worst thing that can be done when solving complex problems is to pick one view and to ignore all others. The individual or the organization that defines its problems narrowly is courting serious trouble.

Thus, the first intellectual challenge that the unthinkable poses is that potential managers must learn how to view the phenomenon from several distinct vantage points. For the most part, business schools do not train people how to do this. Because contemporary business education consists largely of finding the single "right" answer to preformulated, relatively simple exercises, the student is neither encouraged nor trained in the art of problem formulation—that is, in the art of viewing any problem from several different perspectives and looking for multiple solutions to complex problems.

The second intellectual challenge is that students and managers must learn how to handle uncertainty. If they do not, they will fall prey to the worst kind of rigid "either/or" thinking. For instance, although it is true that the exact whereabouts of *the* psychopath who is contemplating an evil action against a business cannot be located, this does not mean that the general behavior patterns of the kind of person who is most likely to engage in such evil acts cannot be known. Because we lack *perfect* knowledge, it does not therefore follow that we have *no* knowledge whatsoever. Wisdom in contrast to mere technical competency consists of making the best use of what one has.

Factor Three: The Tragedy of Current Corporate Cultures. For all the foregoing reasons and more, the unthinkable generally raises great anxiety in individuals and in organizations. If individuals generally are not prepared either intellectually or emotionally to confront the unthinkable, their organizations also do not possess the appropriate culture to confront it. Thus, the current culture of most organizations does not generally support thinking about the unthinkable.

Silent signals exist in all organizations. These constitute the "unwritten rules of the game," and they guide the behavior of people within organizations as powerfully as anything that is written down in formal company manuals. In many ways, they carry the real messages of the company's culture—for instance, what people will really be rewarded for doing, whether it is really okay to disagree with the boss, whether creativity is really valued, whether the organization really believes in equal pay for all, and so on.

Thinking about the unthinkable demands a very different kind of culture from that which governs most organizations. It demands that people be encouraged and rewarded for creative, divergent thinking. It demands that people not be punished for bringing up anxiety-provoking issues. It demands that people be rewarded for anticipating issues of strategic importance to the organization. It demands that people be encouraged to constantly monitor the environment for strange trends, bizarre events, and so on. It demands that organizations bring in outsiders who can shake up and challenge conventional ways of thinking.

The $64 Billion Question: What Can Be Done?

There is much that organizations can do to cope more effectively with the unthinkable. First of all, organizations must recognize the existence of psychopathic behavior. Superficial analysis of the impact of stakeholders on organizations that is based only on the most easily visible properties of people is not sufficient to cope with today's complex world.

Our first suggestion, then, is that managers be able to *think like psychopaths.* They must learn to ask themselves, how does our organization look when it is viewed from the vantage point of a psychopath? What are its strengths and its weaknesses? How can it be protected?

Second, managers need to develop early-warning, environment-scanning systems for monitoring the environment for bizarre acts committed against *any* kind of organization. Very few psychopaths walk up and directly announce either their presence or their intentions to an organization. However, all human beings to one extent or another are influenced by the actions of others, whether it be for good or for evil, and disturbed people are especially susceptible to influence by others. Thus, the fact that even one organization has been attacked by a psychopath is likely to call forth destructive tendencies in other people, as, for instance, in the case of copycat killers. At a minimum, organizations need to develop an inventory of the kind and frequency of evil acts committed against organizations inside and outside of their industry.

Although not all acts committed against organizations are perpetrated by psychopaths, a significant proportion of such acts can be understood by understanding psychopathic behavior. Certainly, this is true in the cases involving Tylenol, Atari, and the P&G logo.

Of all the types of the unthinkable, certain types of undesired projection, such as that in the case of the P&G logo, are the most readily avoided. Organizations can hire specialists in mythology and religious symbolism as consultants to predict beforehand those aspects of their logos that are most susceptible to misinterpretation by religious groups. In fact, guides to undesired religious projection have been used with success to peruse corporate logos and symbols to identify so-called Satanic signs.

The unthinkable can also be avoided by following, for example, some of the new schemes that have recently been developed to help businesses anticipate hazards that might develop in their products. Such schemes can facilitate thinking about cases like that of Rely tampons *before* they occur.

Third, organizations need to develop intellectual "skunk works." The organization needs to set up and reward groups whose full-time occupation is thinking about the unthinkable. Participation in such groups should regarded as an essential step up the corporate ladder.

Since evil is contagious, people participating in such groups need special training to inoculate themselves against catching the very disease they are trying to protect the organization from. For this same reason, the involvement of outsiders is necessary to help the organization deal with the anxiety the unthinkable inevitably raises.

Finally, and most important of all, coping with the unthinkable must be seen as part of a total, integrated program of strategic thinking about the entire range of issues with which the modern organization must deal. Every type of the unthinkable is traceable to the organization's failure to discover, evaluate, and revise a faulty set of assumptions that is held by the members of the organization.

Conclusion

We have the means to think about nearly every aspect of the unthinkable. New and powerful techniques have recently been developed for identifying and challenging the core assumptions that members of organizations hold about themselves and their environment (see Mitroff and Kilmann, 1984, pp. 79-93). We simply must have the will to use these tools to face our deepest fears and anxieties.

In the end, the key question is: does an organization's culture allow it to face its taboos? Taboos are one of the most hidden aspects of a culture; is it possible to have a culture that is more aware of those aspects of itself that it wants to hide? The fact that every culture has taboos does not mean that it is doomed never to be aware of them. The fact that it can never be fully conscious about its taboos does not mean that it cannot attain any consciousness of them.

The fact that we cannot prevent all tragedies from occurring does not relieve us from the basic moral responsibility of *trying* to prevent them. Any culture that does less than this is morally reprehensible.

References

Deal, T. E., and Kennedy, A. A. *Corporate Cultures: The Rites and Rituals of Corporate Life.* Reading, Mass.: Addison-Wesley, 1982.

Leach, E. "Anthropological Aspects of Language: Animal Categories and Verbal Abuse." In P. Maranda (ed.), *Mythology.* Middlesex, England: Penguin Books, 1973.

Leach, E. *Culture and Communication.* Cambridge: Cambridge University Press, 1976.

Mitroff, I. I., and Kilmann, R. H. *Corporate Tragedies: Product Tampering, Sabotage, and Other Catastrophes.* New York: Praeger, 1984.

Moore, T. "The Fight to Save Tylenol." *Fortune,* Nov. 29, 1982, pp. 44–49.

Navarro, M. "Tylenol: A Former Best-Seller Painfully Makes It Back Atop the Market." *Los Angeles Herald Examiner,* Aug. 28, 1983, p. 2.

Peters, T. J., and Waterman, R. H., Jr. *In Search of Excellence: Lessons from America's Best-Run Companies.* New York: Harper & Row, 1982.

Sherrid, P. "Tampons After the Shock Wave." *Fortune,* Aug. 10, 1981, pp. 114–29.

Slater, P. *Earthwalk.* New York: Doubleday, 1974.

"Toxic Shock, Horror Mystery." *The Economist,* Oct. 18, 1980, p. 42.

Twelve

The Cycle of
Cultural Evolution
in Organizations

W. Gibb Dyer, Jr.

Because of recent claims that particular "types" of organizational cultures lead to increased productivity and profits, managers in many organizations have begun to explore ways to change the cultures of their organizations to make them more competitive (Ouchi, 1981; Peters and Waterman, 1982; Deal and Kennedy, 1982). Moreover, a number of writers have begun to develop a variety of theories of culture change that might assist managers in their attempts to "manage" their cultures. For example, Pettigrew (1979) suggests that since leaders are the "creators" of culture, culture change is accompanied by a change in leadership; thus, leadership succession is the essential ingredient in culture change. From a rather different perspective, O'Toole (1979) argues that culture is imbedded in organizational structures such as a company's reward system or hierarchy of authority. Therefore, to change culture the key structures supporting a given culture must be changed. Others, such as Ouchi (1981) and Peters and Waterman (1982), believe that culture can be changed by developing a new set of values, or "management philosophy," which is then inculcated into employees. The change process involves the development of new company goals and ideals and the socialization of both old and new employees to this new set of beliefs. The creation of new symbols as a change strategy has also been discussed by Peters (1978). He argues that leaders can change culture simply by changing their activities, agendas, or interpersonal styles to reinforce new behaviors. Thus, the management of symbols and their accompanying meanings is the agent of cultural change. Other writers, such as Silverzweig and Allen (1976), Baker (1980), Schwartz and Davis (1981), and Sathe (1983), have also outlined similar strategies that might be used to change organizational cultures.

While these writers present a variety of potentially useful approaches to managing culture change, they tend to focus immediately on specific tactics or strategies for change rather than first attempting to uncover the underlying processes of culture change. Rather than present simply another strategy for managing culture change, the purpose of this chapter is to describe the conditions and processes under which such change takes place. After we are able to describe the process of culture change, we can then begin to explore meaningfully how it might be managed.

The model of culture change that will be described was derived by examining the histories of five organizations that have experienced significant changes in their cultures: General Motors, Levi Strauss, National Cash Register, the Balfour Company—an emblematic jewelry firm located in Attleboro, Massachusetts—and the Brown Corporation—a medium-sized ($100 million in sales) materials-handling firm located in the northeastern United States (this is a disguised case). Although the theories of culture change mentioned previously do explain some salient aspects of culture change, the model presented here suggests that each theory explains only a part of a complicated change process consisting of several interconnected "stages," or preconditions for culture change. After the change model has been presented, its implications for managing culture change will then be explored.

Definition of Organizational Culture

Because there are a wide variety of views on the subject of organizational culture, defining what we mean by *culture* is important to understanding exactly what is changing when we discuss culture change. We will define organizational culture by examining the artifacts, perspectives, values, and assumptions in which it appears to reside.

Artifacts. At the highest level are what might be called the verbal, behavioral, and physical artifacts of culture. Verbal artifacts consist of the language, stories, and myths shared by members of an organization; behavioral artifacts are represented in oft-repeated rituals and ceremonies; and physical artifacts are found in an organization's art, accepted working attire, physical layout, and technology. Artifacts are those tangible aspects of culture that a person hears, sees, or feels when entering an organization. Although artifacts often represent the key symbols of an organization's culture, they are only the overt expressions or surface manifestations of socially shared perspectives, values, and assumptions. It is these perspectives, values, and assumptions that are important, for they provide the interpretation of, and deeper system of meaning connected with, the artifacts (Dyer, 1982; Schein, 1981).

Although the terms *perspectives, values,* and *assumptions* appear to be quite similar, they represent three distinct but interconnected levels of organizational culture.

Perspectives. A perspective is a "coordinated set of ideas and actions a person uses in dealing with some problematic situation" (Becker, Geer, Hughes, and Strauss, 1961, p. 34). Perspectives encompass the socially shared rules and norms applicable in a given situation; they involve the way a group defines and interprets various situations in everyday life, and they prescribe the bounds of acceptable behavior. The situations to which perspectives are applied may vary in their degree of concreteness; for example, they include the rather specific encounter involving greeting one's boss appropriately in the morning as well as the more general situation involving what one should do to be advanced to a top management position. Perspectives may entail both formal and informal rules. Standard operating procedures, for example, represent a formal set of rules for managing situation-specific problems.

Values. Inextricably connected with perspectives but broader in their application are values. While perspectives define situations and courses of action, values are the evaluations people make of situations, acts, objects, and people. Such evaluations appear to be quite stable across situations and hence are more abstract than perspectives because of their trans-situational nature. Values reflect the organization's general goals, ideals, standards, and "sins"—"sales growth," "aggressiveness," "career employment," "promote from within," and so forth—and these values are often articulated in statements of organizational identity or management philosophy.

Assumptions. Many scholars in the fields of anthropology, sociology, and psychology have suggested that a group's tacit assumptions about itself, others, and its world are the innermost core of its culture. While often using different terminology to describe these unconscious, core beliefs, they refer to these assumptions as the tacit premises that underlie the overt artifacts, perspectives, and values.

Table 1 illustrates how such tacit beliefs can be uncovered in organizations by examining one cultural artifact of Levi Strauss and the accompanying perspectives and values that had their origin in the Strauss family's assumption that "outsiders are not to be trusted."

Interpretation of this artifact, the yearly ritual of the presentation of the annual report, identifies the perspective that only family members should be allowed to scrutinize the company's annual reports. Nonfamily members are to be given just enough knowledge to meet the requirements of the law.

If we compare this perspective with other perspectives that indicated that employees should not be allowed access to important information about the firm and that the family disdained any actions that might expose the family to public scrutiny, the broader value of "secrecy" becomes apparent. From these data, we can make the inference that this behavioral artifact and its accompanying perspectives and values ap-

Table 1. Levels of Organizational Culture.

Cultural Artifact (annual ritual)	For generations, annual reports had been closely guarded family secrets. To meet the law's requirement that each shareholder see an annual report, every year David Beronio, a trusted family advisor, had typed one copy and personally carried it around the room, showing it to each stockholder attending the meeting. Junior executives and minority shareholders got only a brief glance at the balance sheet before the report disappeared into Beronio's locked drawer. As the board expanded and the company's fiscal problems multiplied, so did the copies of the report—but each was numbered, and all were collected at the end of the annual meeting (Cray, 1978, p. 185).
Perspective	Only family members and trusted advisors are allowed to scrutinize the company's annual reports.
Value	Secrecy regarding the company's affairs is important.
Tacit Assumption	"Outsiders" are not to be trusted.

pear to reflect an assumption that "outsiders should not be trusted."

The key to understanding an organizational culture is found by deciphering the patterning of such tacit assumptions shared by members of an organization and discovering the way these assumptions fit together into a cultural pattern or paradigm to form a unique gestalt or ethos (Dyer, 1982; Schein, 1981). In summary, then, the term *organizational culture* refers here to the artifacts, perspectives, values, and assumptions shared by members of an organization.

Categories of Assumptions

Although there may be many different types of core assumptions held by members of an organization, the works of Kluckhohn and Strodtbeck (1961), Parsons and Shils (1951), and Bem (1970) present us with a number of categories of assumptions that seem quite useful in studying organizational cultures. In this study, five such categories, presented in Table 2,

Table 2. Categories of Cultural Assumptions.

1. *The Nature of Relationships:* Are relationships between members of the organization assumed to be primarily lineal (i.e., hierarchical), collateral (i.e., group oriented), or individualistic in nature?
2. *Human Nature:* Are human beings considered to be basically good, basically evil, or neither good nor evil?
3. *The Nature of Truth:* Is "truth" (i.e., correct decisions) revealed by external authority figures, or is it determined by a process of personal investigation and testing?
4. *The Environment:* Is there a basic belief that human beings can master the environment, or that they must be subjugated by the environment, or that they should attempt to harmonize with the environment?
5. *Universalism/Particularism:* Should all members of the organization be evaluated by the same standards, or should certain individuals be given preferential treatment?

emerged as the most useful in analyzing changing cultural patterns in the five companies studied. Within each category there are a number of different assumptions that might be held by members of an organization at any given point in time. The model of cultural evolution was derived by examining the events surrounding changes in the particular orientations within each category over time.

Data used to decipher the cultures of these organizations and the conditions surrounding culture change were gleaned largely from existing corporate histories, although in some cases, particularly that of the Brown Corporation, information was gathered from interviews, public records (for example, annual reports and minutes of stockholder meetings), internal reports (for example, minutes from board of directors meetings and financial and personnel records) and industry reports.

Changing Cultural Patterns of the Brown Corporation: An Example

As previously discussed, the research process involved mapping each organization's artifacts, explicating significant perspectives and values, and eventually making inferences about the underlying pattern of assumptions. To analyze the process of change, discontinuities in each of these levels of culture were described over each firm's history; for example, those instances where timeworn stories, rituals, or ceremonies were discontinued or new ones started, which might indicate that the culture was changing, were noted, and the events surrounding such changes documented. To illustrate how these cultural periods did change, we will briefly describe the three cultural periods of the Brown Corporation (Dyer, 1984a). The first period, 1922 to 1959, represented the culture as created and nurtured by its founder, John Brown, Sr. The second period, 1960 to 1974, was characterized by Brown employees as the era of "participative management" under the leadership of John Brown, Jr. The final period, 1975 to 1983, featured the introduction of "professional" management into the firm.

Not only did Brown employees assert that these three periods were qualitatively different, but an examination of the artifacts, perspectives, values, and assumptions during each of these periods indicated that the culture had indeed changed. The pattern of core assumptions during each period is summarized in Table 3.

As changes in the orientations within the five categories of assumptions indicate, the culture of the Brown Corporation shifted from one founded on assumptions emphasizing founder and family dominance and a distrust of outsiders, to one based on assumptions fostering a more egalitarian, open, and participative culture; and, eventually, to one based on a set of assumptions favoring individualism and competition between employees, careful compliance to company rules, and reliance on professional codes of conduct. Following is a brief description of each cultural period.

Period 1: 1922-1959. The Brown Corporation was founded by John Brown Sr., who took over a faltering iron works in 1922 and built it into a successful materials-handling firm. Characterized by his co-workers as a dynamic leader, John Sr. was a major force in shaping the company culture during these early years. During Period 1, relationships were lineal or hierarchical. John Brown Sr., as the company father figure, was seen by employees as a benevolent autocrat who "took care" of his employees in return for their loyalty and obedience.

Table 3. Assumptions Underlying the Culture of the Brown Corporation.

Categories of Assumptions	Period 1 (1922–1959)	Period 2 (1960–1974)	Period 3 (1975–1983)
Relationships	Lineal; John Brown, Sr. is the sole leader and father figure for Brown employees	More collateral; power shared between family and nonfamily members; group orientation	More individualistic; people look after their own self-interest
Human Nature	Nonfamily members distrusted, especially those living outside the community	Nonfamily members can and should be trusted	Distrust between top management and workers
Environment	Proactive stance; the company develops a number of innovations	Harmonize with the environment; avoid moving outside of the company's niche in the market	Harmonize with the environment
Truth	Truth resides in the founder; he is the source of all relevant information	Truth discovered via group decisions; participation is important to make good decisions	Truth is found in the principles of management science
Universalism/ Particularism	Particularism; family members given preference	Mixed universalism/particularism	Universalism; competence is the evaluation criterion

Nonfamily members were assumed to be untrustworthy. John Brown, Sr. made all the key decisions, supervised employees closely, and kept information regarding the firm's operations secret. A stock fight with outsiders who tried to take control of the company in the early 1940s increased his distrust of nonfamily members.

John Brown, Sr. fostered innovation by supporting new research and by acquiring new technology, such as one of the first International Business Machines computers; and he gave employees paid vacations before many other companies did. These artifacts reflected a proactive stance toward the organization's environment.

"Truth" resided in the founder, as all key information regarding the firm rested in his hands. Employees assumed that John Brown, Sr. should be granted this prerogative. Finally, the firm's orientation was particularistic, as John Brown, Sr. gave family members preferential treatment and groomed his only son to assume leadership of the firm.

Period 2: 1960–1974. John Brown, Sr. stepped down as chief executive officer (CEO) in 1959 and appointed his son, John Jr., the new CEO. Soon after his appointment, and quite by accident, John Jr.'s wife attended a sensitivity-training group, or T-group, sponsored by the Young Presidents' Organization. Because of her positive T-group experience, she began to encourage her husband to explore the burgeoning field of organizational development (OD). In the early 1960s, John Jr. enlisted the help of Robert Blake in instituting a managerial grid in the Brown Corporation, As a result of grid training and other OD interventions, the culture of the company began to change.

Relationships in Period 2 became more collateral as egalitarianism was increasingly espoused, and the focus shifted to maintaining group solidarity rather than a hierarchical order. Employees were deemed to be basically trustworthy, and time clocks and other control devices were eliminated.

The company's development of a new Product X truck in the 1950s created a unique niche for the company in the materials handling industry. John Brown, Jr. labeled the employees of the Brown Corporation the "Product X People" and preferred to remain in that market niche rather than expand into new markets. This suggests that the basic company orientation was to harmonize with the environment.

Truth no longer resided in the founder but was to be discovered through group decision making. An employee with an organizational problem to solve now assumed that a group should be brought together to solve it; in Period 1, employees had assumed that John Sr. had all the answers, so consulting him was the way to gain knowledge.

The culture also became more universalistic as nonfamily members were given significant authority, but family concerns were still important. The culture's universalistic/particularistic assumption thus was mixed.

This cultural pattern continued until 1974, when a major crisis precipitated further cultural change.

Period 3: 1975-1983. In 1974 the worldwide recession caused the Brown Corporation's sales to plummet, and inventories rose dramatically. To solve this crisis the board of directors looked outside the company and chose Reed Larson, a professional manager trained at International Telephone and Telegraph, to become the new manufacturing vice president. Larson, who had a reputation as a "turnaround guy," took a number of steps that quickly changed the culture. Larson brought with him several other professionals who Brown old-timers described as "ladder climbers." Competition for advancement increased. Group solidarity was no longer so important, and relationships became individualistic. Larson instituted a number of strict controls that increased the distrust between workers and management, and, as a result, union activity intensified. The dominant environmental orientation did not change, although the professionals did emphasize sales growth more than their predecessors did. Truth began to be discovered through formal rules and principles of management science, and participation was increasingly discounted. Finally, universalistic criteria began to be used in evaluation and promotion decisions. Under this new cultural pattern, the crisis was solved; sales grew steadily, reaching their zenith in 1980, when sales reached $113 million. However, worker turnover and alienation increased as company oldtimers decried the "professionalization" of their company.

In summary, this description of the three cultural periods of the Brown Corporation illustrates how culture change over time can be studied systematically and in depth. Using this method of tracking the cultural patterns that evolved in each of the five firms studied and examining the events that precipitated changes, a model of cultural evolution was developed.

The Cycle of Cultural Evolution in Organizations

The cycle of cultural evolution in organizations is presented in Figure 1. The model depicts the change process as composed of sequentially ordered stages that outline the conditions under which culture change will take place. Although the model indicates a temporal ordering of the stages, it is possible for them to overlap or to occur simultaneously.

Before describing this process, a brief explanation of what is labeled in Figure 1 as the *prevailing cultural pattern* must be given. The prevailing cultural pattern is the cultural pattern or patterns (if there are subcultures) present in any given organization. Indeed, without some pattern of shared understandings, organizing cannot take place. But in the case of a new organization, a culture must be created. Schein (1969; 1983), Pettigrew (1979), and Dyer (1984b) all discuss the process of culture creation, and their three major theories on the subject can be summarized as follows:

1. Founders and other leaders bring with them a set of assumptions, values, perspectives, and artifacts to the organization and impose them on their employees.
2. A culture emerges as members of the organization interact with one another to solve the fundamental problems of internal integration of group members and environmental adaptation.
3. Individual members of an organization may become "culture creators" by developing solutions to individual problems of identity, control, individual needs, and acceptance

Figure 1. The Cycle of Cultural Evolution in Organizations.

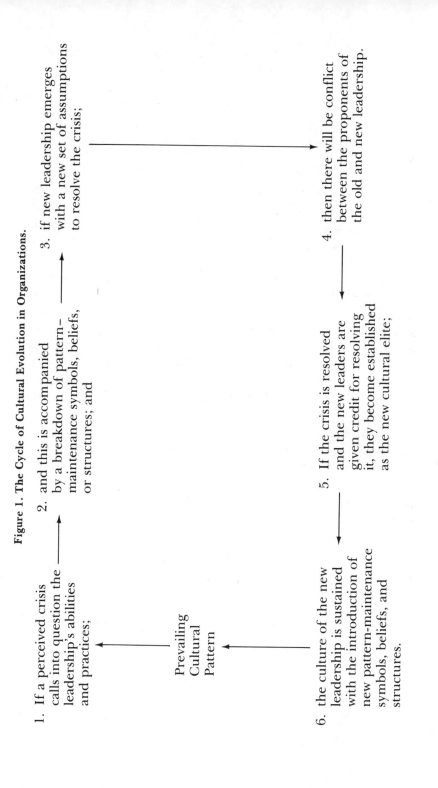

1. If a perceived crisis calls into question the leadership's abilities and practices;

2. and this is accompanied by a breakdown of pattern-maintenance symbols, beliefs, or structures; and

3. if new leadership emerges with a new set of assumptions to resolve the crisis;

4. then there will be conflict between the proponents of the old and new leadership.

5. If the crisis is resolved and the new leaders are given credit for resolving it, they become established as the new cultural elite;

6. the culture of the new leadership is sustained with the introduction of new pattern-maintenance symbols, beliefs, and structures.

Prevailing Cultural Pattern

that are then passed on to succeeding generations of members.

Although the process of culture creation is indeed an important one, the model of culture change presented here focuses on how organizational cultures change *once the initial founder culture is established.* Furthermore, we recognize that an organization's culture may change over time as new artifacts are introduced that are consistent with prevailing culture. For example, in the case of the Brown Corporation, John Brown, Sr. instituted a number of new programs in the 1950s, such as paid vacations and sick leave for employees, but these changes were consistent with the paternalistic culture of that period. Such changes represent only incremental changes in the culture: changes that are generally consistent with the underlying paradigm of assumptions. This model, however, articulates the dynamics accompanying major transformations in the assumptions underlying these higher levels. Thus, it reflects those conditions supporting cultural transformations rather than incremental changes.

With this in mind, the six stages of culture change will be summarized. Data from the five cases will also be presented to illustrate how these stages are applicable to the companies studied.

1. The Leadership's Abilities and Current Practices Are Called into Question. The first stage of the process involves questioning the leadership's ability to solve major problems facing the organization. This questioning is triggered by events that create a crisis that members of the organization perceive cannot be solved by following the traditional practices espoused by the leaders. Hence, a search begins for alternative patterns of behavior that will enable the organization to cope with the crisis.

In each of five cases studied, the process of culture change was initiated by an environmental shock—typically, a major recession or depression. In the case of General Motors, the process of culture change started when a major financial crisis in 1920 forced William Durant, the firm's founder, to relinquish ownership and management of the company to Pierre DuPont and Alfred P. Sloan, Jr. At National Cash Register (NCR), declining dividends in the 1930s caused stockholders to question the abilities of the firm's leadership, which then led to culture change. Levi Strauss began to change its culture when the company's European division lost $12 million in 1973—a period that the firm's president, Walter Haas, Jr., described as "very traumatic" and which caused the Haas family to reevaluate its laissez-faire management style (Cray, 1978). The Brown Corporation's culture changed twice during its sixty-year history—once in the early 1960s after the founder retired and a poor sales record caused the firm's new president, John Brown, Jr., to search for new ideas to run the business, and again in 1973 after the worldwide recession caused sales to drop dramatically. Finally, the Balfour company experienced culture change in the late 1960s when the Federal Trade Commission ordered the firm to stop making the long-term contracts with customers that had led to the company's 98 percent share of the fraternity-ring market. This event, coupled subsequently with the recession of 1973, wreaked havoc on the firm's sales and profits. Thus, in each of the five cases a significant crisis provided the impetus to begin the process of culture change.

   2. *Breakdown of Pattern-Maintenance Symbols, Beliefs, and Structures.* Occurring in concert with the questioning of the leadership's abilities to manage the organization effectively is a breakdown or loss of what we have called the pattern-maintenance symbols, beliefs, or structures that sustain the prevailing culture. For culture to change at all, these must change first.

   Pattern-maintenance symbols are those artifacts that sustain and support the prevailing culture. Pattern-maintenance symbols include rewarding employees who conform to the culture as well as the mere physical presence of a cultural elite in the workplace. Such artifacts serve to remind members of the organization of the importance of conforming to established practices.

   For example, John Patterson, the eccentric and egocentric founder of NCR, was apparently a master at enforcing his desired policies. Stanley Allyn, a Patterson subordinate and future president of the company, describes one encounter with Patterson:

> Even as excited and dedicated an employee as I was had to be wary. Patterson had been known to discharge an employee merely through dislike of the way the man combed his hair. . . . One Saturday noon, certain that . . . Mr. Patterson had departed, I lit a cigar. I had taken one luxurious puff when I heard his unmistakable nervously rapid footfall in the corridor. In his later years Mr. Patterson was a rampaging tyrant about tobacco, convinced that no one was efficient with nicotine contaminating the blood. Across my room, a window was open eight or nine inches. With deadly accuracy, my job depending on my skill, I pitched out the cigar. "Who's been smoking in here?" Patterson asked, his head suddenly in the door, his nose sniffing the air like that of a basset hound. "Uh—it must have been one of the salesmen," I muttered. "No wonder business is off," Patterson growled. "Everyone is full of poison." If he had known the name of the offender, my career at NCR probably would have ended that instant [Allyn, 1967, p. 40].

Such incidents served as a constant reminder to NCR employees of the importance of adhering to Patterson's wishes.

To the extent that an organization's leaders are no longer able to reinforce the culture's values and assumptions, values and assumptions become susceptible to change. In each of the five cases, the declining ability of the leaders to reinforce the company culture with both word and deed was a key factor in culture change. In John Patterson's case, his declining health paved the way for new leadership to establish a new set of symbols that represented a different set of assumptions.

Pattern-maintenance beliefs help sustain a given culture

by stifling opposition and dissent that might lead to questioning the basic premises on which the culture is founded. Contradictions in a belief system or discrepancies between espoused beliefs and actual behavior are common and must somehow be mediated if the leadership is to avoid the questioning of prevailing beliefs and practices. Before culture change occurred in the organizations studied, their members were taught to believe in the essential "goodness" of the leader or owning family and in the ability of the leader, who had helped build and sustain the firm, to cope with any emergency. The following story told by Stanley Allyn illustrates how deeply values were ingrained in NCR employees; they were deemed to be so "right" that they transcended national boundaries even during times of war: "The NCR Paris office on the Champs Elysees was on the line of march when Hitler's Wehrmacht rumbled into the capital of the French in 1940. A tank swerved from the column and halted before the NCR door. Out leaped a German soldier. He pounded for admittance. Finally our French employees decided that discretion required that they open to him. The German smiled and said, 'I'm from NCR in Berlin. I just wondered if you made your quota last year?' " (Allyn, 1967, p. 126). Such stories of employee loyalty and commitment served to strengthen the prevailing company culture at NCR.

When their cultures begin to shift in the face of the overwhelming crises confronting these organizations, those beliefs that served to support the validity and usefulness of established practices became untenable. The undermining of these beliefs eliminated a major stumbling block to culture change.

Certain organizational structures—reward systems, job design, and so on—may also sustain the culture of the organization, since they often reflect the assumptions of the culture and are slow to change. One of the most significant structural barriers to culture change in the companies studied was company ownership. Leaders who both own and operate a business are less susceptible to outside demands for change than are those who must satisfy a number of constituencies. In the cases of General Motors, NCR, and the Balfour Company, culture change was initiated simultaneously with a change in ownership. In the cases of Levi Strauss and the Brown Corporation, culture change began within five years after the companies became publicly held corporations. Since ownership constitutes power, any change in ownership that dilutes the power of the firm's leaders may stimulate culture change.

3. New Leadership Emerges with an Alternative Set of Assumptions. Although the questioning of the leadership's ability to govern and a breakdown of its power-sustaining symbols, beliefs, and structures are necessary conditions for culture change to take place, they are not sufficient to trigger change. Without some alternative set of artifacts, perspectives, values, and assumptions available to test and evaluate, the organization will, in all likelihood, continue to respond to the crisis in ways that proved successful in the past.

In each company, major leadership transitions provided the impetus for change. At General Motors, the culture changed as Alfred Sloan began to gain control of and provide a more formal structure for what had been a rather fragmented group of companies previously allowed by William Durant to operate independently. The contrasting backgrounds and styles of these two men were eventually reflected in the culture change that took place in the 1920s at General Motors. Chandler (1962, p. 130) notes: "The differences between the approaches of the two men to the problems of administration reflects contrasting personalities, education, and experience. Durant was a small, lively, warm man. Nearly everyone called him 'Billy.' Mr. Sloan was tall, quiet, and cool. Increasing deafness heightened his reserve. Nearly everyone called him Mr. Sloan . . . even his closest associates. . . . Where Durant's initial achievements had been in marketing, Sloan's were in production. . . . To this builder of empires [Durant], the details of organization seemed unimportant. But to Alfred Sloan, this lack of attention seemed inexcusable. His rational, precise mind found the promoter's ways of operation wasteful, inefficient, and dangerous."

NCR's culture also changed dramatically as Colonel Edward Deeds began to emphasize teamwork and joint decision making in stark contrast with the autocratic and dictatorial style of John Patterson and his protégé J. H. Barringer. The laissez-faire management philosophy practiced by Levi Strauss and his successors was replaced by strict controls and accountability by Robert Grohman, a company outsider from Playtex and B.V.D. Co., who was brought in to resolve the crisis the company faced in 1973. The death of L. J. Balfour and the subsequent firing of his trusted aide Robert Yeager by the board of directors provided an opportunity for Balfour's new president, Jim Cook, a former vice president at W. R. Grace & Co., to change the culture from one based on paternalism and favoritism to one that was more professional, with decisions based on more universalistic criteria. The Brown Corporation's culture changed twice, first when the son of the founder attempted in the early 1960s to promote participative management in contrast with the autocratic paternalism that characterized his father's tenure, and again in 1974, when Reed Larson, a professional manager, replaced the participative culture of the Brown Corporation with one founded on assumptions that nurtured individual initiative and a reliance on professional decision models to solve organizational problems.

   4. *Conflict—Struggle for Control Between Proponents of Old and New Cultures.* After the introduction of new leadership, a period of conflict ensues between the proponents of the new culture and the old guard, who were either part of or supported the values and assumptions of the previous leadership. These conflicts may be short-lived, as in the cases of General Motors and the Balfour Company, where the old leadership was deposed quickly by new management, or they may last for many years, as in the case of Brown Corporation. The losers in such conflicts feel great resentment toward the new leaders and their values, and therefore they generally are not reeducated to the new beliefs. Most are quickly purged or leave voluntarily. Katz (1983, p. 33) notes that in the Balfour Company, "Yeager's and Cook's management philosophies were at the opposite ends of the spectrum," so Cook fired Yeager's cronies or moved them to other, innocuous positions in the company. Katz concludes that, as a result of these changes, the current management team at Balfour "bears the imprint of Mr. Cook's selective judgment." When Alfred Sloan took over at GM, there was "re-

sentment down the line" between those managers who supported DuPont and Sloan and those who supported William Durant (Cray, 1980, p. 193). One of Sloan's first acts as president was to hire more engineers like himself to supplant Durant's marketing-oriented supporters. Similarly, with the advent of Robert Grohman at Levi Strauss during the 1973 recession, nine of the eleven general managers in Europe and between fifty and seventy-five lower-level managers were fired. This occurred in a firm that traditionally had been known for its paternalism and its emphasis on career employment. Grohman's entry into Levi Strauss was characterized by company oldtimers as a "heart transplant." He began to develop new goals and values that emphasized strict accountability and more impersonal interactions between management and employees. His primary edict was "don't act on your own," whereas the company previously valued independent action. This new set of artifacts, perspectives, values, and assumptions rapidly transformed the Levi Strauss culture. As one oldtimer complained: "Most people working here need a family-type atmosphere. You need to feel involved. But now I feel like Standard Oil or General Motors. I don't feel like I really belong to the whole. 'You're on your own baby. Sink or swim' " (Cray, 1978, p. 239). As a result of these changes at Levi Strauss: "Some of the more entrepreneurial-minded resisted Grohman's constricting pressure. The one-time Levi's salesman who opened Levi Strauss Canada and built it into a $50-million-a-year enterprise could not bend his traditional attitudes, declined a job offer in the home office, and left the company. Two ranking executives shunted aside in the reorganization of the International Group left Levi's for other companies" (Cray, 1978, p. 226).

In the other cases as well, there are similar reports of employees, particularly company oldtimers, being fired, voluntarily leaving, or attempting to sabotage the programs of the new leaders. Indeed, conflict appears to be an integral part of the process of culture change.

5. *The New Leadership Solves the Crisis and Becomes the New Cultural Elite.* Given that the advent of new leader-

ship and the introduction of new ideas and beliefs often create conflicts and resentment among members of an organization, the question arises: How can the new leadership win the conflict and establish a new cultural pattern? There seem to be two conditions that must exist for this to happen. First, the crisis must be resolved—that is, the conditions creating the tension and anxiety in the organization must somehow be ameliorated —and second, the new leadership must be perceived as having resolved the crisis and be given credit for the improvement. This success is generally linked to improved sales and profits after the new leadership takes charge. At Levi Strauss, the proof of the usefulness of the new values espoused by Robert Grohman was found in the company's annual report: "The 1974 annual report validated Grohman's efforts. They had averted further international disasters, confining the decline to a one-quarter lapse. Despite the worldwide recession caused by the Arab oil boycott, Levi Strauss sales increased more than one-third, to $987.6 million. It was the largest increase, both in dollars and as a percentage, in corporate history" (Cray, 1978, p. 227). Once the crisis is resolved, new leaders are often referred to as the "guys who turned things around," or the "saviors" of the firm. Because they are given credit for saving the organization from disaster, the new leaders are given tremendous power and discretion to initiate changes in the company culture.

One interesting point to note, however, is the fact that in each of the cases studied, economic conditions that precipitated the crises also improved after the new leadership emerged. For example, in the case of the Brown Corporation, sales improved from $7 million in 1960 to almost $30 million in 1969 after John Brown, Jr. became CEO in 1959, and they rose from $40 million in 1973 to over $100 million in 1980 after Reed Larson joined the company in 1974. Both executives claimed that their new management practices caused sales to rise, but during both periods, inflation and favorable economic climates probably played a more important role in stimulating sales growth. However, because members of the Brown Corporation believed that, in each case, new leaders caused the turnaround, the power of the new leaders was greatly enhanced, and they were able to take further steps to eliminate rivals and embed their own values and assumptions in the organization. Thus, the leader's ability to persuade members of the organization to attribute improvement to his or her efforts, regardless of whether there is an actual cause-and-effect relationship between the leader's actions and success, is crucial to determining the outcome of the conflicts involved in culture change.

6. *New Symbols, Beliefs, and Structures Institutionalize the New Culture.* As the new leadership establishes its authority, it begins to create new pattern-maintenance symbols, beliefs, and structures to sustain the organization's culture. To symbolize their dominance, the new leaders often promote and hire only employees who are amenable to the new culture. Nonconformists are demoted or fired. Furthermore, they attempt to instill in their subordinates the essential "rightness" of their beliefs. This is often done by pointing out their successes and discrediting the previous regime. History is often reinterpreted by new leaders. After GM head William Durant had fallen from power, he was labeled as "a leader who couldn't control a large corporation." As one of DuPont's men noted: "During Mr. Durant's regime we were never able to get the thing under control. . . . No one knew just how the money had been appropriated and there was no control of how much money was being spent" (Chandler, 1962, p. 127). Such criticism would not have been tolerated during those years when Durant was firmly in control. Durant's unorthodox practices were praised rather than scorned during his tenure as president.

Likewise, John Patterson at NCR was seen as a tyrannical dictator at NCR by the new leadership—a good leader for his time but not for a modern corporation. Robert Grohman was brought in to replace the laissez-faire management that had "failed" at Levi Strauss. Jim Cook turned the Balfour Company into a professional organization, replacing what was viewed as the favoritism and seat-of-the-pants management that previously had prevailed in the company. And Reed Larson debunked the Brown Corporation's participative management of the

1960s, declaring it to be "too groupy—not tough enough" (Dyer, 1984a, p. 157). In each of these cases the juxtaposing of the old, discredited beliefs with the new ideals appears to be one reliable indicator that the culture has indeed changed. (George Orwell's [Orwell, 1949, p. 32] statement that "who controls the past controls the future, [and] who controls the present controls the past" seems quite apropos.)

New structures are often set up to sustain the new culture. In each of the cases where a professional manager was brought in to resolve the crisis, a divisional organizational structure was created. This allowed the professional managers to concentrate power in a corporate headquarters and presented them with opportunities to disseminate their values by creating new divisions led by managers who supported them. At General Motors, for example, the divisional structure was but an artifact of Alfred Sloan's abiding belief that "divisional independence encouraged initiative and innovation," and hence it served to sustain and support these values (Chandler, 1962, p. 133).

Ownership is also frequently restructured to bolster the position of new leadership. New leaders are given shares of company stock or stock options to increase their influence on company affairs.

In summary, this model of culture change suggests that change is triggered by certain crises that call into question the leader's ability to govern. In concert with such crises there occurs a breakdown of the pattern-maintenance symbols, beliefs, and structures that served to sustain the underlying assumptions of the old culture. With the advent of new leadership, a period of conflict between proponents of the old and new cultures ensues. Such conflicts culminate with the new leadership being given credit for resolving the crisis and the expulsion or conversion of adherents to the old beliefs. If the crisis is resolved after the introduction of new leaders and members of the organization attribute this success to the new leaders' efforts, then this firmly establishes the new cultural pattern, and the new leadership is able to take steps to institutionalize the new culture by creating new pattern-maintenance symbols, beliefs, and structures. The new culture is then sustained until some event again calls into question the leadership's abilities and practices, and the cycle of cultural evolution is repeated.

Implications for Managing Cultural Change in Organizations

The model of culture change that has emerged by examining the events surrounding major cultural changes in these organizations appears to have some significant implications for current theory and practice regarding culture change in organizations.

Planning for Culture Change. A number of writers have recently suggested that culture change can be planned and carried out in a more or less rational fashion. Ouchi (1981), for example, outlines a number of steps one might follow to create a "Theory Z" culture. Likewise, Peters and Waterman (1982) present a number of ways to create "excellent" company cultures, and Deal and Kennedy (1982) have their own views about developing new "heroes" or creating new myths to change an organization's culture. Sathe (1983), Schwartz and Davis (1981), Baker (1980), and Silverzweig and Allen (1976) also seem to accept the premise that culture change can be accomplished in a systematic manner by following certain procedures.

However, the events that precipitated changes in the cultures of the companies studied typically were *not* planned. Unanticipated recessions, financial crises, and the illness or death of key leaders were instrumental in triggering cultural change in these companies. Serendipity and historical accidents played critical roles, and while it may be possible to anticipate such occurrences, managers' abilities to control these events are negligible.

It may be possible to manufacture crises, but such attempts are likely to be transparent to employees and thus to prove futile. This implies that to initiate culture change, key leaders must have a sense of timing that enables them to seize those opportunities for change during the crises that inevitably occur over a firm's lifetime. Thus, a certain sense of opportunism is essential to begin the process of culture change.

The Role of Leadership in Culture Change. Despite the fact that certain events stimulating culture change are largely uncontrollable, there are some strategic choices available to those attempting to change a given culture. According to the model of change described here, the most important decision in culture change concerns the selection of a new leader, inasmuch as a new leader who enters an organization during a period of crisis has unique opportunities to transform the organization's culture by bringing and embedding new artifacts, perspectives, values, and assumptions into the organization. Leaders do indeed appear to be the creators and transmitters of culture. In each case cited here, the firm's board of directors had the opportunity to select the kind of leader they believed would be able to resolve the crisis.

One of the common features of the five cases selected is the success of each new leader who emerged during a crisis. After the new leader's arrival, each company's sales and profits rose within a few months or years, and each company became successful. Because economic conditions precipitated many of the crises and the economy improved after each introduction of new leaders, we cannot tell whether the actions of the new leaders were directly or indirectly responsible for the improvement. What is clear, however, is that each leader *believed* he was responsible for the company's success, and he *convinced company employees* that he should be given credit for the improvements. While these beliefs may be incorrect, the power of the new leaders was enhanced by such attributions. Thus, new leaders entering an organization that has encountered a crisis are in a particularly powerful position to initiate change because (1) members of the organization are looking for new ideas to resolve the crisis, and (2) the new leader is likely to receive credit for any subsequent successes, even though exogenous factors may be more significant determinants of improvements in sales or profits than the actions of the new leader. The combination of a crisis and new leadership provides fertile ground for initiating culture change in organizations.

Crisis and Leadership Paradoxes. In each of the corporate histories presented, culture change was precipitated by a major

crisis. However, there were many times during the histories of
these firms when there were crises and the culture did not
change. In fact, in those instances where the organization overcame the crisis, the prevailing artifacts, perspectives, values, and
assumptions were not undermined but further solidified. Resolving the crisis reaffirmed their validity and usefulness; hence,
the culture was reinforced. At Levi Strauss there are many
heroic tales of how Levi Strauss and his descendants were able
to overcome potentially devastating crises and save the firm
from disaster. There are numerous stories of how the family
overcame great obstacles to keep the company operating immediately after the San Francisco earthquake of 1906. The family's ability to weather such crises served to strengthen the
bonds of loyalty and commitment to the family and to the culture that had been created. Thus, paradoxically, a crisis can
serve to either undermine or strengthen cultural values.

There were also a number of times throughout the histories of these firms when the leadership changed but the culture did not. Succession itself did not produce change, for in
times when the organization prospered, new leaders were generally selected on the basis of whether they exhibited and espoused the established beliefs that had led to prosperity. Conformity to honored beliefs, not new ideas, was valued. Thus,
leadership succession, rather than a harbinger of change, can be
a celebration of shared beliefs inasmuch as the new leader is a
symbol of continuity and not change.

Thus, neither a crisis nor leadership succession are clear
indicators that culture change is taking place. Both must occur
in concert, for one without the other is not sufficient to trigger
change.

Conflict and Culture Change. As the model of culture
change illustrates, the change process is fraught with conflict—
managers are fired, employees quit, struggles for power are
common. Such conflicts are largely neglected by those who suggest that culture change can be planned. Human beings are
often perceived as being fairly malleable in learning and adopting new perspectives, values, and assumptions by those who see
planned culture change as possible. But changes in organiza-

tional cultures always accompany changes in the way power is distributed in the organization. Some members of the organization gain by culture change, and others lose. Hence, the potential losers fight vigorously to maintain the status quo, to sustain those values and beliefs on which their positions are based. Because they are unwilling to part with their own beliefs and submit to the ideology of the new leaders—hence relinquishing their power—the old guard is more often purged than socialized to a new set of beliefs.

One key element of culture change connected to the problem of power redistribution and conflict is the elimination of key symbols, beliefs, or structures that sustain the culture. This can be done systematically if those symbols, beliefs, and structures that reinforce the prevailing culture can be identified and if the extent to which these pattern-maintenance factors can be modified or eliminated can be determined. The conflicts inherent in such an undertaking will undoubtably be great.

Thus, to engage in managing culture change, leaders must be willing and able to manage conflicts, exert power, and recognize that all parties are not likely to be happy with the outcome. Some valuable employees may quit, and others may have to be fired or reassigned. This is not likely to be an easy process, but it can be a manageable one.

Culture Change and Adaptation. The five companies that have been highlighted illustrate a variety of different cultural patterns. Some cultures are founded on assumptions fostering founder domination and control, and others rest on more egalitarian relationships and reflect a high degree of trust among members of the organization. Although only a small number of cases were studied, an examination of the relationship between culture and organizational effectiveness reveals that no one pattern is associated with a successful organization. John Patterson was successful at NCR by exerting highly autocratic control, while his successor Deeds was successful by developing an amiable team. With a laissez-faire orientation, Levi Strauss grew quickly. The Brown Corporation grew steadily under both autocratic and participative management, while the Balfour Company prospered under the professionalism brought to it by Jim

Cook. GM grew dramatically under men who operated under a very different set of assumptions.

Although the evidence from these cases does not indicate that a single cultural pattern is likely to be associated with organizational effectiveness, this does not mean that all cultural patterns have similar consequences. For example, the three cultural patterns witnessed in the Brown Corporation had different effects. The culture during founder John Brown, Sr.'s tenure that emphasized founder and family dominance fostered a high degree of dependency among Brown's employees. With most of the power and knowledge regarding the firm's operations in the hands of John Sr., subordinates had few opportunities to exercise independent action or magnify their managerial abilities. This high degree of dependence on the founder left the firm in a precarious position. The sudden departure of the founder could create chaos, and, indeed, John Sr.'s illness in the late 1940s posed a serious problem for the firm and the family. John Jr. admitted that the family would probably have sold the business had John Sr. not recovered. Thus, the culture of that period allowed for little growth and development of John Sr.'s subordinates, and dependence on the founder for direction made the firm vulnerable if the founder were to die or to be disabled. However, the leadership abilities of John Sr. and a favorable economic climate were largely responsible for the company's success during the 1940s and 1950s.

The culture of the 1960s, on the other hand, fostered both independence and collaboration between members of the organization. This proved to be useful as coordinating the various subunits of the company became a key problem because of the company's growth in the sixties. By delegating authority, lower-level managers expanded their ability to act independently, and this mixture of high collaboration and freedom seems to be related to a number of management and technical innovations developed during this period.

The culture nurtured by the professional manager Reed Larson had a different set of consequences. With efficiency as the salient criterion, Larson attempted to improve the organization's performance. Controls were installed and deadwood eliminated. Individual achievement was emphasized, and participation was de-emphasized. These measures appear to have helped the company weather the recession in the early 1970s. Under this cultural pattern, efficiency (based on the company's efficiency measures) seems to have improved. However, worker turnover and dissatisfaction have also increased.

In summary, although each cultural pattern does have different consequences for the organization and the people in it, no single pattern appears necessarily to be related to organizational growth, market share, sales, profits, or other such criteria of organizational effectiveness. Although some writers have suggested that a particular kind of culture is the most effective, the organizations we have studied represent a variety of cultural patterns associated with a successful organization. Factors such as the organization's environment, stage of development, or size may largely determine the type of cultural pattern that would be the most successful. Indeed, the changing cultural patterns in these companies seem to reflect adaptive responses to major changes in their environments or changes within the organization. Thus, assuming that culture change is designed to help the organization adapt to new environmental conditions, these two questions should be asked before any attempt to change a culture is made: (1) Why should the culture of the organization be changed? (2) What should the new culture look like?

Conclusion

Although many of the theories of culture change described at the beginning of this chapter do reflect some facets of culture change, they tend to focus on only certain aspects of the change process and are therefore incomplete. As we have seen, the process of culture change is not often predictable or controllable, and the process may be preempted at any stage of the model. But by becoming aware of the preconditions for culture change, steps can be taken systematically to plan for and manage those stages of the process that are manageable and to take measures to ensure that a given change will have every chance of succeeding. Coping with crises, leadership changes, and conflict are all part of the process of culture change. While managing such a process may be difficult, there are substantial rewards when a new cultural pattern evolves that enhances both individual and organizational development.

References

Allyn, S. C. *My Half Century with NCR.* New York: McGraw-Hill, 1967.

Baker, E. L. "Managing Organizational Culture." *Management Review,* 1980, *69,* 8–13.

Becker, H. S., Geer, B., Hughes, E. C., and Strauss, A. L. *Boys in White.* New Brunswick, N.J.: Transaction Books, 1961.

Bem, D. J. *Beliefs, Attitudes, and Human Affairs.* Belmont, Calif.: Brooks/Cole, 1970.

Chandler, A. D., Jr. *Strategy and Structure.* Cambridge, Mass.: MIT Press, 1962.

Cray, E. *Levi's.* Boston: Houghton Mifflin, 1978.

Cray, E. *Chrome Colossus.* New York: McGraw-Hill, 1980.

Deal, T. E., and Kennedy, A. A. *Corporate Cultures: The Rites and Rituals of Corporate Life.* Reading, Mass.: Addison-Wesley, 1982.

Dyer, W. G., Jr. "Culture in Organizations: A Case Study and Analysis." Working paper no. 1279-82, Sloan School of Management, Massachusetts Institute of Technology, Feb. 1982.

Dyer, W. G., Jr. "Cultural Evolution in Organizations: The Case of a Family Owned Firm." Unpublished doctoral dissertation, Sloan School of Management, Massachusetts Institute of Technology, 1984a.

Dyer, W. G., Jr. "Organizational Culture: Analysis and Change." In W. G. Dyer (ed.), *Strategies for Managing Change.* Reading, Mass.: Addison-Wesley, 1984b.

Katz, D. "Structural Change: Cultural or Strategic." Unpublished masters thesis, Sloan School of Management, Massachusetts Institute of Technology, 1983.

Kluckhohn, F. R., and Strodtbeck, F. L. *Variations in Value Orientations.* Evanston, Ill.: Harper & Row, 1961.

Orwell, G. *1984.* New York: New American Library, 1949.

O'Toole, J. J. "Corporate and Managerial Cultures." In C. L. Cooper (ed.), *Behavioral Problems in Organizations*. Englewood Cliffs, N.J.: Prentice-Hall, 1979.

Ouchi, W. G. *Theory Z*. Reading, Mass.: Addison-Wesley, 1981.

Parsons, T., and Shils, E. A. (eds.). *Toward a General Theory of Action*. New York: Harper & Row, 1951.

Peters, T. J. "Symbols, Patterns, and Settings: An Optimistic Case for Getting Things Done." *Organizational Dynamics*, 1978, 7 (2), 3-23.

Peters, T. J., and Waterman, R. H., Jr. *In Search of Excellence: Lessons from America's Best-Run Companies*. New York: Harper & Row, 1982.

Pettigrew, A. M. "On Studying Organizational Cultures." *Administrative Science Quarterly*, 1979, 24, 570-581.

Sathe, V. "Implications of Corporate Culture: A Manager's Guide to Action." *Organizational Dynamics*, 1983, 12 (2), 5-23.

Schein, E. H. *Process Consultation: Its Role in Organization Development*. Reading, Mass.: Addison-Wesley, 1969.

Schein, E. H. "Does Japanese Management Style Have a Message for American Managers?" *Sloan Management Review*, 1981, 23, 55-68.

Schein, E. H. "The Role of the Founder in Creating Organizational Cultures." *Organizational Dynamics*, 1983, 12 (1), 13-28.

Schwartz, H. M., and Davis, S. M. "Matching Corporate Cultures and Business Strategy." *Organizational Dynamics*, 1981, 10 (1), 30-48.

Silverzweig, S., and Allen, R. F. "Changing the Corporate Culture." *Sloan Management Review*, 1976, 17, 33-49.

Thirteen

How to Decipher and Change Corporate Culture

Vijay Sathe

Two basic arguments will be made in this chapter: first, that behavior change does not necessarily produce culture change, and second, that managers can benefit by taking this into account when conceiving and implementing organizational change. The following topics will be covered:

1. Definition of culture
2. How to decipher culture
3. How to assess resistance to culture change
4. How to influence culture change
5. How to know if the attempted culture change is occurring
6. Alternatives to major culture change

Accounts from the experience of the managers of several companies who have succeeded or failed in creating culture change will be presented for purposes of illustration. In addition, the case of Cummins Engine Company and its operating head, Jim Henderson, will be used to provide one in-depth illustration of successful culture change. A detailed written account of this case, along with two companion videotapes, has been published elsewhere (Browne, Vancil, and Sathe, 1982). Only the essential story line is reported here.

Cummins Engine Company and Jim Henderson

Cummins Engine Company, headquartered in Columbus, Indiana, was incorporated in 1919. From modest beginnings as a machining shop, the company had become a major industrial firm by the mid 1970s, with some 20,000 employees worldwide, net sales of $800 million, and after-tax profit of $25 million. It was at this time that Jim Henderson, the company's operating head, managed a difficult inventory situation and succeeded eventually in modifying the company's management culture.

The company was founded by Clessie Cummins, but it was Irwin Miller, chief executive officer, and Don Tull, chief operating officer, who had the most profound influence on the Cummins organization during the period from the mid 1930s to the mid 1960s. During this time the company was closely directed from the top. Tull was constantly present on the plant floor, checking the work flow, quality control, employee morale, inventory levels, and shipment schedules. Because the company was largely under one roof during these years, costly and cumbersome management systems were not required.

In the mid 1960s, as the company grew and its facilities expanded, Miller saw a need to build a management team. He began to turn top management responsibilities over to younger, more professionally trained managers. When Tull stepped up as chairman of the executive committee in 1969, Jim Henderson became executive vice-president for operations.

Henderson was one of a number of young managers whom Miller attracted into the company in the sixties. Henderson continued this hiring policy, but most of the senior operating management and staff positions were still filled by older managers with proven track records.

As the seventies rolled along, plant capacity in Columbus

was woefully inadequate to meet the rising demands of the engine business. Expansion of plant facilities was first undertaken on a crash basis in Columbus in 1970, but the rationalization and development of formal management and control systems to support a multi-plant operating mode had to wait until later. In the meantime, inventory control for all three plants built in Columbus continued to be carried out at the main engine plant.

In spite of its dramatic growth, in many ways Cummins Engine Company still remained a small-town company in the mid 1970s. It was the largest employer in Columbus, and its history of close relations with an independent local union fostered a sense of special concern for local issues.

Perhaps the most salient management process in the mid 1970s was still the traditional exercise of the art of expediting. The company emphasized extraordinary service to its customers, which gave it an important competitive edge over other suppliers, and a good manager in top management's eyes was one who could always find a way to expedite a special customer request.

Since the mid 1960s top management had been pushing to professionalize management and build a more rational and systematic set of organizational systems. The reality, however, was that demand was growing so fast that only the expert old hands who knew how to coax the last ounce of productivity out of the operating system could keep the production schedule from slipping.

In late 1974, anticipating a sharp downturn, top management viewed the company's rising inventory levels, approaching eighty days' supply, with growing concern. A major discrepancy between the materials management records and the financial accounting records relating to inventory levels also was a source of management concern.

Miller and Tull urged Henderson to take the old, hard-line approach to controlling inventories. During the periodic business cycle downturns that in the past hit the truck manufacturing industry and its component suppliers especially hard, Tull had not hesitated to batten down the hatches. He would let part of the work force go, cut off all capital spending, and cancel orders to suppliers. Tull and the controller could be found on such occasions out on the receiving dock turning away deliveries.

Henderson asked for an opportunity to solve the problem in his own way, however. The practice of managing each downturn in the economy with a top-down "firefighting" approach made it difficult to get managers to take personal initiative for solving such problems; they had learned to wait for the person at the top to tell them what to do. This band-aid approach also delayed the installation of formal systems, such as a materials requisition planning system, that the company needed to prevent the periodic recurrence of this problem. Henderson had concluded that the old way of operating, which had worked in a single-plant environment, would not work in the existing multiplant environment. He wanted to solve the inventory problem in such a way that it also yielded two other desired outcomes: he wanted his managers to take more personal responsibility for solving such problems, and he wanted the company to become committed to installing and using appropriate information and control systems.

Henderson began to meet weekly with his group heads, their plant managers, and the controller to monitor the inventory situation. Henderson also made some unannounced plant visits to draw attention to the inventory problem and to signal to his managers that he was not going to correct this problem for them. These actions helped the company's managers to cope in a manner that went somewhat against the grain of their culture. Over the next several years, two shared assumptions were changed. First, the assumption that "top-management will tell us what to do when there is a problem" was replaced by the assumption that "all managers should take personal responsibility for solving problems." Second, the important shared assumption, "operate informally without systems," was modified to "use systems to do the routine work, operate informally to expedite."

In this case, behavioral changes led to cultural changes. Why this occurred here, but may not always occur, is explained in this chapter. First, we need to better understand culture and how it can be deciphered.

Definition of Culture

There are many definitions of culture (Kroeber and Kluckhohn, 1952). Early authors (for example, Tylor, 1871) defined culture broadly to include knowledge, belief, art, law, morals, and customs. Two major schools of thought in the field of cultural anthropology have influenced later work. Adaptationists view culture as what is directly observable about the members of a community—that is, their patterns of behavior, speech, and use of material objects. Members of the ideational school, on the other hand, define culture as what is shared in community members' *minds*—that is, the beliefs, values, and ideas people hold in common (Keesing, 1974; Swartz and Jordan, 1980).

This is one reason the subject is confusing: different people think of different slices of reality when they talk about culture. Schein (1983) has proposed a three-level model to integrate various views of culture, which we will use here with some modification. First, Schein uses the term *values* to denote espoused values, whereas the terms *beliefs* and *values* are used here to denote those assumptions that people actually hold; that is, the assumptions they have internalized (Bem, 1970; Rokeach, 1968). Second, Schein focuses on preconscious and unconscious assumptions because these are powerful. Such assumptions are hard to discover and debate because they are taken for granted; in fact, people may not even be aware of them until they are violated or challenged. The definition of culture used here includes conscious assumptions because, even though these are easier to detect and debate, they too have a strong influence on behavior and are hard to change. People do not easily give up internalized beliefs and values, whether consciously or unconsciously held (Bem, 1970; Rokeach, 1968), whereas beliefs and values that people merely espouse or comply with are more easily relinquished (Kelman, 1958).

The first of the three levels of culture is composed of technology, art, audible and visible behavior patterns, and other aspects of culture that are easy to see but hard to interpret without an understanding of the other levels. This is the slice of cultural reality that the adaptionists have been most interested in. We will denote this level by the terms *organizational behavior patterns,* or *behavior.* The second level of culture reveals how people explain, rationalize, and justify what they say and do as a community; how they "make sense" of the first level of culture. We will denote this level with the term *justifications of behavior.*

The third level of culture goes deeper still and is the level that the ideational school has been most interested in. It consists of the ideas and assumptions that govern people's justifications and behavior. We will denote this level by the term *culture,* which we will define specifically as the set of important assumptions (often unstated) that members of a community held in common. Two basic types of assumptions are people's beliefs and values—not what people *say* their beliefs and values are or those they comply with because of the demands of others but those beliefs and values people consider to be their own; that is, those they have *internalized.* Because people may not become conscious of the beliefs and values they hold until they are violated or challenged and, even then, will resist changing them (Bem, 1970; Kelman, 1958; Rokeach, 1968), the effects of culture defined in this way are not only subtle and powerful but persistent as well.

This definition does not imply that only the third level of culture is important. Rather, although all three levels are interrelated, they are sufficiently distinct so that combining them is not analytically advantageous (Geertz, 1973). Managers are interested in how people behave as well as in what they believe, but we know a lot more about how to create organizational behavior change (Beer, 1980; Schein and Bennis, 1965) than we do about how to create organizational belief and value change. We will see that behavior change does not necessarily produce a corresponding change in beliefs and values, in part because of the intervening level of justification of behavior. These processes cannot be understood and managed if all three levels are included under the culture label, but organizational insight and analytical power is gained when a different term is used for each level and all three levels are examined separately. Let us now take a closer look at this definition of culture by examining two of its major elements: content and strength.

The content of a culture influences the direction of behavior. Content is determined not by an aggregate of assumptions but by how the important assumptions interrelate and form particular patterns. Among the variety of beliefs and values that the people in a community may hold, the important assumptions are those that are widely enough shared and highly enough placed relative to other assumptions in the community so as to be of major significance to the life of the community. A key feature of the pattern of a culture is the relative importance, or ordering, of its cultural assumptions.

As Schein (1983) has explained, the content of a culture ultimately derives from two principal sources: (1) the pattern of assumptions that founders, leaders, and organizational employees bring with them when they join the organization (which, in turn, depends on their own experiences in the cultures of the regional, national, religious, ethnic, occupational, or professional communities from which they come), and (2) the actual experiences that people in the organization have had in working out solutions to the basic problems of adaptation to the external environment and internal integration. In short, the content of culture derives from a combination of prior assumptions and new learning experiences.

The strength of a culture influences the intensity of behavior. Three specific features of culture determine its strength: (1) *thickness*—how many important shared assumptions there are—(2) extent of sharing—how widely these assumptions are shared in the organization—and (3) clarity of ordering—how clear it is that some assumptions are more important than others. The strongest cultures are thicker, more widely shared, and more clearly ordered and have a more profound influence on organizational behavior. Such cultures are also most resistant to change.

What makes some cultures stronger than others? Two important factors are the number of employees in the organization and their geographical dispersion. A small work force and localized operations facilitate the growth of a strong culture because it is easier for beliefs and values to develop and become

widely shared. But larger organizations with worldwide operations, such as International Business Machines, can also have
strong cultures that derive from a continuity of strong leadership that has consistently emphasized the same beliefs and
values and from a relatively stable and long-tenured work force.
Under these conditions, a consistent set of enduring beliefs and
values can take hold over time and become widely shared and
clearly ordered.

Deciphering a Culture

The internalized beliefs and values that members of a
community share cannot be measured easily or observed directly, nor can what people say about them be relied on when deciphering a culture. Other evidence, both historical and current,
must be taken into account to infer what the culture is.

The managers at Cummins shared five important assumptions, ordered as follows:

1. We provide highly responsive, quality customer service.
2. We get things done well and quickly (to expedite).
3. We operate informally without systems.
4. Top management will tell us what to do if there is a prob-
    lem.
5. The company is part of the family.

The procedure used to decipher the Cummins Company culture
is presented in the following paragraphs.

Inferring the Content of Culture. Each important shared
assumption may be inferred from one or more manifestations of
culture; that is, the shared sayings, shared doings, and shared
feelings members of the organization experience. The aim is to
discover a pattern of important assumptions that help "make
sense" of the cultural manifestations, and the challenge is to in-
sure that the "making sense" is from the point of view of the
"natives," those whose culture is being deciphered (Swartz and
Jordan, 1980). With this in mind, three basic questions can be
explored to infer the content of culture from its manifestations.

1. *What is the background of the founders and others*

who followed them? An understanding of the background and personality of the founders and others who helped mold the culture offer important clues about the content of culture. For example, Irwin Miller at Cummins strongly believed in community service and in "rooting out bureaucratic behavior," which led to two important cultural assumptions: "The company is part of the family," and "We operate informally without systems." Also, most of the Cummins employees came from the local community, and many were from families whose members had previously or currently worked at the company, further reinforcing the cultural belief that the company was part of the family.

2. *How did the organization respond to crises or other critical events, and what was learned from these experiences?* Since culture evolves and is learned, focusing on stressful periods in an organization's history can provide two important clues that help decipher a culture. First, it may reveal how particular assumptions came to be formed. For example, the inventory crisis at Cummins ultimately caused the belief in operating informally without systems to be transformed into a new belief in using systems to do routine work and relying on informal operation to expedite. Second, focusing on stressful periods in a company's history, particularly those that were traumatic for the organization, also reveals the *ordering* of the cultural assumptions, which is otherwise hard to decipher because such assumptions may not ordinarily conflict with each other. During a stressful period, however, the organization may be forced to choose between two important assumptions, thus revealing its priorities.

Although Cummins did not like to lay people off, for example, it did so during periodic downturns. This suggests that the first four cultural assumptions, which were not affected by these traumatic events, were more important than assumption number 5, that the company is part of the family, which was violated to some extent. Similarly, the 1974 inventory crisis brought assumptions 1 and 2 into conflict with assumptions 3 and 4. Since the latter were questioned and were eventually modified but the former were not, assumptions 1 and 2 must be considered more central than assumptions 3 and 4.

The people at Cummins had so thoroughly bought into the values of highly responsive, quality customer service and expeditiousness that these ideals had become more than strategic objectives and operational directives. They had become taken-for-granted, shared assumptions that were a central part of the Cummins management culture. These assumptions were never questioned by the managers at Cummins, even during times of stress. Indeed, the purchasing managers during the inventory crisis of 1974 went so far as to *ignore* higher management directives and ordered extra parts because they believed customer service would otherwise be adversely affected.

3. *Who are considered deviant in the culture? How does the organization respond to them?* In a sense, deviants represent and define a culture's boundaries. An understanding of who and what is considered deviant in a culture helps in deciphering it. For instance, Cummins hired many MBAs from among the brightest and the best in the early 1960s, many of whom did not make it in the company. Those that survived were culturally compatible, and many of those who disappeared were deviants —people who believed in different systems and procedures or who believed their talent and professional education gave them special status in the company ("I am a hot-shot MBA, so I'll teach these guys how to do it right"). These people violated important cultural assumptions (expedite, operate informally without systems, the company is part of the family) which are revealed by examining why these people were rejected by the culture.

A cultural assumption may be so consistently adhered to and taken for granted that almost no one ever violates it. Such an assumption may be particularly hard to discover. Its centrality and power may only be revealed on those rare occasions when someone knowingly or inadvertently violates it, incurring the wrath and fury of the entire community. An example of such an assumption in academia is intellectual integrity. A recent case in point is the disbelief and heated controversy surrounding the chairman of medicine at a prestigious school who has been accused of plagiarism ("Stanford Investigates Plagiarism Charges," 1984). Much can be learned about a culture by looking for such infrequent but critical incidents that deeply offend the people in the community. There is no indication of such a critical incident at Cummins.

Investigator's Skill and Status. When deciphering a culture, it is important to consider who is conducting the investigation because this also determines what is revealed. Some people are more skilled than others at reading culture. Skill comes with practice; those who have been exposed to different cultures will have had greater opportunity to develop these skills because culture is more readily deciphered in contrast to other cultures (Louis, 1980).

The investigator's status relative to the culture being studied also affects what is revealed. A different view of the culture will be seen by established members, newcomers, and outsiders.

The established member of a culture has the benefit of experience in the culture and the native's point of view. This asset is also a liability, however, because some cultural assumptions may be so taken for granted by the established member that he or she may find it difficult to see them. Both newcomers and outsiders can help in this situation.

Since newcomers are not deeply immersed in the culture and can see it in contrast with the culture of the organization they are coming from, they are more likely to notice the cultural manifestations, and *perhaps* the underlying assumptions, than are the established members who take them for granted. The qualifier is important because the newcomer may not as yet have access to all necessary information, especially that which is considered sensitive and embarrassing by the established members, and the newcomer may also misinterpret the culture's content if he or she does not yet understand the native point of view. On the other hand, if the newcomer can team up with one or more established members (and, conversely, if an established member can rely on one or more newcomers) to explore the culture jointly, the advantages that each party brings could make then the process of discovery considerably more efficient (Schein, 1983).

Outsiders are likely to be at an even greater disadvantage

than newcomers in terms of access to sensitive information and in understanding the native point of view, but they have the benefits of greater objectivity and contrast. Outsiders may find it difficult to decipher the cultural content from its surface manifestations, which they can readily notice, unless they can enlist the help of those who are inside the culture. Conversely, established members of a culture can also benefit from help from outsiders in deciphering their culture.

This author is very familiar with the Cummins situation but is an outsider. The culture has been deciphered from information provided by company insiders, including Jim Henderson, now the president of Cummins. However, since the author did not jointly explore the Cummins culture with these people, the description given here may be deficient and might have been improved had a joint exploration been undertaken.

Estimating the Strength of Culture. In inferring the content of culture, how many important shared assumptions the company's culture has and how clearly they appear to be ordered were determined as well. The extent of sharing, the third property that affects the strength of a culture, remains to be assessed.

One clue to the extent of sharing is how extensive the cultural manifestations are from which the inferences are made —what is the *proportion* of people in the organization who demonstrate that they share the same physical attributes, slogans, practices, and feelings? In general, a high proportion indicates that beliefs and values are widely shared. Other clues may be obtained by examining the factors mentioned earlier that influence the strength of culture.

The Cummins culture was relatively strong because there were several important assumptions that appeared to be widely shared and clearly ordered. History, leadership, organizational size, geographical dispersion, and the stability of the work force all had an impact. In its sixty-year history, Cummins had only two generations of top management, and the first, highly influential generation (Irwin Miller and Don Tull) were still serving as chairman of the board and chairman of the executive committee, respectively, at the time of the case. Cummins was medium sized, most of its operations were close together, and employee and management turnover was relatively low.

How To Assess the Resistance to Culture Change

Culture change may involve a change in the content or in the strength of the existing organizational culture. Let us examine each separately before considering their joint effect.

Incremental Vs. Radical Change in Culture's Content. A significant change in a culture's content is involved to the extent that:

1. The change involves a great number of important shared assumptions.
2. The change involves central (high-ranked) shared assumptions.
3. The change involves a movement toward more alien (less intrinsically appealing) shared assumptions.

The fewer and less central the assumptions changed and the less movement there is toward an alien culture, the less significant is the change in the culture's content.

"Alien" Vs. Intrinsically Appealing Beliefs and Values. Three interrelated considerations help determine the intrinsic appeal of the beliefs and values in question. First, beliefs and values that are shared at some level by members of an organization are more intrinsically appealing than those that are not. At Cummins, the value of a close working relationship with the union was not shared widely enough nor was it placed high enough in the company's ordering of beliefs and values to be considered a cultural value. However, this value was more intrinsically appealing for Cummins managers than an anti-union value, because many of them valued the role of the union and desired a close relationship with it.

Second, beliefs and values that were once part of the organization's culture but have since atrophied and are no longer important shared assumptions are more intrinsically appealing than beliefs and values that were never part of the organization's culture. At Cummins, the assumption that "small is beautiful" was part of the company's heritage, but this value had atrophied after the expansion of the war years and was not part of the company's culture by the mid 1970s. This "dormant value" could have been more easily adopted by the people at Cummins than the value "bigger is better," for instance, which was never part of the company's culture.

Third, beliefs and values that are supported by the cultures of the regional, national, religious, ethnic, occupational, and professional communities to which the people in the organization belong are more intrinsically appealing than are beliefs and values that do not find such support in the cultures of the relevant wider communities. For example, "service to the community" was an important value in the local community from which many of those at Cummins came. Accordingly, beliefs and values consistent with the notion of community service were more intrinsically appealing to the Cummins managers than were beliefs and values that ran counter to this notion.

Resistance to Culture Change. A radical change in the content of a culture is more difficult to accomplish than is an incremental change, and cultural resistance to change is greater in a strong culture than in a weak culture. Thus, the degree of cultural resistance to change may be economically represented as follows:

Resistance to culture change	=	Magnitude of the change in the content of the culture; that is, radical versus incremental change in culture's content	X	Strength of the prevailing culture; that is, strong versus weak culture

The culture change at Cummins involved two of the five important shared assumptions. Assumption number 3, "we operate informally without systems," underwent a moderate change to "we use systems to do routine work; we operate informally to expedite." Assumption number 4, "top management will tell us what to do if there is a problem," was substantially altered to "all managers should take personal responsibility for problem solving." Overall, the magnitude of the change in the content of the culture was more than incremental but less than radical because the change involved only two of the five important shared assumptions at Cummins, and the two in question were lower-ranked assumptions. However, because Cummins had a relatively strong culture, the overall resistance was considerable, and these cultural changes took four to five years to accomplish. In general, the greater the cultural resistance, the more difficult and time consuming the culture change will be.

How to Influence Culture Change

Managers interested in producing culture change must understand and intervene in each of the basic processes that cause culture to perpetuate itself. As Figure 1 shows, there are two basic approaches to effecting a desired culture change: (1) getting people in the organization to accept a new pattern of beliefs and values (processes 1, 2, and 3) and (2) adding and socializing people into the organization and removing people from the organization as appropriate (processes 4 and 5). Let us consider each of these processes in turn.

Behavior. The process by which culture influences behavior is consistent with the conventional wisdom; that is, that beliefs and values influence behavior (process 1 in Figure 1). However, the opposite is also true. A considerable body of social science literature indicates that, under certain conditions, to be discussed shortly, one of the most effective ways of changing people's beliefs and values is to first change their corresponding behaviors. The general techniques for creating behavior change are well covered in the existing management literature (Beer, 1980; Schein and Bennis, 1965), but these methods must be used more restrictively if culture change is to be produced. The motivation to change behavior must be based on intrinsic motivators; it cannot rely exclusively, or even excessively, on extrinsic forms. For example, consider the experience of one company and its chief executive officer, Matt Holt.

Figure 1. How Culture Tends to Perpetuate Itself.

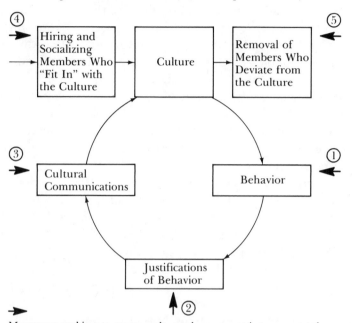

Managers seeking to create culture *change* must intervene at these points. Conversely, managers seeking to *maintain* the prevailing culture must counteract any such intervention by others and prevent any weakening of these processes.

Buffeted by shifting market forces and management turnover, the corporate business strategy had lacked coherent direction. Matt Holt's mandate was to take a longer-term view of the business and to create a technology-driven organization. Analysis conducted with the help of outside consultants indicated that a cultural metamorphosis was needed to accomplish this. A reorganization followed, including changes in the measurement and reward system to encourage the required behavior.

Holt realized there would be a wait-and-see period while people tried to figure out "whether they really mean it." He knew that his true intentions would be judged on the basis of what he did, not just what he said. Accordingly, he tried to ensure that the management systems evaluated and rewarded the required behavior, and he conducted his own affairs—that is, use of his time, visits with company personnel, pats on the back —to reinforce and support what the new formal systems were signalling. Two years later, there had been some improvements. People appeared to be "doing the right things," allocating their time and resources as prescribed by the new systems. Missing, however, was the missionary zeal, the sense of commitment and excitement that Matt had hoped to inject into the life of the company as people came to identify with and share his vision of the mission. Some behavior change had occurred here, but no culture change. One reason for this was Holt's heavy reliance on extrinsic motivation.

Justifications of Behavior. Behavior change does not necessarily produce culture change because of the intervening process of justification of behavior, the second level of culture in the scheme proposed by Schein (1983) (process 2 in Figure 1). This is what happened in the case of Matt Holt. People were behaving as called for by the new formal systems, but they continued to share the old beliefs and values and "explained" their new behavior to themselves by noting the external justifications for it (Aronson, 1976; Bem, 1970)—for example, "We are doing this because it is required of us," and "We are doing this because of the incentives." There was behavior compliance, not culture commitment. In a very real sense, people in this case were behaving the way they were because they felt they had no choice, not because they fundamentally believed in their actions or valued them.

Thus, one reason culture perpetuates itself is that, even if behavior is changed (process 1 in Figure 1), people tend to rationalize it in terms of external justifications (process 2) and continue to adhere to the prevailing pattern of beliefs and values. Managers attempting to create culture change must remain alert to this danger and try to counteract it by taking the following three steps.

The first step, which may appear counterintuitive, is to minimize the opportunity for external justification by inducing the appropriate behavior change with a *minimal* use of rewards, punishments, and other extrinsic forms of motivation (Aronson, 1976, pp. 109–117). This doesn't "feel right" at first to many of us who have become used to offering incentives to get what we want. However, people are likely to cooperate just for the incentives, rather than because they fundamentally believe in what they have been asked to do. This is exactly what happened in the case of Matt Holt. In contrast, Jim Henderson at Cummins offered no financial incentives and relied minimally on other extrinsic motivators (principally, some unannounced plant visits to draw attention to the inventory problems in order to produce the desired behavior). This approach took time and exposed him to personal risk and criticism from his superiors, Irwin Miller and Don Tull, for not acting more forcefully to solve the growing inventory crisis. Henderson understood that the recommended "strong measures" would indeed solve the short-term inventory problems but would not help bring about the new culture he was seeking to create, in which his managers would take more personal responsibility for inventory-control problems (rather than waiting for directives from the top) and in which new systems to prevent the periodic recurrence of inventory-control problems could be introduced and maintained.

The second step follows from the first: to the extent possible, the necessary behavior change should be induced by using intrinsic forms of motivation. Essentially, this means that people must be made to see the inherent worth of what it is they are being asked to do. As Schein (1973) has explained, one way to do this is to persuade people to unlearn or question their current pattern of beliefs and values by helping them to see that their assumptions are not confirmed, or are actually disconfirmed, by reality. This lack of confirmation, and disconfirmation, which are typically accompanied by pain, guilt, anxiety, and lack of self-confidence, provide the necessary intrinsic motivation to learn the new behavior. Holt, for instance, did very little in this area. In contrast, the weekly inventory meetings that Henderson instituted at Cummins provided a forum for joint exploration that led people to see the value of the new approach he was advocating.

Some use of extrinsic motivators may be unavoidable. A third step, then, that managers interested in producing culture change must use is to nullify inappropriate rationalizations of the new behavior. A somewhat drastic technique for doing this is to give people an "out"—those who do not accept the new pattern of beliefs and values may be given the option of leaving the company or transferring to a different organization. If it is perceived as a feasible and a real option, giving people the opportunity to leave can be a powerful tool in producing culture change, not only because it weeds out those who are unlikely to accept the new pattern of beliefs and values (process 5 in Figure 1) but also because those left behind will find it more difficult to come up with inappropriate rationalizations; the perception of choice helps build commitment (Salancik, 1977). This technique is somewhat risky in that some valued people may choose to leave before there has been time to convert them. However, such people tend to be marketable and may leave anyway if they feel coerced.

Another technique is to attempt to nullify inappropriate rationalizations directly. Matt Holt made no attempt to do this. In contrast, Jim Henderson helped remove the inappropriate rationalizations used by his subordinates at Cummins ("Why change? Those above will tell us what to do," and "The guy at the top will act sooner or later to get us out of this crisis.") He did so by demonstrating that he was going to manage the Cummins operations differently from the way Don Tull had during the previous thirty years. Henderson was not going to issue orders in the old way to quickly fix the problem, even if this meant that the inventory problem would worsen and thereby expose him to personal risk and criticism from above for not acting decisively according to the "proven methodology."

Cultural Communications. Managers engaged in culture change must also communicate the new pattern of beliefs and values and get people to adopt them. Culture is communicated via both implicit and explicit forms (process 3 in Figure 1). The former include rituals, customs, ceremonies, stories, metaphors, special language, folklore, heroes, logos, decor, dress, and other symbolic forms of expression and communication (Pondy, Frost, Morgan, and Dandridge, 1983). Examples of the latter are announcements, pronouncements, memos, and other explicit forms of expression and communication. Both forms must be used to persuade people to adopt the new cultural beliefs and values.

If the new pattern of beliefs and values in question is more intrinsically appealing to the people in the organization than is the prevailing pattern, the main problem in getting them adopted is the credibility of the communication, as is the case in much political campaign rhetoric ("I like what I am hearing, but is this what the communicator really believes?"). However, if the new pattern of beliefs and values being communicated is *less* intrinsically appealing to the audience than is the prevailing pattern, as it was in the cases of both Matt Holt and Jim Henderson, credible communications about the new pattern of beliefs and values makes people believe these to be true intentions rather than mere corporate propaganda (for example, "I think management is really serious about this"), but it does not mean that the new pattern will be adopted. The audience may remain aware of the new beliefs and values, and even comply with them, without internalizing them. Let us consider each of these processes in turn.

Credibly communicating new beliefs and values is a difficult task; explicit communications by managers of the new beliefs and values that they hope the people in their organization will accept may fall on deaf ears or be seen as mere corporate propaganda. How can communications be made more credible?

First, backing up words with deeds gains credibility, especially for individuals who in the past have consistently lived by what they said. A leader who has lost his or her reputation for credibility cannot reestablish it immediately. A considerable period of demonstrated consistency between the communicator's espoused beliefs and actual behavior must elapse before explicit communications are accepted as true intentions rather than mere fluff.

Second, communications tend to be accepted with less skepticism when they are not apparently espousing something that is in the communicator's self-interest. Explicit communications about new beliefs and values are more credible if their advocates apparently stand to lose in some meaningful way if the organization adopts these beliefs and values, or when they entail significant personal sacrifice for their proponents.

Given the difficulties and limitations of explicit communication, two indirect means may more effectively convey a new pattern of beliefs and values and make them seem credible. One is to spread the word by more informal means of communication, such as through a neutral intermediary, especially one who formerly had been cynical about the new beliefs and values. This works because people receive communications less skeptically when they do not feel that the communicators are trying to persuade them (Aronson, 1976). Second, research shows that communications are not only more memorable but also more believable when implicit forms, such as stories and anecdotes from company history or individual experience, are used (Martin, 1982). This is because stories make concepts seem concrete as well as the fact that the morals of stories are usually not explicitly stated. The listener draws his or her own conclusions and so is more likely to believe them. The problem with such communications is that a different moral must be inferred from the one intended. One way to guard against this danger is to use stories with minimal potential for misinterpretation. Ultimately, however, the way to increase the credibility of communications is to ensure that they are backed by consistent action that is in keeping with the intended beliefs and values. Both Matt Holt and Jim Henderson did a good job in this area.

Credible communication can also encourage the internalization of new beliefs and values. If it is credibly communicated, a new pattern of beliefs and values that is more intrinsically appealing than the existing pattern will be accepted and eventually internalized. However, to the extent that the new pattern of beliefs and values is *less* intrinsically appealing—that is, perceived to be alien by the people in question—communications about it must be not only emphatic and credible but persuasive as well. Such culture persuasion cannot rely on statistics and other facts alone, for alien beliefs and values are not necessarily accepted and internalized on the basis of hard evidence (McMurry, 1963, p. 139; Pfeffer, 1981, p. 325). This was the challenge that both Matt Holt and Jim Henderson faced.

There are two basic approaches for getting people to accept and eventually internalize new beliefs and values, especially alien ones: identification and "Try it, you'll like it."

The first approach relies on the audience's identification with one or more people who credibly communicate their attachment or conversion to the pattern of beliefs and values in question. Such a person could be the manager directing the culture change, or it could be anyone else whom the audience not only believes but identifies *with*. For example, in a company with a long tradition of authoritarian management, a new CEO with a strong belief in participative management was having difficulty getting managers to do more than go through the motions of managing their departments. Then one of the senior executives from the old school, who was widely respected and admired as a company folk hero who would never say or do anything he did not really believe, began to change. As word of his "conversion" spread informally, others began to change their beliefs. Eventually, this manager's department became a model of the intended culture. The belief in participative management began to seep into the rest of the company and gradually became more widely shared. There was no indication that this mechanism was at work in the case of either Matt Holt or Jim Henderson.

This manager came to change his belief in participatory management because he "tried it and liked it." He was a company loyalist who had an even stronger value: "I owe the new boss a fair shake." He was skeptical at first but then came a few fairly dramatic changes that resulted in improved morale of certain valued but difficult employees, changes that he attributed to the new philosophy. Gradually, he changed his mind about participative management. Advocacy followed, and eventually he became a champion of the new culture.

If people can be persuaded to give the new system a fair chance and if they like the experience that they attribute to it, they may accept the new beliefs and values being advocated. This is the approach that Jim Henderson used successfully at Cummins. As mentioned previously and as illustrated by contrasting the cases of Matt Holt and Jim Henderson, persuasion to try new behaviors must not rely too heavily on financial and other extrinsic forms of motivation; otherwise, the incentives may serve merely as external justifications for the new behavior and may produce no changes in the prevailing beliefs and values. This is especially important when the beliefs and values in question are alien. Where the intrinsic appeal of the beliefs and values in question is greater, extrinsic motivators can be used to induce the new behavior with less risk of inappropriate rationalizations. Further, both appeals and challenges can be effective tools in getting people to give a new behavior a try without heavy reliance on extrinsic motivators and their attendant risk of external justification.

In the case just cited, the value of participative management was not intrinsically appealing to the "folk hero," but he decided to give it a try because it appealed to his higher value ("I owe the new boss a fair shake"). A more general form of this appeal is to ask people to try new behaviors in more tentative, exploratory, and relatively nonthreatening ways ("Let us try this as an experiment," or "Let us try this; we can always go back to the old way if it doesn't work"). Another general way to appeal to people is to show them that the proposed changes are really nothing new ("We have done it before; it is part of our heritage"). People may also be convinced to try the new behavior without heavy reliance on incentives by challenging them to do so.

A final set of processes that are important to consider if culture change is being attempted is the hiring and socialization of newcomers to fit into the intended culture and the "weeding out" and removal of existing members who do not (processes 4 and 5 in Figure 1). Neither of these processes were relied on to any great extent in the cases of Matt Holt and Jim Henderson.

Changes in the *content* of culture—in the number of important shared beliefs and values and the way they are ordered—requires appropriate changes in administrative philosophy: changes in human resource management policies and practices that alter the "breed" of people hired and socialized into the company as well as those who are removed. *Strength* of culture is increased by adhering to a consistent philosophy to guide human resource management policies and practices over time. Keeping down the rate at which people are brought in and turned over also strengthens the culture. With a more stable work force, there is more opportunity for beliefs and values to become more clearly ordered and widely shared.

There is a limit to how rapidly culture can be changed by adding, socializing, and removing people from the organization. It is difficult to assimilate a large number of new people effectively in a short period of time. A large influx of people can also lead to political infighting, ploys, and counterploys in the organization as people jockey for position, especially when large numbers of new people are brought in at higher levels.

How to Know If Culture Change Is Occurring

If the prevailing culture is fairly open, as it was in the cases of both Matt Holt and Jim Henderson, it will be easier to see whether people are accepting the new beliefs and values. Where the culture is not so open, people may only appear to accept the new beliefs and values because they feel they must, thus making the detection of culture change difficult. For instance, over a period of three years, Winn Hughes, an innovative division general manager responsible for 2000 people and $200 million in annual revenues, attempted to create an entrepreneurial culture within his division. Several new ventures were launched by the division during this period, and one was highly successful. When Hughes was promoted to a different part of the company, he felt he had left several promising ventures behind in the pipeline and, more important, he felt, many "product champions." Within one year of his departure, however, he learned that all these ventures had died or had been killed.

It was not the case that Hughes' replacement had ordered these actions nor even that his successor was anti-entrepreneurial. Instead, the new head, who called himself a "balanced asset and growth" manager, said he would fund deserving projects and starve others—it was up to the people who believed in their projects to stick their necks out for them. No one had come forward. "Where are my product champions?" Hughes asked himself with great disappointment when he heard about this. "They have disappeared into the woodwork!" he thought.

The real answer was that there never were any product

champions in that division, which had experienced three general managers in five years. Under Hughes' predecessor, a cost-cutting "hatchet man," these managers played the "cost and efficiency game"; during Hughes' tenure, they played the entrepreneurial game; and under Hughes' successor, the "balanced asset and growth" manager whom they perceived was an asset manager "deep down," they played the "this year's return-on-investment" game. In short, these managers believed in playing whatever game happened to be in town. That was their principal shared value, along with security consciousness and risk aversion; these were the underlying constants that explained these people's actions under three different general managers over a period of five years. Hughes had been fooled because he mistook compliance for commitment.

Behavior change does not necessarily indicate a corresponding culture change because the organization's leadership and systems (structures, measurements, controls, incentives, and so on) can effect behavior change without effecting any culture change, as they did in the case of Matt Holt. It is also what happened in the case of Winn Hughes. Culture change can be positively inferred only if the new behavior can be attributed to neither the organization's leadership nor to its systems. A good test of culture change is whether the new behavior persists after the leaders that helped create the culture change leave or after the systems used to create the culture change are further altered.

Although this is a good test of culture change, it is of little use to current leaders who want to know if the culture change they are attempting to create is in fact taking hold. That is what Winn Hughes should have asked himself and, in retrospect, says he would have liked to have known. They are not foolproof, but three types of tests may be used to make some reasoned judgments about whether culture change is occurring.

1. *Is there evidence of intrinsically motivated behavior?* Would the new behavior persist if extrinsic motivators, those administered by the organization's leadership and systems, were diminished? Hughes could have eased off a bit on the bonuses and the public recognition he was giving to "product championing" to see how many people really were committed to his con-

cept. If this is deemed too risky a test ("let's not mess with what is working well"), opportunities that impose greater demands on the organization can be sought to see if people respond appropriately without a corresponding increase in the extrinsic motivators. In the Winn Hughes case, the deadlines on two key projects had to be advanced for competitive reasons. The managers involved argued that the new deadlines could not be met without additional resources, resources that were not forthcoming because of a budget crunch. They said they would "do their best," but there was no indication that they were stretching themselves to try. No one was putting in longer hours, for example. Both the projects failed to meet the slightly advanced deadlines.

2. *Is there evidence of "automatic-pilot" behavior?* If a crisis or a novel situation is encountered, do the people involved automatically do what seems to be appropriate in light of the desired culture without waiting for directions from the organization's leadership or prodding from the organization's systems? In Hughes' case, one of the new ventures was an outdoor product that unexpectedly broke on one particularly cold winter night during its first year on the market. Rather than acting immediately and offering free replacements, the managers involved took forty-eight hours to investigate the problem and reached a decision only after consulting with Hughes—who was on an overseas field trip and was difficult to reach—while irate customers waited. Hughes was upset that his managers had waited to consult with him on this relatively straightforward issue, but he didn't probe further for the significance of this critical incident. Had they truly been product champions, these managers would have taken the modest personal risk of acting without the boss' input to do what had to be done.

3. *Is there evidence of "countermandated" behavior?* Do people behave in ways that run counter to established cultural values or organizational directives but that make sense in light of the desired culture? There was no evidence of such behavior in Hughes' division. For example, the managers involved might have bootlegged resources from other parts of the company (which would have been counter to the company culture) or ig-

nored certain policy directives (for example, 20 percent of engineering time had to be devoted to research projects rather than development projects) in an attempt to meet the advanced project deadlines, but they did not.

While it may not be feasible or advisable to conduct planned experiments to determine if culture change is in fact occurring, leaders can look for occasions and situations to serve as "natural experiments" through which they can observe the telltale signs of culture change, or the lack of them. Thus, with detective work and opportunistic testing, a manager can make reasoned judgments about whether culture change is occurring.

The Alternatives to Major Culture Change

Since major culture change is difficult to effect and generally takes a relatively long time to accomplish, why bother to create such change? Why not rely on the organization's leadership and systems instead to create the necessary changes in organizational behavior patterns?

The answer is that, under certain conditions, creating behavior change without culture change may not work at all or may work but at very high costs to the organization. The reason for this is that creating culture change in the organization is analogous to gaining the commitment of the individual. Just as it is possible to secure an individual's compliance without gaining his or her commitment, so also it is possible to secure behavior change without culture change and with essentially the same kinds of costs and risks. There are basically three types of costs: inefficiency, insufficiency, and irrelevancy.

Inefficiency is the result of monitoring behavior to secure compliance with the desired behaviors and administering rewards and punishments to sustain it. The costs of these inefficiencies rise sharply as the organization gets larger and geographically more dispersed, because monitoring and rewarding and punishing appropriate behavior becomes increasingly difficult. In contrast, these costs are much smaller when behavior change is accompanied by appropriate culture change, because the behavior is self-monitored and the rewards and punishments driving the behavior are at least partly self-administered.

Insufficiency is the result of the fact that compliance is often characterized by the "just enough" syndrome—people will do just enough to get by. Committed people, on the other hand, will put in the energy, time, and effort to do what needs to be done, not just what they are minimally required to do. Compliance can be a problem also because the organization's leadership and systems can never fully anticipate every contingency that can arise. When something novel or unforeseen happens, the organization is at the mercy of the individual to do what is appropriate, which may be different from or even contrary to the specified behavior. Thus, where energy and commitment are critical and where novel or unplanned responses are frequently called for, behavior change without a corresponding culture change may be inadequate.

Finally, irrelevancy results because there are considerations that are simply not addressed by behavior change alone. These relate to mental processes, such as perception and thinking, which are only affected by culture change, not by behavior change. Where changes in such mental processes are an important aspect of the organizational changes being sought, behavior change by itself is not a viable option.

Unless these criteria make it essential, a major culture change may not be worth the time, costs, and risks associated with it. Whenever possible, it makes sense to ask whether the desired results can be achieved without a major onslaught on the prevailing culture, especially when the culture is a strong one. Indeed, this is one of the creative aspects of management. It is recommended that the following questions be seriously considered before embarking on a radical transformation of a strong culture.

1. *Can the desired results be obtained by behavior change without culture change?* This is a particularly attractive option where only temporary changes in behavior are required to deal with a transient situation. It may also be a better alternative where the culture is weak, but appropriately so, because the business environment is unstable and requires abrupt changes in the organization's behavior patterns.

There are also times when the necessary behavior changes must be effected quickly, and culture change is less critical. At

Citibank in the early seventies, for instance, John Reed converted the operating group from a service-oriented "back office" to a "factory" in order to cope with a rising tide of paper (Seeger, Lorsch, and Gibson, 1975). Reed had little time to spare and relied on a core group of managers with expertise in production management (many of them recruited from the Ford Motor Company), heavy use of extrinsic motivators (threats and punishments), and the removal of several middle managers to effect the required behavioral changes. Culture change did not follow, but this was not essential in this case, as is evident when the three critical tests just described are applied. Inefficiency was not great because all people were located on two floors in one building and behavior compliance thus could be relatively easily monitored. Insufficiency was not a big problem because the change involved implementation of a predictable, routine technology with little room for novelty or the possibility of having to deal with the unexpected once the operations were debugged and running. Finally, irrelevancy was not a major consideration because the important changes involved skills and behavior rather than perceptions and other mental processes.

2. *Can the desired results be obtained by creatively utilizing the existing potential of the prevailing culture?* Rather than viewing culture as something to be changed, it can be looked on with the frame of mind that says: "Culture is my friend. How can I rely on it to accomplish my desired ends?" For example, in a professional consulting group with a "Lone Ranger" culture ("everyone is on his or her own"), several attempts to transform the culture into a more collaborative one failed. Finally, the organization was reconceptualized as a group of independent entrepreneurs, each with his or her own "fiefdom." Results were dramatically better and were sustained for a longer period of time than ever before.

3. *Can the desired results be obtained by utilizing the latent potential of the prevailing culture?* Rather than look upon culture as something to be changed, a manager can ask: "What hidden part of this culture can I awaken to achieve the intended results?" If appropriate dormant values can be detected and activated (constituting an incremental rather than a radical

change in the culture's content, as explained earlier), the desired results may be more easily achieved. For example, the newly appointed head of a demoralized unit ("we are not as good as the competition") decided to challenge the group on what he correctly perceived to be their two hidden "hot buttons": values of self-confidence and pride in the group. The group responded tentatively at first, but these values were strengthened and reinforced in the group as the new leader repeatedly showed the group how performance improved when these dormant values were adhered to.

4. *Can the desired results be achieved via a culture change toward more intrinsically appealing beliefs and values rather than toward more alien ones?* This also constitutes a less radical change in the culture's content. For example, a highly successful family business in the United States that had built a strong corporate culture around the central value of family spirit ("this company is a family") had considerable difficulty getting people in new offices in southeast Asia to accept this value. When the head of international operations, a son of the founder, took it upon himself to build a stronger international culture by preaching the company value in his visits to the new offices, he met with reactions ranging from apathy to hostility. He learned that most of his host-country employees viewed "family" as an almost sacred symbol of kinship ties and resented its use in the context of their employment with a foreign company. There was greater receptivity to the notion that the employees were "invited guests" of the U.S. company, and eventually these people accepted the values of concern and caring for the U.S. "host," which helped to generate the spirit the company was seeking.

An understanding of these approaches and methods thus can help managers decide how best to utilize the prevailing culture to the extent possible and how to transform it to the extent necessary to most effectively achieve the desired results.

References

Aronson, E. *The Social Animal.* (2nd ed.) San Francisco: W. H. Freeman, 1976.

Beer, M. *Organization Change and Development.* Santa Monica, Calif.: Goodyear, 1980.

Bem, D. J. *Beliefs, Attitudes, and Human Affairs.* Monterey, Calif.: Brooks/Cole, 1970.

Browne, P. C., Vancil, R. F., and Sathe, V. *Cummins Engine Company: Jim Henderson and the Phantom Plant,* Harvard Business School Case 9-182-264, 1982. (There are two videotapes accompanying the case: "Managerial Philosophy, Personal Style, and Corporate Culture" [videotape 9-880-001] and "The Phantom Plant" [videotape 9-880-002].)

Geertz, C. *The Interpretation of Cultures.* New York: Basic Books, 1973.

Keesing, R. M. "Theories of Culture." *Annual Review of Anthropology,* 1974, *3,* 73–79.

Kelman, H. C. "Compliance, Identification, and Internalization: Three Processes of Attitude Change." *Conflict Resolution,* 1958, *2,* 51–60.

Kroeber, A. K., and Kluckhohn, C. *Culture: A Critical Review of Concepts and Definitions.* New York: Vintage Books, 1952.

Louis, M. "Surprise and Sense Making: What Newcomers Experience in Entering Unfamiliar Organizational Settings." *Administrative Science Quarterly,* June 1980, 226–251.

McMurry, R. N. "Conflicts in Human Values." *Harvard Business Review,* May–June 1963, pp. 130–136, 139–142, 145.

Martin, J. "Stories and Scripts in Organizational Settings." In A. Hastorf and A. Isen (eds.), *Cognitive Social Psychology.* New York: Elsevier, 1982.

Pfeffer, J. *Power in Organizations.* Marshfield, Mass.: Pitman, 1981.

Pondy, L. R., Frost, P. J., Morgan, G., and Dandridge, T. C. (eds.). *Organizational Symbolism.* Greenwich, Conn.: JAI, 1983.

Rokeach, M. *Beliefs, Attitudes, and Values: A Theory of Organization and Change.* San Francisco: Jossey-Bass, 1968.

Salancik, G. R. "Commitment Is Too Easy." *Organizational Dynamics,* Summer 1977, pp. 62–80.

Schein, E. H. "Personal Change Through Interpersonal Relationships." In W. G. Bennis, D. E. Berlew, E. H. Schein, and F. L. Steele (eds.), *Interpersonal Dynamics.* Homewood, Ill.: Dorsey, 1973.

Schein, E. H. *Organizational Psychology.* (3rd ed.) Englewood Cliffs, N.J.: Prentice-Hall, 1980.

Schein, E. H. "Organizational Culture: A Dynamic Model." Working paper no. 1412-83, Massachusetts Institute of Technology, Feb. 1983.

Schein, E. H., and Bennis, W. G. *Personal and Organizational Change Through Group Methods.* New York: Wiley, 1965.

Seeger, J. A., Lorsch, J. W., and Gibson, C. F. *First National City Bank Operating Group (A) and (B),* Harvard Business School Cases 9-474-165 and 9-474-166, 1975.

"Stanford Investigates Plagiarism Charges." *Science,* Apr. 6, 1984, *224,* 35.

Swartz, M., and Jordan, D. *Culture: An Anthropological Perspective.* New York: Wiley, 1980.

Tylor, E. B. *Primitive Culture.* London: J. Murray, 1871.

Fourteen

You Can't Get There From Here: What Will Make Culture-Change Projects Fail

Alan L. Wilkins
Kerry J. Patterson

About every five years a new management theory falls out of the ivory tower and finds its way into the popular press. The path to public acceptance is quite predictable. What may begin as a relatively conservative model postulated by careful scholars is translated by eager management specialists into a modest promise. The promise is then gobbled up by front-line practioners and turned into a boast or even a panacea.

Of course, when faced with complex organizational demands, the panacea fails miserably. No sooner is the failure evident, than the victims of the oversimplifications turn on the crazy "eggheads" who came up with the simplistic notion in the first place. The theorists, by now familiar with the predictable distortions, argue that they were misquoted, that their model only deals with a very small piece of a very large and complicated pie.

The current fascination with organizational culture seems

headed for a similar fate. The theories postulated by Peters and Waterman (1982), Ouchi (1981), and Deal and Kennedy (1982) have been strained, reframed, and simplified into "quick fixes" to cure the ailing American corporation. The promise seems to be that if companies will just get new cultures, they will become more productive, innovative, and humane. In fact, the current trend is to order up culture-change projects as though culture can be installed in the same way that a new cooling system or a compensation plan is installed.

Our concern is that many approaches to culture change are too simplistic. They promise too much. And yet managers seem willing to believe. Why? Perhaps they are not as gullible as they are desperate. Recent business conditions could make anyone a believer in any promise that appears attractive enough.

No wonder books like *Theory Z* (Ouchi, 1981) and *In Search of Excellence* (Peters and Waterman, 1982) have been successful. They describe organizations that have remained healthy, even robust, in the face of adversity. When they suggest that success has been a function of a specific culture, it is little wonder that readers run off and attempt to order cultural characteristics as if they were items on a menu.

However, eager attempts to turn companies around by implanting new cultures are destined to failure. Changing culture involves much more than simply making sure that a company is instilled with the eight basic attributes of "excellence." It is even more complex than the planned-change processes recommended by many contemporary consultants.

What We Can Learn from the Concept of Culture

Of course, characterizing organizations as cultures has its virtues. Exploring the values and assumptions of organizational participants is a very useful response to the overly rational focus of past management theory. The concept of organizational culture suggests to us that metaphors and stories from the past might be as useful in deciding how to think about a management problem as a strategic planning model.

The concept of culture helps us remember that we cannot

always count on being able to implement any business plan that comes off the drawing board. Organizations are human institutions, not mechanical systems. Consequently, in order for an organization to change significantly, its members must develop new skills, assumptions, and values—and not just as individuals, but as a group as well. They must learn to work and relate in different ways. The correlative tugging and pulling within organizations undergoing large strategic changes (for example, AT&T; see "AT&T Marketing Men . . . ," 1984) is thus rarely smooth and systematic.

Finally, the specific kinds of cultures currently held up as ideals remind us that an adversarial relationship between management and labor may be a relationship organizations can no longer afford. When we explore the Japanese clan-like organization, with its "holistic concern" for its employees, and then note the employees' loyalty, effort, and flexibility, we can see why certain cultures appear to be more attractive than others, particularly when we also note the fact that clan-like organizations seem to best traditional forms of organization in every market they enter (Ouchi, 1981; Pascale and Athos, 1981).

Concerns About Current Culture Change Efforts

Although there is much to be gained from taking a "cultural perspective," we believe that many of the current applications of the concept will fail to deliver what the concept implies. First, in spite of current suggestions that cultures are not likely to be changed merely through careful planning (see, for example, Quinn, 1980), we have yet to see a culture-change project that does not begin by asking the following questions in one form or another:

1. Where do we need to be going strategically as an organization?
2. Where are we now as a culture?
3. What are the gaps between where we are as a culture and where we should be?
4. What is our plan of action to close those gaps?

Of course, the implication of such a list of questions is that culture can be changed to fit specific objectives in ways that are under the control of management. Culture actually develops more often through evolutionary growth over the years (as was the case with International Business Machines (IBM), for example) or through revolutionary changes (for example, the recent changes at Chrysler). Rational architects of the programs mentioned earlier little attention to the frustration a manager experiences when asked to influence culture with such precision.

Second, we observe that current attempts to reform culture typically overlook the clear message that the cultures associated with "excellent" and "Theory Z" companies encourage a feeling of fairness and teamwork. Instead, change agents seem more enamored with the recommendation to be "hands-on and value-driven" (Peters and Waterman, 1982). Indeed, we think this injunction is often taken out of context and misapplied.

One company, for example, currently engaged in a self-proclaimed effort to "change our culture," invited a large number of executives to a three-day training program. A significant portion of the program was devoted to discussing how to "drive openness and candor through the organization." Can openness and candor be "driven" or forced into an organization? If the culture is an imposed one, will it provide the kind of unobtrusive, internalized control and committed energy that recent descriptions of culture extol? We think not.

Third, although almost everyone who writes about culture gives lip service to how hard culture is to change, we still hear people saying things like: "Well, if our future success means we have to change our culture, then that's just what we'll do!" It would be nice if complex and difficult problems like changing a company's culture could be resolved with enthusiasm and commitment alone. With few exceptions, however, we see companies going through the exercise of writing a philosophy statement and producing slick and glossy brochures to announce that the culture is changing. Some companies even worry about starting new ceremonies to celebrate heroes and plan a ceremony for every Thursday, whether they have a hero or not ("we'll create them"). They seem to believe that by focusing on culture, even though only superficially, they can make culture change more quickly than it usually does.

To summarize, it seems that current attempts to change organizational culture make one or more of the following assumptions: (1) that through clear and careful planning, cultures can be changed in precisely intended directions, (2) that by acting in value-oriented ways, executives will present clear signals that everyone will want to follow and will know how to follow, and (3) that if enough emphasis is put on changing a culture, the culture can be changed much faster than would ordinarily be the case.

"You Can't Get There from Here"

We know of one chief executive officer (CEO) who, after hearing about the success of excellent company cultures, pounded the desk and ordered: "I want one of those cultures, and I want it on Monday!" Perhaps this CEO should be told what one of the authors often heard when asking for directions in the highlands of Peru: "de aquí no se puede"—roughly meaning, you can't get there from here.

We have come to realize that these Peruvians did not mean that the destination was unattainable. Instead, they meant that the terminal destination cannot be reached without first passing through other villages. It is a way of recognizing the importance of what must be done first before a goal can be reached.

Changing cultures is much the same. Individuals desiring to change their organizations probably ought to consider the fact that sometimes they simply "can't get there from here." In some cases, of course, changes are so drastic that they are virtually unattainable. In other cases, where the change is possible, attaining the new characteristic will require that the organization first go through some critical transformations. Just as when a person travels on a Peruvian roadway, organizations must first pass through some crucial junctions—changes of orientation or culture rather than physical locations, in this case. "You can't get there from here" could mean, then, that the "you" that arrives at the destination of an "excellent" culture will have changed enough that "you" can no longer be considered "you."

In short, our argument is that cultures cannot be changed by methods that focus on rational planning, imposing the values of the few on the many, or eliminating the muddling and growing time required to change human institutions.

In order to develop this argument, we will first discuss in global terms what the "there"—the ideal culture—looks like. Our intent will be to examine the popular literature, particularly the work on excellent companies and Theory Z, and see what light it sheds on culture change. The final section of the article will address ways of "getting there."

Before we can describe the basic elements of an "ideal culture," we need to define culture in general. If ever there was a time not to oversimplify theory, it is now when the fact that changing organizations means changing culture is beginning to be accepted. Few theories have been broader-reaching in their implications for those responsible for change. Now is the time to slow down and take a close look at what culture really is and what, if anything, can be done to bring about culture change.

What Is Culture?

Culture consists of the conclusions a group of people draws from its experience. An organization's culture consists largely of what people believe about what works and what does not. A group's beliefs range from conventional practices (for example, particular ways of making decisions or of recognizing and managing low performers), to values (judgments about what is good and bad; for example, "you should always be thorough in preparing to make a recommendation"), to assumptions ("maps" in people's heads about what the world is like and how to get things done in it; for example, "if you take risks and fail, you will be fired," or "all problems are basically marketing problems").

People are typically less aware of assumptions than they are of their common routines and practices; values fall somewhere in between. Our concern is that contemporary efforts to understand and change organizational culture focus on the more overt values and practices of culture and leave the tacit assumptions relatively unexplored. One result of neglecting the tacit level is that an organization may adopt practices, such as the Japanese quality control circle, without understanding how they fit with its underlying assumptions (Schein, 1981). As a result, the new practice is interpreted differently and produces different outcomes in the new setting than it did in the old. For example, a recurring complaint of employees involved in quality control circles is that no one really seems to care or do much about the ideas they generate. Apparently, companies see the benefits of having committed employees who take initiative, but they are less experienced in implementing ideas put forth by lower levels of the hierarchy than are the Japanese (Johnson and Ouchi, 1974).

The real power of culture resides in the tacit assumptions that underlie it. These habitual ways of seeing and thinking about the world are like automatic pilots. They are powerful because people rarely think about them, though they influence almost everything people do.

Perhaps the chief message of anthropologists is that people in different places live by very different assumptions, values, and practices. Compared to most animals, human beings are born quite unprogrammed. Most animals, for instance, can function relatively independently shortly after birth. Their instinct provides the programming. However, most of what human beings come to know is learned from the family and from society. Because they are so dependent, then, human beings adopt an almost infinite array of different cultural forms to adapt to different conditions.

Why Culture Is So Hard to Change

Paradoxically, once people have created a particular way of understanding the world, they tend to hold to it quite tenaciously. There are at least three reasons why this is the case.

First, people typically form routine practices, values, and assumptions over a long period of time. People's conclusions, although not the only ones they could have developed, thus feel like reality, or "what is obvious about the world." Nystrom and Starbuck (1984) recently reported a study of organizational crises in which they found that most crises result because managers cannot unlearn old ways of seeing the world and operating within it quickly enough. They seem to go on automatic pilot and just keep solving problems the same way, even when the problems change; when they are confronted with poor results, they cling to the old ways even harder.

In one case, a company that had been a leader in the production of mechanical calculators for fifty years eventually went bankrupt because its managers did not respond to the fact that the world had changed with the introduction of electronic calculators. Management thought it knew how to produce mechanical calculators better and for less than anyone else. It may have been right, but that soon became a moot point. As electronic calculators replaced mechanical ones, top management decided to shut down and even sell plants producing office furnishings and typewriters (where sales demand was two to three times capacity) in order to devote more attention to what it knew how to do best: make mechanical calculators. After going bankrupt, the company was acquired by a larger organization, and the entire top-management team was fired. The new company put in a new management team, changed mechanical-calculator plants into electronic-calculator plants (several good models had already been developed by "deviants" in the company), and encouraged growth in office furnishings and typewriter production and sales. Thus, only crisis, failure, and the complete change of top management permitted an alteration in the culture to occur.

It can be concluded from this example that a way of seeing the world—a culture—will be tenacious when the people who hold this view have had a relatively stable history in which they have experienced few challenges to their assumptions, values, and practices. In this case, the company had enjoyed fifty years of leadership in a particular market, which resulted in a view of the world that was well-developed. This view of the world was extensive in that it applied to the way top management thought about all aspects of its business: the way it thought about strategy, customers, production, risk, and so on. All of these aspects of the business seemed to be interconnected in top management's mind.

Hence, when a company culture forms through a stable history, is extensive, and is interconnected, we say that it is deeply held and that it will therefore be very difficult for members to be able to see alternatives with much clarity.

The second reason that culture is so difficult to change is that people often do not *want* their cultures to change. Beyond the lack of ability to see the world in alternative ways, many decision makers in the calculator company who began to see the necessity for change, did not want to change; that is, they had developed personal stakes, pride, reputation, and a sense of assurance that a particular approach to their world would bring them personally the best results. They therefore did not want to accept change in cherished, well-worn assumptions, values, and practices.

Finally, some people, like the top management of the calculator company, have power because of their organizational position, reputation, and control of resources that allows them to enforce their particular views of the world, values, and practices.

One tentative axiom would thus be that culture changes just about as fast as its most recalcitrant powerful members change. When these powerful figures do not *have* to change, it may not matter much whether the reason they do not change is because they cannot see new ideas or because they do not want to see them. On the other hand, if recalcitrance is the result of lack of knowledge, not lack of motivation, education—rather than a carrot or a stick—may be used to motivate people to change.

In summary, culture is hard to change when it is deeply held. Because of long experience, people often are unable to see alternatives easily. Many will have developed personal stakes in the current way of operating and thus do not want to change. And when those who have both a long history and a personal stake in current ways are powerful, they do not have to change, and they can enforce their reticence on the company.

The implication of our definition of culture is that culture is most powerful when it is least obvious; that is, when it is taken for granted because it has worked in the past as a way of seeing the world and operating within it. Further, unless culture is changed at all three levels—assumptions, values, and practices—and especially at the level of assumptions, an organization's culture has not really been changed.

As we consider the elements making up an "ideal culture," we will focus on assumptions, because these are the component of culture most difficult to change. However, our examples will also suggest values and practices consistent with the assumptions of an ideal culture.

Being "There": The Ideal Culture

We posit that in order to provide the kind of committed energy found in current examples of excellent company cultures, people in an ideal culture need to share at least two assumptions: (1) relationships among members must be seen as equitable; that is, members must feel that they can trust one another because they see their personal interests as congruent with corporate interests; and (2) as a group, members must have a unique competence or skill and each individual must be able to see how his or her work fits into this broader whole; they would be good at something and know it.

These two basic assumptions provide motivation (because of the assumptions that personal and corporate interests are congruent and because people have a sense of pride in contributing to something excellent) and direction (because of the shared assumptions about how work gets done). However, because the business world in which corporations exist changes frequently and often unexpectedly, we add a third assumption: (3) people will also share some assumptions about how to apply their work assumptions to new situations and how to develop and learn new ways of working together. Only if the culture permits and encourages learning and growth will it stay viable when the world it competes in changes.

This cultural adaptability is something like the movement of the earth near fault lines. If the earth is able to adjust positions frequently as pressures change, it is rare that a major upheaval will occur; however, if the earth is rigid and unable to make adjustments, eventually pressure will build up along the fault and result in a major earthquake. Organizational cultures that constantly make minor adjustments thus can be viewed as more stable and long-lasting than those that do not.

The ideal culture, then, is characterized by a clear assumption of equity (a feeling of "we're in this together and will rise and fall together"), a clear sense of collective competence ("we know how to do something very well"), and an ability to continually apply the collective competence to new situations as well as to alter it when necessary. The first two assumptions are, in a sense, in potential conflict with the third. There is a tension between the cultural values of "sticking to your knitting" and fostering autonomy and entrepreneurship (Peters and Waterman, 1982).

There is also a relationship, as we see it, between the assumption about the congruence of personal and corporate interest and the other two assumptions. We posit that individuals are inherently self-interested. They may learn to obtain their goals in different ways or to see themselves as altruistic, depending on the culture they grow up in, but they still would rather experience pleasure than pain. Individuals entering an organization may not initially want to move as often, be paid as little, or do as much as the best interests of the organization require. This reluctance must be overcome before participants will give loyal service to the corporation for a long enough period to be able to learn and contribute to the collective competence of the whole.

Thus, every organization provides clues to new recruits about the kind of relationship they can expect to have with the company. People learn through direct or vicarious experience whether the company is fair or selfish and whether they should cooperate or protect themselves. When people assume that they must protect themselves, they tend to develop countercultures that work to put down and sabotage (Martin and Siehl, 1983; Wilkins, 1984). Hence, we suggest that the cooperation needed to develop and continually update a collective competence will only come about if assumptions about equity already exist.

To show how each of the three assumptions relates to recent observations of successful cultures, we will now examine each of them more closely. We will also discuss how each seems to be violated by current attempts to change culture.

Equity Assumptions. Several recent writers express the hope that culture will serve as a powerful, though unobtrusive, control mechanism in organizations. Ouchi (1981) is most explicit in this regard. He claims that in the Theory Z organization, as well as in many Japanese firms, people are so convinced that the organization has a "holistic concern" for them, or is concerned about them as a whole person, that they are willing to give their intense loyalty to the firm. These firms select people whose values and assumptions are similar enough to those of the firm that acculturation is easily achieved. They also encourage long-term employment. This gives employees time to feel a part of and to learn the firm's culture.

Peters and Waterman (1982) suggest that excellent companies share the value of "productivity through people." These companies are able to motivate their employees by helping them "shine" and feel like winners. Employees come to feel that the company cares about them and will reward them and recognize them. Peters claims that the only way to achieve an "excellent" corporate culture is to start with the assumption that excellence is an "all-hands effort": "Thus virtually all of these [excellent] institutions put at the head of their corporate philosophies a bone-deep belief in the dignity and worth and creative potential of *all* of their people. Said one successful Silicon Valley chief executive officer recently, 'I'll tell you who my number one marketing person is. It's that man or woman on the loading dock who decides *not* to *drop* the box into the back of the truck.' " (1984, pp. 15–16)

The hope for unobtrusive control from culture (which helps people who are not able to be otherwise watched or controlled by external sources) can only come if all hands feel respected and treated fairly. Managers who think that they can obtain the promise of culture by putting on a better public relations campaign need to take a serious second look. We have observed several companies where managers were trying to develop "excellent" or "Theory Z" companies. Our conclusion is that employees eventually find out whether a serious attempt is being made to collaborate with them, or whether they are just being tricked into higher productivity.

For example, many employees at one major electronics company delight in the story about their president, whom we will call George Johnson. One afternoon Johnson was doing some photocopying after hours in the research and development (R&D) laboratories. He was dressed in a very unpresidential white lab coat because he had spent the day working with R&D people. As he was copying some paperwork he wanted to review that night, he was suddenly accosted by an obviously new secretary.

"Were you the one who left the lights and the xerox machine on last night?" she inquired almost scathingly.

"Uh . . . Well, I guess I did," was the sheepish reply.

"Don't you know that Dan (the CEO) and George (the sheepish photocopier) have implemented an energy-saving program in the company and have particularly emphasized turning off equipment and lights?"

"I'm very sorry; it won't happen again."

Two days later the secretary passed Johnson, now dressed in a suit and wearing a name tag. "Oh no," she thought, "I chewed out the president of the company!"

The most important point for those who tell the story is that George (as most of them called him) did not pull rank. He really seemed to mean what he had said previously about downplaying status differences and treating each individual in the company as important. He practiced what he preached.

We have also noticed the skepticism with which employees greet slick and glossy announcements of a new management philosophy that they believe contradicts the way things really work. Sometimes the past history of employee-organization relationships is so poor that even well-intentioned managers who really want to change things do not get a chance. Without assumptions of equity, "you can't get there"; that is, you cannot achieve an "ideal culture."

Competence Assumptions. If culture is to provide the unassailable competitive advantage that some claim it will, it must somehow help the organization's participants define how they uniquely relate with one another; that is, the culture must clarify what participants can do together better than anyone else. Achieving this goal requires more than one person's vision. It requires multiple insights and efforts. It may be that primarily one person articulates the dream and even symbolizes it, but people from all parts of the organization must interpret it and define how each person fits into the vision.

The task for the organization leader is to take the odd-shaped building blocks of particular people, particular geography, particular contacts, and so on and fashion them into an edifice. No existing blueprint will provide the model for this edifice because the materials are unique. Using the blueprint from some other building (from IBM or Hewlett-Packard, for example) may be illustrative if your situations are comparable, but to blindly follow another's blueprint will produce a mediocre result. That is no way to get maximum contribution from each component. The true work of art, the real excellence, is only achieved as the materials and creator interact to produce what they together are uniquely able to do. It is said that when Michelangelo saw a certain block of marble, with its particular coloring, grain, faults, and shape, he saw David inside waiting to be released. His task was to let David out rather than to impose his vision upon the marble. Managers need to practice seeing the unique genius within a finite collection of people and resources rather than imposing a formula from some other company on their raw materials.

This claim that organizations need to establish a unique set of assumptions about what the particular tasks and methods of the organization are is consistent with Peters and Waterman's (1982) finding that excellent companies do not try to be all things to all people. Rather, they tend to "stick to their knitting" and be "hands-on and value-driven" in the service of maintaining their particular skills or competences. These authors cite the comprehensive study conducted by Richard Rumelt (1974), which demonstrated that the most successful firms over a twenty-year period were unquestionably those that diversified by building on some particular strength, skill, or resource associated with their original dominant activities. Ouchi (1981) also suggests that Japanese-like American Theory Z firms have an informal sense of their particular businesses, which is learned and passed on to successive generations of employees.

And yet we see companies acquiring businesses far removed from their traditional domains and then expecting to create a common culture for the conglomeration. It may make very good economic sense for American Can or United Technologies or Bendix or US Steel to move into industries where the possibilities of growth are greater; our point, however, is that such arrangements are very unlikely to produce a culture of excellence (however, Haugen and Langetieg [1975] showed that mergers of unlike companies also are riskier for stockholders—the stock price is more variable—than are mergers of companies in the same business). A consistently superior performance is much more likely to result from building on a unique cultural strength or skill (Barney, 1984).

Of course there is some good and some bad news associated with this particular attribute of the ideal culture. The good news is that every company has the potential to develop a unique combination of values and resources that no one else can duplicate; the bad news is that not every unique combination will lead to the same success. In fact, it is possible for an organization to have a culture that promotes a sense of equity and unique organizational competence but still be relatively unsuccessful as a company.

It is also possible that an organizational competence can lead to success at one point and disaster at another (recall our example of the mechanical calculator company). That is why we suggest that the third component of the ideal culture must be a set of assumptions that facilitate the company's ability to adapt, apply, and change the culture without threatening the basic sense of equity in the company.

Assumptions About Adaptation and Change. If culture were something we could put on casters so that the whole of it could be moved about from one emphasis or competence to another, we could solve a major problem in organizations. But then we would not be as interested as we currently are in culture. Culture is interesting not only because it provides unobtrusive control and motivation, but also because it can provide a virtually unassailable competitive advantage. If it were easily changed or adopted, competitors could "install one on Monday" and it would cease to be a competitive advantage.

All the talk about how companies can adopt a Theory Z culture or an excellent-company culture is, of course, misguided from this point of view. That is, if an organization really could become just like Hewlett-Packard or IBM or McDonald's, then those organizations would not be as unique nor as prosperous. They are useful as models because they have preserved their uniqueness and have not tried to be exactly like another organization, and no other company should try to be precisely like them.

But all this is merely a way of summarizing the implications of the previous claim that ideal cultures develop unique competencies. That some aspects of excellent cultures are unique and hard to copy points up how important those aspects are and how hard they might be to adapt. Ideal cultures must continually try to adapt and evolve their competencies, and the only way for them to do so is for the culture to provide assumptions about how to change and values favoring change and adaptation.

Peters and Waterman (1982) suggest this idea when they describe excellent companies as valuing autonomy and entrepreneurship as well as being close to the customer. This allows them to sense and respond to changing needs. Ouchi (1981) merely implies this idea by suggesting that the presence of informal controls and a relative absence of tight formal controls allow employees to take initiative and make decisions at their own levels.

An example from our own observations in the same company Ouchi used as an example of Theory Z culture comes to mind in this regard. One very high-ranking human resource executive recalled his experience in the Far East when he and the operations manager were confronted with an emergency decision for which there were no formal company policies. Since they were the two ranking managers in the area, they were expected to make the decision. Unfortunately, they were unable to get in touch with company headquarters for advice. They sat down and asked themselves, "Well, what would Grant [a fictitious name for the company president five levels above them in the hierarchy] do?" They almost immediately recalled a general concept the president had taught. Their decision became quite clear in light of this insight, and they later discovered that their decision met with complete approval from headquarters. As another executive told one of us in this same company, "We basically just try to teach our people a general philosophy. If they get the right basic ideas, they will generally do the right thing."

Culture, if it is passed on as broad assumptions and values rather than as rigid rules and practices, allows for flexibility. Given the motivation and general sense of the business that people have in "excellent" cultures, people are usually very willing to do whatever it takes to make the company successful. If this includes adapting to a changing environment, this too can be built into the value system. In some sense, then, the assumptions and values needed to facilitate adaptation can develop naturally, if the equity and competence assumptions are in place.

Assumptions about how to deal with change should help people understand and feel good about applying the collective competence to new areas. They should also assure people that risks and failure are part of the natural order of change. Without an acceptance of some failure, no one will try to learn anything new. Accepting a view of the world that encourages experimentation and learning can certainly facilitate the adaptation and evolution of a cultural competence that can remain distinctive as well as keep up with the times.

Getting "There"

Up to this point we have argued that organizational cultures are not changed with the simple pronouncement of a corporate command, an emotion-laden description of a new vision, or the careful calculation of a rational plan. We suggest, in contrast, that an organization's culture is more like a person's character or personality and is therefore changed through processes of growth rather than engineering; that is, cultures grow as organization members develop extensive cognitive maps and value systems that are based on a steadily maturing, complex, and interwoven matrix of shared history.

If it is the case that cultures develop over an extended period of shared experience, the question becomes: If the current culture is not working, how can a new one be grown?

It has frequently been argued that individuals are best motivated by tapping into their existing motives rather than creating new ones. The problem then is how to use these existing motives to promote organized change.

Pruning: What Are You Willing to Let Grow? Changing cultures is similar to pruning trees. A gardener does not engineer a tree but, rather, shapes and directs existing energy. This energy manifests itself in shoots that go in many directions. Essentially, the gardener decides what to let grow.

People who attempt to redirect a culture also need to think about letting things grow in alternative directions rather than dramatically altering, or even directly attacking, the current culture. Indeed, perhaps the quickest way to change a culture without destroying it is to look for opportunities to release pent-up energy and let the culture grow in ways in which it is already trying to grow but which have previously been inhibited. Consider the following example.

We were recently asked to help an organization rebuild a long-standing but somewhat battered corporate value of "concern for the customer." Even a cursory investigation of the institution under study revealed that the staff members already had a great desire to serve clients in a sensitive, humane way. In fact, the typical employee explained that most of the staff were frustrated because they were unable to deliver the kind of service they would like.

In this case, the change process involved letting people develop in ways they were already motivated to develop—to allow the existing branches to grow towards the dominant energy source rather than hacking back limbs, grafting on new branches, or forcing the growth towards the dark. In fact, the project met with tremendous emotional support. Within six months, the local community talked of how the company had turned around. The fact was that it had not turned around so much as it had just headed in the direction the existing staff was already facing.

When growing a new culture, it makes much sense to build on the old. Cultures grow in the soil of existing, deeply held values and assumptions much more quickly than they do on totally new ground.

Know Thyself: Finding the Roots of "Genius." Using current values, assumptions, and motivations as stepping stones to new ones requires a knowledge of what the current ones are. Unfortunately, as we argued earlier, cultural assumptions are something that are usually taken for granted and therefore are difficult to see. Thus, organizations must find ways to identify core values and assumptions if they expect to grow in new directions.

We suggest here that a reasonable first step is to provide a means for key actors to talk about their views of what is unique and valuable about the company. The roots or core of any culture rest in its assumptions about equity, competence, and adaptation. In the beginning, it may be difficult for employees to articulate their views of employee-organization relationships, of organizational competence, and of assumptions about adaptation, but, with time, key organizational members can arrive at a shared understanding.

The possibility that these managers will overlook certain subcultures within the company, however, suggests the value of a study of cultural orientations. The purpose of such a study is to understand the operating, rather than the espoused, culture of various groups to facilitate the incorporation of these different orientations.

Some companies have found that by involving representatives of various subcultures in discussions about "Who are we?" and "Where should we be going?" is very useful. It can accomplish the important goal of discovering the different orientations in operation, and, if representatives are also informal opinion leaders, it can also help those represented understand and accept new directions.

It should be recognized that some people and subgroups are likely to feel snubbed when cultural changes seem to favor the interests of others over their own. As a consensus among key managers and other groups forms, managers must try to involve less favored groups and to use their own influence to overcome the resistance of those who continue to oppose changes.

However, we hasten to add that the greatest influence an executive can have comes through gentle persuasion rather than force. In speaking of the power of the president of the United States, Neustadt (1980) observes that most people believe that the most powerful president is one who, figuratively, dresses in shiny riding boots and full military uniform and rides a white charger while commanding and leading the troops into battle. On the contrary, argues Neustadt, the president who really influences the direction of the country and its politics in the face of multiple, and often conflicting, interest groups is better portrayed dressed in blue jeans and sneakers and holding the stirrup inviting others to get on board. Thus, the leader in this image does have a force, a "horse he's pushing," but his principal form of influence is persuasion and involvement.

Capturing Faith Through Metaphors. Of course, people are not exactly like trees; after all, they do think about their futures. In fact, a person's view of the future can, in many ways, be a self-fulfilling prophecy. The problem for cultural change agents in this regard is how faith in the future can be fostered. If members believe that a new culture is unachievable, they are right. Their actions will inhibit the development of new cultural norms. In order to avoid resistance of the new, change agents must find ways to relate the old, traditional ways and values to the new. When people see such connections, they develop faith and overcome the inherent fear of the unknown.

Louis Pondy (1983) argues that metaphors can facilitate and give direction to change while still reinforcing appropriate traditional values. A metaphor, as he defines it, is the assertion that two things are the same when they manifestly belong to two different categories (for example, the notion that "our accountant is a cold fish"). As a result, metaphors help people understand that which is unfamiliar or complex (our accountant) by asserting its identity with, or similarity to, something that is more familiar or less complex (a cold fish). The presentation of the unfamiliar in terms of the familiar facilitates understanding and action.

Hsia's (1961) example of the use of extended metaphor in China is cited by Pondy as an example of the way metaphor can be used to facilitate change. In the case of the Chinese, the goal was to communize and industrialize a nation used to working intensively on rice paddies in extended families. Because of the recent success of the revolution and Mao's Long March, they were able effectively to use an extended military metaphor to inform people and help them understand the unfamiliar organization and behavior required for industrial production. Sometimes the metaphor was used explicitly: "We have won the victory of the Revolutionary War under the direction of the brilliant strategic thinking of Chairman Mao. Production is another kind of war, and the 'enemy' to be engaged in production is the contradictions, difficulties, and other unfavorable factors" (p. 7). Other times the metaphor was used implicitly and partially as in the following two examples: "Literary workers are sentinels on the revolution-battle-line. . . . I am a new soldier [a recruit] on the literature-battle-line" (p. 7). "The tailors who have learned new designs and cutting methods are said to have 'changed their old chen-ti [battle positions] which they have held for more than one thousand years' " (p. 10).

According to Pondy, such an extended metaphor works in this case to facilitate change because it places explanation beyond doubt and argumentation—the success of the revolution, the very detail and richness of the language that evokes the recent success, is persuasive and hard to argue against—and the shift to unfamiliar industrialization is cast in terms of traditional values of "a long struggle against difficult odds [which] has been a motif in Chinese thought for centuries" (Pondy,

1983, p. 163). Hence, the metaphor can simultaneously map new, unfamiliar territory and deepen and reinforce traditional values.

In a slight variation on this theme, Simplot Company, a major producer of french fries for the McDonald's restaurant chain, has recently undertaken a campaign to "return to the example of our founder, Jack Simplot, who was a true entrepreneur." Business had skyrocketed when the company became associated with McDonald's. Accompanying this growth, however, was a sense of security and a lack of innovation that the company would now like to overcome. The strategy is to hold up Jack Simplot's entrepreneurial example for emulation by other employees. BankAmerica Corp. is trying a similar tactic as it attempts to retell and make salient the entrepreneurial bent of its founder, A. P. Giannini.

Growing a "New Way." Growing an organization's culture according to its distinctive competence only begins with trying to develop a consensus about what that competence is and how it fits with current practices, values, and assumptions. Once key actors have a feeling for where they want to go, they face the challenge of growing the rest of the organization in the desired direction. This growth actually requires reorienting the shared "maps" in peoples' heads and is not likely to come about by simply giving stirring speeches or by writing new philosophy statements. After all, these maps resulted from years of experience, so why should they be changed by "cheap talk?"

The assumptions or maps in peoples' heads are best altered by altering corporate experience. People need to actually have different experiences and also to recognize that these experiences are different in order for them to change. Let us consider some examples of companies that have managed to create or recognize teaching moments for the corporation and then have used these moments effectively.

IBM's recent success with its personal computer is a marvelous example of how a company can encourage learning and new experience. Afraid that the new computer would be sabotaged by company traditionalists before it could prove itself, the company created a separate division far from company headquarters and gave it a large budget and considerable autonomy. The subsequent success of the effort gave key actors the opportunity to tell a story that may now influence the way people in the company think about their business.

Of course, not every company has the resources of an IBM, but almost any company can learn to protect people with new ideas, to let them experiment and grow for a while. Minnesota Mining and Manufacturing Company has made history by encouraging experiments. "Make a little, sell a little," is one of their mottos. They also try to keep alive stories of past entrepreneurs in the company who bucked the system and won.

Another example of how culture might be grown is a major real estate development company whose senior partners were worried because they were planning to break with tradition by promoting their first partner from the staff group. Traditionally, partners had come only from the marketing side of the business. The senior partners feared that other staff people would develop unrealistic expectations, which eventually would be dashed when they did not gain partner status. They also worried that some people would interpret this event as license to neglect their main tasks in order to devote full time to contributing financial advice to partners, thus superficially following the example of their partner colleague with the hope of becoming a partner themselves. Given the potential for misinterpretation of their action, the senior partners wanted to know how to make sure everyone had the correct view of the situation. In other words, they wanted to create a culture that made people see things the way they did.

Our advice was that everything cannot be taught at once, and very few messages go through an organization ungarbled anyway. The best way for the senior partners to make their point of view clear, we believed, was for them to become teachers. We advised them first to clarify for everyone just how significant the contribution of the promoted staff person had been. We advised against attempting to downplay the possibilities of advancement for others because this would make the

message too complex. They were then told to observe how people responded. If some people began to act irresponsibly by
shirking certain aspects of their jobs, they were to act decisively
to demonstrate their view of the problem. Of course, people
may not respond in just the way the senior partners anticipated,
so they will have to stay on their toes to try to understand how
staff people seem to be seeing the world as implied by their actions. As time passes, a dynamic new view of the individual-
organization and staff-organization relationships will form. It
will be the result of a collage of events that are complexly related. The resulting culture will be much clearer, however, if the
understandings of participants are built on clear statements
made by uncomplicated and straightforward executive actions.

There is a temptation to try to make culture change happen and to use brute force to move it along more rapidly. The
excellent-company and Theory Z–company managers we have
observed realize that things will not happen exactly as planned.
When managers give people some autonomy and encourage innovation based on certain principles and skills, they must expect occasionally to be surprised. They also must be willing to
put up with some mistakes because that is the way people
learn. Punishing honest mistakes and pushing too hard destroys
the very lifeblood of the kind of adaptation we have observed.

Managers who have a passion for communicating a vision
and a view of the world through clear and sometimes dramatic
action statements are likely to have a significant influence on
what their cultures become. However, they will look more like
teachers who are "winging it" and "learning as they go" than rational planners who are using scientific and carefully developed
organizational tools.

Pruning: What Do You Have to Let Go? Once changes
are under way, change agents must find ways to emphasize the
contrast between what is being kept and encouraged and what
no longer fits the organization. Growth in new directions, as
discussed earlier, can be encouraged by showing the relationship between the old ways and the new. However, as learning
and consensus for change develop, change agents must use clear

contrasts in order to show what must be left behind. Merely talking about the "new way" without changing actual practices will not work.

Differences can be made salient by taking actions that demonstrate that new values have higher priority than those that once seemed sacrosanct (morale is chosen over profit, cost cutting is given priority over chain of command, clear communication is given preference over traditional authority).

Sometimes the problem is how to nip inappropriate practices in the bud before they cause deviation in the general thrust of the organization. An example of this can be seen in a high-technology company we have observed. This company wanted to balance its relatively high-risk research effort with its conservative financial policy. Executives therefore had decided to avoid long-term debt. However, while the president was away on a three-year leave of absence to work with the government, values and assumptions began to change in favor of rapid growth. When the president returned, he found that the company was getting ready to borrow $100 million in long-term debt to cover a cash shortage that had resulted from rapid growth. Shocked at the violation of philosophy, the president buried himself in his office for two days and pored over company accounting records. On emerging, he called an emergency meeting of the top 200 managers in the company and made a dramatic speech: "Many have said we need to take on long-term debt. I don't believe it. Look at these figures. They tell me that our inventories and receivables have grown faster than our sales. No wonder we are cash short! We don't need long-term debt, we need *management*! And if you can't manage your inventories and receivables better than this, heads will roll! Now if we can pull together, we can work our way out of this problem within a couple of years without incurring any new long-term debt. Let's get to work!" Within six months the company had not only made up the shortage but posted a $40 million surplus.

In this case, the pruning proved salutory. It showed clearly what was not acceptable and what was (see Wilkins, 1984). Of course, such dramatic pruning must be handled judiciously lest the members of the culture learn that changes are threatening, incomprehensible, and to be resisted through fight or flight. It is to these concerns that we now turn.

The Culture of Change

In line with our suggestion that one of the key elements of any ideal culture is its valuing and facilitation of adaptation, we believe that any culture can be thought of as having a "culture of change." In other words, every culture has a way of viewing change. Change and adaptation can be valued or not. Certain kinds of change may be viewed as good (change through democratic process or through a scientific invention, for example) and other kinds may be seen as bad (for example, changes that are autocratic and imposed). It seems critical that in any culture where change is contemplated would-be change agents must consider what kinds of processes, key figures, and issues will most facilitate change.

Most critically, we suggest that managers should give primary attention to the implications of current change efforts on future efforts. If, indeed, culture is the outgrowth of a company's history, then companies are always tied to their past. Current efforts will provide the seeds of future approaches to change. Can employees trust what leaders say? Will employees have time to implement changes? Should employees take risks or be very cautious in trying new ideas? What works and what does not? The answers to these and many other questions will come from experience and are to some extent controlled by the way current attempts are managed.

We are aware of a very successful retail company that has become a model of adaptability. Paradoxically, the company has cultivated a culture that facilitates such flexibility by not pushing people too fast. In the past, when company managers saw the need for more decentralized control of stores, they realized that their division managers had developed administrative styles and a culture that encouraged too much centralized control. Rather than instituting massive demotions and firings, they invested in training and gave people time to see the need for a change and to attempt to make the change. Some, of course, chose not to change and found positions elsewhere in the company or in more compatible companies, but many were able to make the change successfully. Today, memories of a reasonable approach to change in the past have helped create a culture where change is welcomed.

Evolution or Revolution?

Our suggestions for growing a new culture look far more like evolution than revolution, and there is a good reason for this. It is hard to undo years of history and corporate memory. Existing cultures, no matter how ineffective, have a way of perpetrating themselves in the face of resistance. Organization members hold to their old ways in spite of past failures. After all, the old organization is better than an unknown organization or no organization at all.

We are aware that many executives will feel that they do not have time to wait while a new culture grows. They will feel that their choices are limited and that action must be taken with haste or there will not be a company left to change. The example of the adaptive retail company should give pause, however. Sometimes "biting the bullet" in the short run to develop something as valuable as the character of an institution is worth the time.

Of course, revolutionary changes such as bringing in an entire new top-management team, firing large numbers of staff, and selling off whole businesses are very likely to bring about cultural change. But will this kind of change develop a clear collective competence, feelings of equity and trust, and a willingness to adapt and change in the future? It seems to us that the chances of developing such a culture from revolutionary means are not good. In spite of the seeming rapidity of revolutionary change, it still takes a long time to help people, whether brought in from the outside or reorganized from within, to learn to relate to others in new ways—to come to take for granted that they will be treated fairly and to build a collective competence.

Further, it is likely that many people in the organization

other than those who are fired or whose jobs are directly at risk will feel threatened by revolutionary change. We have worked with one company that over ten years ago instituted massive layoffs and reorganization. This company has still not been able to regain a sense of trust and a sense of its competence.

This is not to suggest that a cultural revolution would never be appropriate. Desperate times sometimes require desperate means. Indeed, we can imagine situations where there is a consensus in the organization that major change is necessary and in which revolutionary change is the only viable solution. Some claim, in fact, that the only change attempts that will really affect a culture are revolutionary efforts (see Chapter Twelve). Our observations lead us to a different point of view. Most of the current culture-change efforts we have observed appear to assume a middle ground; they are neither wholly revolutionary nor wholly evolutionary. Our suggestion is that only if they are one or the other will they have much of a chance of effecting change. Further, we suggest that their chances of effecting change that leads to a culture of excellence are significantly better if evolutionary strategies are chosen.

Summary

Current efforts to change organizational culture seem to lack an understanding of the kind of culture that was described by *In Search of Excellence* (Peters and Waterman, 1982) and *Theory Z* (Ouchi, 1981) and to emphasize efforts to impose change on superficial cultural manifestations rather than efforts to change the experiences people have and what they learn from them so that assumptions and values are altered. We have suggested that if the kind of cultural ideals suggested by these popular works is the goal and if such superficial efforts are the means, "you can't get there from here."

We have proposed that the ideal culture consists of shared assumptions in three basic areas: (1) equity, (2) competence, and (3) adaptability. These assumptions must be developed and learned rather than directly imposed because they must be internalized and shared to provide the kind of unobtrusive control that the concept of culture suggests is possible. We have thus suggested several ways in which culture may be developed or grown. The role of the executive in these efforts is analogous to that of a master teacher.

Implementing these suggestions requires "starting from where you are" but most likely will create enough change that it is still accurate to say *"you* can't get there from here."

References

"AT&T Marketing Men Find Their Star Fails to Ascend as Expected." *Wall Street Journal,* Feb. 13, 1984, pp. 1, 6.

Barney, J. "Economic Profits from Organizational Culture." Working paper, Department of Management, University of California at Los Angeles, 1984.

Deal, T. E., and Kennedy, A. A. *Corporate Cultures: The Rites and Rituals of Corporate Life.* Reading, Mass.: Addison-Wesley, 1982.

Haugen, R., and Langetieg, T. "An Empirical Test for Synergism in Mergers." *Journal of Finance,* Sept. 1975, *30* (4), 1003-1014.

Hsia, T. A. *Metaphor, Myth, Ritual and the People's Commune.* Center for Chinese Studies, University of California at Berkeley, 1961.

Johnson, R. T., and Ouchi, W. G. "Made in America (Under Japanese Management)." *Harvard Business Review,* Sept.-Oct. 1974, *52* (5), 61-69.

Martin, J., and Siehl, C. "Organizational Culture and Counterculture: An Uneasy Symbiosis." *Organizational Dynamics,* 1983, *12* (2), 52-64.

Neustadt, R. E. *Presidential Power: The Politics of Leadership from FDR to Carter.* New York: Wiley, 1980.

Nystrom, P. C., and Starbuck, W. H. "To Avoid Organizational Crises, Unlearn." *Organizational Dynamics,* 1984, *12* (4), 53-65.

Ouchi, W. G. *Theory Z.* Reading, Mass.: Addison-Wesley, 1981.

Pascale, R. T., and Athos, A. G. *The Art of Japanese Management.* New York: Simon & Schuster, 1981.

Peters, T. J. "Symbols, Patterns, and Settings: An Optimistic

Case for Getting Things Done." *Organizational Dynamics,* Autumn 1978, pp. 3–23.

Peters, T. J. "Strategy Follows Structure: Developing Distinctive Skills." *California Management Review,* 1984, *26* (3), 111–125.

Peters, T. J., and Waterman, R. H., Jr. *In Search of Excellence: Lessons from America's Best-Run Companies.* New York: Harper & Row, 1982.

Pondy, L. R. "The Role of Metaphors and Myths in Organization and in the Facilitation of Change." In L. R. Pondy, P. J. Frost, G. Morgan, and T. C. Dandridge, *Organizational Symbolism.* Greenwich, Conn.: JAI, 1983.

Quinn, J. B. *Strategies for Change: Logical Incrementalism.* Homewood, Ill.: Richard D. Irwin, 1980.

Rumelt, R. B. *Strategy, Structure and Economic Performance.* Graduate School of Business Administration, Harvard University, 1974.

Schein, E. H. "Does Japanese Management Style Have a Message for American Managers?" *Sloan Management Review,* 1981, *23* (1), 55–68.

Wilkins, A. L. "Management by Stories: What Every Executive Should Know." Working paper, Department of Organizational Behavior, Brigham Young University, 1984.

Fifteen

Cultural Change: Opportunity, Silent Killer, or Metamorphosis?

Terrence E. Deal

Early into the night that was September 8, 1971, my strong and spirited wife died. She was forty years old, and in the sixteen years of our marriage she had been sick only once. Without a clear warning, without even a foreboding, I was suddenly alone with our three children. In this terrible moment, I brought them together in our family room. I heard myself say, "Mom didn't make it. She died" [Lindeman, 1974, p. 275].

But now that I know that I no longer live as a Catholic in a Catholic world, I cannot expect the liturgy—which reflects and cultivates my faith—to remain what it was. I will continue to go to the English mass. I will go because it is my liturgy. I will, however, often recall with nostalgia the faith that I have lost. And I will be uneasy knowing that the old faith was lost as much by choice as it was

> inevitably lost. . . . The Catholic church of my
> youth mediated with special grace between the
> public and private realms of my life, such was the
> extent of its faith in itself. That church is no longer
> mine. I cling to the new Catholic church. Though it
> leaves me unsatisfied, I fear giving it up, falling
> though space [Rodriguez, 1982, pp. 107-109].

In the personal and religious aspects of life, it is easy to recognize the wrenching emotional and spiritual impact of loss. We become attached to people we love, and the death of a loved one leaves a personal void. We attach ourselves to the enduring symbols of religion, and any change in them creates a spiritual vacuum. Most of us can recall vividly the pain such experiences cause. Memories of loss haunt us throughout our lives, despite conscious or unconscious defenses or denial. We grieve over the loss of anything we value long after the object or symbol is actually gone.

In our work lives, however, we rarely think about loss in this way. Organizations, after all, are rational instruments, and they are created primarily to accomplish goals. In pursuing goals, people are assigned to formal roles with specific responsibilities. In many organizations, what people contribute to the bottom line is more important than who they are or what they represent. When we leave our spiritual, fraternal, or personal lives and cross the boundary of work organizations, the awareness of basic human needs tends to diminish or vanish beside goals and tangible outcomes (Argyris, 1984). We become employers, managers, or executives—ostensibly immune to deeper emotions. We rarely recognize that changes in the nature of work also create losses that trigger powerful individual or collective reactions. The costs may not be immediately obvious nor reflected directly in tangible ways, but left unattended over time, pressure builds up and can become a silent killer in organizations—much like hypertension in the human body. The unresolved loss of title or office can cause personal maladjustments, such as depression or excessive drinking; the substitution of a computerized system for manual procedures can create uncertainty, confusion, and a loss of identity. Wholesale changes in an organization can dramatically affect overall morale, productivity, and turnover. Most often, however, we fail to link these effects to the real cause. We attribute the blame to personal or other intangible sources, rather than to changes in the work setting.

In *Corporate Cultures* (Deal and Kennedy, 1982) Allan Kennedy and I discuss the difficulty of changing organizations:

> Change always threatens a culture. People form strong attachments to heroes, legends, the rituals of daily life, the hoopla of extravaganza and ceremonies—all the symbols and settings of the workplace. Change strips down these relationships and leaves employees confused, insecure, and often angry. For example, the simple installation of a computerized inventory system can dramatically alter work rituals and can cause great anxiety. . . .
>
> Many times the hidden cultural barriers to change are overlooked. New CEOs may realign their organizations, but in the process may topple heroes that people have revered since the company began. A strategic review may launch a new business strategy or new acquisition, but may miss the fact that these new initiatives undermine important values that have guided a company for years and years. Unless something can be done to reduce such threats and provide support for transitions from old to the new, the force of the culture can neutralize and emasculate a proposed change [pp. 157-158].

In those two short paragraphs, my coauthor and I introduced a germ of an important idea: cultural change typically creates significant individual and collective loss. We did not then fully realize the power of the idea. The deeper realization came during a presentation to a Bell operating company shortly after the announcement of the divestiture of American Telephone and Telegraph (AT&T). Addressing an audience of 200 Bell managers, I talked about corporate culture and the potential impact of its loss. I amplified the points from the book without fully knowing the situation or the actual sentiments within the group. In the midst of the session, I realized that this was not a typical presentation to a detached crowd. Most of the people in the audience had tears in their eyes. The room was painfully hushed. At the end of the presentation, several of the participants lined up to continue the conversation; they wanted to tell me how the change was affecting them personally. Many were visibly anguished. All reported the agony of "being pulled apart inside." I was overwhelmed with the pain the people reported and very concerned about how their loss might be resolved.

My experiences in the subsequent year and a half, as I visited companies across the country, have revealed even more dramatically these deeper issues of cultural change. AT&T, because of its strong culture nourished over more than 100 years, offers a most poignant example: "A large division of AT&T. Several hundred people attending an occasion to mark the transition from comfortable tradition to an uncertain future. The final night was an elaborate ceremony of food and frolic. At the height of the festivities, a group entered with a small coffin with the words 'Ma Bell' written on the outside. The reaction was electric, but unspoken. Some laughed, some cried. That night I had a death dream. Hearses carrying loved ones I'd known passed in review, each person waving goodbye. Then a dark form leaped at me. I awoke in a cold sweat. I had somehow internalized the collective sentiments" (Deal and Kennedy, 1984, p. 16). But other companies in the aftermath of merger, executive succession, innovation, growth, or decline have shown that the power of cultural change is not confined to the Bell system.

> A maverick hero retired from a West Coast company. He refused to have a going away party in his honor—a wake to mark his departure. A visit to the company six months later revealed a large number of people who still had not come to terms with his departure. People were hanging on when they

needed to let go and move on. They conspired to bring him back, "strap him in a coffin," and mourn his "passing."

During a three-day retreat for a group of executives from a large manufacturing firm, an issue arose. They were all happy; I was very depressed. At lunch on the third day, I discovered why. The group was engaged in animated lunchtime chatter. The chairman of the board turned to me and said, "Companies are strange. When we dedicated the new plant several weeks ago, people came from all over the world and cried." I responded: "John, maybe they needed a funeral." The group suddenly became hushed. When the seminar reconvened I said, "I think your corporate landscape is littered with dead bodies—people lost in the merger. Before you can move on, you must bury the old and celebrate the new." From the back of the room, a brother of one of the old heroes yelled, "You sonofabitch, my brother is alive and well." "To me, he's not," responded a vice president. "Your brother to me is dead." For the next two hours, the group engaged in a spirited debate filled with anger, tears, and nostalgia. At the end, the chairman rose to his feet and, with obvious emotion, said a few words that most of us in the audience could not actually hear. Yet people rose in standing ovation [Deal and Kennedy, 1984, p. 24].

In these examples, the two themes of this chapter begin to crystallize. The first theme is the deep sense of individual and collective loss and grief that lurks below the surface of cultural change. Death or life without meaning are fundamental fears of the human species (Becker, 1973). Cultural change can tap into both. The second theme is the need for cultural rituals—collective events that assuage deep fears, heal wounds, mend tears in the fabric of shared meaning, and graft onto old roots new forms equal to contemporary challenges. Historically, rituals and ceremonies have helped humans create and celebrate the social fictions culture expresses. Symbolic events create collective energy that heals and bonds (Katz, 1982). Their absence in modern society and corporations has thrust the brunt of creating meaning onto isolated individuals, a task to which only the most heroic among us are equal.

This chapter will attempt to develop both of these themes: change as loss, and ritual as respite or repair. The discussion will draw from several bodies of literature as well as from the author's ongoing experiences working with businesses, hospitals, schools, and other organizations. It will attempt to fuse organizational theory with the phenomenology of organizations, to link the literature with clinical observations. A moral emerges from the fusion: Ignoring the silent, deep consequences of cultural change causes unnecessary personal suffering and pain. Over time, a succession of unresolved changes and experiences can unravel the fabric that holds a society or company together. Even in a culture like America's, where innovation is a core value, too much change too fast can sever the connection between past and present and future. In the absence of social devices to reconnect roots with immediate experience and long-term vision, a people can falter—or fall. Ultimately, a way of life can perish—a reminder or lesson of history.

The Escalating Pace of Change

For the past two decades, most American organizations have conducted business or rendered services in a fast-moving, turbulent environment. This is not surprising, given America's preoccupation with new things and the challenge of new frontiers. But the ongoing cultural press for newness and growth has fused with some sharp new economic, demographic, and political developments. These contemporary shifts are not confined within the boundaries of the United States; they are global trends that affect organizations throughout the world.

The result is what many commentators describe as a dizzying carousel of circumstances. Among these are technical advances, new government policies, soaring inflation rates, fierce competition, and a new breed of employers and managers. The revolution brewing since the introduction of computers into the workplace and the confusion caused by government deregulation provide striking examples. But countless numbers of equally powerful events have created a topsy-turvy world outside organizations that requires constant attention within (Toffler, 1970).

A few organizations—mostly large, multinational companies—strive actively and often effectively to influence external events, but the majority tries to keep pace by adapting internally to outside challenges. The strategies employed are common across sectors. Jobs are reorganized. New products and programs are launched. Executives come and go. Long-term employees are reassigned or leave. New management techniques are introduced and replaced quickly by others. Acquisitions, mergers, strategic planning, and cost containment are attempted. These are familiar scenarios, very well known to nearly anyone who works for a living.

In the past few years, however, the pace of change has quickened, and the stakes appear to have risen. The impact of the divestiture decision on the Bell System is the most graphic example (Tunstall, 1985), but banks, insurance companies, and airlines are all struggling to respond to the intensified pressure of competition. The automotive and steel industries are trying to regain a competitive edge—or to survive. Such struggles are not confined only to the private sector. The field of health care is going through a revolution—notably evident in hospitals— with the introduction of prospective payments and diagnostic reference groups. Educational institutions, both public and private, are facing their own battles of survival. We live in an era where most organizations are changing—not by choice but of necessity. Our modern reality is fleeting and elusive. Organizations and people have to change in order to compete and survive in a changing world.

There would be some solace if the turmoil was temporary. But if the predictions of John Naisbitt (1982) are even roughly on target, we can expect the future to be even more tumultuous than the present or past. Naisbitt's key points suggest that this is only the beginning:

- We have changed to an economy based on the creation and distribution of information (even though we think otherwise).
- We are moving in both high-tech/high-touch directions, matching each technology with a compensatory human response.
- We must now acknowledge that we are part of a global economy. We have begun to let go of our ideas and must remain an industrial leader as we move on to other tasks.
- We are restructuring from a society run by short-term considerations and rewards to one that emphasizes long-term considerations.
- We have rediscovered the ability to act innovatively and to achieve results from the bottom up.
- We are shifting from reliance on institutional help to self-reliance.
- We are giving up our dependence on hierarchical structures in favor of informed networks.
- More Americans are leaving behind the old industrial cities of the North in favor of the South and the West.
- From a society confined by the limited range of personal choices embedded in the narrowly defined world of the city, state, or other political entity, we are exploding into a free-wheeling, multiple-option society.

All of these predictions imply that what we are experiencing now is only the tip of the iceberg underneath. These trends suggest a major restructuring of organizations. They will require a major revolution in our thinking and behavior. We seem to be on the brink of having to transform ourselves and the culture of our organizations and society. This is not a task that human beings have ever relished, let alone enthusiastically embraced.

Culture and Change: A Basic Contradiction

It is often easier to meet unique challenges with fresh, new institutions. New organizational forms are the groundwork for new ways, unencumbered by assumptions and patterns of the past. Tandem and other newly formed computer companies, for instance, have set examples for both productivity and forward-looking ways of organizing work; Nissan of America has shown in its new automobile factory in Smyrna, Tennessee, that Americans can meet and surpass Japanese standards of automobile quality. Unfortunately, however, the opportunity to start from scratch is the exception rather than the rule; most companies have to begin where they are, with what they already have. They will, of necessity, face new challenges with traditions developed and nourished under different conditions. The old ways will not be transformed easily, unless the old ways are clearly inadequate for a majority of people. Lee Iaccoca did not inherit a vigorous and productive company (Iacocca, 1984); Chrysler was in a crisis, and most inside the company knew it. Chrysler was certainly more malleable than the Bell System, a company that over a long period delivered successfully the most advanced telephone service in the world (Tunstall, 1985; Von Auw, 1983). The difference between Bell and Chrysler was the strength of the existing cultures. Weak cultures are tough to change; strong cultures are nearly impossible. They move as easily as a large oil tanker at dock can be pushed by someone standing on a pier. They change so slowly that it almost requires a Rip Van Winkle figure to witness a complete turnaround. The difficulty and pace are predictable. Changing an organization runs afoul of the very human creation that provides stability and contributes to success: the culture of the workplace.

Organizational culture is not a new concept. The symbolic side of organizations has a long tradition in the literature and lore of organizational studies under a variety of names: climate (Halpin and Craft, 1962), institutions (Selznick, 1949), ideology (Weber, 1946), saga (Clark, 1975), ethos (Rutter and others, 1979), or clans (Ouchi, 1980). Culture is a concept that captures the subtle, elusive, intangible, largely unconscious forces that shape a society or a workplace. Culture is a social fiction created by people to give meaning to work and life (Barnard, 1938). It is a potent shaper of human thought and behavior within a company—and even beyond a company's boundaries.

Others, including Allan Kennedy and myself, have offered definitions of culture. These range from more scientific definitions (Schein, 1985), on the one hand, to common sense definitions on the other: "the way we do things around here" or "what keeps the herd moving roughly west" (Deal and Kennedy, 1982). At the heart of most of these definitions of culture is the concept of a learned pattern of unconscious (or semiconscious) thought, reflected and reinforced by behavior, that silently and powerfully shapes the experience of a people. Culture provides stability, fosters certainty, solidifies order and predictability, and creates meaning.

Change, on the other hand, creates instability and ambiguity and replaces order and predictability with disharmony and surprise (Hoffer, 1963). Even in organizations such as Digital Electronics or Antioch University, where innovation is among the core values, how far an individual or group may deviate from "the way we do things around here" is constrained by other shared values and norms.

Culture is the human invention that creates solidarity and meaning and inspires commitment and productivity (Deal and Kennedy, 1982; Peters and Waterman, 1982). It actively and forcefully begins to work against a company when changes become necessary for survival. All human beings have a basic need to make sense of this world, to feel in control, and to create meaning (Kegan, 1982). When events threaten meaning, human beings react defensively; when events rupture meaning, people will do almost anything to recapture the status quo, to restore their existential pillars. A simple example of this can be found in perception experiments where suits and colors are altered on playing cards: red clubs and spades, black diamonds and hearts. As people are shown the cards quickly on a screen, they become uncomfortable. As the sequence of cards is slowed, most reverse the colors in their minds. As the sequence is slowed still further, discomfort increases—some people even leave the room (Kuhn, 1970). We see in this simple example the human reaction to changes even in an innocuous belief such as the color of suits of cards. Much stronger reactions occur when core values or beliefs are threatened or challenged—for example, when scientists are required to question paradigms (Kuhn, 1970), when people are asked to change eating or smoking habits, when new educational practices are developed to replace old ones, or when the techniques of modern management are substituted for intuition or judgment.

On the positive side of organizational change lie some institutional patterns far superior to their predecessors in confronting the challenges of tomorrow—and possibly even those of today. But lurking on the negative side of change is the reality of human suffering and turmoil and the possibility that natural reactions to uncertainty and loss may prevent us from ever moving far beyond ourselves. Unless we understand the process of cultural change and recognize that many of the changes we seek will result in the loss of existing cultural patterns and of individual or collective meaning, we may never fully attain the organizational forms necessary to meet modern challenges.

Reconsider the language of John Naisbitt in *Megatrends* (1982) from this perspective: "We have changed (even though we think otherwise) . . ." "We are moving . . ." "We must let go . . ." "We are restructuring form in favor of . . ." "We have rediscovered . . ." "We are shifting . . ." "We are giving up . . ." "More Americans are leaving behind . . ." ". . . from narrow city/state into a multiple option society . . ." Each prediction is a prophesy of transition, and each transition means the loss of tradition. Moving on always involves giving up and letting go. The phrases embedded in the predictions of *Megatrends* underscore the challenges of the next decade: (1) How can we deal with the uncertainly of transition? (2) How can we cope with giving up what we need to in order to move on? These issues strike at the very heart of the key existential dilemmas of the human species. That is one of the reasons why we have not dealt with loss as the core issue of change (Becker, 1973; Marris,

1974). We attribute resistance to a lack of needed skills, problems of coping with new role expectations, or conflicts arising from shifts in power (Bolman and Deal, 1984). We have defined resistance as a fundamental barrier to change without realizing what the resistance is all about. We forget the epicenter of change: shifts in cultural patterns—values, heroes and heroines, rituals, ceremonies, and priests and priestesses—that create existential loss and pose a threat to meaning. From the perspective of culture, organizations need to attend to transition issues, to find ways of moving effectively through the rough waters of change. If they do not, most will either become stuck in an unworkable past or mired in a meaningless present.

Change As Loss:
A Brief Synopsis of the Literature

Attachment is a fundamental human tendency (Freud, [1915] 1937). We attach ourselves to other people, to places, to possessions, to roles, to relatives, to pets, to cars, to work (Bolman, 1980). We form attachments for a number of reasons. Attachment brings happiness and fellowship. Attachments confer status and power. Attachments head off loneliness. But in the most profound sense, attachments create meaning, without which people lose their existential orientation and their will to go on. When attachments are broken, we lose important objects, and even more important, we often lose what these objects represent. Attachments make meaning; loss creates disequilibrium and grief. The process is rarely acknowledged or discussed. Marris (1974) documented the sense of loss and grief among widows and city dwellers displaced by urban renewal projects. He generalizes from these studies, arguing that similar reactions occur in response to other social or personal changes.

Changes stem from a number of different sources, each with its own set of challenges. One of the most widely documented life changes is death—unanticipated or otherwise. Death as loss of life is a moot issue for the victims (Weisman, 1976), but it is a significant issue for the survivors. Their bubble of meaning temporarily bursts. Marris's (1974) study of grieving widows illustrates how survivors react to the rupture of existential reality. They are caught between two primary impulses: one to follow the victim into the grave (clinging to the past); the other, to immediately embrace the present (denying the loss). Either impulse reduces the ability of the survivor to resolve the loss of the spouse and to move ahead.

Studies of other life changes reveal similar patterns. The process of individual development or growth—moving from one ego state to another—involves letting go of one conception of the self and moving on to another. In the process, people become ambivalent, alternating between ego levels until the transition is made (Kegan, 1982). In the later stages of human development, aging, (Neugarten and Weinstein, 1976; Warren, 1976), retiring, and entering a retirement home (Hughes, 1976), raise disconcerting transition issues. Again, the key issue is how a person moves from one state to another, how the process of letting go and moving ahead proceeds. As one man recently put it: "I wondered why I got so depressed during my fortieth birthday party. I saw my youth slipping away and I didn't want it to pass. So many memories. I find myself holding back from aging. At the same time, I'm looking forward to the first Christmas my granddaughter rides her new bike."

Think of other life transitions:

- Educational transitions—moving from elementary school to high school to college to graduate school—involve leaving one life (or one institution) behind and adapting to another (Signell, 1976).
- Adoption (Kadushin, 1976), living together (Lobsenz, 1976), marriage (Raush, Goodrich, and Campbell, 1976), and parenthood (Dyer, 1976)—happy events in one sense—involve significant changes in life circumstances. Less happy events—divorce (McDermott, 1976) or other broken relationships—create equally significant transition crises. Many people are simply unable to come to terms with the fact that an important relationship has been lost. They either deny that it is lost or quickly find a replacement.
- Moving (Fried, 1976) or changing a place of residence (Le-

vine, 1976) causes extreme disorientation. When the move is involuntary and the transition is to an unpleasant set of circumstances, the transition can be particularly painful, as studies of prisoners of war (Spaulding and Ford, 1976) and concentration camp inmates (Chodoff, 1976; Dimsdale, 1976; Ostwald and Bittner, 1976) dramatically document; and often the readjustment following release is as difficult as the initial adjustment (Spaulding and Ford, 1976).

• Man-made disasters, such as the explosion of the atomic bomb in Japan (Janis, 1976), and natural disasters, such as tornadoes (Schanche, 1976) and floods (Birnbaum, Coplon, and Scharff, 1976), create multiple losses for survivors. Adjustments after skyjacking incidents (Jacobson, 1976), the isolation of duty on a nuclear submarine (Earls, 1976), and rape (Sutherland and Scherl, 1976) are comparable.

Through all of these transitions, the core proposition stands out: change produces loss, and the loss creates grief.

Individuals or organizations respond to change and loss in predictable ways. Kubler-Ross (1969) has outlined the sequence of responses of survivors in situations where someone has died. The same sequence probably prevails anytime a significant change occurs.

1. Denial—a psychologically cushioning reaction that avoids confronting the reality of the loss.
2. Anger—the response immediately following denial: Why did this happen to me (or us)? How could the person have done this to me (or us)?
3. Depression—once the anger subsides, the reality of the loss begins to sink in, producing waves of anguish and depression.
4. Bargaining—the psychological struggle to recapture or return to the lost state or object.
5. Acceptance—coming to terms with the loss and moving ahead.

There are several explanations of why people react so

negatively to change. First, change produces loss, and loss creates wounds. "When an untimely death penetrates our sense of reality, we often respond like a microorganism punctured by a painful injury. We withdraw, finding a psychological counterpoint to physical avoidance in denial. By denying a painful portion of immediate reality, we protect our own presence and consciousness. We simply disbelieve, repudiate anything that would threaten our enduring assumptions about reality and its key relationships. Denial is an emergency response that closes off further perceptions by means of physical and psychological numbness. Quite literally, we are wounded, having come to grief before we are prepared to mourn" (Weisman, 1976, p. 267).

Second, change shatters reality, causing us to feel out of control and undermining our sense of efficacy. Under normal circumstances, most people create for themselves a feeling of psychological control. We feel that we are in control and that we can affect our surroundings. Change often creates a sense of being out of control and undermines our feeling of being able to make any difference. Thus, we often withdraw from change and try to shrink our psychological space in order to recapture feelings of control and efficacy. In concentration camps, for example: "Each [person] seemed to have constructed a small world within which he could live with a sense of native autonomy and security precisely because of its narrow boundaries" (Ostwald and Bittner, 1976, p. 369).

Third, change alters our relationships with objects, activities, and symbols that give meaning to our lives and create a world that makes sense to us. In reaction to the announcement of the death of the mother cited at the beginning of this chapter the teenage son replied, " 'You know, Dad,' . . . in a clear, steady voice and with his clear blue eyes as dry as a bone, 'If we think long enough and hard enough about this, I suppose some day it will make sense.' His statement was in reference to his mother's death—also his feelings about his world" (Lindeman, 1976, p. 279).

Victor Frankl (1963), whose experiences in Auschwitz represent the most wrenching loss imaginable, suggests the fundamental reason why change is so disorienting: "[T]he striving to find a meaning of one's life is the most profound motivational force in man. . . . Man is able to live and even to die for the sake of his ideals and values. Man is a being whose main concern consists in fulfilling meaning and in actualizing values, rather than in the mere gratification and satisfaction of desires and instincts . . ." (pp. 154–155, 164).

The bedrock of our lives is the symbols we create to give life meaning: "Rob the average man of his life illusion and you rob him of his happiness at the same stroke" (Ibsen, [1884] 1967, p. 217).

When attachments to objects or symbols are broken, people experience deep feelings of hurt, loss of control, and an existential vacuum that threatens their toehold on the life's meaning. But the impact is more than psychological. A scale of social readjustment also links change to physical illness (Holmes and Masuda, 1976). In this schema, life changes are assigned numerical values (life change units) based upon estimates of the degree of readjustment required: death of a spouse = 100 units, divorce = 63 units, marital separation = 65 units, jail term = 63 units, marriage = 50 units, change in line of work = 36 units, son or daughter leaving home = 29 units, begin or end school = 26 units, change in residence = 20 units, and so forth. High scores are highly predictive of the onset of disease. Thus, change not only causes psychological pain; it can also trigger disease and other pathologies such as excessive drinking or mental illness.

Change and Loss in Organizations

The literature links change to loss, and loss results in some sort of human reaction. In theory, when symbols, activities, or objects are changed in organizations, people experience loss, but their feelings are unconscious and usually unacknowledged or displaced. In our society, more than in many others, the existence of loss and grief tends to be denied (Becker, 1973).

The change-loss-reaction sequence is especially applicable to cultural changes. Culture's primary function in organizations is to give meaning to human activity. The elements of culture—values, heroes, rituals, ceremonies, priests, priestesses, stories—are important as tangible expressions, representations, and symbols of deep, unconscious thoughts and assumptions (Jung, 1958; Langer, 1951). People become attached to the elements of culture as the foundation of individual and collective meaning. When cultural elements change or are changed, people experience loss and react in much the same way as they would to the death of a spouse or the loss of a home (Marris, 1974). A shift in organizational philosophy, a succession in upper management, the alteration of management techniques or work procedures, the cancellation of an annual conference, or the retirement of a number of old-time employers silently places individuals, divisions, or entire companies in grief—without anyone recognizing or understanding the symptoms. Several examples from the author's own work follow.

Values. Slogans are shorthand expressions of deep-seated organizational values. Values evolve from trial and error. Slogans such as "Do It Right," "Respect for the Individual," "You Can Do It," or the "H-P Way" make values accessible to both insiders and the outside world.

For the Bell System, "universal service" was a core value for over a hundred years (Von Auw, 1983). Philosophy statements developed following divestiture often eliminated "universal service" or "service" as top-seated values. After reading new mission statements, Bell managers and employees often reported feelings of discomfort and disorientation. The absence of a long-standing phrase from the company's statement of philosophy created a sense of loss.

New diagnostic reference group arrangements for hospitals mean government reimbursements for services are no longer tied to patients' length of stay but are predetermined by the severity of the illness; hospitals receive the same funds whether patients stay for one day or five. Thus, cost containment has assumed a position at par with the value of quality care. Many professionals and front-line employees are concerned that quality patient care, so long the goal of health organizations, will suffer. Behind their concern is a deeper reaction to what this new emphasis will mean for both their collective mission and their individual work.

The values of insurance companies and banks are also in transition. The shift from attention to detail to risk taking is producing a disorientation similar to other types of loss.

Heroes and Heroines. Heroes and heroines embody and personify values; they provide tangible role models for others and highlight the core values the company wishes to reinforce.

When a key figure in upper management steps down, moves on, or is moved out, a company often loses a hero or heroine. When Ed Land retired from Polaroid, when Lee Iaccoca left Ford, when John DeLorean left General Motors, those who looked up to these men as visionary heroes or role models felt a disjunctive jolt and a collective loss.

In one company, a new chief executive officer (CEO) has been on the job for two years. In style and temperament he is radically different from his predecessor. Many of those in upper management consciously or unconsciously retain their connection to the "old man," and they still tell stories about him. No one knows any stories about the new CEO (except for those people he brought with him). The new CEO represents a new set of values for the company: aggressiveness and competitiveness. But until the loss of the old CEO is recognized or resolved, the new CEO's ability to move the company ahead will be severely constrained.

A department chairmanship changed in a large university. At the first meeting under the new leadership, three decisions were made by a unanimous vote and in record time. Prior to adjourning the meeting, the new chairman announced a mundane decision he had made without consulting the faculty. A faculty member jumped to his feet, announced his resignation from the faculty, and stomped out of the meeting, slamming the door as he left. Unknown to everyone, the new chairman still stood in the shadow of the departed hero. His acceptance awaited a collective rite of passage.

In a large insurance company, a maverick vice-president challenged the image that the conservative executive wanted to project. His office resembled a college fraternity house—a Pink

Panther doll sat in a rocking chair, beer cans littered the floor, strange pictures hung on the wall. He was a marketing and sales genius, however, and he captured the imagination and loyalty of the field agents. His departure from the company in the wake of a dispute with upper management left a void for many field sales people that is hard to fill.

When heroes and heroines who embody core values approach retirement, organizations become worried and restless. People up and down the ranks of Mary Kay Cosmetics verbalize their concern for "what will happen when Mary Kay is no longer around." She embodies the spirit of the company in such a powerful way that her absence will be difficult for everyone to come to terms with.

As well as heroes, many organizations also create devils. Heroic action is attributed to events that go right; devils are assigned responsibility for things that go wrong. One major U.S. company was thrown off balance by the retirement of the executive who had served as their corporate devil. His departure took away the primary explanation for mistakes and problems. A number of managers noted, "It is just not the same without old George around. I hated him while he was here, but I kinda miss him now. Remember the time when. . . ." People develop attachments even to cultural devils.

Rituals. Rituals are physical expressions of cultural values and beliefs—the dance of culture. People ritualize approaches to work: doctors scrub for seven minutes even though germs are destroyed in thirty seconds. Work itself is highly ritualized. Strategic planning, for example, may not produce a tangible plan known across a company, but during the planning process, people learn, celebrate, and reshape core values. (More will be said about rituals of transformation later.)

Changes in work or management rituals also create loss. The introduction of computers at a large newspaper, for example, made the reporters' traditional Remington typewriters obsolete. For a long time the publisher wondered why the new system, designed to shorten the time from story to print, seemed to require more time than the old. He later found out that reporters were first secretly typing stories on their Remingtons and then entering the stories into the computers. The comments of a corporate executive suggests why: "Where we used to do one planning projection in two days, we now do ten in an hour. It doesn't necessarily lead to better decisions, but you feel more secure." "I can't help mourning the death of the educated guess," says another. People become attached to work rituals.

In a recent merger, the unique management meetings of one company were replaced by the more formal sessions of the acquiring company. In private, executives from the acquired company grumbled about a number of things that displeased them, and in a year most left the company. In a later interview most were able to trace their discontent to the replacement of their management meetings, a ritual that had always symbolized the special approach of the company. The loss of the meetings represented the loss of their culture. Imagine the turmoil at Tandem Computer if the weekly popcorn feed was cancelled indefinitely.

Ceremonies. Ceremonies are episodic occasions when the culture of an organization is put on display. Values are reasserted. Heroes are anointed, reanointed, and celebrated. Rituals are recreated. Stories are told and retold. Symbols are exchanged. The cultural network of priests and priestesses, gossips, spies, and storytellers becomes actively visible.

In one large company a cost-curtailment program forced a major scaling down of the annual Christmas party. In the months following the holidays, a series of unexplained conflicts and erratic behavior stimulated the CEO to investigate the causes. The problems were traced back to the changes in the Christmas party, an event that earlier had signaled that the company cared about its employees. The revised version was interpreted to mean, "They don't care about us anymore; they only care about costs."

In a large hospital, a formerly annual management retreat had not been held for three years. In its absence, the strength and isolation of subcultures had increased, and new employees had little idea of the rich heritage of the organization. When a retreat finally was held again, the overwhelming energy and enthusiasm displayed demonstrated how much the annual get-together had been missed and how powerfully its absence had eroded cohesion and meaning.

In a southern company, a trucking strike prohibited the annual distribution of turkeys to employees. Initial employee reaction was vigorous, but not prolonged. In subsequent months, however, employee grievances increased, and productivity decreased. Although no one could document a link between the cancelled event and employee reactions, a number of people suggested that "things haven't been the same around here since last December's fiasco. That has always been the highlight of the year. The CEO himself gave out the turkeys. It was a special event. It was really missed, and people are still pissed."

Priests, Storytellers, and Other Characters. The informal network of priests and priestesses, storytellers, gossips, and spies is well known in most companies. The collective, informal task of these people is to carry on and protect the culture. When one of these characters leaves or retires, this person's departure leaves a tear in the fabric of meaning. One insurance employee described the "excitement around the water cooler when old Harold was around. We never really appreciated his stories enough. Now that he's gone, we realize how much his yarn-spinning meant."

In another company, a new CEO surveyed the personnel resources of the corporate headquarters. Everyone seemed productive and well placed except for one older, shuffling man whose job no one could really describe. "People seemed to drop into his office, but I don't know exactly why." "He always seems busy, but it's not always clear what he does; he's always reminding us in meetings about the 'way things used to be.' " After superficial consideration, the executive demoted the man by memo, offering him the option of early retirement. The old man left his office and cleaned out his desk. That evening the entire company hosted him at an extravagant, tear-filled party. The CEO was unable to turn the company around and left two years later.

Symbols. Company logos or symbols often summarize or condense what a company stands for: the eagle of Anhauser Busch, the bumblebee of Mary Kay Cosmetics, the bell of

AT&T. When symbols are changed or replaced, a significant reaction is triggered. In response to the new AT&T logo, one frustrated phone user emotionally asked, "Where's the bell? That's
the way I've known the phone company all my life."

A recent modernization of the logo of a large multinational company prompted a swift response from employees.
The controversy soon went underground and still is a topic of
informal conversation several months after the change was
made.

The Legacy of Change. As is evident in all of these examples, changes in the elements of culture create a deep sense of
personal and collective loss. The feelings are usually unconscious; the anguish churns well below the surface of the organization. Explicit discussions about the relationship between
change and loss typically trigger an "aha!" or "oh, my god!" response. When the link is called to their attention, people often
break through their denial and become conscious of the hidden
impact of cultural change. They are often surprised that they
had not seen the relationship before. "I know something was
wrong; I just couldn't put my finger on what it was." Figure 1,
used in presentations with Bell operating companies, graphi-
cally depicts the wholesale shifts among the elements of the culture of AT&T. When shown to groups, the slide visibly involves
an emotional reaction. A personnel manager, reviewing the slide
prior to a presentation, held the slide up to the light and winced,
lowered the slide, and, with tears in his eyes, remarked, "My
god, that's powerful."

Figure 1. Cultural Change at Bell: Defining the New.

	Old	*New*
Values:	Universal Service	?
Heroes:	The Committed Installer	?
Ceremonies:	The Operation's Conference	?
Rituals:	The Budget	?
Communications:	The Memo	?

Our failure to associate cultural change with loss and to
help individuals or groups move through the stages of grief has

created a legacy of emotional baggage in many organizations. Wounds from changes of five years or a decade ago fester or lie open. People struggle to find meaning in a situation that changed several years ago. People shrink their world to find control they once had and lost. Some people find comfort in memories; others find solace in the pell-mell of the present, on the job or in their personal lives. Change thus can be a silent killer; its effects gnaw at the marrow of American organizations. The pace of change will probably increase, however. What can be done to help organizations or people change without incurring such significant hidden costs?

Death and Bereavement: Transition Rituals

> After about a half hour or so, a few of the abangans began to chip half-heartedly away at pieces of wood to make grave markers, and a few women began to construct small flower offerings for the want of anything better to do; but it was clear that the ritual was arrested and no one knew what to do next. Tension slowly rose. . . . The first requisite was stripping the corpse (which was still lying on the floor, because no one could bring himself to move it). But by now the body was rigid, making it necessary to cut the clothes off with a knife, an unusual procedure which deeply disturbed everyone, especially the women clustered around. . . . Before the washing [of the body] began, however, someone raised the question as to whether one person was enough. Wasn't it usually three [Geertz, 1973, 156–158]?

The confusion underlying this account of a confused burial service for a young Javanese boy was a divisive, country-wide political feud. Because of the political beliefs of the boy's family, the local Modin, or holy man, would not supervise the burial preparations. The boy was finally buried in the appropriate manner, but the disorganized ritual left his relatives and the community confused and divided long after the event was over.

Death as the ultimate transition is marked by ritual in all cultures. In the ritual, the community comes together to grieve the loss and to reinforce the symbolic bond among the living. Without bereavement, it would be impossible to accept loss or to find real meaning in the present or the future: "The process of bereavement is a problem of coping with a wounded reality. Its aim is to facilitate healing—namely, resolution, relief, and restoration of a corrective equilibrium between reality sense and reality testing" (Weisman, 1976, p. 267).

Every culture specifies a process of bereavement. In Japan, for example, grieving widows go daily to the household altar. On the altar is a picture of the deceased and an urn holding the ashes.

In Japan, the deceased become ancestors who are fed, watered, given gifts, talked to, and so the tie between the widow and the dead husband remains through the concrete medium of the husband's picture on the altar. The family altar is almost universal and is a cultural cultivation of the idea of the presence of the deceased. The rituals appeared to aid the widows, and although they are acutely grieving, they seemed to be adapting to the loss. They certainly required no special fantasy making since they could literally look at the picture and feel that he is alive and look at the urn of ashes and realize that he is dead. Over time the regular reminder of both the presence and departure of the husband helps the widows to adjust to the loss [Yamamoto, Okonogi, Iwasaki, and Yoshimura, 1976, p. 302].

Loss, as noted, triggers two impulses. One is to hold onto the past, the other is to rush headlong into the present to avoid the anguish. In ritual, the prescribed physical alteration between the two impulses helps people to fuse past and present and to move into a meaningful future. The bereavement ritual heals, unites, repairs, and transforms. "Bereavement has become an individual matter, with an attendant deritualization of mourning. As institutional patterns diminish, the bereaved are left increasingly to fend for themselves, with concomitant growth of uncertainty" (Harrison, Davenport, and McDermott, 1976, p. 85).

Studies of death and bereavement document the importance of having small children regularly visit the grave sites of lost parents and of having widows and widowers go through the rituals of wake, funeral, and resurrection (Lindeman, 1976). When the loss of a loved one is not marked by ritual, survivors become stuck between the disorganized state of wanting to recapture what they have lost and wanting to move ahead. The example of the disjointed Javanese funeral rite is applicable to our own culture. Here, however, it is not political turmoil that typically mars the bereavement process; it is our own culture's denial of death and loss (Becker, 1973).

Loss from death, however, is not the only transition that needs to be marked by ritual. Differences between the long-term reactions of Korean prisoners of war and those of the imprisoned crew of the U.S.S. *Pueblo* were traced to the way in which the two groups reentered the culture (Spaulding and Ford, 1976). Korean POWs were sent home on a ship, a process that lasted for weeks. The Pueblo crew was flown home immediately and thereby denied the opportunity to symbolically let go and move on. The same pattern was noted among concentration camp inmates who immediately reentered their society following their internment (Hunter, 1976).

Whether the loss is the result of a move (Fried, 1976), a disaster (Janis, 1976; Schanche, 1976; Birnbaum, Coplon, and Scharff, 1976), a graduation, a terminated relationship, or the natural process of human development in which a person "loses one self and replaces it with another" (Kegan, 1982), it must be accompanied by an individual or collective process of mourning. The old is grieved at a wake and laid to rest, and, after a specified period of time, a new reconnection is celebrated. The process keeps the past and present connected as movement into the future evolves.

Within rituals, rules specify particular sequences of events and often call for different behavior on the part of different participants (Moore and Meyerhoff, 1977). The physical action and underlying sentiments objectify and reinforce collective beliefs and values. In mourning rituals, for example, the events and symbols are designed to evoke sadness (Weisman, 1976). As people cry together over their loss, they come together in the will to go on, to enter a future of new meaning. In death and other losses, bereavement rites are either specified or arise spontaneously. Where ultimate loss is not collectively mourned, the survivors either cling to the past or spin frenetically in a meaningless present. Change in organizations is typically not seen as loss. When change is experienced as loss, the feelings are repressed or denied. As a result, rituals seldom develop to transfigure change. When rituals arise spontaneously, they are often discounted or aborted.

A central point of this chapter is that unless transition rituals permit participants to mourn loss and to transform old meaning into new, organizations unknowingly get stuck in the past or mired in the meaningless activity of the present. A vital management task thus is to consciously plan rituals and to encourage ritualistic activities that arise from the spontaneous actions of individuals or groups as they struggle to come to grips with the ambiguity and loss that change produces.

Transition Rituals: Some Contemporary Examples

In the past two years this author has had the opportunity to be part of transition rituals in companies, hospitals, and schools. The events are never labeled formally as transition rituals or funerals. They are labeled more conventionally as meetings, management retreats, executive seminars, or annual conferences. The stated purpose is to accomplish some task; their implicit, unstated purpose, however, is to deal with the psychological aftermath of significant change. The events begin to depart from typical retreats, seminars, or conferences in the early stages of planning. There is an unspoken tension and an underlying sense that the event is something special. While this is rarely addressed directly, the planning process is filled with an air of drama that is evident to a sensitive outsider, if not to the participants themselves. Even when the underlying issue of loss is explicitly addressed, participants seldom anticipate the dramatic character of the event they are planning.

A group of administrators attending a two-week-long institute for public school principals held a closing ceremony after discussing the theory of cultural change and loss. They were losing the temporary culture created during the institute. The principals covered a table with a bedspread from one of the dormitory rooms and set two candles on it. They seated the faculty behind the table and grouped themselves in front. The room was darkened. Two people came forward to light the candles, and a tape recording of Pachelbel's *Canon* was turned on. Two other individuals walked to the back of the room and took down a large banner that read, "Principals' Institute, 1984." The banner was unfurled across the table, and the participants arranged themselves in a circle, each ceremonially donning his or her official Principals' Institute cap. Each person then "passed in review," signing the banner. When the procession was finished, the banner was folded and given to the director of the institute. During the event, everyone became aware of the power of the ritual. People were obviously moved and touched. The luncheon that followed seemed like an after-funeral gathering. Voices were hushed. People finished lunch, hugged or shook hands, and left. The event was dramatic and unforgettable. Those who planned it had not anticipated the power of a well-designed transition ritual.

Although the meaning of such events can often only be inferred from participants' conversations immediately afterward, follow-up conversations usually reveal that the interpretation of these events as important transition rituals is shared by others. In the example of the management retreat cited at the beginning of this chapter, the two-hour event helped a group of executives come to terms with the significant cultural losses following a merger. Some other examples of transition rituals reveal similar benefits to organizations and their members.

Two years ago, for example, a new president took over the reins of a large Midwestern manufacturing company. Where his predecessor was solid and conservative, the new CEO was mercurial and highly innovative. He instituted a series of changes to make the culture more competitive and forward looking. In planning the management retreat, the group wanted to have a discussion of a case study, followed by a presentation on cultures. The CEO was to close off the conference. During the planning session I expressed some concerns about leading a case discussion with 300 managers. They persevered; I finally agreed. We selected General Electric (GE) because the succession of Jack Welch to the presidency closely resembled the new CEO's experiences within the manufacturing firm. In the small-group session where people began to discuss the case, groups began to realize the circumstances at GE were similar to their own. Most groups seemed to sense the issues although they found them hard to articulate. In the large group session, the issues started to emerge and the tension in the room began to grow. During the presentation on culture, I could sense people were consciously beginning to understand the issues. The section on change and loss created an obvious emotional reaction. I left and the CEO closed the meeting. Two weeks later, an older man with long tenure in the company and who had vied with the new CEO for the presidency and lost voluntarily left the company for another position. In letters, the CEO and other executives noted that the situation had changed significantly. The event was a transition ritual that marked the passing from one CEO and culture to another.

In the Bell example mentioned earlier, a gathering of employees from three regions recently grouped into a new AT&T division featured skits by people from each of the regions. Each skit represented the cultural essence of the region. Implicitly, the event was designed to meld the diverse parts into one cohesive new unit. The final skit introduced the unspoken piece: the loss of the Ma Bell culture, which had to be recognized and accepted before a new entity could be formed. The presentation on the final day put the loss of the Ma Bell culture in perspective and evoked again the feeling of loss. The closing remarks by the division vice-president recognized the past and then articulated the future, evoking the best of the past and linking this with the new demands of the future. The event was emotion-laden and moving. Conversations with people afterwards documented the intense feelings and suggested a deeper transformation of meaning.

At the newspaper cited earlier, the introduction of computers did not have the anticipated result of reducing the time required to produce a story. After a series of training sessions had failed to yield any improvement, a consultant was retained to investigate the matter. He spent two days observing and talking with individuals and groups. He then went to the publisher and asked for an old Remington typewriter, the name of a local firm that bronzed baby shoes, and the scheduling of a Friday beer party in two weeks. The consultant arrived at the beer party with a bronzed Remington typewriter and presented it to the oldest reporter, who served as the employee's informal priest. There was a stunned silence when the priest placed the bronzed Remington on his computer console. The act was then greeted with a loud ovation. In successive weeks, the typewriter passed from desk to desk. Eventually, the efficiency of the computerized process was realized. The transition event helped the reporters recognize their loss and move ahead.

The annual management retreat in the large hospital mentioned earlier had not been held for three years, and the rifts and divisiveness among different factions that emerged during those three years made executives worry that reinstituting the retreat might produce a full-scale war. As time passed, however, executives began to notice signs of deepening chasms and individual withdrawal. The symptoms seemed to worsen as changes were made and even more significant changes loomed on the horizon. The executives formed a planning group to formulate a retreat. The planners were extremely worried about how the retreat would proceed, but their fears were unfounded. During the two days of the retreat, a series of sessions and skits brought the past into the present. The group officially discussed what they had lost and gained during the past three years. They specifically noted how much the annual retreat had been missed and pointed to specific instances where the "lost" ceremony had created intergroup hostility, weakened common bonds, and made it difficult for new managers to find their way into the culture. Task forces continue to meet to develop new ways to strengthen the culture—including extending attendance at the transition rite to other employees.

A large electronics firm had introduced numerous changes during a two-year period: a new CEO; a new company slogan; and a number of other new values, symbols, and cultural rituals. Again, a management conference was planned, and the process of planning it was filled with tension. Although none of the planners could articulate the main issues, there was a clear sense that the stakes were high. The conference opened with a general discussion of culture and then continued with three successive small-group sessions of thirty participants each. When asked for metaphors to capture the essence of the company, the groups overwhelmingly came up with transitive images: afloat in a stormy sea without an anchor, a two-headed animal, and so on. Each group specifically addressed the issue of loss. In the last session, the CEO was present; the word had spread that the discussions were yielding some significant perceptions. The tension in the room was obvious. At one point, the participants were asked to name what they had lost, and these were written on a flip chart. The list included values, symbols, rituals, ceremonies, priests, and heroes. As people contributed specific losses, someone got up and dimmed the lights. The emotion was obviously high. The group then launched into a discussion of the positive features of the company in its new incarnation. The CEO incorporated much of the preceding discussion into an excellent closing speech, and the company moved ahead—again illustrating the need for, and power of, a transition ritual following cultural change.

Managing or Dancing?
Alternative Approaches to Transition

The tranquility of an unchanging status quo is a state few people experience anymore. Whether one is the president of a business, the administrator of a hospital, the superintendent of a school system, or the head of a household, the key challenge today is how to cope with changing circumstances. Struggling with transition is a central feature of life in any organization. Most predictions suggest that social and technological innovations will continue and intensify in the years and decades ahead. Rather than slow down, the scope and pace of change will quicken.

This endless series of transitions has two dimensions. One side of change is positive: by changing, human organizations continue to evolve, adapt, and rethink old ways. On many fronts, we have come a long way in the past decades, and the potential for progress in the future is limited only by our ability to imagine the possibilities. Change is an ideological and managerial preoccupation in America. As a people, we are continually engaged in improving, reforming, renewing, transforming, and tinkering with organizations of all kinds. We enjoy the excitement and adventure of changing. We seek new forms with enthusiasm, hope, and an optimism that innovations will make our work lives more productive and enjoyable. We long for the opportunities that line the future.

The other side of change, however, is less obvious and less positive. Its negative effects are hidden beneath the newness and sense of progress that change brings. We rely on social and cultural patterns for stability and meaning. Work—whether in a factory, hospital, government agency, school, or business—becomes an extension of our identities. We expect and need to be able to count on organizations like the telephone company, family, local pub, or Marine Corps. As circumstances shift, our individual and collective equilibrium is upset. Change creates ambiguity. Change undermines social solidarity. Change wounds, both spiritually and physically. Change results in loss and calls life's meaning into question. Even change agents—those members of organizations who support the change process—feel this effect of transition.

Our natural reaction to transition has become a modern epidemic for which we have no ready remedy. We cannot be inoculated against the effects of change; there is no pill available to mute or cure the symptoms. We cannot even label the feelings or pinpoint the sources of this discomfort. Excitement can temporarily mask the effects of change. As modern people, we believe we should be on the cutting edge, forever in flux. We deny or avoid the deep suffering that accompanies transitions.

Consequently, as organizations change, we unknowingly become stuck—either as whirling dervishes caught up in the high-speed carousel of change or as nostalgic anachronisms who hunker down and cling to the past. In either case, we cause problems for ourselves and for organizations. We need instead to move ahead without losing our roots, to transform old forms and practices into new ones without jeopardizing individual or collective meaning. How to do this is one of the most significant challenges of our century. Introducing computers into the workplace, women and minorities into the mainstream, cost consciousness into medicine, and risk taking into banks and insurance companies are necessary initiatives that trigger unwanted reactions. We need to pay attention to the process of changing and to find ways of moving ahead without accumulating the residual effects of transitions.

How do we this? There are unlimited numbers of experts who appear to have the answers. Their answers typically are managerial recipes that outline how changes should be made. The problem is that most of the recipes will not work. They fail because they do take into account neither the working mental maps of managers responsible for transitions nor the local terrain in which the changes are being made. All strategies reflect the assumptions of the people who develop them. We need to begin our search for better approaches to change with an examination of the various perspectives that influence our initial questions, our formulation of key issues, our remedies, and our assessment of how well changes have worked. The critical issue is how managers think about change and how well their images capture the essence of transition. Becoming more conscious of our images of change is a necessary first step toward developing more effective strategies (Baldridge and Deal, 1975).

One popular approach looks at how change can be managed. This view relies heavily on the rational assumptions and techniques of modern management. Changes can be made successfully if we define the objectives clearly, plan sufficiently, control the process carefully, monitor the progress systematically, and assess the outcomes objectively.

From the earlier discussion, it should be clear that this approach is not equal to the challenge. The heavy emphasis on rationality minimizes the symbolic aspects of change. Why should people become disturbed when transitions are designed to move toward exciting new horizons and opportunities? Managerial emphasis on control discourages events that become too messy and emotional. It is not wise to let things get out of hand. The emphasis on instrumental logic rules out expressive events that may be required to deal with existential, symbolic issues. "Get the job done, we'll talk about it later," is the attitude often taken.

There are times when management practices may unknowingly ameliorate the trauma of change. Specifying objectives may induce a temporary vision to bolster confidence and hope. Planning may implicitly provide occasions where people can vent their grief. Task forces and meetings may help recreate shared meaning. Reports may reduce ambiguity and symbolize that changes are on the right track. But the benefits are not intended; they are accidental. And when drama begins to encroach on the task at hand, many managers rush quickly to restore order and return to their main agendas. In short, managing while changing may be counterproductive.

A second approach is reemphasizing the symbolic side of change, leaving modern management tools behind and rediscovering more fundamental structures. Flowing with transitions may symbolically be more important than trying to manage or control change. A shift in language is important. Leaders need to think about how they can convene, encourage, and become active participants in rituals, social dramas, and healing dances as a means of transforming modern organizations.

Ritual arises around the boundaries of the unknown. In organizations, rites take several forms: rites of passage (induction), rites of degradation (firing), rites of renewal (annual retreats), rites of enhancement (seminars), rites of conflict reduction (collective bargaining), and rites of integration (birthday or holiday parties) (Trice and Beyer, 1984). Ritual has several important properties: repetition, acting, stylized behavior, order, evocative presentational style, and a collective dimension of shared meaning (Moore and Meyerhoff, 1977). Ritual also has consequences. In rituals we experience a transpersonal bonding essential to the human species (Rappaport, 1978). Ritual is particularly important in transitions because of its ability to repair, soothe, and transform (Langer, 1951). Ritual is never imposed; it arises naturally. Leaders can convene occasions and encourage symbolic transformations; they cannot make them happen independent of the collective will.

Social drama offers still another means of expressive and effective transition activities (Turner, 1982). A social drama begins with a breach of the norm. A crisis follows in which antagonisms become visible. To limit the crisis, adaptive and redressive mechanisms spontaneously emerge. The conclusion is a reconciliation, a rapproachment among the conflicting parties. Social dramas arise naturally around transitions. They need to be choreographed and dramatized to work. Leaders need to be both directors and actors in order to move effectively from breach to reconciliation.

A final means of symbolic transitional activity is the dance. In *Boiling Energy,* Katz (1982) describes the healing dance of the !Kung, a tribe in the Dobe area of Africa straddling the borders of Namibia and Botswana. Dances are held regularly for the tribe to promote wellness, and more frequently when someone is sick. The healing dance centers around the concept of Num, a spiritual energy that can heal. Num is activated by the dance and intensified through an altered state of consciousness called Kia. With healers as media, Num becomes available to the tribe in the dance. As Katz notes: "The healing dance is a way to deal with transitions, and the uncertainties as well as opportunities they release. Whether a person seeks to transit from sickness to health or from a known state of consciousness to an unknown one" (p. 300). Those who manage change in modern organizations need to learn to dance, to become healers capable of releasing collective energy to heal the wounds of change.

The clinical observations cited earlier document how rituals, social dramas, and healing dances arise spontaneously around transition events. In these experiences, a script emerges, behavior becomes stylized, emotions rise, and a drama unfolds. The experiences seem to have a life of their own, a momentum that individuals unconsciously follow, a scenario that is larger than the sum of the individual parts. It is a cocoon of human experience that produces a metamorphosis of past, present, and future. Within the behavioral cocoon, the organization is transformed, wounds are healed, new meaning is grafted onto the old, and a new organization emerges. It is a natural process that is neither consciously planned nor formally controlled. It begins on a signal; it ends on a cue. Thereafter, the organization is "never the same." Social dramas, human dances, cultural rituals —all have the power to heal and transform the issues around change.

When these processes arise spontaneously, they can be orchestrated and encouraged. Many managers undoubtedly try to be in control, but special events require an ability to be temporarily out of control and a faith that everything will be all right. Changing and managing are incompatible. But dancing and changing may be complementary: the change requires the dance; the dance transforms the change. For many, this proposition will sound preposterous, but keep in mind that Thomas Watson, Sr., the founder of International Business Machines, once remarked, "You must put your heart into the business and business into your heart." Heart is not an integral part of the modern management lexicon. Yet it helps to crystallize what happens when organizations change. To lose heart is to lose confidence and meaning. For many people, the rapid pace of change has torn the heart out of work. Heart will not be restored by knowledge; it can only be restored by dancing and healing. But this will require a significant shift in our thinking about how organizations can be changed.

References

Argyris, C. *Integrating the Individual and the Organization.* New York: Wiley, 1984.

Baldridge, J. V., and Deal, T. E. *Managing Change in Educa-*

tional Organizations: Sociological Perspectives, Strategies, and Case Studies. Berkeley, Calif.: McCutchan, 1975.

Barnard, C. *Functions of the Executive.* Cambridge: Harvard University Press, 1938.

Becker, D. *The Denial of Death.* New York: Free Press, 1973.

Birnbaum, F., Coplon, J., and Scharff, I. "Crisis Intervention After a Natural Disaster." In R. H. Moos (ed.), *Human Adaptation: Coping with Life Crises.* Lexington, Mass.: Heath, 1976.

Bolman, L. G. "Organization Development and Limits to Growth: When Smaller Is Better, Can O.D. Help?" Unpublished paper, Graduate School of Education, Harvard University, 1980.

Bolman, L. G., and Deal, T. E. *Modern Approaches to Understanding and Managing Organizations.* San Francisco: Jossey-Bass, 1984.

Chodoff, P. "The German Concentration Camp as a Psychological Stress." In R. H. Moos (ed.), *Human Adaptation: Coping with Life Crises.* Lexington, Mass.: Heath, 1976.

Clark, B. "The Organizational Saga in Higher Education." In J. V. Baldridge and T. E. Deal, *Managing Change in Educational Organizations: Sociological Perspectives, Strategies, and Case Studies.* Berkeley, Calif.: McCutchan, 1975.

Deal, T. E., and Kennedy, A. A. *Corporate Cultures: The Rites and Rituals of Corporate Life.* Reading, Mass.: Addison-Wesley, 1982.

Deal, T. E., and Kennedy, A. A. "Tales from the Trails." *Hospital Forum: The Journal of the Association of Western Hospitals.* May–June, 1984, pp. 16–26.

Dimsdale, J. E. "The Coping Behavior of Nazi Concentration Camp Survivors." In R. H. Moos (ed.), *Human Adaptation: Coping with Life Crises.* Lexington, Mass.: Heath, 1976.

Dyer, E. D. "Parenthood as Crisis: A Re-Study." In R. H. Moos (ed.), *Human Adaptation: Coping with Life Crises.* Lexington, Mass.: Heath, 1976.

Earls, J. H. "Human Adjustment to an Exotic Environment: The Nuclear Submarine." In R. H. Moos (ed.), *Human Adaptation: Coping with Life Crises.* Lexington, Mass.: Heath, 1976.

Frankl, V. *Man's Search for Meaning.* New York: Washington Square Press, 1963.

Freud, S. "Mourning and Melancholia." In *The Complete Psychological Works of Sigmund Freud.* Vol. 14. London: Hogarth Press, 1937. (Originally published 1915.)

Fried, M. "Grieving for a Lost Home." In R. H. Moos (ed.), *Human Adaptation: Coping with Life Crises.* Lexington, Mass.: Heath, 1976.

Geertz, C. *The Interpretation of Cultures: Selected Essays.* New York: Basic Books, 1973.

Halpin, A. W., and Craft, D. B. *The Organizational Climate of Schools.* St. Louis: Washington University Press, 1962.

Harrison, S. I., Davenport, C. W., and McDermott, J. R., Jr. "Children's Reactions to Bereavement: Adult Confusions and Misperceptions." In R. H. Moos (ed.), *Human Adaptation: Coping with Life Crises.* Lexington, Mass.: Heath, 1976.

Hoffer, E. *The Ordeal of Change.* New York: Harper & Row, 1963.

Holmes, T. H., and Masuda, M. "Life Change and Illness Susceptibility." In B. S. Dohrenwend and B. P. Dohrenwend, *Stressful Life Events: Their Nature and Effects.* New York: Wiley, 1974.

Hughes, E. Z. "Angry in Retirement." In R. H. Moos (ed.), *Human Adaptation: Coping with Life Crises.* Lexington, Mass.: Heath, 1976.

Hunter, E. J. "The Prisoner of War: Coping with the Stress of Isolation." In R. H. Moos (ed.), *Human Adaptation: Coping with Life Crises.* Lexington, Mass.: Heath, 1976.

Iaccoca, L. *Iaccoca.* New York: Bantam Books, 1984.

Ibsen, H. "The Wild Duck." In O. G. Brochett and L. Brochett (eds.), *Plays for the Theater.* New York: Holt, Rinehart, & Winston, 1967. (Originally published 1884.)

Jacobson, S. R. "Individual and Group Responses to Confinement in a Skyjacked Plane." In R. H. Moos (ed.), *Human Adaptation: Coping with Life Crises.* Lexington, Mass.: Heath, 1976.

Janis, I. L. "Aftermath of the Atomic Disasters." In R. H. Moos (ed.), *Human Adaptation: Coping with Life Crises.* Lexington, Mass.: Heath, 1976.

Jung, C. G. *Psyche and Symbol.* New York: Doubleday, 1958.

Kadushin, A. "Reversibility of Trauma: A Follow-up Study of Children Adopted When Older." In R. H. Moos (ed.), *Human Adaptation: Coping with Life Crises.* Lexington, Mass.: Heath, 1976.

Katz, R. *Boiling Energy.* Cambridge, Mass.: Harvard University Press, 1982.

Kegan, R. *The Evolving Self.* Cambridge: Harvard University Press, 1982.

Kubler-Ross, E. *On Death and Dying.* New York: Macmillan, 1969.

Kuhn, T. *The Structure of Scientific Revolutions.* (2nd ed.) Chicago: University of Chicago Press, 1970.

Langer, S. *Philosophy in a New Key.* Cambridge: Harvard University Press, 1951.

Levine, M. "Residential Change and School Adjustment." In R. H. Moos (ed.), *Human Adaptation: Coping with Life Crises.* Lexington, Mass.: Heath, 1976.

Lindeman, B. "Widower Heal Thyself." In R. H. Moos (ed.), *Human Adaptation: Coping with Life Crises.* Lexington, Mass.: Heath, 1976.

Lobsenz, N. M. "Living Together: A Newfangled Tango or an Old-Fashioned Waltz?" In R. H. Moos (ed.), *Human Adaptation: Coping with Life Crises.* Lexington, Mass.: Heath, 1976.

McDermott, J. F. "Parental Divorce in Early Childhood." In R. H. Moos (ed.), *Human Adaptation: Coping with Life Crises.* Lexington, Mass.: Heath, 1976.

Marris, P. *Loss and Change.* London: Routledge & Kegan Paul, 1974.

Moore, S. F., and Meyerhoff, B. G. *Secular Ritual.* Amsterdam: Van Gorcum, 1977.

Naisbitt, J. *Megatrends: Ten New Directions Transforming Our Lives.* New York: Warner, 1982.

Neugarten, B. L., and Weinstein, K. K. "Developmental Life Transitions: Retirement and Aging." In R. H. Moos (ed.), *Human Adaptation: Coping with Life Crises.* Lexington, Mass.: Heath, 1976.

Ostwald, P., and Bittner, E. "Life Adjustment After Severe Persecution." In R. H. Moos (ed.), *Human Adaptation: Coping with Life Crises.* Lexington, Mass.: Heath, 1976.

Ouchi, W. G. "Markets, Bureaucracies, and Class." *Administrative Science Quarterly,* 1980, *25,* 129-141.

Peters, T. J., and Waterman, R. H., Jr. *In Search of Excellence: Lessons from America's Best-Run Companies.* New York: Harper & Row, 1982.

Rappaport, R. "Adaptation and the Structure of Ritual." In N. Blurton Jones and V. Reynolds (eds.), *Human Behavior and Adaption.* Vol. 38. London: Taylor & Francis, 1978.

Raush, H. R., Goodrich, W., and Campbell, J. R. "Adaptation to the First Years of Marriage." In R. H. Moos (ed.), *Human Adaptation: Coping with Life Crises.* Lexington, Mass.: Heath, 1976.

Rodriguez, R. *Hunger of Memory.* Boston: David R. Godine, 1982.

Rutter, M., and others. *Fifteen Thousand Hours.* Cambridge: Harvard University Press, 1979.

Schanche, D. A. "The Emotional Aftermath of 'The Largest Tornado Ever'." In R. H. Moos (ed.), *Human Adaptation: Coping with Life Crises.* Lexington, Mass.: Heath, 1976.

Schein, E. H. *Organizational Culture and Leadership: A Dynamic View.* San Francisco: Jossey-Bass, 1985.

Selznick, P. *TVA and the Grass Roots.* Berkeley: University of California Press, 1949.

Signell, K. A. "Kindergarten Entry: A Preventive Approach to Community Mental Health." In R. H. Moos (ed.), *Human Adaptation: Coping with Life Crises.* Lexington, Mass.: Heath, 1976.

Spaulding, R. C., and Ford, C. V. "The Pueblo Incident: Psychological Reactions to the Stresses of Imprisonment and Repatriation." In R. H. Moos (ed.), *Human Adaptation: Coping with Life Crises.* Lexington, Mass.: Heath, 1976.

Sutherland, S., and Scherl, D. J. "Patterns of Response Among Victims of Rape." In R. H. Moos (ed.), *Human Adaptation: Coping with Life Crises.* Lexington, Mass.: Heath, 1976.

Toffler, A. *Future Shock.* New York: Random House, 1970.

Trice, H. M., and Beyer, J. M. "Studying Organizational Cultures Through Rites and Ceremonies." *Academy of Management Review,* 1984, *9* (4), 653–669.

Tunstall, W. B. *Disconnecting Parties: Managing the Bell System Break-up—An Inside View.* New York: McGraw-Hill, 1985.

Turner, V. *From Ritual to Theater.* New York: Performing Arts Journal Publications, 1982.

Von Auw, A. *Heritage and Destiny.* New York: Praeger, 1983.

Warren, H. H. "Self-Perception of Independence Among Urban Elderly." In R. H. Moos (ed.), *Human Adaptation: Coping with Life Crises.* Lexington, Mass.: Heath, 1976.

Weber, M. *From Max Weber: Essays in Sociology.* (H. B. Gerth and C. W. Mills, eds.) New York: Oxford University Press, 1946.

Weisman, A. D. "Coping with Untimely Death." In R. H. Moos (ed.), *Human Adaptation: Coping with Life Crises.* Lexington, Mass.: Heath, 1976.

Yamamoto, J., Okonogi, K., Iwasaki, T., and Yoshimura, S. "Mourning in Japan." In R. H. Moos (ed.), *Human Adaptation: Coping with Life Crises.* Lexington, Mass.: Heath, 1976.

Sixteen

Four Phases for Bringing About Cultural Change

Robert F. Allen

Have you heard the one about the two managers driving in the desert? One looks out the window and notices a group of men dressed in identical outfits, dancing furiously around a campfire. He rolls down the window and hears their voices as they shake their fists at the sky, pleading for rain.

"Do you believe these guys," he says, settling back into the real leather seat. "They think they can change the weather by doing some jogging around a bunch of burning branches. What a waste of energy. This is the twentieth century, after all."

"I don't know about that," says the driver, accelerating into the horizon. "Reminds me a lot of last week's management meeting."

For those of us who have been involved in them, efforts to bring about change can be as frustrating as rain dances in the desert, and much more costly. Much of the futility involved in these attempts seems to revolve around a lack of understanding both of how lasting change takes place and what needs to be done to bring it about.

This chapter describes a norm-based methodology for helping people to create and maintain cultural environments that are supportive of what they are trying to achieve in their lives and in their organizations. Normative systems methodology has evolved over the past twenty-five years through its application in a wide variety of change programs with a range of different-sized groups and organizations. It is based on the premise that the needs of many groups can be met by a systematic, humanistic, participative change process. This change process focuses on culture and makes use of the power of culture to bring about positive changes.

There is no end to the litany of problems faced by organizations, ranging from readily quantifiable issues such as low productivity and absenteeism to more elusive issues such as lack of teamwork and low morale. The normative systems approach to change can and has been used by organizational leaders in a number of different ways: as a comprehensive approach to organizational development, as a way of addressing particular organizational problems and opportunities, and as a method for sustaining the influence of training programs and other organizational interventions.

As managers, we can be the architects of cultural change in our organizations. Anyone who has tried to build a structure, whether it be a small shack or a monolithic office tower, knows that it can only be built one step at a time. In this chapter the overall normative concept to be used in the construction will first be described, followed by the principles that underlie it and that provide the foundation upon which the structure of change is built. The structure itself is a four-phase, systematic program for cultural change, and each of these phases will be described in sequence. Following the description of each of the phases, potential problems, or barrier norms, will be discussed so that they can be taken into account in the construction process.

We explore norm-based methodology not so much to discover a blueprint, but because it can serve as an illustration to aid in the design of change projects. This methodology can be used by work teams, departments, divisions, whole corporations

—in fact, any group of people who are committed to a participative process of social change.

As the architects of change projects, we are the creative overseers, but we must keep in mind that a good architect involves in the planning process not only the craftspeople who will do the building, but the people who will live in the building as well. The effective architect also is attentive to detail, flexible and able to make alterations in the plans for the good of the project as it progresses without losing sight of the original vision.

Why Norms?

Although cultures have many component parts, a normative basis was chosen for the change system discussed here because this is a concept that people from a broad range of backgrounds and educational levels can understand and apply successfully. Since norms are the elements of culture least dependent upon abstractions, most readily recognizable in all aspects of our daily lives, and most general in their applications, they provide an excellent vehicle for helping people understand and manage the cultural aspects of organizational life.

The definition of norms used here is a simple one. When people come together over time, they bring with them, or create, certain expectations regarding one another's behaviors. Every culture has ways of doing things that influence its members, and we call these norms. Many social scientists, psychologists, and anthropologists have studied the stated rules and standards—the norms—that govern what people should or should not do, say, or think within a given context. As the term is used here, norms encompass all behavior that is expected, accepted, or supported by the group, whether that behavior is stated or unstated. The norm is the sanctioned behavior, and people are rewarded and encouraged when they follow the norms, and chastised, confronted, and ostracized when they violate them.

Norms influence all of us in every aspect of our lives, from the ways we dress and the hairstyles we choose, to the houses we live in and how we furnish them, to the topics of conversation that we engage in with different people. They also influence our organizations.

Let us consider the following widespread norms and try to project the reaction if we (or one of our peers) deviated from them:

- Golfers do not speak during a golf tournament while their opponents are putting.
- Bathing suits are not worn to work or to formal parties.
- Employees do not openly criticize their boss in an organization that does not practice open communication.
- Employees are expected to arrive on time (or late or early) for work.

Norms are all around us, and, like stress, they can be either positive or negative. They are so much a part of our lives that often we do not recognize their importance. But without norms, our lives would be in chaos, unstructured, and disorganized; simple decisions would demand our undivided attention. Norms can help us accomplish our goals, but they can also be barriers to personal and organizational fulfillment. Norms are the building blocks of any culture, and it is important that we focus on them when we seek to change our behaviors or our organizational environments.

Is the Problem Cultural?

It is important to recognize from the outset that not all problems and opportunities in our organizations are culture based. There are situations that can be remedied and changes that can be made by dealing with one employee, one machine, one aspect of production. However, in most cases, if a situation can be dealt with simply, it usually is. We rarely become perplexed or concerned about easily solvable problems—we just solve them. It is the more difficult and chronic problems that most frequently cause organizational concern.

When we consider a perceived problem, it is essential to determine whether it is culture based or nonculture based. If it is not culture based, a relatively simple solution such as writing a memo, holding a training session, or changing a procedure may solve it. If it is culture based, however, a more systematic and sustained culture-based strategy will be required.

Three relatively simple questions can help us decide whether or not a given problem is cultural. These questions are:

- Is the problem chronic?
- Is the problem widespread?
- Has the problem resisted prior change efforts?

Affirmative answers to these questions suggest that the problem may be a cultural one and that an opportunity for culture-based change exists.

If we try to change culture-based problems with nonculture-based solutions, most often our efforts will result in little lasting change. Our efforts will be like punching into a giant pillow: if we punch hard enough (with enough dollars, energy, and so forth), we will create an indentation (some change in the situation), but soon after we remove our fist, the pillow will puff up and return to its old shape.

Once we understand and appreciate the influence of norms and are certain that the problem is a cultural one, we can proceed to lay the foundation for our program. This framework is made up of certain key principles, each of which needs to be directly applied within the normative systems change process.

The Normative Systems Change Process

The normative systems change process is depicted in Figure 1. It consists of four phases.

During Phase I, the organizational culture, including the cultural norms as they currently exist is analyzed, and preliminary objectives are set. An overall plan is developed, and obstacles that need to be overcome are identified.

Once this is accomplished, the system is introduced to those most directly affected, thus involving them in the change process. This is Phase II. People get a clear idea of what the

Figure 1. The Normative Systems Change Process.

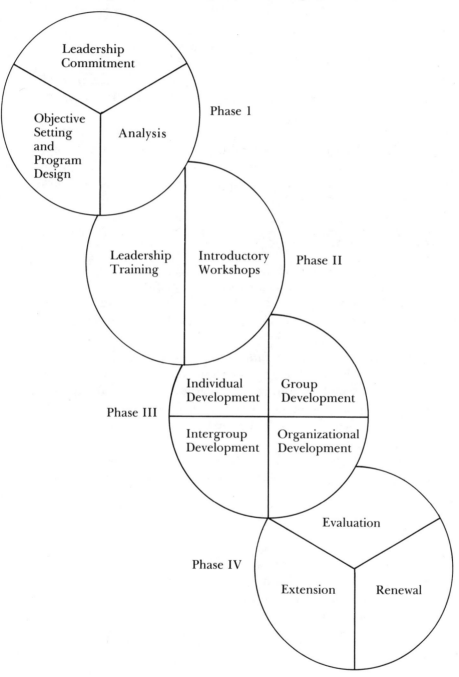

Phase 1

Leadership
Commitment

Objective
Setting
and
Program
Design

Analysis

Leadership
Training

Introductory
Workshops

Phase II

Individual
Development

Group
Development

Phase III

Intergroup
Development

Organizational
Development

Evaluation

Phase IV

Extension

Renewal

existing norms are and what the organization's normative objectives might be. They also learn the basic principles that will guide the change process.

Phase Three calls for the systematic modification of the organizational culture. During this phase, four key elements of the culture must be considered: individuals; work teams; leaders; and the policies, programs, and procedures of the organization.

In Phase IV, feedback is provided about what has and has not worked well and what modifications and corrections might make the program work better. Results are evaluated, and the program is extended to other appropriate areas of the organization.

The Principles

Understanding of the principles that underlie the system is crucial if applications are to be successful. These principles form the basis upon which adjustments and alterations in the system can be made, and without them, little of positive value will be accomplished.

Focus on Both the Individual and the Culture. The change process emphasizes the importance of the individual in creating and supporting the culture, and of the culture in creating and supporting the individual. Through this process, a synergy and interdependence is developed that can assure the success of both.

Involvement of People. The system encourages, develops, and rewards participation on all levels. People will not believe in a change effort unless they have the opportunity to plan it, experience it, provide feedback, and own it. Involvement supports and sustains motivation, the essential ingredient for change.

Systematic Strategies and Tactics. A fully integrated plan for change is needed to address the complexity of culture-based problems. A well-planned approach breaks a problem into key component parts so that attention can be systematically directed toward solutions.

Win-Win Solutions. All individuals and groups in the organization need to benefit from positive changes, and positive change is the responsibility of each individual. Since there will be no losers in this contest, there is no room for blame placing. The energy wasted trying to find the villain or the culprit to be blamed for past failures may be parlayed into increased movement toward change goals.

Results Orientation. Organization members focus on the results to be achieved. They observe their own progress and reward themselves for it, and this in turn motivates further progress. Short- and long-range goals are established and results are promptly noted. Visible accomplishments help keep participants in touch with progress toward objectives.

Sustained Effort. For success to be achieved, the organization must commit itself to a long-term, sustained effort. Inherent in this principle is the concept of enjoyment, of taking pleasure in day-to-day progress and in the enriched relationships that result from working together. People who are not enjoying the process do not stick with any plan for long.

Freedom. Last, but far from least, the principle of freedom is basic to the normative systems approach. People must feel, understand, and trust that their organization respects and encourages their freedom to mold and create their organizational environment. We create culture as it creates us. Cultural analysis and change make us both powerful and free.

The Four Phases

The four phases that comprise this conceptual model are intended to serve as a generic framework for change in organizations of any size and in any setting. The model depicts a systematic process through which solutions can evolve. Because culture is an intangible entity that involves people and their relationships, application of the system must remain flexible and organic.

The four phases often overlap and must stretch to accommodate the unique qualities and structure of each organization. The system described here is presented as a guideline within which managers can creatively formulate programs that suit the needs of their own particular situations.

Phase I: Analysis and Objective Setting. Phase I is the preparation phase of the program. Without sound preparation, it is unlikely that any change program can be effective. It provides us with an opportunity to determine:

- What is now happening in the organization and why?
- What do we want to have happen?
- What do we need to do to bring about the desired change?

In order to respond constructively to these questions, we must involve ourselves in a process of fact finding and study to ensure that our change program is based on sound information and that it is headed in the desired direction. To do this we carry out a conceptual analysis of the culture, identify the key norm influences affecting the culture, and set tentative objectives for our change program.

A useful analysis is not only wide but deep. It goes beneath the surface of the problem to discern the latent causes of any manifest negative behavior. It aims for a deep understanding of the environmental issues that are often articulated in simplistic, negative descriptions of behavior ("we don't communicate," "we have no team work"). Without a careful and sensitive scrutiny of the underlying norms of the culture, we set ourselves up for recurrent failure, and we set our objectives out of despair rather than from positive planning.

During Phase I we plan for action, not reaction. It is crucial during this period to enlist and demonstrate the support of both the appointed and indigenous organizational leaders. A visible public commitment for change from the leaders of the organization is the foundation upon which successful work can progress. If employees hear or sense a lack of commitment on the part of the leadership of the organization, this negative strain will infect and undermine all future efforts.

In this analysis phase we review systematically the key influences that impact on any given culture: (1) we take a critical look at the formal documents, manuals, and organizational statements that publicly express desired behavior; (2) we use confidential interviews and observations to help evaluate both the manifest and latent norms of the culture; (3) we conduct a cultural audit, making use of an opinion-survey instrument such as the one illustrated in Figure 2, designed to examine cultural norms and norm influences throughout the organization. The overall purpose of this review is to get a feeling for "the way things are around here." Particular attention is given to the following nine areas that frequently are influential in a culture:

1. *Rewards*. What behaviors are supported? Rewarded? What behaviors lead to confrontation and formal or informal penalties?

2. *Modeling Behavior*. Which people have the greatest influence, and what type of behavior do they model for the organization? Are others expected to model this behavior, or is the philosophy projected, "Do as we say, not as we do"?

3. *Information and Communication Systems*. What information is being communicated? Do mixed messages sometimes cause confusion? Is it the norm for people at all levels to seek out the ideas and opinions of others?

4. *Interactions and Relationships*. In what ways do present interactions and relationships influence the culture? What opportunities exist for improving these interactions and relationships? Do organizational units and teams work effectively together?

5. *Management and Supervisory Skills*. Do managers and supervisors have the skills necessary for effective leadership? How can they be helped to develop these skills if they do not have them?

6. *Organizational Structures, Policies, and Procedures*. Is the organization structured in a way that helps it achieve its objectives? Are there ways that the organizational structures, policies, and procedures can be modified to help them contribute more to the achievement of the cultural goals?

7. *Training*. Are training opportunities sufficient to support the desired culture? Are skills developed in the training process supported in the day-to-day life of the organization?

8. *Orientation*. Are the right things being communicated during the orientation process? Do the people responsible for

Figure 2. Extract from a Cultural Audit.

Instructions:
Norms are expected or usual ways of behaving in groups or organizations. This survey asks for your opinions concerning the norms that exist in your organization. You are to fill in the blank that best describes your agreement or disagreement with each of the statements in the survey. Some examples are given below. After completing the sample items, continue with the remaining survey items.

	Strongly Agree	Agree	Neutral	Disagree	Strongly Disagree	Don't Know
Example It is a norm around here:						
A. for people to be rude to each other.	( )	( )	( )	( )	( )	( )
B. for people to be comfortably dressed.	( )	( )	( )	( )	( )	( )
C. for coffee breaks to be pleasant.	( )	( )	( )	( )	( )	( )
It is a norm around here:						
1. to maintain the progress that is made.	( )	( )	( )	( )	( )	( )
2. for people to regularly plan their work goals and review progress.	( )	( )	( )	( )	( )	( )
3. for new people to be properly oriented and trained for their jobs.	( )	( )	( )	( )	( )	( )
4. for leaders to take time to follow up on the jobs they've assigned to people.	( )	( )	( )	( )	( )	( )
5. for organizational policies and procedures to be helpful, well understood, and up-to-date.	( )	( )	( )	( )	( )	( )
6. for people to confront negative behavior or norms constructively.	( )	( )	( )	( )	( )	( )
7. for people to avoid blame placing and concentrate on looking for constructive solutions.	( )	( )	( )	( )	( )	( )
8. for people to feel satisfied with their pay.	( )	( )	( )	( )	( )	( )
9. for people to feel that their work is important.	( )	( )	( )	( )	( )	( )
10. for people to feel that the organization offers good job security.	( )	( )	( )	( )	( )	( )

the orientation process exhibit positive behavioral norms, attitudes, and work habits?

9. *Allocation of Resources.* On what are money, time, and resources spent? Are expenditures in line with the cultural goal?

By asking the right questions, we begin to see that answers are possible. Norms are made by people, and they can be changed by people. The energy stemming from that recognition helps us to establish our objectives.

Another important element of the Phase 1 process is the establishment of three types of objectives: (1) performance objectives to assess such quantifiable factors as production results, sales figures, and profitability; (2) program objectives to ensure the institution of such activities as training programs and reward systems needed to bring about the desired change; and (3) cultural objectives to measure the presence or absence of the cultural norms that are desired. The first two types of objectives are common in most change programs. The third, however, is often neglected, but, with the other two, it is essential to the norm-based strategy presented here. Without all three types of objectives, change programs are likely to be less successful than they otherwise might be; all three provide the focus for subsequent phases and are formally evaluated during the Phase IV evaluation of program success.

Phase II: Systems Introduction and Involvement. In the second phase, each group and work team, beginning with the top of the organization, has an opportunity to become involved in the change process. All of the people directly affected by the change program must have an opportunity to experience the new culture. Often a workshop provides an appropriate atmosphere for the introduction of new norms, because people are generally more open to trying new norms when they are away from familiar surroundings and requirements. In this way, possibilities for change are perceived as real.

People involved in the change program are first given the opportunity to gain an understanding of the importance of the program, the impact of cultural norms on themselves and the

organization, and the possibilities for change. People next identify the nature of the existing and the desired cultures, focusing
on the norms they want and need to develop in order to reach
the objectives that they have set. Finally, the change agents plan
the action steps necessary to ensure that all of the key influences are modified so that they support the objectives of the
change process.

Ownership is an essential concept throughout the four-
phase process, and it is given special emphasis during Phase II. If
people feel their ideas have been considered in preparing the program, they will be more likely to take on responsibility for
change and to feel in control of their situations. Two aspects of
the ownership concept are vital: it must be *genuine,* and it must
be *felt.* If it is merely felt but not genuine, the program is
manipulative. If people do not feel a part of the process, however, even if they have been invited to participate in its development, ownership will make little difference. Meaningful change
occurs when people both *feel* themselves to be and truly *are* in
control of the process.

At the conclusion of Phase II, participants have the opportunity to ask themselves:

- What can I do to aid in the cultural change process?
- What can our group do, both on its own and in relation to
  other groups, to aid in the cultural change process?
- What can our organization do to aid in the cultural change
  process?

It is with these questions in mind that we move on to the
Phase III implementation of the change program.

Phase III: Systems Implementation and Change. Phase III
allows each individual, group, and the overall organization to
apply to their actual work environment what they have learned
and experienced in the Phase II. Members of the various organizational units focus on those areas of influence that were identified in the Phase I analysis (rewards, modeling, orientation, and
so forth) and begin to modify and strengthen those influences
so that they contribute to the achievement of the goals that

have been set. During this implementation phase, four key elements of the culture are addressed: the individual, the group, the leaders, and the organization.

In all four areas, people are helped to put into practice and reinforce the necessary changes. Let us look at some of the ways each element in the organization can facilitate the change process.

Individuals are oriented to the performance, program, and cultural goals of the organization and to each person's role in the change process. Each person is helped to develop the skills and understandings necessary for the achievement of these goals and rewarded for his or her achievements. As new goals are set, each individual is helped to achieve them. Performance planning and review become a positive, ongoing process, and individuals receive the constructive support and feedback that they require.

Group development is an important part of Phase III. New work teams are established, and existing teams have the opportunity to develop and sustain a constructive group culture with congruent individual and group goals. Work groups meet regularly to discuss issues and problems that affect them and to measure progress toward their goals. Regularly scheduled, carefully planned meetings set the stage for results-oriented sessions, efficient use of time, and enhanced group efforts. Work groups also have an opportunity to improve their intergroup interfaces so that synergism can be achieved.

All cultures are strongly influenced by the perceived behavior of their leaders. Organization leaders are involved in the change process on a continuing basis. Soon after being introduced to the program, leaders are helped to strengthen existing positive norms and to put positive new norms into practice. Use of norm feedback instruments and training modules helps leaders better understand how those they supervise perceive them and strengthens the behavior they project for others to model.

The organizational policies, procedures, and programs that were examined in the Phase I analysis process are modified and strengthened during Phase III so that they provide support for the newly established goals. Where necessary, task forces are formed to explore specific problems, recommend changes, and monitor the effectiveness of the changes that are made.

Phase IV: Evaluation and Renewal. No matter how successful a change effort has been, continual renewal and reassessment are required so that the change program gradually becomes part of the ongoing culture.

Regular evaluation of each of the three types of objectives set in Phase I provides the opportunity to assess what has and has not been accomplished so that necessary modifications can be made. Renewal meetings are scheduled from the outset, and this built-in assessment and renewal process lends weight and credibility to the commitment to change. This phase provides an opportunity for all participants to:

- Recognize achievements.
- Identify areas that need improvement.
- Plan ongoing strategies for further improvements.
- Integrate new people into the process.
- Keep the focus on results.

Information and statistics are examined and evaluated so that progress can be measured, achievements can be recognized, and problems that need to be addressed can be identified.

Barrier Norms

As a change program progresses, it is important to identify those negative norms that might, if overlooked, interfere with the success of the change process. These norms, which we call interfering or barrier norms, can stand in the way of cultural change and must be detected and modified if the change program is to be successful and long lasting.

Most organizations include at least some of the barrier norms discussed here.

Blame Placing. When a problem arises, we often devote our energies to finding a culprit rather than to finding solutions and preventing a recurrence of the problem. In many organizations, there is a tendency to view problem solving as finding someone to blame; a scapegoat for our anger. This fosters frustration and fear rather than efforts to find the best solution to the problem at hand.

Win-Lose Confrontations. We often construct situations in our organizations, groups, and personal relationships in which one side comes out the winner, the other, the loser. Rather than actively seeking win-win solutions, we expend our energy in clashes that create an environment in which everyone loses in the end.

Simplistic Solutions. We often count on, wish for, or talk ourselves into easy answers to complex questions. Our anxiety to "do something" causes us to forge ahead before we fully understand the real nature of a problem, and our simplistic, single-variable solutions become important links in the vicious cycle of organizational frustration and failure.

Crash Programs. Related to simple solutions, crash programs burst upon the scene with the energy and flash of fireworks. Unfortunately, they fizzle out as quickly, with more at stake. These brief, enthusiastic attempts at problem solving die almost as they appear. An organization often energetically jumps into a crash program like an overweight person committing to a fad diet, but crash dieters know that they have lost the same pounds many times over. In an organization, crash programs sap energy and create disappointment. A change program without commitment can induce even deeper feelings of negativity and hopelessness than those that existed before the crash program was undertaken.

Learned Helplessness. A feeling of helplessness is often the result of constant exposure to simple solutions and crash programs. When not combated, learned helplessness can nurture a pervasive negativity that presents a formidable obstacle to cultural change.

Promises, Promises. In an effort to encourage participation, we often make promises that we cannot keep. We underestimate the intelligence and sensitivity of employees, who most often are as aware of difficulties and obstacles as we are. It is best whenever possible to share these difficulties and obstacles with employees, because promises without visible results lead to disillusionment and mistrust.

A Caveat

All of us who are interested in cultural change programs need to remain sensitive and objective about our efforts in this arena. We know that the power of culture is awesome, it governs so many areas of our lives. When we enlist that power for the good of our organizations, it can greatly enrich the lives of all individuals involved.

We must, however, reflect critically and constantly upon the goals and objectives that we set for ourselves and the openness of the process we employ. We must be wary of programs and plans that merely substitute one form of manipulation or control for another, or, like the rain dancer, we will end up tired and dry in the end. By emphasizing the concept of ownership at all levels, we can protect our programs from our own sabotage.

History has given us too many examples of top-down cultural changes in the service of negative goals. Nazi Germany is one illustration of how extremely successful change programs resulted in one of the world's most horrifying eras. Cultural change can be destructive and dehumanizing. This is neither worthwhile nor acceptable, and is more likely to be avoided if those who are affected by change are involved in the change process.

Managerial Checklist

Asking the following questions can help us evaluate our change programs as they proceed:

- Have we defined our management objectives in terms of the desired performance, program, and cultural outcomes? Are these objectives clear?
- Do we have a workable plan for involving all people within the organization?

- Is the leadership commitment to the change program visible? Can we make it more visible?
- Are leaders prepared, willing, and able to model the behavior we desire?
- Do we have a plan for giving feedback as to our progress toward our desired goals?
- Do we have a system to ensure that people will be rewarded for desired behavior?
- Is the organizational structure one that supports the achievement of our goals?
- Are our relationships and communications such that people can work well together?
- Have we provided a framework within which people at all levels will have the opportunity to develop the knowledge and skills they need to meet both individual and organizational goals?
- Will the organization's orientation procedure reflect and support our new cultural objectives?
- Do we have a systematic plan for implementing each phase of the change program at each level of the organization?
- Have we developed strategies for achieving win-win solutions through constructive problem solving?
- Is our program results oriented?

Conclusion

The normative systems methodology for cultural change can be a valuable tool for managers and their organizations. It can be used to help people at all levels of the organization—from top managers to the lowest-paid employees—become involved in creating their own positive environments instead of being unwilling victims of whatever currently exists.

Implementing this methodology is, however, complex—there are no easy answers to complex cultural problems—and it is time consuming, though not as time consuming as consistent failure. The exact amount of time the process will take depends on the size and complexity of the organization and the problems being confronted, but it takes time to create norms, and so it also takes time to change them.

Is it possible for this methodology to work? Yes; people and organizations can shape the cultures that influence their success if they are willing to expend their time, energy, and commitment. This investment, however, is not only worthwhile, but energizing, and the alternative—continuing to live and work in cultures that are less than what we would like them to be—is not a viable choice for people who want to make a difference in their organizations.

Seventeen

Five Steps for
Closing Culture-Gaps

Ralph H. Kilmann

The likelihood that an organization will achieve success in a
dynamic and complex environment is not determined just by
the skills of its leaders, nor by the strategies, structures, and reward systems that make up its visible features. Rather, the organization itself has an invisible quality—a certain style, a character, a way of doing things—that may be more powerful than
the dictates of any one person or any formally documented system. To understand the essence or soul of the organization requires that we travel below the charts, rulebooks, machines, and
buildings into the underground world of corporate cultures.

What exactly is culture? Nobody knows for sure, nor will
there ever be a clear definition that meets with everyone's approval. William B. Renner (1981, p. 1), vice-chairman of the
Aluminum Company of America, mentions the problem of defining culture: "Culture is different things to different people.

Adapted from *Beyond the Quick Fix: Managing Five Tracks to Organizational Success* (San Francisco: Jossey-Bass, 1984).

For some, it's family, or religion. It's opera or Shakespeare, a
few clay pots at a Roman dig. Every textbook offers a definition, but I like a simple one: culture is the shared values and
behavior that knit a community together. It's the rules of the
game; the unseen meaning between the lines in the rulebook
that assures unity. All organizations have a culture of their
own."

Most definitions of culture disagree mainly on *what* is
shared among the members of an organization. Is it rules, norms,
beliefs, expectations, values, philosophies, or all of these things?
For most purposes, these intangibles are so interconnected that
it makes little sense to argue about how each is similar to or different from the others. However, it is worthwhile to learn how
these intangibles become shared among the members of any
group, and why this creates such a powerful force that guides
behavior. Thus, the most exciting thing about culture is discovering how it first captures and then directs the collective will of
a group's members.

Culture provides meaning, direction, and mobilization—it
is the social energy that moves the corporation into action. A
person has to experience the energy that flows from shared
commitments among group members to know it: the energy
that emanates from mutual influence, "one for all, and all for
one," and "esprit de corps." Can management tap this source of
energy for organizational success, or will the energy remain immobilized? Or, worse yet, will this social energy be working
against the mission of the organization?

There are many organizations in which this social energy
has barely been tapped. The energy has been diffused in all directions or even deactivated; it is not mobilized toward anything. Most organization members seem apathetic or depressed
about their jobs. They no longer pressure one another to do
well. Pronouncements by top management that the situation
will improve fall on deaf ears. The members have heard these
promises before. Nothing seems to matter. The soul of the organization is dying.

In other cases, even though the energy is actively flowing,
it is moving members in the wrong direction. The organization

lives in a culture lag, or *culture-gap*—the social energy pressures members to persist in behaviors that may have worked well in the past but that clearly are dysfunctional today. The gap between the outdated culture and what is needed for success gradually develops into a *culture rut*—people pursue behaviors out of habit without asking any questions. There is no adaptation or change; routine motions are made again and again, even though success is not forthcoming. Here, the social energy not only works against the organization but is contrary to the private wishes of the members. Nobody wants to be ineffective and dissatisfied, but everyone pressures one another to comply with the unstated, below-the-surface, behind-the-scenes, invisible culture. An organization can proceed in this rut for years, even though morale and performance suffer. Bad habits die hard.

Culture shock occurs when the sleeping organization awakens and finds that it has lost touch with its mission, its setting, and its assumptions. Today's world has left the insulated company behind—it is a Rip Van Winkle story on a grand scale. Rather than experience this shock, the organization may decide not to wake up; its managers may simply continue to believe the myth of erroneous extrapolation: what made the organization successful in the past will make it successful in the future.

The first part of this chapter explores three interrelated questions: (1) What are adaptive—in contrast to dysfunctional—cultures? (2) How do cultures form; what brings cultures into being? (3) How are cultures maintained; what forces keep cultures intact? Understanding the answers to these questions is necessary for assessing and changing cultures. In these discussions, we will see how cultural norms provide the leverage points for creating and maintaining adaptive cultures more directly than any of the other manifestations of an organization's way of doing things.

The second part of this chapter presents five steps for managing culture: (1) surfacing actual norms, (2) articulating new directions, (3) establishing new norms, (4) identifying culture-gaps, and (5) closing culture-gaps. These five steps show how the organization can gain control over its culture rather than vice versa. The members can decide on what new norms are needed for today's complex problems and then can proceed to energize their work groups toward the new directions they envision, thereby closing the corporate culture-gap.

What Are Adaptive Cultures?

Even if we accept the idea that the term *culture* will always be a bit vague and ill defined, unlike the more superficial and tangible aspects of organizations, it is still important to consider what makes a culture good or bad, adaptive or dysfunctional. Wallach (1983, p. 32) provides a summary of what cultures do for the organization: "There are no good or bad cultures, per se. A culture is good—effective—if it reinforces the mission, purposes and strategies of the organization. It can be an asset or a liability. Strong cultural norms make an organization efficient. Everyone know what's important and how things are done. To be effective, the culture must not only be efficient, but appropriate to the needs of the business, company, and the employees."

Why does one organization have a very adaptive culture while another has a culture that reflects only the past? Is one a case of good fortune, and the other a result of bad luck? To the contrary, it seems that any organization can find itself with an outdated culture if its culture is not explicitly managed.

If left alone, a culture eventually becomes dysfunctional. Human fear, insecurity, oversensitivity, dependency, and paranoia seem to take over unless a concerted effort to establish an adaptive culture is undertaken. People have been hurt at one time or another in their lives, particularly in their childhoods. It is, therefore, easy to scare people into worrying about what pain or hurt will be inflicted in the future, even in a relatively nonthreatening situation. As a result, people cope by protecting themselves, by being cautious, by minimizing their risks, by going along with a culture that builds protective barriers around work units and around the whole organization.

A dysfunctional culture also helps explain some of the self-defeating behaviors that have been observed in many organizations, behaviors that persist in spite of their many disruptive effects. These behaviors include doing the minimum to get by, purposely resisting or even sabotaging innovation, and being generally negative about the organization's capacity to change. Worse yet, behaviors may even include lying; cheating; stealing; and intimidating, harassing, and hurting others. While these behaviors may seem unthinkable, they often do receive cultural support even though they cause difficult problems for the organization. They also significantly undermine both morale and performance.

The most detrimental behavior in the long run, however, is continuing to see and act out what made the organization successful in the past rather than adapting to the dynamic complexity of today and tomorrow. AM International, for example, found itself caught in a culture rut because it fell into the trap of erroneous extrapolation: "The common denominator of our problems at AM International has been the corporate culture. When a company has been in business for a long time and enjoyed a long history of success, such success reaffirms the validity of the way things have been done, of the corporate culture, in the minds of the company's managers and other employees. It's as though they were saying to themselves, 'If we have been that successful, we must be doing something right.' But it too often turns out even when the company is no longer successful, employees persist in doing things the old way" ("Conversation with Roy L. Ash," 1979, p. 54). The company is now faced with the challenge of developing a new, functional culture.

Emerson Electric is faced with a similar need for cultural change in order to break out of its old behavior patterns: "Emerson's very success in building a culture that focuses so thoroughly on year-by-year returns may hamper its quest to deliver the new technology its markets demand. A culture that was built on cost-cutting and total dedication to the bottom line must be made flexible enough to encourage the development of technologies and products whose payoff may be years down the road. . . . But so deeply embedded is Emerson's old culture that some company officials still question whether top management will stick to its new policy if success does not come quickly" ("Emerson Electric . . . ," 1983, p. 58).

Alternatively, an *adaptive* culture entails a risk-taking, trusting, and proactive approach to organizational as well as individual life. Members actively support one another's efforts to identify all problems and to implement workable solutions. There is a shared feeling of confidence: the members believe, without a doubt, that they can effectively manage whatever new problems and opportunities will come their way. There is widespread enthusiasm, a spirit of doing whatever it takes to achieve organizational success. The members are receptive to change and innovation.

How Do Cultures Form?

Cultures often form quickly, depending on the organization's mission and setting and what is required for the organization's success: quality, efficiency, product reliability, customer service, innovation, hard work, loyalty, and so forth. When an organization is born, a tremendous energy usually is released as members struggle to make the company work. The culture reflects everyone's drive and imagination. As the reward systems, policies, procedures, and rules governing work are formally documented, they begin to have a more specific impact on shaping the initial culture, suggesting what behaviors and attitudes are important for success in each work unit.

Such forces in shaping culture, however, cannot compete with either the bold or the subtle actions of key individuals. For example, the objectives, principles, values, and especially the behavior of the founder of the firm provide important clues as to what is *really* wanted from all members both now and in the future. Other top executives follow the founder's lead and pass on the culture of the company to their subordinates. Edson W. Spencer, chief executive officer and chairman of Honeywell, discussed his impact on the corporate culture: "Most of us, very humbly don't wish to acknowledge that fact, but nonetheless the chief executive's tone, his integrity, his standards, his way of dealing with people, his focusing on things that are important or not important can have a profound impact on the rest of the organization. What I am saying is that the way the chief executive and senior managers of the company conduct themselves as individuals has a more profound impact on how other people in the company conduct *themselves* than anything else that happens" ("Conversation with Edson W. Spencer . . . ," 1983, p. 43).

Employees also take note of all critical incidents that stem from any management action, such as the time that so-and-so was reprimanded for doing a good job just because he was not asked to do it beforehand or the time that so-and-so was fired because she publicly disagreed with the company's position. Incidents such as these become the folklore that people remember, indicating what the corporation really wants, what really counts in getting ahead, or, alternatively, how to stay out of trouble—the unwritten rules of the game. Work groups adopt these lessons as norms of how to survive and make it, how to protect oneself from the system, and how to retaliate against the organization for its "sins."

As a culture forms around a recognized need, setting, and specific task requirements, it may be very functional at first. But, over time, the culture becomes an entity unto itself, independent of the initial reasons and incidents that formed it. The culture becomes distinct from the formal strategy, structure, and reward systems of the organization. As long as it is supportive of and in harmony with these formally documented systems, the culture remains in the background.

Culture also becomes distinct from its members. All members throughout the organization are taught to follow the cultural norms without questioning them. By the time employees have been part of the organization for even a few years, they will have "learned the ropes." Even new top executives who vow that things will be different soon find out—often the hard way—that culture is more powerful than they are. Single-handed efforts by an executive to counter the "invisible social hand" are met with constant frustration. For example, a top manager can get verbal commitments for some new policy or plan from every individual subordinate; however, when each person moves back into the corporate culture, the manager finds that the new plan is bitterly opposed.

The strength of the culture is even more apparent when management attempts to make a major strategic shift or tries to adopt entirely new work methods and the culture does not support the changes. Management cannot pinpoint the source of apathy, resistance, or rebellion and is puzzled as to why the new work methods are not automatically and enthusiastically embraced. To management, it is obvious that these proposed changes are necessary and desirable. Why cannot everyone else see this? The reason is that the changes run counter to the culture that underlies the organization.

At the same time, top management is also caught in the grip of the firm's separate and distinct culture. Employees from below wonder why managers "play it so safe," why they refuse to approach things differently, why they keep applying the same old management practices even though these simply do not work. Employees wonder why management is so blind to the world around them. They wonder if management is "mean" or just "stupid."

How Are Cultures Maintained?

The force controlling behavior at every level in the organization—the force that can make members believe that what they are doing is automatically good for their company, their community, and their family—must be very powerful indeed. That such dysfunctional and self-defeating behaviors can persist for years again suggests that some powerful force is at work. Is it magic, or is it the result of people's need to affiliate themselves with a group? We must understand the invisible force that is operating if we wish to control it rather than have it control us. A deeper knowledge of norms and how they are enforced is essential.

Social scientists speak of norms as the unwritten rules of behavior. In a company, for example, a norm might be: don't disagree with your boss in public. These norms are embedded in the organization when a strong consensus exists among organization members concerning what constitutes appropriate behavior. If a norm is violated—if someone behaves differently from what the norm dictates—there are immediate and strong pressures to get the offending party to change his or her behavior. Consider, for example, an individual who persists in presenting his or her reservations about the company's new product at a group meeting just after his boss has argued strongly for investing heavily in an advertising campaign for the product. The individual is stared at, frowned at, looked at with rolling eyes, and given other nonverbal messages to shut up and sit down. If these efforts do not silence the individual, he will hear about it later, either from his co-workers or from his boss.

Every person's need to be accepted by a group—family, friends, co-workers, or neighbors—gives a group leverage to demand compliance with its norms. If people did not care about acceptance at all, a group would have little hold, other than formal sanctions, over individuals. The nonconformists and the mavericks who defy pressures to adhere to group norms always do so at considerable risk.

A simple experiment conducted by Asch (1955) demonstrates just how powerfully the group can influence its deviants. The experiment was presented to subjects as a study in perception. Three lines—A, B, and C—all of different lengths, were shown on a single card. Subjects were asked to indicate which of these three lines was identical in length to a fourth line, D, shown on a second card. Seven people sat in a row. One by one they indicated their choices. While line D was in fact identical to line C, each of the first six people, confederates of the experimenter, said that line D was identical to A. The seventh person was the unknowing subject. As the six confederates each gave the agreed-upon incorrect response, the actual subjects usually became increasingly uneasy, anxious, and doubtful of their own perceptions. Subjects agreed with the six confederates almost 40 percent of the time. When no other individuals were present, subjects chose the wrong line less than 1 percent of the time.

In this experiment, which has been duplicated many times, there was no opportunity for the seven people to discuss the problem among themselves. If there had been such an opportunity, the effect would have been stronger, because the six confederates would attempt to influence the seventh person. It is not easy to be a deviant in a group when everyone else is against you. People need acceptance from others so much that they will deny their own perceptions when confronted with the group's norms of "objective" reality. Objective reality thus becomes *social* reality.

Imagine just how easily such socially defined and distorted perceptions of reality can be maintained when backed by formal sanctions such as pay, promotions, and other rewards. The group or the entire organization can reward its members so that they ignore not only the changes taking place in the environment but also the disruptive behaviors of various troublemakers inside the organization. The members collectively believe that everything is fine, and they continue to reinforce this myth and reward one another for maintaining it. In essence, everyone agrees that the dysfunctional ways can continue without question. Any deviant who thinks otherwise is severely punished and eventually "banished from the tribe."

Assessing and Changing Cultural Norms

While culture manifests itself through shared values, beliefs, expectations, and assumptions, it is most easily controlled through norms, the unwritten rules of the game. Even norms that dictate people's behavior, opinions, and facial expressions can be surfaced, discussed, and altered: "Norms are a universal phenomenon. They are necessary, tenacious, but also extremely malleable. Because they can change so quickly and easily, they present a tremendous opportunity to people interested in change. Any group, no matter its size, once it understands itself as a cultural entity, can plan its own norms, creating positive ones that will help it reach its goals and modifying or discarding the negative ones" (Allen and Kraft, 1982, pp. 7-8).

A good way to assess an organization's culture is to ask members to write out what previously was unwritten. Members usually are willing and able to write out their norms under certain conditions: (1) no member will be identified as stating or suggesting a particular norm, and (2) no norm will be documented when members' superiors are present. Further, the members must believe that the list of norms will not be used against them but will be used to benefit them as well as their organization. The consultants and managers who guide members to state norms, therefore, must generate trust and commitment throughout all steps of the five-step process.

Step 1: Surfacing Actual Norms. The first step is for group members, usually in a workshop setting, to list the actual norms that currently guide their behaviors and attitudes. This can be done with just one group or with many groups, departments, and divisions, depending on how many individuals can be included and managed in one setting. Sometimes it takes a little prodding and a few illustrations to get the process started, but once it begins, members are quick to suggest many norms. In fact, they seem to delight in being able to articulate what beforehand was never stated in any document and rarely mentioned in any conversation.

For an organization whose culture is dysfunctional, some of the norms people may list are: don't disagree with your boss, don't rock the boat, treat women as second-class citizens, put down your organization, don't enjoy your work, don't share information with other groups, treat subordinates as incompetent and lazy, cheat on your expense account, look busy even when you are not, don't reward employees on the basis of merit, laugh at those who suggest new ways of doing things, don't smile much, openly criticize company policies to outsiders, complain a lot, don't trust anyone who seems sincere. One norm that may exist and that must be violated so that this list can be developed is: don't make norms explicit.

When norms are listed for everyone to see, there usually is considerable laughter and amazement as members become aware that they have been seducing one another into abiding by these counterproductive directives. But each individual did not make a conscious choice to behave this way; rather, as each individual entered the organization, each was taught the expected behavior, often in quite subtle ways. The more cohesive the group, the more rapidly this learning takes place and the more strongly the sanctions are applied. In an extreme case, a highly cohesive group that has been together a long time may have members that look, act, think, and talk like one another.

Step 2: Articulating New Directions. The next step is for all group members to discuss where the organization is headed and what type of behavior is necessary to move forward. Even when a company has a very dysfunctional culture from the past, members, as individuals, usually are aware of what changes are needed for organizational success. Similarly, members are aware of what work environment they prefer for their own well being and satisfaction.

A certain amount of planning and problem solving, however, may be needed to help members articulate the new directions in which the company should head. In work groups that have been in a culture rut, members often are so absorbed with the negative aspects of their situation that they have not spent much time thinking about or discussing what they desire. Sometimes it is useful to ask members to reflect upon their ideal organization: if they could design their own organization from scratch, what would it be like? This generally develops into a discussion of how the present organization could be different and what aspects of the organization should not be accepted just because they have existed for a long time.

Step 3: Establishing New Norms. The third step is for all group members to develop a list of new norms that would lead to organizational success. At this point, the members usually recognize the impact that unwritten rules have had on their behavior. They experience a sense of relief as a new way of life is considered. They realize that they no longer have to pressure one another to behave in dysfunctional ways. The members can create a new social order within their own work groups and within their own organization. Part of this sense of relief comes from recognizing that their dissatisfaction and ineffectiveness are not the result of their being incompetent or bad individuals. It is much easier, psychologically, for members to blame the invisible force called *culture.*

Some of the new norms that are often listed as necessary to help an organization adapt to modern times are: treat everyone with respect and as a potential source of valuable insights and expertise, be willing to take on responsibility, initiate changes to improve performance, congratulate those who suggest new ideas and new ways of doing things, be cost conscious so that the organization remains efficient relative to its competitors, speak with pride about your organization and work group, budget your time according to the importance of tasks for accomplishing objectives, don't criticize the organization in front of clients or customers, enjoy your work and show your enthusiasm for a job well done, be helpful and supportive of the other groups in the organization.

Step 4: Identifying Culture-Gaps. The difference between the desired norms identified in Step 3 and the actual norms identified in Step 1 can be immense. This difference can be called a *culture-gap*. The Kilmann-Saxton Culture-Gap Survey (Kilmann and Saxton, 1983) is a measurement tool that can be used to detect the gap between what the current culture is and what it should be.

This survey was developed by first collecting more than four hundred norms from employees in more than twenty-five different types of organizations. Many of these norms were also developed through culture-change projects. The final set of twenty-eight norm pairs that appear on the survey were derived from statistical analysis of the norms that were most frequently cited in the organizations studied. An example of a norm pair is: (A) Share information only when it benefits your own work group, versus (B) Share information to help the organization make better decisions. Each employee is asked to select the item in each norm pair that indicates, first, the pressures the work group puts on its members (actual norms) and, second, the norms that should be operating to promote high performance and morale (desired norms).

The differences between the actual norms and the desired norms represent culture-gaps. Culture-gaps occur in four areas, each revealed through seven norm pairs:

1. Task Support: norms for sharing information, helping other groups, and being concerned with efficiency; for example, "Support the work of other groups" versus "Put down the work of other groups."
2. Task Innovation: norms for being creative, being rewarded

for creativity, and doing new things; for example, "Always
try to improve" versus "Don't rock the boat."

3. Social Relationships: norms for socializing with one's work
    group and mixing friendships and business: for example,
    "Get to know the people in your work group" versus
    "Don't bother."

4. Personal Freedom: norms for expressing oneself, exercising
    discretion, and pleasing oneself; for example, "Live for
    yourself and your family" versus "Live for your job and
    career."

Using the Kilmann-Saxton Culture-Gap Survey in numerous profit and nonprofit organizations has revealed distinct patterns of culture-gaps. For example, in some high-technology
firms, lack of cooperation and information sharing across
groups has resulted in large culture-gaps in Task Support. In the
automotive and steel industries, not rewarding creativity and innovation has resulted in large culture-gaps in Task Innovation.
In some social service agencies, where work loads vary greatly,
large negative gaps in Social Relationships are found, indicating
that too much time is spent socializing rather than getting the
next job done. In extremely bureaucratic organizations, such as
some banks and government agencies, large gaps in Personal
Freedom are evident; members feel overly confined and constrained, which affects their performance and morale.

The most salient finding to date is the widespread presence of large culture-gaps in Task Innovation. It seems that
American industry is plagued by significant differences between
actual and desired norms in this area, a finding that is supported
by the general acknowledgment of the existence of a productivity problem in the United States. An industrial culture that
pushes short-term financial results is bound to foster norms
against efforts at long-term work improvements, regardless of
what formal documents and publicity statements claim.

Do all members in the same organization see the same
culture-gaps? Apparently not. The smallest culture-gaps are
found at the top of the organization's hierarchy. Managers believe their own publicity; they say that they reward creativity

and innovation but do not recognize that their actions speak louder than their words. Culture-gaps are largest at the bottom of the hierarchy, where the gaps also reveal alienation and distrust. Here the work groups can explain what is meant by the norm: don't trust management. In essence, work groups see management as up to no good, caught up in fads to fool and manipulate employees, or viewing workers as too stupid to see what is behind management's latest whim.

This sort of grass roots culture not only describes a culture rut but suggests why developing an adaptive culture must precede any other effort to promote change and improvement. Without an adaptive culture, every action by top management will be discounted, or ignored by the groups below. Even top-down efforts to change the culture will be unsuccessful; executives may try to dictate a new culture by making dramatic changes in their own behavior and symbolic gestures and fiery speeches, but only when work group members encourage one another to be receptive to overtures by other groups—as a result of the five-step process for closing culture-gaps—will culture change take place. For example, various work groups could include such new norms as: give management another chance and assume good intentions. Managers and consultants, therefore, need to work especially hard to encourage work groups, including executive groups, to meet one another half way.

Just as the size of culture-gaps can vary according to the shape of the organization pyramid, the type of culture-gaps can differ from division to division in the same organization. Divisions have different histories, critical incidents, strategies, markets, and managers. As a result, each division in a multiproduct firm may require a different culture to be effective. Let us look at the case of an international conglomerate, General Telephone and Electronics (GTE): "GTE is a conglomerate that includes operations as diverse as a light-bulb manufacturer and a high-tech microcircuit manufacturer, as well as telephone companies —each with its own cultural norms. In fact, it is such a diversified organization that another question enters the fray: Does it make sense to try to create some sort of 'unified' GTE culture?" (Lee, 1984, p. 31).

In contrast, a very centralized, single-product firm may have an identical culture-gap profile in every work group, department, and division. For example, International Business Machines (IBM) is often cited as a firm that has a very strong, unified culture because of its highly focused mission in the computer industry. Only if the success of IBM's different products—such as mainframe computers and personal computers—depended on different employee behaviors would unique cultures be desirable for the company's various divisions.

Step 5: Closing Culture-Gaps. How can culture-gaps be closed? How can an organization achieve its desired culture? Can a company be freed from a culture rut and put back on a track that will allow it to solve present and future problems? Will the organization survive the culture shock that accompanies such change?

When members of the current culture are at least open to change, it is almost miraculous what impact survey results or lists of desired norms can have on the members of a work unit. As mentioned before, there is often a great sense of relief as people become aware that they can live according to different norms and that they have the power to change their work environment. Surprisingly, some change can be brought about just by listing desired new norms, because members often start acting out the new norms immediately after they are discussed.

When members of the current culture are cynical, depressed, and in a rut, the response to survey results is quite different. Even when large gaps are shown to exist and when a tremendous difference between actual and desired norms is revealed, the members are often apathetic and listless. Members respond by saying that their work units cannot change for the better until the level of management above them and the rest of the company changes. Members believe that it is the external system that is keeping them down.

Curiously, when a culture-gap survey is conducted at the next highest level, the very same arguments are heard again: "We have no power to change; we have to wait for the next level to let us change; *they* have the power." It is shocking, after conducting a culture-gap survey for an entire organization, to present the results to the top management group only to find the same feelings of helplessness. Here, top management is waiting for the economy to change. In reality, it is the corporate culture that is saying: don't take on responsibility; protect yourself at all costs; don't try to change until everyone else has changed; don't lead the way, follow; if you ignore the problem, maybe it will go away.

This is a perfect example of a company in a culture rut, where the shock of acknowledging the discrepancy between actual and desired norms is just too great to confront. Instead, the organization buries its head in the sand and hopes everything will sort itself out. Even in the face of strong evidence of a serious problem, this organizational denial persists, and it is a much more powerful and perhaps destructive force than any individual denial. The group's power to define reality clouds each person's better judgment. The dysfunctional culture "wins" again.

One large industrial organization asked the author to present a three-day seminar to the top executive group—the chairman of the board, the chief executive officer, and the ten corporate officers—on the topic of corporate culture. I suggested that a representative survey of culture-gaps be conducted for all divisions in the company. In this way, I could report on the culture of the organization specifically, which would generate a more interesting and lively discussion than an abstract lecture would. In a couple of weeks, the vice-president of human resources gave me his response: "No, we better not do this. I don't think the executive group really wants to know what is going on in the company. Besides, we can't take the chance of surprising them with your survey results." Who is protecting whom?

At another meeting with a major company on the same topic, I shared this anecdote as an example of the culture problem in American industry, without, of course, mentioning any names. The response to my story was: "That must be *our* company you're talking about!" It was not the same company, but the message was the same.

A major lesson to learn from corporate cultures that have successfully changed, especially from cultures that were very dysfunctional and depressed—those in a culture rut—is that people do not have to feel powerless and inept. If managers and organization members decide that change should occur, then changes can be brought about. Power and control are more a social reality than an objective, physical reality. Many times, individuals and organizations have moved forward and achieved great success when everyone else "knew" this was impossible.

Merely listing and stating desired new norms, however, is not enough to instill them in the organization. Also, norms cannot be altered by just declaring a norm change. Members have to develop agreements that the new norms will indeed replace the old norms and this change must be monitored and sanctioned by the work groups. Group members must reward one another for enacting the new behaviors and attitudes and confront one another when the dysfunctional norms creep back into the work group. Assume that one new norm is: congratulate those who suggest new ideas and new ways of doing things. If any member notices that a co-worker frowns when some new product idea is suggested, the co-worker should be given suitable stares and reminders of the new norm. The member might even be confronted with some statement such as: "I thought you were part of the team and had agreed to make the switch. What's your problem?"

In another major company implementing a change program, I suggested that each new norm should be written on an index card and given a number. Each member in a work group was then responsible for monitoring several norms and calling attention to behavior that did not conform. Eventually, group members no longer needed to cite the norms—only the numbers. Co-workers would state: "You just committed a number twelve," or "You pulled a seven on me." These people were able very effectively to enforce their new norms in this lighthearted manner. When "outsiders" heard such interchanges, they were confused, and this added to the group's cohesiveness, because the members now had their own secret code.

Conclusion

Any organization that determines the extent of its culture-gaps using the steps described here is in a position to chart the direction of a culture change. Conducting workshops for each work group, department, and division to present the new norms and the ways in which they will be monitored and enforced will begin the change process. However, the new culture will gradually revert to the old dysfunctional ways if it is not supported by all of the formally documented systems—the strategy, structure, and reward systems—and by top management's behavior. Leaders in each work unit must display such behaviors as risk taking, openness, and flexibility, and employee job descriptions must specify information sharing and cooperation, both within and between all work units. Also, the reward system must encourage members to follow the new cultural norms and suppress the old ones. In these ways, the social energy and the formal system will work together—precisely what is required for organizational success.

References

Allen, R. F., and Kraft, C. *The Organizational Unconscious: How to Create the Corporate Culture You Want and Need.* Englewood Cliffs, N.J.: Prentice-Hall, 1982.

Asch, S. E. "Opinions and Social Pressure." *Scientific American,* Nov. 1955, pp. 31-34.

"Conversation with Edson W. Spencer and Foster A. Boyle." *Organizational Dynamics,* Spring 1983, pp. 30-45.

"Conversation with Roy L. Ash." *Organizational Dynamics,* Autumn 1979, pp. 48-67.

"Emerson Electric: High Profits from Low Tech." *Business Week,* Apr. 4, 1983, pp. 58-62.

Kilmann, R. H., and Saxton, M. J. *The Kilmann-Saxton Culture-Gap Survey.* Pittsburgh, Penn.: Organizational Design Consultants, 1983.

Lee, C. "Raiders of the Corporate Culture." *Training,* Feb. 1984, pp. 26-32.

Renner, W. B. "The New Corporate Culture." *Alcoa's Public Relations and Advertising Department,* 1981, pp. 1-4.

Wallach, E. J. "Individuals and Organizations: The Cultural Match." *Training and Development Journal,* Feb. 1983, pp. 29-36.

Eighteen

Using
Six Organizational Rites
to Change Culture

Harrison M. Trice
Janice M. Beyer

When corporations are viewed as cultural entities, many of the organized activities they pursue can be seen as having a combination of both practical and expressive consequences (Trice, Belasco, and Alutto, 1969; Trice and Beyer, 1984c). Cultural anthropologists refer to such organized activities in other cultures as rites or ceremonies; they study them to discover the shared beliefs and values that characterize the cultures involved (Geertz, 1971).

Similarly, by examining the organized activities in their corporations as rites, managers can uncover many of the beliefs and values underlying their current corporate cultures. This chapter will discuss how managers can use rites to change their companies' cultures.

Views on Culture Change

How easily corporate cultures can be deliberately managed and changed is a matter of considerable controversy. Some of the reasons given by those who argue that cultures are not easy to manage or change are:

1. Cultures are too elusive and hidden to be accurately diagnosed, managed, or changed (Uttal, 1983).
2. It takes such difficult techniques and rare skills and such a long time to understand a culture (Uttal, 1983) and then so much more time to change it (Schwartz and Davis, 1981), that culture change is not a practical endeavor.
3. Cultures arise spontaneously and cannot be consciously created or managed (Dorson, 1972).
4. Corporations have multiple, not single cultures, and it is hard to imagine how all of these diverse cultures can be homogenized (Barley and Louis, 1983).
5. Cultures sustain people through life's difficulties (Beyer, 1981; Boje, Fedor, and Rowland, 1982), and one of the chief ways they do this is by providing continuity; thus, it is natural for people to resist changes in their culture ("Corporate Culture . . . ," 1980).

Other analysts imply that cultures can be readily manipulated, suggesting that managers can use direct, intentional actions not unlike those used in other management tasks to change their corporate cultures (Peters and Waterman, 1982; Deal and Kennedy, 1982; Kilmann, 1982).

The reality probably lies somewhere between these two extremes. Like all other social phenomena, cultures inevitably change, and it is natural for managers and others to attempt to initiate and manage such changes (Jones, 1984). However, it now seems clear that if cultures can be and are deliberately changed, doing so requires a gradual and difficult process. One view emphasizes that cultural change is likely to be incremental: "The most that can be expected is that a manager can slightly modify the trajectory of a culture, rather than exert major control over the direction of its development" (Martin and Siehl, 1983, p. 53). Another view is that changing cultures is difficult because it involves replacing existing social learning processes with new ones (Schein, 1984). Other cautions could be cited. The outlook for change efforts that employ rites, however, is more optimistic, perhaps because rites are concrete leverage points that can be used to bring about change (Trice, 1985).

Other analysts have suggested two major ways that cultures can be changed: through top management behaviors and through more general socialization processes. Proponents of the first approach argue that how managers spend their time and what managers do symbolize the values of the corporate culture; if manager behavior changes, the culture's symbols—and, hence, the culture itself—will also be changed (Peters, 1980; Pfeffer, 1981). Proponents of the second approach suggest that cultures are the result of social learning (Schein, 1984) and therefore can be changed by changing what is taught (Van Maanen and Schein, 1979). One of the customary ways that people learn work-related cultures, for example, is through the socialization processes by which newcomers are inducted into work organizations (Van Maanen, 1973); if these processes are changed, the organization itself will begin to change. These arguments are not wrong, but they are incomplete.

Van Maanen (1973) noted the similarity of socialization processes among police recruits to the rites of passage identified in many different societies by anthropologists. Several other kinds of rites are also practiced in modern corporations (Trice and Beyer, 1984c). All of these rites do much more than mirror existing social arrangements; they also reorganize and even create them. Indeed, secular ceremonies are often assembled and performed precisely for that purpose in modern societies (Moore and Meyerhoff, 1977, pp. 5, 10; Lane, 1981). Rites, as we will see here, can be used to bring about culture change in business organizations.

Organizational Rites

The term *rites* will be used here to refer to organized and planned activities that have both practical and expressive consequences. The activities involved are usually "relatively elaborate, [and] dramatic, . . . [and] consolidate various forms of cultural expression into one event, which is carried out through social interactions, usually for the benefit of an audience" (Trice and Beyer, 1984c, p. 654). When this definition is applied to corporate life, such diverse activities as personnel testing, organizational development programs, and collective bargaining can be seen as rites that have not only practical consequences but also express important cultural meanings. For example, when they were in vogue, personnel tests were used to create an aura of scientific rigor around the important and difficult process of choosing competent personnel (Trice, Belasco, and Alutto, 1969, p. 46). Test use represented deeply held American managerial ideologies and values that centered around rationality (Moore, 1962; Staw, 1980). The current preoccupation with computers and other information systems can be seen as an expression of the same cultural ideologies and values today (Feldman and March, 1981). Similarly, the array of what Peters (1980) called "management systems" now in use manifest rites that communicate a variety of either reinforcing or conflicting cultural messages.

Using both the anthropological and the management literatures as bases, six types of rites that are found in modern organizations can be identified. These can be differentiated according to their intended expressive consequences (Trice and Beyer, 1984c), as shown in Table 1. Like rites in tribal societies, all of these rites also have intended practical consequences. (The term "intended" is used because not all rites actually have either the intended expressive or practical consequences.) Also, as indicated in Table 1, rites often result in not only intended consequences but in less obvious, unintended consequences as well. To use these rites as change mechanisms, therefore, requires careful analysis. Each rite must be analyzed in terms of its potential for stimulating and supporting not only desired change but also impediments to desired change.

We will now examine each of the six specific types of rites that exist in organizations and discuss how they can be used to facilitate organizational change.

Rites of Passage

The most commonly recognized rites in modern society are those that facilitate the transition of new recruits from the status of outsiders to the status of members in some group. A

Table 1. A Typology of Rites by Their Manifest, Expressive Social Consequences.

Types of Rites	Example	Manifest, Expressive Social Consequences	Examples of Possible Latent, Expressive Consequences
Rites of passage	Induction and basic training, U.S. Army	Facilitate transition of people into social roles and statuses that are new for them.	Minimize changes in ways people carry out social roles. Reestablish equilibrium in ongoing social relations.
Rites of degradation	Firing and replacing top executive	Dissolve social identities and their attendant power.	Provide public acknowledgment that problems exist and what their details are. Defend group boundaries by redefining who belongs and who does not. Reaffirm social importance and value of role involved.
Rites of enhancement	Mary Kay Cosmetics seminars	Enhance social identities and their attendant power.	Spread good news about the organization. Provide public recognition of individuals for their accomplishments and motivate others to similar efforts. Enable the organization to take some credit for individual accomplishments. Emphasize social value of performance of social roles.

Rites of renewal	Organizational development activities	Refurbish social structures and improve the ways they function.	Reassure members that something is being done about problems. Disguise nature of the problems. Defer acknowledgment of problems. Focus attention on some problems and away from others. Legitimate and reinforce existing systems of power and authority.
Rites of conflict reduction	Collective bargaining	Reduce conflict and aggression.	Deflect attention from solving problems. Compartmentalize conflict and its disruptive effects. Reestablish equilibrium in disturbed social relations.
Rites of integration	Office Christmas party	Encourage and revive shared feelings that bind people together and keep them committed to a social system.	Permit venting of emotion and temporary loosening of various norms. Reassert and reaffirm, by contrast, moral rightness of usual norms.

prominent feature of genuine rites of passage is some sort of ordeal by which the initiate is symbolically separated from past identities so that the new identity and its obligations can be better assumed. The long ordeal of basic training in the military is the prototypical example of such rites in modern societies (Bourne, 1967; Trice and Beyer, 1984c). Occupations that have a military flavor tend to have somewhat similar, extensive rites of passage.

Another example of a rite of passage is the occupational training required of novice smokejumpers, a specialized group of firefighters who parachute into isolated areas of forests to suppress fires. The first month rookies spend on the job "is one of almost total submission to a strict regimen of physical conditioning, parachute handling, landing techniques, tower jumps, equipment construction and repair, tree climbing, mental conditioning, and physical harassment from experienced jumpers, squadleaders, and pilots" (McCarl, 1976, pp. 49-50). Ordeals of one type or another are also required of police recruits (Van Maanen, 1973), Mormon missionaries (Wilson, 1981), and even college professors (Lortie, 1968).

It is striking that all of the published accounts of well-developed rites of passage initiate people into *occupational* cultures rather than into the cultures of specific organizations. Although orientation and initiation programs are common in work organizations, they rarely seem to have the bite and drama of occupational rites. Perhaps this is one reason that many people in modern societies like the United States appear to be more committed to their occupational identities than to their organizational ones.

This is not necessarily the case in Japan, however. Managerial trainees for one Japanese bank, for example, undergo ordeals similar in intensity to those experienced in the military and in tribal societies. Their ordeals include actual military drills on an army base, Zen meditation exercises in which they are hit with a paddle if their concentration flags, begging for work among strangers, and a grueling endurance walk of twenty-five miles. As many as one-third of all medium- and large-sized Japanese companies employ training rites similar to these (Rohlen, 1973, p. 1542).

There are no accounts of which we are aware of American companies subjecting their managerial trainees to such physical rigors, but the extensive testing, screening, and training required for managerial positions in some corporations has all of the elements of genuine rites of passage. Outcroppings of the three classical phases of rites of passage (Van Gennep, [1909] 1960) were observed in one managerial training program in a large corporation. The separation phase was marked by a two-week period of testing in an assessment center; the transition phase was marked by sensitivity training; and the incorporation phase was marked by a brief shutdown of the plant, during which the production superintendent explained to an assembly of all managers what the trainees had been through, followed by a cocktail party in a nearby club (Trice, 1985). We do not know how widely such extensive rites of passage for managers are practiced but it is unlikely that the one observed was an isolated example.

These examples suggest that rites of passage are presently used primarily to maintain the continuity of existing organizational and occupational cultures. The question is whether they can be used equally successfully to change cultures. There seems to be no inherent problem in using them to instill new cultural beliefs and values in new members of the organization. This becomes more problematic, however, when new members encounter the existing cultural beliefs and values held by veteran members. Will the new recruits be able to sustain their new beliefs and values if their co-workers do not share them? It seems likely that, by themselves, rites of passage used with new recruits will produce cultural change only in special circumstances; for example, if the new recruits are very numerous compared to the existing organizational membership, or if new recruits are isolated from the influences of the present culture, perhaps because they form a special subunit that is physically separated from the rest of the organization.

But why confine the important benefits that can be gained from rites of passage to new recruits? Other rites of passage can be devised so that existing members can also be indoctrinated with the new desired ideologies and values. They could be used, for example, to mark any changes in status—promotions, for example, or steps from one skill level to another within a grade. Unfortunately, rites of passage at present are largely neglected as a means of instilling new values and beliefs into current members.

Of course, rites of passage do not have to be used alone to accomplish cultural change. Other rites are available to reiterate and reinforce the cultural indoctrination experienced during rites of passage. In particular, rites of enhancement, degradation, and passage form a mutually supportive cluster.

Rites of Enhancement

Rites of enhancement are public celebrations of the positive accomplishments of some members of the organization. They provide opportunities for managers to dramatize and emphasize the accomplishments and behaviors they value. By themselves, the rites are a reward for the people singled out to receive special recognition. But usually, more than praise and recognition are bestowed; honored employees are also rewarded with material awards and new statuses.

Clearly, rites of enhancement serve as reinforcement mechanisms. They can help produce cultural change because managers can use them selectively to reinforce only those behaviors most in accord with desired cultural values. Psychologists have demonstrated that intermittent reinforcement is a powerful force in shaping behavior (Skinner, 1971).

Although rites of enhancement can only act as reinforcements for those who receive some sort of rewards, they also inform, motivate, and inspire other employees in ways that can help to produce cultural change. Such rites send messages to all employees about which behaviors, old and new, can help them to reach personally desired goals. In the language of path-goal theory (House, 1973), they help to clarify paths to desired goals. They can also inspire by creating and advertising desirable role models.

At a Diamond International plant in Massachusetts, the personnel director devised a "100 Club" to emphasize the cultural value of good performance. Employees are awarded points according to such factors as their attendance, accident, and error records. On the program's birthday every year, a ceremony in which employees receive awards according to the total number of points they have earned during the year is held. All those with 100 points are publicly recognized and presented with a jacket emblazoned with the company's logo and a membership patch to symbolize their accomplishment. Those with more than 100 points receive additional rewards and recognition as well ("Hot 100," 1983, p. 46).

Another example of a rite of enhancement is the "You want it when?" award at Versatec in Santa Clara, California. This award recognizes the exceptional efforts of those who frequently work overtime and late at night. The president of the company composes scrolls expressing the company's appreciation, and these are presented at a special luncheon that features the mottos, "We appreciate this" and "You did not go unnoticed" ("It's Not Lonely Upstairs . . . ," 1980, p. 111). Another example that has been widely publicized is the "Atta-Boy" award described in *Corporate Cultures* (Deal and Kennedy, 1982, p. 61).

Rites of enhancement are most effective when they are not isolated events but are used in conjunction with other rites. Ideally, the behaviors that are reinforced and advertised as desirable in rites of enhancement should have already been instilled in at least some employees through rites of passage. By themselves—without the socialization and indoctrination that rites of passage can accomplish—rites of enhancement will not be as effective as they could be in facilitating culture change.

One organization that seems to use these two rites in mutually reinforcing ways is the Mary Kay Cosmetic Company. Mary Kay saleswomen receive extensive training when they begin working for the company, and the same cultural themes and values are celebrated in the company's famous, elaborate Mary Kay Seminars, which consist of three days of recognition, entertainment, and training (Ash, 1981, p. 191). One of the other strengths of the Mary Kay rites is that so many members receive some form of enhancement during them. Thus, the rites serve as more than inspiration; they provide direct reinforcement for many employees of the company. Obviously, the larger the proportion of employees who can be reinforced in such rites, the greater the opportunity to shape behavior. Of course, the rewarded behaviors must support the desired culture and must be exceptional enough so that the rewards carry some distinction.

Another reason that rites of enhancement can facilitate cultural change is that they usually change the statuses of those who are enhanced. To the degree the enhanced members gain visibility, authority, and control of financial resources and information channels, they are likely to influence others to conform, as they do, to the desired cultural values.

Rites of Degradation

Rites of degradation are used relatively infrequently by social groups; their purpose is to dissolve the social identities and power of certain members. A complete rite of degradation includes the following elements: (1) the collective attention is focused on the people being degraded and their behaviors are publicly associated with failures and problems, (2) the degraded people are discredited by some supposedly objective report or analysis, and (3) the degraded people are publicly stripped of their positions and statuses. In a sense, rites of degradation combine the opposites of both rites of passage and rites of enhancement. Not only are the singled-out members degraded rather than enhanced, but they may be expelled from membership in the group.

A good example of a rite of degradation is provided by Pfeffer's (1981) description of the firing of chief executive officers (CEOs) at the Gulf Oil and Northrup Corporations. To justify their being told to leave the company, the status of these officers had to be reduced and their practical power dissolved. To accomplish this, consultants were hired to produce data and analyses linking the CEOs to their corporations' problems. They became "symbolic victims" who had to be replaced before their companies' crises could end (Starbuck, Greve, and Hedberg, 1978, p. 132). In neither case was it clear that there was actual wrongdoing on the part of the CEOs that justified their expulsion.

In political bodies, dramatic rites of degradation are sometimes used to punish members who have clearly transgressed group norms. Two U.S. congressmen who were censured by the House of Representatives for deviant sexual behavior with young congressional pages, for example, were subjected to rites of degradation that included long public hearings exposing the deviant behaviors of the two men, a debate over the extent of their guilt, and a ceremonious rebuke by the House membership delivered by the Speaker of the House in a public, televised session. "Both men were made to stand before grim colleagues while the pronouncements of censure . . . were read aloud and broadcast on TV nationwide" ("Congress Metes Out a Rare Punishment," 1983, p. 48). The cumulative emotional impact of this degradation rite was such that one of the target congressmen broke down in tears and admitted his guilt and remorse before the assembled House and a national television audience.

The most obvious way in which rites of degradation can facilitate cultural change is by removing those members who are most likely to resist the desired change or who symbolize prominent features of the old culture to many other members. In 1971, the U.S. Postal Service used an abbreviated rite of degradation to try to change its culture when it changed from a government agency to a public corporation. To purge many of the postal officials who represented the old culture, employees with high seniority were offered a one-time bonus of six months' pay if they would retire immediately. Many took the offer, and subsequent retirement ceremonies functioned as rites of degradation communicating that the values of the retiring members were being supplanted by a new set of values. With this one stroke, much of the former leadership was destroyed, thus clearing the way for newer employees who might be more receptive to the new culture (Biggart, 1977, p. 422).

Similar rites often follow corporate mergers as management attempts to integrate the often disparate corporate cultures involved. In merger situations, members of one culture are likely to win out over the other, and those members of the corporation who represent the losing culture are likely to be forced to leave (Walter, 1984). These forced leavings have become sufficiently prevalent that new mechanisms, popularly dubbed *golden parachutes,* have been devised to soften the landings of those expelled (Hirsch and Andrews, 1983).

If members of the old culture—or of a new competing one—cannot be removed, organizations sometimes try what have been called rites of intimidation, in which members are discredited in a variety of ways but are not necessarily forced to leave the organization (O'Day, 1974). Although this type of rite has been documented primarily as a method of dealing with whistle blowers, there is no inherent reason it could not also be used to discredit champions of an existing culture that management seeks to replace. For example, in nonmerger situations where cultural conflict breaks out in response to attempted cultural change, rites of intimidation may be useful in discrediting leaders of the factions that are resisting the change.

In all rites of degradation, the audience is dramatically informed of who won and who lost, of what behavior is good and what behavior is bad, and thus learns, if it does not already know, which values and behaviors are likely to lead to public humiliation and expulsion and are therefore to be avoided. Like all punishment, rites of degradation do not communicate clearly which behaviors and values are desired; this is done much more effectively by rites of passage and rites of enhancement. Thus, when all three of these rites are used together, they can exert a powerful force to help induce cultural change.

Rites of Conflict Reduction

Rites of conflict reduction help restore equilibrium in disturbed social relations. Cultural change inevitably generates conflict; these rites can be used by management to express and acknowledge these conflicts so as to avoid the breakdown of collective efforts.

Union-management committees are one vehicle for holding rites of conflict reduction. The practical achievements of such committees are typically unimpressive (Kochan, 1980), but through them, the level of trust between management and labor, the degree to which power is shared in the organization, and the various goals that exist within the organization can be expressed (Trice and Beyer, 1984b). The very existence of union-management committees symbolizes a willingness to explore specific problem areas and consider alternative solutions, although the history of union-management cooperation in introducing change in U.S. corporations is disappointing (Kochan, 1980, p. 414).

Rather than eliminating conflict altogether, rites of conflict reduction can lead to acceptance of the existence of conflict and then try to keep it at a level that is not disruptive (Kochan and Dyer, 1976). When circumstances are dire enough, unions and management can be made to cooperate, as was evidenced in the cutbacks that the United Auto Workers were willing to take in the auto industry a few years ago. Now that circumstances are improved, union members would like to regain some of what they gave up. Current prospects are that another, powerful rite of conflict reduction—collective bargaining—will be the next step in trying to resolve the persistent conflicts in the auto industry.

Of course, unions do not represent the only source of conflict over change. Whenever change is attempted, some members of the organization will feel threatened because the changes call into question their own past accomplishments and present behaviors (Beyer and Trice, 1982, p. 608). Some way must be found to reduce these feelings of threat and anxiety if the desired change is to be fully implemented and institutionalized. Some examples of rites of conflict reduction that may help include internal appeal systems, ritual spoofs of high-status members at public social events, and vigorous sports contests that pit members of the warring factions against one another.

One of the authors witnessed the use of ritual spoofs to express the inevitable social cleavages and tensions between doctoral students and faculty in the psychology department of a large university. After the annual dinner sponsored by the psychology fraternity and attended by most of the doctoral students and the faculty and their spouses, students presented elaborate skits in which they portrayed prominent faculty members, usually provoking much merriment by exaggerating the faculty members' personal mannerisms. The skits usually portrayed the faculty as having callous disregard for student feelings and unrealistically high academic standards. Although we have encountered no descriptions of similar rites in corporations, we suspect they exist. Through the spoofing process, the disgruntled are able to express their dissatisfactions and thus have them acknowledged to some degree. Since humor is usually also evoked during such skits, all in the audience are encouraged to laugh at their collective predicament, rather than to despair over it (Gluckman, 1963).

Internal appeal systems also act as conflict reducers, especially if they operate as close to the source of the conflict as possible. The grievance mechanism is perhaps the best-known example. It is widely recognized as an effective, informal way of reducing work-related conflicts in U.S. industry and other organizations. In one law school, a joint student-faculty committee hears grievances filed by either students or faculty. Students consider the committee useful, both for resolving conflicts and as an experience relevant to the careers of student members and student grievers (Coleman, 1984, p. 19). In a study of the use of a national ombudsman in New Zealand, only 18 percent of over 10,000 complaints handled over a thirteen-year period were judged by either party to be justified to the extent that they warranted continued action after the ombudsman had completed an initial inquiry (Hill, 1976). One factor considered important to the success of these conflict-reduction rites is their promptness; in both of the examples cited here, the rites took place as close to the time of the grievances as possible. This factor may outweigh any relative advantages that could be gained if the rites were carried out in a more ceremonious and public manner, such as a courtroom trial. Pomp and ceremony usually involve advance planning and, therefore, delay.

Sports contests can also be used as rites of conflict reduction. One business school, for example, holds an ice hockey game pitting faculty against students. One important feature of this contest is that women, who are only minimally represented on the faculty, are better represented on the student team and are thus publicly seen competing and holding their own against male faculty in a tough, "macho" sport. Similar faculty-student contests involving various team sports are held at many other professional schools as well. Some less-developed societies, however, may be wiser in how they carry out such rites. Andaman Islanders hold dances in which dancers shake one another. Members of conflicting factions are not allowed to form opposing sides, however; rather, members of each faction are randomly designated as people who do the shaking and people who are shaken (Radcliffe-Brown, 1964, p. 238). Sports contests would probably be more effective as rites of conflict resolution if they also mixed members of opposing factions on each of the teams.

Rites of Integration

The major purpose of rites of integration is to encourage and revive common feelings that bind members of a cultural group together and keep them committed to the group's continuity. Differences within the group are lessened as members increase their social interactions with one another during these rites; ideally, therefore, these rites are inclusive rather than exclusive. Usually they involve eating, drinking, dancing, music, and other recreational activities. They may incorporate some elements of rites of conflict reduction; for example, an office picnic may include a baseball game between managers and workers.

It seems obvious that rites of integration can be very helpful during cultural changes, when group cohesion can break down over both ideological and power-related issues. Clearly, in times of change, organizations have a greater need than at other times for mechanisms that can help to build and maintain cohesion.

Several examples of this type of rite have been observed and described by Dandridge (1983) and by Ritti and Funkhouser (1977). In one company, an annual layoff of production workers occurred just before Christmas. This layoff was usually announced in late November and was followed by a management-financed and employee-prepared Thanksgiving dinner held in the production areas of the plant. The management group served the employees as they filed by. This particular rite of integration had been traditional in this company for many years (Dandridge, 1983). Another rite of integration in the same company was a Great Race that was held in the company parking lot. Outlandish vehicles built especially for the occasion and powered by teams of six people were raced against one another for prizes. Many other examples could be described and cited.

Although there is no shortage of cocktail and other parties among people who work together, few of these are very effective rites of integration. Status differences within and between groups seem to militate against members mingling as freely as genuine rites of integration require. People's status differences include not only their positions in the organizational hierarchy, but also their race, ethnicity, and gender. Whenever a group is especially heterogeneous, it is difficult to hold successful rites of integration. In heterogeneous work forces, many rites of integration do not gain the widespread participation that is required to make them effective. Rites that involve smaller groups may be more cohesive, but because they are not fully inclusive, they also fall short of being truly integrative.

New, more potent rites must be devised to replace present ones, which are too often seen as chores instead of as meaningful and enjoyable experiences. In any rite of integration, the activities themselves (like the Great Race described earlier) should be so absorbing that people forget status differences. Also, such rites include activities that are attractive and enjoyable to employees' families. This would serve not only to acknowledge the part that families play in supporting the organization's efforts (Kanter, 1977) but would also remove one obstacle to employees' attending such rites and staying more than just a short time.

One format for such an event is the festival that commemorates or celebrates some occasion of special significance to the corporation. Such occasions provide natural opportunities for people to celebrate accomplishments, to rejoice and feel good together, in an atmosphere of acceptance and conviviality. In 1980, the Hawthorne plant of the Western Electric Company held a celebration in honor of the company's involvement in the historic Hawthorne studies.

Another example of a celebratory rite of integration is the annual picnic that IBM used to hold. This event lasted several days, during which time some of the company's employees lived in tents on the company grounds, as employees had done when the company was new. Such informality can encourage the kind of conviviality that stimulates feelings of integration.

Another promoting type of festival held in one California company was a year-long ethnic identity festival, in which members of all ethnic groups were encouraged to explain and express their ethnic heritage to other employees during a series of extended lunch periods. Groups prepared and sold foods, performed dances and music, and displayed cultural artifacts (Samuelson, 1983). In sharing their cultural backgrounds, employees revealed the similarities beneath their apparent differences and thus become a more cohesive group.

What is important for managers and others to realize in planning and staging rites of integration is that the activities should be enjoyable to as many participants as possible and should be inclusive rather than exclusive. If these elements are present, such rites should help companies restore any cohesion lost and attain new levels of cohesion during periods of cultural change.

Rites of Renewal

More than other rites, rites of renewal may interfere with cultural change efforts. Their intended purpose is to refurbish social structures and help them function effectively again. Rites of renewal can also, however, disguise the nature of problems, defer the acknowledgment of problems, reinforce existing systems of power and authority, and reassure members that something is being done about problems when what is being done may not be sufficient or focused in appropriate directions. Some ostensible change efforts are actually rites of renewal because the changes they attempt are too piecemeal to change anything of importance. Sometimes in such instances change may be intended but not achieved, and sometimes it is doubtful that change was intended at all. In the latter case, rites of renewal may merely be substitutes for meaningful problem solving.

A good example of a rite of renewal is the Employee Assistance Program (EAP). The overt purpose of EAPs is to help employees cope with their personal problems, especially when these problems adversely affect work performance. Troubled employees are either referred by their supervisors or come on their own initiative to an EAP counselor within the company; these employees are, if appropriate, referred by the counselor to outside treatment facilities for help with their problems, and their supervisors are trained in how to deal with troubled subordinates. The reaction of top management and supervisors to these programs in seven locations of a large corporation was recently studied (Trice and Beyer, 1984a). In relatively unstructured interviews, managers at the top two levels indicated that they believed that EAPs helped improve existing social arrangements and relations within their organizations, provided support and protection to lower-level managers who have troubled subordinates, and renewed confidence in the company among rank-and-file employees. The success of these programs in resolving personal problems that impair job performance has yet to be assessed, but it is clear that these programs and their observed outcomes are valued within organizations.

Organizational development (OD) activities and other activities of consultants may also qualify as rites of renewal. Often, if they have consequences of any lasting kind, OD activities tend to be expressive, rather than technical (Bower, 1973; Burke, 1980). Many OD programs tend to emphasize rites that fine tune the system (Burke, 1980, p. 431) rather than change it. One such rite is called *team building*. In this rite, typically, employees go on a retreat, held away from the workplace, where they are asked to discuss and rank work-related issues, generate and decide upon alternative solutions to problems, and specify action steps for implementing these solutions. There seems to be little question that such efforts have expressive consequences, but there is little agreement about their technical effects in promoting organizational change.

Rites of renewal can use up many resources and much good will to arrive at a point not very far from where they started. For example, it could be argued that many academic curriculum reviews ostensibly conducted with change in mind instead actually legitimatize and freeze existing curricula. One reason for this is that, often, new curricula cannot be adopted without a vote of the faculty. Such a democratic process rarely results in genuine change because change may upset existing systems of power and advantage.

Another example of the sometimes unintended consequences of rites of renewal is the Glacier project, a corporate program whose goal ostensibly was to give more power to workers through worker-management councils. When the new councils were in place, "rather than reducing managerial authority, this system enhanced it because the managers 'acted with the sanction of all groups within the enterprise.' For this reason, it may be argued that the managers have greater real authority because it is legitimated by the representation system" (Warner, 1981, p. 172).

Rites of renewal tend to be essentially conservative, rather than creative, in nature. Any genuinely new ideas tend to get diluted in efforts to accommodate diverse interests and preferences. This problem is greater in large organizations, where many people are involved, but it exists in relatively small companies as well.

Possible New Rites

A new type of rite is badly needed to set genuine change processes in motion. Genuine change requires the invention and establishment of new patterns of behavior; new roles or scripts must be devised, accepted, learned, and enacted. The social interactions required to invent and establish new scripts could be called "rites of creation—rites for establishing new roles and embedding them in ongoing social arrangements" (Trice and Beyer, 1984c, p. 33). Once these rites have been established, people could be resocialized to fill the new roles through special rites of passage and rewarded when they performed well in them through rites of enhancement.

Rites of creation are more likely to succeed if they initially are carried out on a small scale. Limiting participation will make it easier to choose participants whose beliefs and values are congenial to the changes contemplated or to change in general. Also, this initial change effort can be treated as a pilot project; if it does not achieve what was expected of it, they can be dismantled with less expense, embarrassment, and disruption than could a broader program.

When such relatively radical change efforts are set in motion, what should be done about the rites of renewal that are already present and functioning? It is probably unwise to try to dismantle them immediately. They are probably serving at least an expressive function if they have adherents. If the rites of creation are successful and new roles are established and seem to be working well, the old rites of renewal can gradually be eliminated. If the rites of creation have worked well, this may not even be necessary; the old rites of renewal may just fade away from lack of interest and attention.

The Role of Rites in Culture Change

Having considered a number of different rites separately, it is now appropriate to consider whether there are any general implications and cautions about the use of rites to foster culture change. The first and most obvious concern about the use of rites is their generally conservative nature. Regardless of their potential for facilitating change efforts (Moore and Meyerhoff, 1977), change is clearly not the usual purpose of cultural rites. Their usual purpose is to maintain rather than to change, to preserve and celebrate current and traditional cultural patterns.

There are three other reasons to suspect that existing rites, especially well-established ones, can interfere with, as well as facilitate, change efforts (Trice and Beyer, 1984c, p. 31). First, rites are such public and collective cultural expressions that those that have persisted over time are likely to celebrate areas of cultural consensus. Second, corporate rites usually reflect the ideologies and values of top management; otherwise, management would not provide the considerable resources that rites often require. Unfortunately, management may have the biggest stake in maintaining the status quo and thus may resist genuine change. Third, most organizations include many different occupational groups, and some of these will have their own cultural traditions, including rites. Some of these rites may express ideologies and values incompatible with those that are the goal of the cultural-change effort.

For all of these reasons, it may be unrealistic to expect that any rites that are composed entirely of elements expressing new cultural values can be successful. People expect their cultures to provide continuity, and to be successful, rites must therefore combine any new messages with familiar and accepted cultural elements. There are two obvious ways to do this: existing rites can be modified to incorporate the new values, or entirely new rites that consciously combine elements of the old and the new can be established.

One factor to consider in choosing between these two strategies is the prevalence and vigor of existing rites. If rites are numerous and have many staunch adherents, it may be most practical to try to modify them to incorporate the new values. Obviously, those rites that are most consistent with or complementary to the new cultural values make the best candidates for such modification. The chief danger in pursuing this strategy is that the new cultural messages may be missed by the audience or twisted to fit into the existing cultural understandings associated with the old rites. Thus, the modified rites must be designed to give the new values a prominent place within them.

Another approach is to eliminate any rites that express those ideologies and values that are seen as no longer desirable. However, it could be risky to try to dismantle or supplant well-established rites that have many adherents. This course of action is likely to provoke antagonisms that could solidify into general opposition to the change effort. The less risky strategy when numerous vigorous, competing rites exist is to build new rites to compete with them. This solution may result in a busy calendar, but it is unlikely to violate existing expectations and values. As time passes, if the new rites are very successful, the undesirable older rites may lose some of their adherents, and company support for them can be withdrawn. However, if undesirable rites persist and there is evidence they are hampering the change effort, the more direct action of pruning or dismantling them may become necessary.

If rites are numerous but not vigorous, the challenge will be to try to discover a central theme or core of values that is congenial to the desired new culture and that can be used as a basis for integration and further development. Again, judicious pruning may be necessary.

If rites are neither numerous nor vigorous, it is easy to establish new ones. It may be difficult to awaken the workers from their lethargic response to the relatively few anemic rites with which they are already familiar, but some rites are especially useful for this purpose. Rites of integration may be poorly attended, but a rite of enhancement on company time is hard to resist, especially if everyone knows someone who will be receiving an award. A rite of passage, both for newcomers and oldtimers, also held on company time, should be well attended, too. The fact that rites take place on company time has practical and symbolic benefits; it helps to ensure attendance, and it also demonstrates that the company cares enough about the rite to pay people to attend.

In general, it seems that altering or establishing new rites of passage and rites of enhancement may be the best way to initiate cultural change. Rites of degradation logically complete this cluster of rites, but they probably should ordinarily not follow until members have had a chance to learn the new expectations. Even when a jolt would be desirable to signal that quick change is imperative and rites of degradation look like a logical starting point, it is risky to use them to begin a cultural change. Members of the organization are likely to feel that those degraded are being treated unfairly, unless their conduct has clearly been in violation of old as well as new norms. If firings must take place, it may be better to try to gloss over them as quickly as possible (Gooding, 1972) and move on to positive celebrations of the new culture.

Rites of conflict reduction and integration comprise the

next logical cluster of rites. As discussed earlier, together these two rites provide ways to deal with the strains and conflicts generated when new and old cultural values collide and to build cohesion around an amalgam of what is desirable in the new and the old. Their creation and modification should probably therefore wait until the exact nature of resultant strains and conflicts is evident. All rites, but perhaps most importantly these two rites, should be designed around the strains, conflicts, and cleavages they are supposed to help people to manage (Chapple, 1967).

Fortunately, rites include many different cultural forms that can be used to convey desirable new and old cultural messages. Table 2 presents a list and definitions of some of the forms available. Because rites easily accommodate such an array of forms, it is relatively easy to add, subtract, or change elements to arrive at an effective mixture of the old and the new. For example, some of the meanings conveyed by existing rites could be changed simply by changing one or two elements, such as the setting and the performers. For instance, the cultural meaning of an internal appeals committee might be changed by moving the group's meeting place from near the general manager's office to somewhere on the plant floor and changing the participants to include lower-level employees as well as managers. Similarly, the cultural meaning of an existing rite of passage could be changed by incorporating into the rite hitherto neglected sagas and stories about the organization and its early heroes that reflect desired beliefs and values. A previously moribund office Christmas party could be enlivened and made to express more concern for employees by having a member of top management dress as Santa Claus and give appropriate and funny presents to all assembled, especially if those assembled include employees' children.

Rites thus clearly can be used to facilitate cultural change. To use them effectively, however, managers and others must recognize the rites and ceremonies already occurring around them and become aware of both their intended and latent consequences. With such an awareness, combined with a healthy respect for the power of rites to help people maintain some sense

Table 2. Other Culturally Expressive Forms
Often Incorporated in Rites.

Form	Definition
Symbol	Any object, act, event, quality, or relation that serves as a vehicle for conveying meaning, usually by representing another thing.
Language	A particular form or manner in which members of a group use vocal sounds and written signs to convey meanings to each other.
Gesture	Movements of parts of the body to express meanings.
Physical setting	Those things that surround people physically and provide them with immediate sensory stimuli as they carry out culturally expressive activities.
Artifact	Material objects manufactured by people to facilitate culturally expressive activities.
Ritual	A standardized, detailed set of techniques and behaviors that manage anxieties but seldom produce intended, technical consequences of practical importance.
Myth	A dramatic narrative of imagined events, usually used to explain origins or transformations of something. Also, an unquestioned belief about the practical benefits of certain techniques and behaviors that is not supported by demonstrated facts.
Saga	An historical narrative describing the unique accomplishments of a group and its leaders, usually in heroic terms.
Legend	A handed-down narrative of some wonderful event that is based in history but has been embellished with fictional details.
Story	A narrative based on true events—often a combination of truth and fiction.
Folktale	A completely fictional narrative.

Source: Adapted from Trice, 1985.

of stability in the midst of change, managers can begin to use rites creatively and effectively to achieve desired cultural change.

References

Ash, M. K. Mary Kay. New York: Harper & Row, 1981.

Barley, S. F., and Louis, M. R. "Many in One: Organizations as Multi-Cultural Entities." Paper presented at the 43rd annual meeting of the Academy of Management, Dallas, Tex., Aug. 14, 1983.

Beyer, J. M. "Ideologies, Values, and Decision-Making in Organizations." In P. C. Nystrom and W. H. Starbuck (eds.), *Handbook of Organizational Design.* New York: Oxford University Press, 1981.

Beyer, J. M., and Trice, H. M. "The Utilization Process: A Conceptual Framework and Synthesis of Empirical Findings." *Administrative Science Quarterly,* 1982, *18,* 591–622.

Biggart, N. W. "The Creative-Destructive Process of Organizational Change: The Case of the Post Office." *Administrative Science Quarterly,* 1977, *22,* 410–426.

Boje, D. M., Fedor, D. B., and Rowland, K. M. "Mythmaking: A Qualitative Step in OD Interventions." *Journal of Applied Behavioral Science,* 1982, *18,* 17–28.

Bourne, P. G. "Some Observations on the Psycho-Social Phenomenon Seen in Basic Training." *Psychiatry,* 1967, *30,* 187–196.

Bower, D. "O.D. Techniques and Results in 23 Organizations." *Journal of Applied Behavioral Science,* 1973, *9,* 21–43.

Burke, W. W. "Organizational Development and Bureaucracy in the 1980s." *Journal of Applied Behavioral Science,* 1980, *16,* 423–437.

Chapple, E. D. Personal Communication to H. M. Trice, Feb. 24, 1967.

Coleman, D. F. "The Law School Culture." Class term paper, School of Management, State University of New York at Buffalo, June 1, 1984.

"Congress Metes Out a Rare Punishment." *U.S. News & World Report,* Aug. 1, 1983, p. 48.

"Corporate Culture: The Hard-To-Change Values that Spell Success or Failure." *Business Week,* Oct. 27, 1980, pp. 148–160.

Dandridge, T. C. "Ceremony as an Integration of Work and Play." Paper presented at the University of California Conference on Myths, Symbols, and Folklore: Expanding the Analysis of Organizations, Los Angeles, Mar. 1983.

Deal, T. E., and Kennedy, A. A. *Corporate Cultures: The Rites and Rituals of Corporate Life.* Reading, Mass.: Addison-Wesley, 1982.

Dorson, R. M. "Introduction: Concepts of Folklore and Folklife." In R. M. Dorson (ed.), *Folklore and Folklife: An Introduction.* Chicago: University of Chicago Press, 1972.

Edelman, M. *The Symbolic Uses of Politics.* Urbana: University of Illinois Press, 1964.

Feldman, M. S., and March, J. G. "Information in Organizations as Signal and Symbol." *Administrative Science Quarterly,* 1981, *26,* 171–184.

Geertz, C. "Deep Play: Notes on the Balinese Cockfight." In C. Geertz (ed.), *Myth, Symbol, and Culture.* New York: Norton, 1971.

Gluckman, M. *Order and Rebellion in Tribal Africa.* New York: Free Press, 1963.

Gooding, J. "The Art of Firing an Executive." *Fortune,* Oct. 1972, pp. 22–30.

Hill, L. B. *The Model Ombudsman.* Princeton, N.J.: Princeton University Press, 1976.

Hirsch, P. M., and Andrews, J. Y. "Ambushes, Shootouts, and Knights of the Roundtable: The Language of Corporate Takeover." In L. R. Pondy, P. J. Frost, G. Morgan, and T. C. Dandridge (eds.), *Monographs in Organizational Behavior and Industrial Relations: Organizational Symbolism.* Vol. 1. Greenwich, Conn.: JAI, 1983.

"Hot 100." *Time.* July 4, 1983, p. 46.

House, R. J. "A Path-Goal Theory of Leader Effectiveness." In E. A. Fleishman and J. G. Hunt (eds.), *Current Developments in the Study of Leadership.* Carbondale: Southern Illinois University Press, 1973.

"It's Not Lonely Upstairs: An Interview with Renn Zaphiropoulos." *Harvard Business Review,* Nov.–Dec. 1980, *58,* 111–132.

Jones, M. O. "Is Ethics the Issue?" Paper presented at the Conference on Organizational Culture and Meaning of Life in the Workplace, University of British Columbia, Vancouver, Apr. 3, 1984.

Kanter, R. M. *Men and Women of the Corporation.* New York: Basic Books, 1977.

Kilmann, R. H. "Getting Control of the Corporate Culture." *Managing,* 1982, *3,* 11–17.

Kochan, T. A. *Collective Bargaining and Industrial Relations.* Homewood, Ill.: Richard D. Irwin, 1980.

Kochan, T. A., and Dyer, L. "A Model of Organizational Change and the Context of Union-Management Relations." *Journal of Applied Behavioral Science*, 1976, *12*, 59-78.

Lane, C. *The Rites of Rulers—Ritual in Industrial Society: The Soviet Case.* Cambridge: Cambridge University Press, 1981.

Lortie, D. C. "Shared Ordeal and Induction to Work." In H. S. Becker, B. Greer, D. Riesman, and R. Weiss (eds.), *Institution and the Person.* Chicago: Aldine, 1968.

McCarl, R. S. "Smokejumper Initiation." *Journal of American Folklore*, 1976, *89*, 49-66.

Martin, J., and Siehl, C. "Organizational Culture and Counterculture: An Uneasy Symbosis." *Organizational Dynamics*, 1983, *12*, 52-64.

Moore, S. F., and Meyerhoff, B. F. "Secular Ritual: Forms and Meanings." In S. F. Moore and B. G. Meyerhoff (eds.), *Secular Ritual.* Amsterdam: Van Gorcum, 1977.

Moore, W. E. *The Conduct of the Corporation.* New York: Random House, 1962.

O'Day, R. "Intimidation Rituals: Reactions to Reform." *Journal of Applied Behavioral Science*, 1974, *10*, 373-386.

Peters, T. J. "Management Systems: The Language of Organizational Character and Competence." *Organizational Dynamics*, 1980, *9*, 3-26.

Peters, T. J., and Waterman, R. H., Jr. *In Search of Excellence: Lessons from America's Best-Run Companies.* New York: Harper & Row, 1982.

Pfeffer, J. "Management as Symbolic Action: The Creation and Maintenance of Organizational Paradigms." In L. L. Cummings and B. M. Staw (eds.), *Research in Organizational Behavior.* Vol. 3. Greenwich, Conn.: JAI, 1981.

Radcliffe-Brown, A. R. *Andaman Islanders.* New York: Free Press, 1964.

Ritti, R. R., and Funkhouser, G. R. *The Ropes to Skip and the Ropes to Know: Studies in Organizational Behavior.* Columbus, Ohio: Grid, 1977.

Rohlen, T. P. "Spiritual Education in a Japanese Bank." *American Anthropologist*, 1973, *75*, 1543-1562.

Samuelson, S. "Improving Conditions, Increasing Awareness:

An On-Site Ethnic Display Event." Paper presented at the University of California Conference on Myths, Symbols, and Folklore: Expanding the Analysis of Organizations, Los Angeles, Mar. 1983.

Schein, E. G. "Suppose We Took Culture Seriously." *O.D. Newsletter,* 1984, pp. 2-7.

Schwartz, H. M., and Davis, S. M. "Matching Corporate Culture and Business Strategy." *Organizational Dynamics,* Summer 1981, pp. 30-48.

Skinner, B. F. *Beyond Freedom and Dignity.* New York: Knopf, 1971.

Starbuck, W. H., Greve, A., and Hedberg, B. L. T. "Responding to Crisis." *Journal of Business Administration,* 1978, *9,* 111-137.

Staw, B. M. "Rationality and Justification in Organizational Life." In B. M. Staw and L. L. Cummings (eds.), *Research in Organizational Behavior.* Vol. 2. Greenwich, Conn.: JAI, 1980.

Trice, H. M. "Rites and Ceremonials in Organizational Culture." In S. B. Bacharach and S. M. Mitchell (eds.), *Perspectives in Organizational Sociology: Theory and Research.* Greenwich, Conn.: JAI, 1985.

Trice, H. M., Belasco, J., and Alutto, J. "The Role of Ceremonials in Organizational Behavior." *Industrial and Labor Relations Review,* 1969, *23,* 40-51.

Trice, H. M., and Beyer, J. M. "Employee Assistance Programs: Blending Performance Oriented and Humanitarian Ideologies to Assist Emotionally Disturbed Employees." In J. R. Greenley (ed.), *Research in Community and Mental Health.* Vol. 4. Greenwich, Conn.: JAI, 1984a.

Trice, H. M., and Beyer, J. M. "A Study of Union-Management Cooperation in a Long-Standing Alcoholism Program." *Contemporary Drug Problems,* 1984b, *11,* 295-317.

Trice, H. M., and Beyer, J. M. "Studying Organizational Cultures Through Rites and Ceremonials." *Academy of Management Review,* 1984c, *9* (4), 653-669.

Uttal, B. "The Corporate Culture Vultures." *Fortune,* Oct. 17, 1983, pp. 66-72.

Van Gennep, A. *Rites of Passage.* Chicago: University of Chicago Press, 1960. (Originally published by Emile Mourry in Paris in 1909.)

Van Maanen, J. "Observations on the Making of Policemen." *Human Organization,* 1973, *32,* 407-418.

Van Maanen, J., and Schein, E. H. "Toward a Theory of Organizational Socialization." in B. M. Staw (ed.), *Research in Organizational Behavior.* Vol. 1. Greenwich, Conn.: JAI, 1979.

Walter, G. H. "Strategic Goals for Mergers and Acquisitions." Working paper no. 296, Faculty of Commerce and Business Administration, University of British Columbia, Vancouver, 1984.

Warner, M. "Organizational Experiments and Social Innovations." In P. C. Nystrom and W. H. Starbuck (eds.), *Handbook of Organizational Design.* New York: Oxford University Press, 1981.

Wilson, W. A. *On Being Human: The Folklore of Mormon Missionaries.* Logan: Utah State University Press, 1981.

Nineteen

Arriving at Four Cultures by Managing the Reward System

Nirmal K. Sethia
Mary Ann Von Glinow

Everyone knows that if the results aren't
there, you had better have your resume up to date.
—a former PepsiCo manager

Some workers expect us to be papa and
mama, and aren't motivated enough to help themselves.
—a J.C. Penney manager

These two quotations, taken from a *Business Week* cover
story on corporate culture ("Corporate Culture . . . ," 1980, pp.
151, 154) suggest that two very different types of corporate

Suggestions received from Arvind Bhambri and Erik Jansen were of
invaluable help in the preparation of this chapter. We also benefitted from
the comments offered by Edward E. Lawler and Patricia Riley on our preliminary work in this area.

cultures prevail at PepsiCo and J.C. Penney. The article describes the cultures of these two companies in some detail and draws attention to the fact that in these companies, as well as in a host of others, a key managerial challenge is changing the culture. To become a successful challenger to the Coca-Cola Company, PepsiCo had to systematically change the emphasis of its culture from passivity to aggressiveness. Similarly, Penney will have to overcome the limitations of its paternalistic culture if it is to prevent loss of market share to more aggressive discounters such as K-mart. These companies are representative of an increasing number of organizations experiencing the powerful impact of one or more of the following factors that provide major impetus for culture change:

- Change in business strategy
- Change in core technology
- Change in the regulatory environment
- Acquisition or merger
- New leadership vision

Observing the widespread efforts of major corporations to change their cultures in response to such forces, a *Fortune* analyst recently exclaimed, "U.S. business is in the throes of a cultural revolution" (Uttal, 1983, p. 66). Thus, a very important question is: How can we change organizational culture? Or more generally, how can we *manage* organizational culture—that is, create and sustain a desirable culture, and change the culture when it becomes dysfunctional?

In day-to-day organization life a very concrete and powerful lever for managing culture is the organizational reward system. The reward system can be effectively used as a means of influencing culture because the culture and the reward system of an organization are highly interdependent. For example, the two quotations cited at the beginning of this chapter are suggestive not only of different types of cultures but also of different types of reward systems. At PepsiCo, rewards are highly contingent on performance, and failure results in punishment. In contrast, at J.C. Penney, poor performers are likely to be treated with consideration and given easier jobs.

In this chapter, we will first explore the nature and extent of interdependence between the culture and the reward system of an organization. It will then be argued that because the culture and the reward system must remain in a state of dynamic balance, mutually compatible or congruent cultures and reward systems form distinctive patterns in organizations. Because such patterns are easier to interpret and manage when they are meaningfully classified, a simple, fourfold typology of congruent patterns of cultures and reward systems is presented. Finally, we will examine the ways in which reward systems can be used to manage cultures.

The primary focus of this chapter is on the cultures and reward systems of managerial groups in large business organizations, but the arguments presented can easily be extended to other employee groups and to other types of organizations.

The Core Concepts

Before we can begin our discussion of the intricate relationship between organizational culture and reward systems, we must first define these terms. There is nothing absolute or rigid about the definitions offered here, however; our purpose is only to clarify the meaning and the scope of these terms in the present discussion.

Organizational Culture. Peters and Waterman (1982, p. 75) regard culture as representing the shared values of an organization's members. Kilmann (1982, p. 11) calls culture "the collective will of members" and argues that it indicates "what the corporation *really wants* or what *really counts* in order to get ahead" in the corporation. Schein (1983, p. 4) refers to culture as "the sum total of the collective or shared learnings of a group." Schwartz and Davis (1981, p. 33) regard culture as "a pattern of beliefs and expectations shared by the organization's members" that produces "norms that powerfully shape the behavior of individuals and groups in the organization." Finally, Tunstall (1983, p. 1) describes culture as "a general constellation of beliefs, mores, customs, value systems, behavioral norms, and ways of doing business that are unique to each corporation." Consistent with these various formulations, organizational culture will be defined here as *the shared and relatively enduring pattern of basic values, beliefs, and assumptions in an organization.*

Organizational Reward Systems. The term *reward system* is frequently used to describe, singly or jointly, the following interrelated elements: (1) the types of rewards that are available in an organization, (2) the conditions according to which different rewards are made available to individual members, and (3) the ways in which these rewards and the criteria for their allocation are selected and administered in the given organization (see, for example, S. Kerr, 1982; J. L. Kerr, 1984; Lawler, 1984). In the present discussion, the term *reward system* is used to refer to *the rewards available in an organization and the criteria according to which members can qualify to receive these rewards.*

Most organizations usually offer a mix of four kinds of rewards: financial, job content, career, and status. Some of the specific rewards that represent each of these four kinds are listed in Table 1. In considering the rewards available, it is also important to consider some basic attributes of the rewards, such as whether they are superior or inferior, frequent or infrequent, large or small, and optional or standard. Examples of the particular rewards for which these attributes are likely to be relevant also are presented in Table 1.

Criteria for the rewards indicate the basis on which rewards are offered or withheld in the organization. Usually, three types of criteria govern such decisions in organizations: performance in terms of tangible output or results, performance in terms of actions and behaviors that are expected to be directly or indirectly instrumental in bringing about organizationally desirable outcomes, and considerations of contractual obligations or customary practices. How these criteria are often defined in practice is indicated in Table 1.

We can now examine the interdependent nature of organizational culture and reward systems in organizational settings.

Table 1. Elements of a Reward System.

1. Rewards and Their Attributes
    a. *Kinds of Rewards Available*
        Financial: salary, raises, bonuses, stock options, profit sharing, various benefits
        Job Content: challenge, responsibility, freedom, meaning, feedback, recognition
        Career: job security, training and development programs, promotion opportunities
        Status: special facilities and privileges, titles, committee memberships
    b. *Attributes of the Rewards Available*
        Superior or Inferior: salary, benefits, training
        Frequent or Infrequent: raises, promotions, feedback
        Large or Small: bonuses, raises, benefits
        Optional or Standard: benefits, privileges, training
2. Criteria for Rewards
    a. *Performance: Tangible Outcomes or Results*
        Performer: individual, group, organization
        Performance: quantity, quality, timeliness
        Perspective: day-to-day, short-term, long-term
    b. *Performance: Instrumental Actions or Behaviors*
        Such as: cooperation vs. competition, risk taking vs. playing it safe, initiative vs. conformity, innovation vs. compliance, helping vs. hindering, communication vs. secrecy
    c. *Nonperformance: Considerations of Contract or Custom*
        Such as: membership, nature of work, external equity, internal equity, tenure, hierarchical position, ease of replacement, terms of employment, contractual obligations

The Culture–Reward System Relationship

The interdependence of an organization's culture and its reward system arises from a set of relationships portrayed in Figure 1. This figure illustrates that (1) an organization's culture can influence its reward system both directly and via a mediating human resource philosophy, and, reciprocally, (2) the organization's reward system influences its culture both directly and via the quality of human resources in the organization; that is, the caliber of people in the organization. The manner in which these relationships operate is explained in the following sections.

Influence of the Culture on the Reward System. Because an organization's culture relates to the basic values, beliefs, and

Figure 1. Culture-Reward System Relationship.

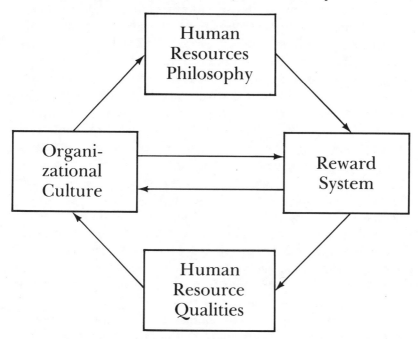

assumptions of its members, it necessarily influences the type and the qualities of rewards that are available in the organization as well as the conditions according to which the rewards are allocated to individuals. Often, this influence is quite direct. In the ruthlessly performance-oriented culture of PepsiCo, in the words of a former vice-president, "Careers ride on tenths of a market share point" ("Corporate Culture . . . ," 1980, p. 151). By contrast, United Press International had, until recently, a decidedly more easy-going culture in which jobs were usually for life and, according to a company manager, "You had to shoot the president to get fired" ("A New Era for Management," 1983, p. 60). Another example is Texas Instruments, whose autocratic and intense culture has come to mean "management by fear" for many managers who believe that they are more likely to be rewarded if they tell their bosses what their bosses want to hear than if they speak their minds (Uttal, 1982, p. 44).

Culture also can influence the reward system indirectly by contributing to the organization's human resource philosophy. Companies such as International Business Machines (IBM), American Telephone and Telegraph (AT&T) and Hewlett-Packard have well-articulated human resource philosophies, and these have a major impact on the reward systems of these companies. A particularly illustrative example is Analog Devices, a medium-sized high-tech company whose corporate culture has been examined in great detail by Davis (1984). According to Davis, a key element in this company's credo is its beliefs about people: "They believe that people are honest and trustworthy, are most satisfied when working to their fullest potential, and perform best when they feel a sense of purpose. They believe people want a say in how their jobs are done, want to be accountable, and want recognition . . ." (p. 106). These beliefs are translated into policies that include "above average wages and benefits; profit sharing, stock and bonus plans; equal opportunity, job security; promotion from within; and dual career ladders for technical and managerial personnel" (p. 106).

A specific aspect of the human resource philosophy that is relevant to many organizations is egalitarianism versus hierarchy consciousness, which is reflected in the absence or presence of various status-oriented rewards such as reserved parking areas, exclusive wash rooms and dining areas, choice office locations, and so forth. Some companies, such as Digital Research, Tandem, and Intel, tend to be quite egalitarian, while other companies, such as General Motors and AT&T, traditionally have been very hierarchy-conscious.

Influence of the Reward System on the Culture. An organization's reward system influences its culture directly by selectively reinforcing certain beliefs and values. This influence of reward systems has been explained by Lawler (1983, p. 111), who observes: "The behaviors they [the reward systems] cause to occur become the dominant patterns of behavior in the organization and lead to perceptions and beliefs about what an organization stands for, believes in, and values." The appropriateness of this reasoning is evident in many organizations. Until recently, for example, Chase Manhattan Bank was not a particularly performance-driven organization; it used to be a genteel company that "rewarded people more for appearance than performance," and that resulted in "inbreeding and a smugness that made the bank loathe to grapple with competitors" ("Corporate Culture . . . ," 1980, p. 158). By contrast, companies such as Emerson Electric and PepsiCo have fostered strong performance-oriented cultures by making significant rewards contingent on the results achieved.

Reward systems indirectly influence cultures by affecting the quality of human resources in organizations. Reward systems greatly determine the type of people organizations are able to attract and retain (see, for example, Lawler, 1983; Von Glinow, 1985). An organization that offers rewards that are superior by market standards and provides significant incentives for high performance can attract and retain individuals who have the best qualifications and strong achievement orientation. Such individuals then can set the pace for others in the organization and thereby contribute to the creation of an inspiring and productive culture in the organization. On the other hand, an organization that offers relatively inferior rewards and has few incentives tied to performance is likely to attract people with lesser talents. Moreover, its members are likely to exhibit low levels of commitment and motivation, resulting in an uninspiring and unproductive culture. Companies such as IBM and Hewlett-Packard deliberately offer higher-than-market salaries so that they can attract people with superior qualifications. Moreover, the reward systems of these companies make them attractive places to work for people who are strongly self-motivated and who look for high levels of challenge and excitement. On the other hand, AT&T traditionally had attracted people who preferred secure and stable careers over the pressure-filled life characterizing highly dynamic and strongly competitive organizations.

From this discussion, it can be seen that the cultures and reward systems of organizations are strongly interdependent and will have a tendency to alter each other until they reach a state of mutual balance. This perspective is the basis of the argument that reward systems can be an effective tool for managing culture. A systematic understanding of the specific cultures and specific reward systems that are compatible with each other is needed, however, to provide a sound basis for managerial action. Such understanding can be facilitated by a meaningful scheme for classifying cultures and their related reward systems.

A Typology of Cultures and Reward Systems: A Framework of Orientation for Managerial Action

The major underpinnings of an organization's culture are provided by its human resource orientation. Therefore, useful insights for differentiating and classifying cultures of different organizations can be obtained by examining their human resource orientations. Two basic criteria that define an organization's human resource orientation are the level of concern for people and the level of concern for people's performance in the organization. *Concern for people* refers to the organization's commitment to the well-being of its members and respect for their dignity. *Concern for performance* refers to the organization's expectation that its members will give their best on their jobs and make full use of their talents. A low or high level of concern for people in conjunction with a low or high level of concern for performance suggests four generic types of organizational culture that are grounded in the organization's human resource orientations. These four cultures, depicted in Figure 2, are the Apathetic culture, the Caring culture, the Exacting culture, and the Integrative culture. The Apathetic culture exhibits little concern for people and indifference to their performance. The Caring culture exhibits high concern for people but relatively undemanding performance expectations. The Exacting culture exhibits little sensitivity to people but extremely demanding performance expectations. The Integrative culture exhibits high concern for people as well as high performance expectations. Each of these cultures is compatible only with specific types of reward systems. The patterns of reward systems generally consistent with each of these four cultures is summarized in Table 2.

The Apathetic Culture. Lack of concern for people and

Figure 2. A Framework of Human Resource Cultures.

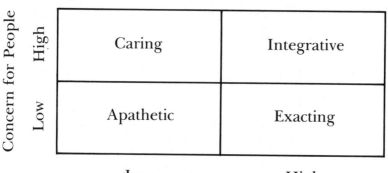

indifference to their performance together symbolize the Apathetic culture. This culture reflects the general state of demoralization and cynicism that permeates organizations with inept or alienated leadership. The long-term viability of such organizations is problematic, but they may survive if they have entrenched positions in their industries, momentum because of size, or a protected environment.

One example of the Apathetic culture is the culture that prevailed until just a few years ago at RCA Corporation. According to a recent *Business Week* cover article on the company ("RCA . . . ," 1984), for many years the company's history was dominated by "Byzantine cabals, factions, and schisms," and during this time, "talk of who was up and who was down occupied the troops far more than the company's business" (p. 53). Maximum rewards at that time appeared to have accrued to some individuals who were merely getting hired and fired at the company; Edgar H. Griffiths, who was chairman of the company from 1975 to 1981, "hired and publicly fired top aides, compensating them handsomely both coming in and going out" (p. 54). This denigration of people and neglect of performance for many years sapped the vitality of this company that had been a pioneer of radio and television.

Another example of the Apathetic culture is the First National Bank of Chicago, the tenth largest bank in the United

Table 2. Summary of Reward Systems in Four Cultures.

Reward-System Dimensions	Human Resource Cultures			
	Apathetic	Caring	Exacting	Integrative
1. Kinds of Rewards				
Financial Rewards	Poor	Average	Variable	Superior
Job-Content Rewards	Poor	Average	Good	Superior
Career Rewards	Poor	Good	Average	Superior
Status Differentiation	High	High	Moderate	Low
2. Criteria for Rewards (Examples)				
Performance: Results	Individual success Illusory	(Reasonable effort) Day-to-day	Individual success Short-term	Group/company success Long-term
Performance: Actions and Behaviors	Manipulation Politicking	Compliance Cooperation	Efficiency Competition	Innovation Independence
Nonperformance Considerations	Contract Patronage	Membership Position	Nature of work Replaceability	Equity Potential

States. As observed by Davis (1984), during the troubled times during the late 1970s the atmosphere inside the bank was one of growing "mistrust and contentiousness [combined] with uncertainty and confusion," and "people lost confidence in both the institution and the leadership." Further, Davis notes, "There was a strong belief that favoritism ruled, that success was not rewarded, and that risk-taking was penalized. From top to bottom workers lost their enthusiasm and disregarded any performance orientation" (p. 22).

The workings of organizations with the Apathetic culture, as illustrated in these examples, are frequently governed more by vested interests or political expediencies than by the concerns of efficiency or effectiveness. In such organizations, financial rewards usually are poor to average, through in some particular cases they also can be generous to the point of being irresponsible. Job-content rewards are the hardest to find in this culture. As for career rewards, job security is low, growth opportunities are limited, and promotions are given capriciously. Status rewards are highly visible, but they are likely to be limited to the privileged few.

By definition, performance is not an important criterion for rewards, and most rewards are likely to be based on contractual obligations or on patronage. However, some clever individuals can use their personal accomplishments—which usually are more illusory than real—as bargaining chips. In addition, actions and behaviors that get rewarded in this culture are often dysfunctional ones, such as playing politics, manipulating rules and policies, "managing" impressions, and so on.

The Caring Culture. An organization with the Caring culture carefully looks after the well being of its members but does not impose very high standards of performance on them. The traditional cultures of companies like J.C. Penney, Corning Glass, AT&T, and Bank of America are representative of this type. This culture is usually the expression of the paternalistic philosophy of the organization's founders or key leaders. So long as the competitive environment is not very threatening, organizations with this culture function quite smoothly because of employees' ready compliance with organization leaders; and they can survive, and even prosper at times, because of the loyalty and steadfastness of their people.

In this culture, financial rewards are average by market standards, but career rewards are usually very good: job security is high; training and development programs are good without being high-pressured; and promotions, even if they are infrequent, are usually the means by which open positions are filled. Status rewards also are relatively high in this culture, but job-content rewards are average to poor; most people do not enjoy a high degree of freedom, have limited responsibilities, and are not "burdened" with challenging or difficult tasks.

Conditions for rewards in the Caring culture are not strongly related to performance, although people are expected to make reasonable efforts in their day-to-day work. Certain types of actions and behaviors, such as teamwork, cooperation, conformity, and receptivity to guidance from superiors, can influence an individual's rewards. At J. C. Penney, for example, "a store manager once was severely rebuked by the company's president for making too much profit. That was considered unfair to the customers, whose trust Penney seeks to win" ("Corporate Culture . . . ," 1980, p. 148). Major determinants of rewards in this culture often are considerations unrelated to performance. Many of the rewards are available simply on the basis of membership, while other rewards are governed mainly by tenure and position in the organization's hierarchy. For example, the traditional personnel policies of Bank of America have been compared to those of the civil service; as one corporate lending officer of the bank observed, "everybody at a certain grade could expect about the same salary and the same increase" (quoted in Zonana, 1984, p. 1).

The Exacting Culture. Companies with the Exacting culture are performance driven or success oriented. In these companies, performance is what counts, and individuals are, at times, expendable. Some likely candidates for this category are PepsiCo, Texas Instruments, ITT during the reign of Harold Geneen, Emerson Electric, where nothing is more sacred than the bottom line ("Emerson Electric . . . ," 1983)—and Intel—where, according to a former executive, "there are no sissies" (quoted in Levering, Moskowitz, and Katz, 1984, p. 154). Such organizations compete aggressively in the marketplace and live by the code, "survival of the fittest."

In this culture, financial rewards usually are very good, but the highest rewards tend to be in the form of bonuses and other performance-based incentives and therefore, are highly variable. At Emerson Electric, for example, "Superachievers are rewarded handsomely. Divisional managers can increase their annual compensation up to 81 percent by exceeding preset goals" ("Emerson Electric . . . ," 1983, p. 61). Job-content rewards—challenge and responsibility—are high in this culture. Status rewards vary from organization to organization, but they are not considered particularly important here. Career rewards tend to be least attractive in this culture because job security is heavily dependent on performance, and the emphasis on results mitigates against any meaningful development opportunities, which in turn leads to rapid burn-out.

The availability of rewards in this culture is highly contingent on the tangible outcomes of people's efforts. Moreover, the short-term competitive success of the individual usually counts most. At Texas Instruments, President J. Fred Bucy is "never far from a computer rating of the performance of each of his operating managers" (Uttal, 1982, p. 41). The Exacting culture at times provides mixed signals as to the actions and behaviors that are valued. While risk taking and creativity are ostensibly important here, they can be discouraged by the penalties of failure. On the other hand, many dysfunctional activities, such as hoarding resources, withholding information, or being insensitive to the needs of others, often are rewarded because they can lead to short-term competitive success. Finally, the nonperformance factors prominent here are the nature of the work and the relative ease or difficulty of replacing people.

The Integrative Culture. In this last culture category, the Integrative culture, high concern for people is matched with strong performance expectations, and these two aspects of the culture tend to reinforce one another. This culture is likely to measure up to Peter Drucker's definition of the organization's responsibility toward its people, expressed by him as follows:

"People are weak. . . . People cause problems. . . . And people are a cost and a potential 'threat.' But these are not the reasons why people are employed. The reason is their strength and their capacity to perform. And . . . [t]he purpose of an organization is to make the strengths of people productive and their weaknesses irrelevant" (Drucker, 1974, p. 307). The Integrative culture similarly values people, and it brings out their best by challenging them meaningfully. Some of the widely noted embodiments of this culture are IBM, Hewlett-Packard, Minnesota Mining and Manufacturing, and Tandem Computers. Another example is Lincoln Electric Co., as described by Martin in Chapter 9 of this book. The concern for people in this culture is not paternalistic as it is in the Caring culture but is characterized by a genuine respect of the dignity of people. This in turn shapes the organization's expectations about its people: They are considered capable of making significant contributions to the performance of the organization, and therefore they are expected to do so.

In this culture, financial rewards are usually superior by market standards, because organizations with this culture are serious about attracting and retaining talented people. IBM and Hewlett-Packard, as has been mentioned, consciously maintain higher-than-market pay levels. Job-content and career rewards also are very attractive in this culture. Companies with this culture offer their members challenging jobs, considerable freedom, significant responsibilities, and generous recognition. These companies also emphasize job security, maintain high-quality training and development programs, and mostly promote from within. Hewlett-Packard, for example, is widely admired for its "ability to recruit the best talent from the best engineering schools and to move young engineers quickly into significant jobs in an informal environment" ("Can John Young . . . ," 1982, p. 78). In fact, sense of fulfillment from meaningful and challenging work is one of the more important rewards in this culture. Analog Devices, referred to earlier, also has the Integrative culture, and as Davis describes the situation in this company, "Analog's guiding beliefs about people focus on allowing them to be all they can be, more than on the organizational rewards for being so. People sign up for the trip, not because of the money" (1984, p. 108). Status-oriented rewards are usually downplayed in the Integrative culture because the general tendency here is toward egalitarianism and informality (though for some organizations, such as IBM, this is not necessarily the case).

Because performance is a core value in this culture, significant rewards are contingent on performance, but unlike the Exacting culture, emphasis here usually is on group or company success rather than on individual success. Moreover, performance is not viewed solely in terms of the current bottom line, but long-term implications are also taken into consideration. Actions and behaviors that are valued in the Integrative culture include self-management, cooperation, risk taking, innovation, experimentation, and skill building. Nonperformance criteria taken into consideration pertain to issues such as internal and external equity and the individual's potential.

A Framework of Orientation for Managerial Action. This typology of cultures presents *generic* categories. Therefore, it is not an easy task to place an organization into any single category exclusively, nor can a particular category convey everything about an organization that is placed in it; however, most organizations can be meaningfully characterized with relative ease as being closer to one particular cultural type than the rest. Hence, this typology can function as a basic framework to orient managerial actions for shaping cultures.

Another point to be kept in mind is that the typology does not recommend a "best" culture. As Gordon observes in Chapter Six of this book, there is no one "winning culture." "Rather," he clarifies, "factors such as the characteristics of the industry and the marketplace and the diversity, size, and market position of the organization define the broad outlines of an appropriate culture." Extrapolating from Gordon's analysis, the following arguments can be made: For monopolistic, protected utilities or other similar organizations, the Caring culture, with its emphasis on security and long-term stability, might be more appropriate, while for dynamic-marketplace companies engaged in a free-wheeling competition, the Exacting culture, with its short-term incentives and high-risk compensation, is likely to be more appropriate. Thus, definition of "best" culture is dictated more by realism than idealism. The utility of the typology presented here, therefore, again rests mainly in its being a convenient frame of reference for managerial analysis and action.

Guidelines for Managerial Action

Today an increasing number of organizations are finding it necessary to modify their cultures in order to prosper and, in some cases, just to survive. Whenever efforts are made to strengthen or alter an organization's culture, accompanying changes in the organization's reward system usually become critically important. The experiences of many organizations readily support this argument.

Cultural Adaptation and Reward-System Change. Some organizations that offer illuminating cases of significant culture change are AT&T ("Corporate Culture . . . ," 1980; Tunstall, 1983), Bank of America (Fierman, 1983; Zonana, 1984), Chase Manhattan Bank ("Corporate Culture . . . ," 1980; Fierman, 1983), and the Marine Midland Bank (Louis, 1982). It appears that AT&T, Bank of America, and Chase Manhattan Bank generally have been striving to shift their cultures from the Caring pattern to the Integrative pattern. To accomplish the hoped-for changes in their cultures, these organizations are making appropriate changes in their reward systems. They are changing the rewards offered as well as the criteria for rewards. There may be considerable differences in the specific steps each organization is taking, but there are some common trends in their efforts. All are offering more attractive compensation, enhancing job-content rewards by creating more challenge and more responsibility in managerial jobs, improving career rewards by providing more opportunities for growth and development, and, to some extent, reducing status differentiation. Further, these organizations are making rewards more contingent on performance; addressing the issues of equity and of potential worth of their people; and encouraging risk taking, initiative, and innovation.

Another kind of cultural transition is discernible in the

case of Marine Midland Bank, which ranks fourteenth among all banks nationwide in assets. From the analysis of its corporate culture offered by Louis (1982) it appears that Marine's culture was similar to the Apathetic pattern through most of the 1970s, but efforts lately have been under way to change its culture, and it is likely that the "New Marine" will follow the Exacting cultural pattern. Marine had not shown particularly high concern for its people in the past, and even today its sensitivity to the human element is limited; however, as Marine pursues an ambitious program to change its culture—or "style"—it is becoming significantly more performance oriented than before. Several changes in the reward system that correspond to Marine's new cultural emphasis are already evident. As Louis (p. 44) points out, in the past the bank had been "relatively tight fisted even in the best of times"; but now "both salaries and fringe benefits are being sharply boosted," and a broad variety of new incentive programs are being created. Job content rewards also have improved at the bank; specific goals and achievement targets are being defined, and decision-making power is more widely shared. In setting its criteria for rewards, "Marine is trying to relate compensation directly to performance, something it had hardly tried before" (p. 44). Correspondingly, great emphasis is now being placed on productivity and assertiveness.

Guidelines for Action: Managing the Culture of Organization O. Guidelines for managerial action that follow from the preceding discussion can be illustrated by the case of hypothetical organization O. The approach recommended here involves a diagnosis phase followed by an action phase.

- *Diagnosis Phase*
  - Step 1: Identify the current culture of O using the cultural typology described here.
  - Step 2: Ascertain whether the current culture of O is desirable and viable.
  - Step 3: Ascertain, by referring to Table 2, if the culture and the reward system of O are compatible.
- *Action Phase*
  - Alternative 1: If the culture of O is desirable and viable

and is adequately supported by the current reward system, then initiate no action in this sphere at this time.

Alternative 2:   If the culture of O is considered undesirable or not viable, then initiate efforts to change the culture. For this, first use the typology presented here as a general reference for selecting the type of culture desired, and then selectively redesign the reward system to support the culture-change objectives, using Table 2 as a guide.

Alternative 3:   If the culture of O is desirable and viable, but the reward system is not fully consistent with the culture, then redesign the reward system. Use Table 2 as a guide to the types of changes in the reward system that can make it a proper support for the culture.

Summary

Managerial efforts to create, strengthen, or change culture will have a high probability of success only if such efforts are accompanied by parallel efforts to design (or redesign) the organizational reward system for cultural compatibility. The reason for this is that if the reward system is in harmony with the culture, it will reinforce and invigorate the culture, but if it is inconsistent with the culture, then it will undermine and stultify the culture. In this chapter, a framework of four types of cultures and their matching reward systems have been described. Managers can use this framework to diagnose the current situation in their organizations and create appropriate reward systems to ensure the vitality of the cultures in their organizations.

References

"Can John Young Redesign Hewlett-Packard?" *Business Week,* Dec. 6, 1982, pp. 72–78.

"Corporate Culture: The Hard-To-Change Values That Spell Success or Failure." *Business Week,* Oct. 27, 1980, pp. 148-160.

Davis, S. M. *Managing Corporate Culture.* Cambridge, Mass.: Ballinger, 1984.

Drucker, P. F. *Management: Tasks and Responsibilities.* New York: Harper & Row, 1974.

"Emerson Electric: High Profits from Low Tech." *Business Week,* Apr. 4, 1983, pp. 58-62.

Fierman, J. "Cultural Therapy for Anxious Bankers." *Fortune,* Oct. 17, 1983, p. 71.

Kerr, J. L. "A Framework for Understanding Reward Systems." Working paper, School of Business, Southern Methodist University, 1984.

Kerr, S. "Some Characteristics and Consequences of Organizational Reward Systems." Working paper, School of Business Administration, University of Southern California, 1982.

Kilmann, R. H. "Getting Control of the Corporate Culture." *Managing,* 1982, (3), 11-17.

Lawler, E. E. "The Design of Effective Reward Systems." Working paper, Center for Effective Organizations, University of Southern California, 1984.

Lawler, E. E. "The New Pay." Working paper, Center for Effective Organizations, University of Southern California, 1984.

Levering, R., Moskowitz, M., and Katz, M. *The 100 Best Companies to Work for in America.* Reading, Mass.: Addison-Wesley, 1984.

Louis, A. M. "In Search of Style at the 'New Marine.' " *Fortune,* Sept. 20, 1982, pp. 40-45.

"A New Era for Management." *Business Week,* Apr. 25, 1983, pp. 50-86.

Peters, T. J., and Waterman, R. H., Jr. *In Search of Excellence: Lessons from America's Best-Run Companies.* New York: Harper & Row, 1982.

"RCA: Will It Ever Be a Top Performer?" *Business Week,* Apr. 2, 1984, pp. 52-62.

Schein, E. H. "Corporate Culture: What It Is and How to Change It." Working Paper ONR TR-26, Sloan School of Management, Massachusetts Institute of Technology, 1983.

Schwartz, H. M., and Davis, S. M. "Matching Corporate Culture and Business Strategy." *Organizational Dynamics,* Summer 1981, pp. 30–48.

Tunstall, W. B. "Cultural Transition at AT&T." *Sloan Management Review,* 1983, *25* (1), pp. 1–12.

Uttal, B. "Texas Instruments Regroups." *Fortune,* Aug. 9, 1982, pp. 40–45.

Uttal, B. "The Corporate Culture Vultures." *Fortune,* Oct. 17, 1983, pp. 66–72.

Von Glinow, M. A. "Reward Strategies for Attracting, Evaluating and Retaining Professionals." *Human Resource Management,* 1985.

Zonana, V. F. "Stirring Giant: Bank of America, Seeking Turnaround, Seems to Gain Ground." *Wall Street Journal,* Jan. 27, 1984, p. 1.

Twenty

Conclusion:
Why Culture
Is Not Just a Fad

Ralph H. Kilmann
Mary J. Saxton
Roy Serpa

There is a religious side to American industry. It is forever seeking salvation, never sure what form the messiah will take.

And just how does salvation manifest itself? Certainly not in the form of fads or gimmicks. We would certainly never put up with such nonsense! Salvation for American Industry comes in the form of new or revised techniques, procedures, and methods to improve performance—"to impact the bottom line," as the current jargon would have it. Whatever ills exist, whatever weaknesses, the newest and latest will cure everything—particularly if it is imported from Japan. Last year it was Quality Circles; this year it is Zero Inventories.

421

> The truth is, one more panacea and we will
> all go nuts [Gittler, 1985, p. 98].

Corporate culture has been the rage for several years now, and people are wondering how much longer it will last. There is the expectation that it is just a matter of time before the culture fad will be dropped, and a new "hot" management topic will emerge. After all, that has been the pattern for several decades now: in the 1940s, human relations training was the new management tool; in the 1950s, management by objectives was heralded as the new solution to performance problems; in the 1960s, organization structure was believed to be the best solution; in the 1970s, corporate strategy was considered the new panacea; by the mid 1980s, hundreds if not thousands of firms had implemented quality circles to improve performance.

We believe that the topic of corporate culture is too important to be dismissed as just another fad. As the chapters in this book have shown again and again, culture *is* the social energy that drives—or fails to drive—the organization. To ignore culture and move on to something else is to assume, once again, that formal documents, strategies, structures, and reward systems are enough to guide human behavior in an organization— that people believe and commit to what they read or are told to do. On the contrary, this book argues that most of what goes on in an organization is guided by the cultural qualities of shared meaning, hidden assumptions, and unwritten rules.

Another possible development is that culture will continue to be studied but will be called something else. We believe that the study of corporate culture or, more generally, the human side of the organization has been fragmented because of this tendency to put old wine in new bottles. For example, the human relations movement in the 1940s and 1950s was directly relevant to today's efforts to understand and manage corporate culture. Further, bringing sensitivity training groups to organizations and efforts concerned with participative management, humanizing the workplace, quality of work life, and democratization of work are approaches related to what we now call corporate culture. Such relabeling, although often effective in capturing research attention and news headlines, does little to help us integrate all that we have learned about managing people at work. Perhaps when both academics and practitioners resist the temptation to call something "new" every few years, they will be able to add to our store of knowledge rather than to keep reinventing the wheel.

Actually, what makes anything a fad—culture included—is the promise of a quick, single remedy to a complex problem. We believe that it is virtually impossible to improve the functioning of a complex organization by any quick fix, no matter how appealing this is. Complex problems can only be solved by complex solutions—approaches that take into account the full range of interconnected variables that operate in a problematic situation. Thus, to improve the bottom line requires an explicit management of culture along with all the other controllable variables in the organization: strategy, structure, rewards, skills, teams, and so on (Kilmann, 1984).

In the introductory chapter of this book we defined three levels of depth comprising the concept of corporate culture: behavioral norms, hidden assumptions, and human nature. Norms occur at the surface level, where culture can be readily discussed and altered, although any culture change at this level is difficult to sustain. Assumptions occur at the next level of depth, at a somewhat unconscious level, and are more difficult and time consuming to change. Last, shared human nature—fears, anxieties, defense mechanisms, and power motives, for example—are most difficult to address. These deeper aspects of human nature, however, can help to explain why people resist change.

In this concluding chapter, we will examine the consequences of two recent—potentially faddish—approaches to organizational growth: (1) bringing entrepreneurship into large organizations and (2) merging organizations. In both cases, an understanding of all levels of corporate culture is necessary, and a "quick-fix" approach will not suffice.

"Intrapreneurship": New Fad or Integrated Approach?

Pinchot (1985) coined the term *intrapreneuring* to suggest a strategy to help large, bureaucratic organizations become creative and innovative once again by developing new ideas and bringing them to the marketplace much like an *entre*preneur does. In the early months of 1985, there was a wave of articles on this topic, suggesting the new management craze of the mid 1980s (Geltner, 1985; Gupta, 1985; "Harold Geneen...," 1985; "Here Come the Intrapreneurs," 1985; Lee and Zemke, 1985; "Secrets of *Intra*preneurship," 1985; Vicere, 1985). We are sure that many firms have rushed to establish venture programs so that intrapreneurship will flourish.

Massive barriers to successful intrapreneuring derive from the complex assortment of organizational properties that are typically ignored when any new panacea comes on the scene: strategy, structures, reward systems, skills, team efforts, union-management relationships, and so forth. In essence, merely establishing one or more separate venture groups and giving each sufficient capital to proceed with new product ideas is not enough.

Will the leaders of the new venture groups come from the ranks inside the company, or must they be recruited from outside? If an established firm has continually selected and trained its members to abide by its long-standing conservative practices, for example, what will inspire these members suddenly to become risk takers and innovators? If the firm does go outside to hire entrepreneurial employees, will the rest of the corporation accept these people? Will the reward system, which does not recognize exceptional performance or allow wide fluctuations in the distribution of rewards, be able to keep intrapreneurs happy? In all likelihood, if the existing reward system is not adjusted to allow intrapreneurs to reap substantial benefits from their risks, and the incentives for innovation are minimal, the intrapreneurs will leave the company and venture out on their own—and become *entre*preneurs. This migration—a sort of brain drain—could mean that the organization loses its best people. Furthermore, will the established reward system allow mistakes, which must be expected in any innovative effort? Alternatively, if the reward system *is* adjusted to meet the needs of the new venture group, will the rest of the organization members understand why their reward system is different?

Bringing entrepreneurship inside a large corporation,

therefore, can create major culture problems. If cultural issues are not managed explicitly, it seems clear that the old culture will have its way. On the other hand, if a program of culture change that includes all relevant aspects of the organization is designed and implemented, perhaps the members can accept a different organizational approach for the venture groups.

Consider the first level of culture, behavioral norms. Perhaps some new "rules of the game" will allow differences to exist with minimum interference. Possible new rules include: allow two reward systems to exist in this company to keep the company competitive, encourage new venture groups to operate differently than the other groups in the organization, do not be negative about venture groups, accept new blood in the organization, do not distinguish between old-timers and newcomers. If a systematic discussion of norms does not occur, and if these new norms are not established, intrapreneuring is likely to fail.

Gradually managing the second level of culture, hidden assumptions, should help firms successfully digest new people, approaches, and venture groups. The hidden assumptions that hamper intrapreneurial activity first must be exposed. These may include: innovation is not needed in today's world, smaller firms will not develop new products and services that will compete with ours, efficiency of operations is more important than creating new products and services, foreign competition is no threat to our markets, and loyalty to our firm will discourage our brightest and most able members from moving to firms that provide more rewards and greater freedom for innovation. The members of any corporate group or division can be encouraged to entertain a set of assumptions that are the opposite of these and actively to participate in culture change. This exercise can help convince members that the old, established assumptions are no longer valid and that assumptions that foster intrapreneuring are needed.

At the deepest level of culture—human nature—people's resistance to change or even active efforts at sabotage can undermine intrapreneurship. The organization may have to establish programs that encourage its members to discuss their fears and concerns. The reward system may have to be modified to encourage new attitudes and behaviors which, ultimately, might encourage change—at least at the surface level—despite members' anxiety about the new venture groups in their organization.

As suggested in the introductory chapter and discussed in several chapters in this book, creating culture change in large organizations can be approached in a top-down or in a participative manner. First, for example, top management can legislate the new behaviors and attitudes that are required for intrapreneuring to work. Management can change rituals, conduct ceremonies, or adjust the formal reward system. Such changes signal that some of the old norms will have to change. Then, as the various venture programs proceed, a more participative approach can be used. Members who interface with the venture groups can be asked to revise their assumptions of what is needed for the competitive world today. Some of these discussions could touch upon the natural tendency of people to resist change and be threatened by differences, thereby surfacing some of the deepest aspects of the corporate culture. With a well-planned, systematic effort toward culture change, the membership of a large organization will be more likely to give intrapreneuring a chance to succeed.

Corporate Mergers: Just on Paper or for Real?

The last five years has witnessed a tremendous increase in the number of corporate mergers and acquisitions. This strategy for growth allows firms to increase their efficiency of operations and to provide new products and services on a large scale without having to spend the time and energy necessary to develop these internally. Merger decisions assume that some kind of synergy will develop, whereby the combination of resources, talent, economies of scale, integrated technologies, and know-how will yield more than the sum of the two separate organizations. However, this is not always the case. Decades after a merger, discussions at corporate headquarters concerning the need to integrate the two corporate entities often still abound.

It is slowly being recognized that the merger of two companies may result in a clash of two distinct corporate cultures (Arnold, 1983; "A Star Is Born," 1985; Darlin and Guiles, 1984; Feldman, 1985; Geltner, 1985; Magnet, 1984; Smith, 1985; Wells and Hymowitz, 1984). Most mergers are evaluated according to economic and financial criteria, as if these aspects fully account for the effective functioning of organizations. It is the finance people who are generally involved in decisions to merge. Given their personalities, background, and training, it is not surprising that they emphasize the number aspects and not the people aspects of the decision before them.

What if the two firms involved in a merger have very different cultures and ways of doing business? If the benefits of the merger can be realized only if the two companies truly consolidate their particular advantages, the different cultures may get in the way. In fact, the two companies may have been successful in different ways in the same marketplace precisely because of their different strategies and cultures.

Picture two icebergs in the ocean, where the tip of each represents the top-management groups—primarily financial people—deciding the fate of the two companies and how the merger will work. As these top-management groups set the merger in process, the two icebergs begin moving toward one another until the tips meet and mesh as one. Such a consolidation, however, can never take place. As the icebergs approach one another, it is not the top that meets; rather, it is the much larger mass below the surface of the water, the respective cultures of the organization, that collide. Instead of synergy, there is culture clash. If the cultures of the two merging firms are not articulated before they are integrated, clashes will continue to occur. In addition, industrial concentration in society is increased without the benefits of greater efficiencies and innovation.

Consider how merger decisions might benefit from a deeper understanding of corporate culture. If a company considering growth by merger analyzed the cultures of all possible target firms, then, assuming that each company satisfies appropriate financial criteria, the actual target firm can be chosen according to the ease with which the cultures of the two companies would mesh. In some cases, it might even be more advantageous to trade off some financial pluses for cultural benefits, thus helping the merger to work with minimal transition costs and headaches. Last, if a target firm has exceptional financial and economic possibilities, but if its culture is radically different, the organization might decide not to pursue a merger.

Of course, using cultural assessments as well as financial assessments assumes that an organization's culture can be measured in a reliable and valid manner. While progress is being made, a reliable tool for assessing culture does not yet exist. A culture survey that measures gaps in behavioral norms (actual versus desired norms) (Kilmann and Saxton, 1983) can be applied to each company in a merger, but assessing either the deeper levels of hidden assumptions or human nature still can be done only impressionistically. Furthermore, it is easier to obtain financial data (which is often public information) than to obtain the kind of information revealed by a cultural audit, especially during a takeover attempt.

If culture can be reliably measured, a critical issue to consider in merger decisions is how easily cultures can be changed or meshed. If both cultures have been fixed for a long time, then any merger decision must assume that the cultures will stay the same, and financial projections must be made accordingly. What must be considered is whether the cultures of the two companies will severely interfere with the productive activity expected of the two firms in combination. Alternatively, if the acquiring company believes that at least one of the cultures can be changed, then any current culture clash does not have to be taken as a given. Instead, the acquiring company can estimate the amount of time, effort, and resources needed to mesh the respective cultures and so to realize the benefits of the merger. Actually, if the cost of culture change is factored into the overall equation in estimating the benefits derived from merging the two firms, a more accurate decision model emerges. Further, it might be that the culture change has benefits as well as costs. A meshing of cultures that leaves both firms more adaptive, innovative, and energized clearly results in synergistic *cultural* effects in addition to the projected financial benefits. A merger might even be used as a means of challenging both organizations to change and to become revitalized.

As with all culture change, the level on which culture is approached affects the way the change process is conducted. When two corporate cultures (not to mention the different cultures within each firm) are meshed, the first concern is with changing behavioral norms to support the merger. Here, a top-down approach is feasible if the top managers can agree on the behaviors they wish to encourage. Again, by rites, rituals, ceremonies, and some changes in the reward systems, critical signals can be sent that will bring some overt compliance to the new situation. In time, through a more participative process involving team members from both firms, the assumptions behind the merger and what has to change to make the merger work can be examined. Discussions can consider whether either firm could operate as an independent entity, how a lack of cooperation can create havoc for both firms, whether it is important for the two firms now to accept different ways of operating, and whether the firms can set examples for each other. In most cases, if the merger decision was sound, assumptions about the marketplace and what is needed for success are the reasons behind the merger, as are assumptions about the synergistic benefits of meshing the two firms.

At the deepest level of culture lies the human tendency to resist any movement from a relatively certain state to an uncertain one. Peoples' sense about what the final organization will be like may rest upon their deepest fears of losing all meaning and purpose in life or of dying. Having extensive discussions—call them counseling sessions—with organization members, particularly the more tenured members, might help to facilitate change during the difficult transition period before much is known about the final outcome. Recognizing the human need to understand and make sense of changing circumstances is a central part of managing the deepest levels of corporate cultures.

Conclusion

If innovation, growth, and revitalization are mandatory in a world characterized by rapid change and world-wide competition, organizations must find a way to breath new life into their procedures, management styles, and cultures. Otherwise, the large, established firms in America will continue to lose ground to the more vibrant smaller companies in this country and to the newer firms in other nations. At the same time, if the large, established firms attempt to foster innovation by acquiring smaller, more dynamic companies, ways must be found to mesh the two merging firms so that innovation is realized. Otherwise, the large firms will stifle the innovation of the acquired firms just as they have done repeatedly in themselves.

For both intrapreneurship and corporate mergers to succeed, corporate culture—the missing link to moving forward in today's world—must be managed, and all our other strategies for managing complex organizations must be implemented as well. The time has come to fight against the lure of the next "quick fix," the next key to management salvation. The danger of accepting panaceas is slowly being recognized, but the defenses necessary to ward off temptation are not yet firmly implanted in the way corporate America thinks and acts. Let us look at the case of quality circles, for example, which promised increased productivity and worker satisfaction. In the past few years, many companies in the United States have taken the plunge and learned the hard way that quality circles are not enough, by themselves, to salvage organizations.

A *Fortune* article underscores the difficulty of implementing quality circles: "Many American companies are discovering that, unlike a new piece of machinery, quality circles cannot simply be acquired, installed, and left to run on their own. This lesson was brought home repeatedly to managers and workers at General Motors' Chevrolet plant in Adrian, Michigan, southwest of Detroit, where they're now trying to make quality circles work for the third time . . . It's just a lot harder than many fix-it-quick, fix-it-once Americans thought it would be" (Main, 1984, pp. 50, 56).

Hinrichs puts the quality circle in its proper place as he convincingly argues for integrated approaches to planned change:

Now, American managers in desperation are rediscovering participation. It's ironic, though, that they're going to Japan to do so. And it's also unfortunate that they're putting it into place with an oriental cast rather than ensuring that it fits with American systems. Once again, it's the quick fix, the bandwagon mentality. Predictably, many American quality control circle programs being introduced today with such ballyhoo, will soon quietly fold their tents and steal away.

It seems that American managers still haven't learned that, if they're really serious about changing their organizations and enhancing productivity, they can't be simplistic. They can't willy-nilly grab the latest gimmick, and they must devote some serious thought and effort to sustaining any gains.

What's essential is a systematic assessment of just what is needed (where and what are the problems, what changes are possible, what support systems are required, and so forth). They must look at their total organizational system (management; work and the way it's organized; design of the organization; workers, technology, and the potential for investment in new facilities). They will probably have to focus on multiple change efforts rather than counting on the quick fix from something like quality circles. And they'll have to continually monitor and provide tender loving care to nurture any innovations and new systems [1983, pp. 40–41].

Managing corporate cultures is now possible. If we continue to improve our understanding of this important concept, we will be able to develop new methods that increase our control of corporate cultures, instead of vice versa. We should refrain from latching onto the next panacea and be careful not to overlook what we have already learned because it is called by a new name. If the current interest in corporate culture is taken seriously and lasts, we will not be reading about the demise of intrapreneuring, corporate mergers, or any other efforts toward innovation and revitalization. Rather, we will see that an integrated approach to managing organizations is possible with people—and culture—at center stage.

References

"A Star Is Born." *Business Week,* Apr. 1, 1985, pp. 74-81.

Arnold, J. D. "Saving Corporate Marriages: Five Cases." *Mergers and Acquisitions,* Winter 1983, pp. 53-58.

Darlin, D., and Guiles, M. G. "Whose Takeover? Some GM People Feel Auto Firm, Not EDS, Was the One Acquired." *The Wall Street Journal,* Dec. 19, 1984, pp. 1, 21.

Feldman, M. L. "The SWAT Team Approach to Acquisition Analysis." *Mergers and Acquisitions,* Winter 1985, pp. 61-63.

Geltner, S. "Putting Adventure into Business Ventures." *Human Potential,* Mar. 1985, pp. 16-19.

Gittler, H. "One More Panacea and We'll All Go Nuts." *Industry Week,* Mar. 4, 1985, pp. 98, 104-105.

Gupta, U. "Redefining the Intrapreneur." *Venture,* Mar. 1985, pp. 44-48.

"Harold Geneen: Why Intrapreneurship Doesn't Work." *Venture,* Jan. 1985, pp. 46-52.

"Here Come the Intrapreneurs." *Time,* Feb. 4, 1985, pp. 36-37.

Hinrichs, J. R. "Avoid the 'Quick-Fix' Approach to Productivity Problems." *Personnel Administrator,* July 1983, pp. 39-43.

Kilmann, R. H. *Beyond the Quick Fix: Managing Five Tracks to Organizational Success.* San Francisco: Jossey-Bass, 1984.

Kilmann, R. H., and Saxton, M. J. *The Kilmann-Saxton Culture-Gap Survey.* Pittsburgh, Penn.: Organizational Design Consultants, 1983.

Lee, C., and Zemke, R. " 'Intrapreneuring': New-Age Fiefdoms for Big Business?" *Training,* Feb. 1985, pp. 27-41.

Magnet, M. "Acquiring Without Smothering." *Fortune,* Nov. 12, 1984, pp. 22-30.

Main, J. "The Trouble with Managing Japanese-Style." *Fortune*, Apr. 2, 1984, pp. 50–56.

Pinchot, G., III. *Intrapreneuring.* New York: Harper & Row, 1985.

"Secrets of *Intra*preneurship." *Inc.*, Jan. 1985, pp. 69–76.

Smith, L. "Merck Has an Ache in Japan." *Fortune*, Mar. 18, 1985, pp. 42–48.

Vicere, A. A. "Managing Internal Entrepreneurs." *Management Review*, Jan. 1985, pp. 31–32.

Wells, K., and Hymowitz, C. "Takeover Trauma: Gulf's Managers Find Merger into Chevron Forces Many Changes." *The Wall Street Journal*, Dec. 5, 1984, pp. 1, 22.

Name Index

Subject Index

A

A. M. Best Co., 152, 160

AM International, and culture rut, 355

Academy of Management, x

American Can, and mergers, 276

American Multiple Industries, and corporate tragedy, 189-190

American Psychological Association, x

American Society for Training and Development, x

American Telephone and Telegraph Company (AT&T): attitude survey by, 56-58; background on, 44-48; as Caring culture, 411; Communications, 52, 63; Consumer Products, 63; continuum for change at, 62-63; cultural elements at, 49; cultural viability at, 124; cultural wheat from chaff at, 49-50; and culture change, 14, 45-64, 264; culture clash at, 67-68; effecting change at, 50-53; environmental challenges to, 157; findings on, 58-60; functional integration of, 115; Information Systems, 63; job enrichment at, 173; joint ventures by, 52, 63; leadership at, 60-62; and loss, 294-295, 298, 300, 308, 313, 319-320; Merlin Communications System of, 52-53; pluralistic process at, 63-64; reward system of, 406, 407, 411, 416; study of impact by, 53-56; Technologies, 52, 63

Analog Devices: as Integrative culture, 414-415; reward system of, 406

Andaman Island, and rites of conflict reduction, 385

Anhauser Busch, symbol of, 312

Antioch University, and innovation, 301

Apple Computer Company, and competition, 192

Artifacts, in corporate culture, 202, 204

443